This book examines a small geographical area in order to illuminate large issues in national society. By looking at the Elizabethan scene from the viewpoint of county politics, not only is greater depth given to some of the main themes of the history of the period (the rise of Puritanism, the origins of the Civil War), but some of the issues are seen in a novel and revealing light. Such regional studies, as it is now commonly recognized, are among the most fruitful lines of investigation into early modern history, and our understanding of English politics is very effectively deepened by research of this kind.

COUNTY AND COURT

COUNTY AND COURT:

Government and Politics in Norfolk, 1558-1603

BY

A. HASSELL SMITH

CLARENDON PRESS
OXFORD
1974

Oxford University Press, Ely House, London W.1

GLASGOW NEW YORK TORONTO MELBOURNE WELLINGTON
CAPE TOWN IBADAN NAIROBI DAR ES SALAAM LUSAKA ADDIS ABABA
DELHI BOMBAY CALCUTTA MADRAS KARACHI LAHORE DACCA
KUALA LUMPUR SINGAPORE HONG KONG TOKYO

ISBN 0 19 822407 9

Printed in Great Britain
by W & J Mackay Limited,
Chatham

To

Elsie & Jennifer

Preface

THE principal theme of this book is the interaction between local and central affairs. Early modern historians have tended to write about politics and administration from a central and national viewpoint: political issues have emerged in parliament; administration has been controlled from London; what went on locally has been greatly affected by decisions at the centre, but those decisions do not appear to have been much influenced by local factors. This view of the Tudor and Stuart scene has been generally accepted by historians of county society and administration, despite the challenge presented by Sir John Neale's *The Elizabethan House of Commons.* I believe our understanding of administration and politics can be deepened by looking at national politics and central administration from a county viewpoint. I have therefore tried to explore the way in which local administration engendered local politics, which, in turn, generated issues in parliament and distorted, if not dictated, many of the policies and decisions of the central administration.

Because the slant of this book is rather different from that of the normal county study I have omitted much that others have treated extensively. Thus, there is no consideration of crime and punishment, of order and disorder, and only a partial account of local administration which omits all consideration of the activities and problems of borough government. For the same reason I have not made a thorough study of the Norfolk gentry; my account ignores many members of this group and pays little attention to their economic activities and even less to their educational background. For these omissions I am unrepentant. I do, however, greatly regret that the loss of the assize records for the Norfolk circuit during the sixteenth century has prevented any consideration of the role of assizes in Norfolk administrative and political affairs.

In the preparation of this book I have accumulated an immense debt to a great number of people. My thanks go first to Professor S. T. Bindoff, Sir John Neale, and Professor R. Ashton. Professor Bindoff stimulated my interest in research, Sir John Neale supervised my postgraduate studies, and, more recently, Professor Ashton has read drafts of the entire manuscript, persuading me to make fundamental revisions to a much revised text.

The Master and Fellows of Corpus Christi College, Cambridge, enabled me to begin this book by electing me to a Schoolmaster Fellow Commonership. Their generosity was matched by the Headmaster and Governors of Woolverstone Hall School, who granted me leave of absence. Subsequently the Council of the University of East Anglia has twice given me study leave. To all these bodies I express my gratitude. Their investment would, however, have been wasted but for the help of others. Professor J. Hurstfield gave me valuable advice on how to turn a thesis into a book, while Dr. H. C. Lewis, Mr. S. W. Goetzee, Mr. B. Bodington, Mr. R. B. Woodings, and my wife have all provided constructive criticism over a number of years. Miss Gillian Baker has typed the several drafts of each chapter, as well as giving invaluable academic assistance and unstinting help. Finally, Dr. R. T. Spence and Miss Norah Fuidge have read the entire text, making many positive suggestions as well as drawing my attention to errors. I alone appreciate fully the extent to which this book is the result of a team effort and I take this opportunity to thank all those who have been involved.

My work has been facilitated both by owners of manuscripts, who have deposited papers or given me access to their muniment rooms (not to mention hospitality in their homes), and by guardians of archives who have helped me in searching for privately owned historical sources. I am especially grateful to Mr. T. S. Blakeney, the late Mr. H. L. Bradfer-Lawrence, Mr. B. Cozens-Hardy, the Hon. Richard de Grey, the Rev. H. G. B. Folland, Mr. B. Hall, Captain A. Hamond, Dr. W. O. Hassall, Mr. D. E. H. James, Miss Jean M. Kennedy, the Earl of Kimberley, the Earl of Leicester, Mrs Joy Rowe, Mr. and Mrs. P. Rutledge, the Marquess Townshend of Raynham, and Lt.-Col. Lord Walsingham.

The bulk of the material for this study, however, is preserved in libraries and record offices. In this connection I wish to thank the following people: the Trustees of Amherst College and Dr. L. B. Wright, who awarded me a Fellowship at the Folger Shakespeare Library; the Norwich City Librarian (Mr. P. Hepworth), the Archivist of the Norfolk and Norwich Record Office (Miss Jean M. Kennedy), and the Librarian of the Colman and Rye Libraries of Local History (Mr. F. D. Sayer), who, with their respective staffs, have constantly attended to my needs over many years; the Mayor and Corporation of King's Lynn; the Mayor and Corporation of Great Yarmouth; the Dean and Chapter of Norwich and their Archivist (Miss Barbara Dodwell); the Master and Fellows of Corpus Christi College, Cambridge, and of Pembroke College, Cambridge; and His Grace the Archbishop of Canterbury and the Trustees of Lambeth Palace Library. I also acknowledge the help and attention I have received from the staff of the British Museum, the Public Record Office, the House of Lords Record Office, Cambridge University Library, the Bodleian Library, the Ipswich Public Library, and the Institute of Historical Research.

This study has benefited from my close association with the work of the History of Parliament Trust. I have to thank the Trustees and the editorial board for permitting me to consult their manuscript biographies. Indeed, I have drawn so freely upon their material that it would have been tedious to acknowledge this source on almost every page. Readers should therefore understand that where biographical information appears without reference it comes from the files of the Trust. I have greatly appreciated the friendship accorded me over many years by its staff, and I can only hope that, in return, the Elizabethan section of the History will have gained a little from my labours.

The following scholars have kindly allowed me to quote from their unpublished theses: Dr. J. K. Allison, Professor P. Collinson, Dr. J. L. Stern, Professor R. J. W. Swales, Dr. F. X. Walker, and Dr. N. J. Williams. Most of Chapter V appeared in *Norfolk Archaeology* XXXIV, and I record my thanks to the editor (Mr. M. V. B. Riviere) for allowing me to reproduce it here. I am also most grateful to Mr. J. L. B. Todhunter and Mr. Bryan Hall for permission to reproduce portraits in their possession. Finally, in ways not previously specified, I have benefited from the scholarship and friendship of Mr. B. Burnham, Mr. R. C. Gabriel, Mr. F. R. Grace, Mr. P. Hasler, Dr. E. W. Ives, Mr. D. Kirby, Mr. V. Morgan, Dr. Joyce E. Mousley, Mr. J. F. Pound, Mr. J. Roberts, and Dr. R. Virgoe.

Centre of East Anglian Studies
University of East Anglia.
June 1973

Contents

APPENDICES

List of Plates

Note: This portrait of an old man is a late seventeenth or early eighteenth century copy of a portrait which can be dated by the costume to 1610–15. It is one of a group of Bacon portraits at Gillingham Hall and has traditionally been supposed to be Henry Bacon, the builder of the Hall. This is most unlikely since he was a young man when the portrait was painted. When Prince Frederick Duleep Singh examined it in 1921 he recorded that it was undoubtedly Nathaniel Bacon of Stiffkey. His identification is probably correct since Nathaniel would have been in his mid 60's when this portrait was painted, and all other members of the Bacon family can be eliminated either on grounds of age or because they are known from identified portraits. Dr. Roy Strong has kindly examined a photograph of this portrait and considers that Duleep Singh might well be right.

LIST OF MAPS

Abbreviations

AHR	*Agricultural History Review.*
APC	*Acts of the Privy Council of England*, ed. J. R. Dasent.
Allison, 'Wool Supply'	K. J. Allison, 'The Wool Supply and the Worsted Cloth Industry in Norfolk in the Sixteenth and Seventeenth Centuries' (Leeds PhD thesis 1955).
BIHR	*Bulletin of the Institute of Historical Research.*
BM	British Museum.
Barnes, *Somerset*	T. G. Barnes, *Somerset 1625–1640: A County's Government During the Personal Rule*, 1961.
Birch, *Memoirs*	*Memoirs of the Reign of Queen Elizabeth...*, ed. T. Birch, 1754.
Blomefield	F. Blomefield & C. Parkin, *An Essay towards a Topographical History of the County of Norfolk*, 11 vols, 1805–10.
Bodl	Bodleian Library.
Boynton	L. Boynton, *The Elizabethan Militia, 1558–1638*, 1967.
CPR	*Calendar of Patent Rolls.*
CRS	*Catholic Record Society.*
CSPD	*Calendar of State Papers Domestic.*
CUL	Cambridge University Library.
Camb.HJ	*Cambridge Historical Journal.*
Collinson	P. Collinson, *The Elizabethan Puritan Movement*, 1967.
Collinson, 'Classical Movement'	P. Collinson, 'The Puritan Classical Movement in the Reign of Elizabeth I' (London PhD thesis 1957).
DNB	*Dictionary of National Biography.*
Davies, *Enforcement*	M. G. Davies, *The Enforcement of English Apprenticeship: A Study in Applied Mercantilism, 1563–1642*. Camb. Mass. 1956.

D'Ewes	*A Compleat Journal of the Votes Speeches and Debates Both of the House of Lords and House of Commons Throughout the whole Reign of Queen Elizabeth*, ed. S. D'Ewes, 1708.
EHR	*English Historical Review.*
Econ.HR	*Economic History Review.*
FSL	Folger Shakespeare Library.
GEC	*The Complete Peerage*, ed. G.E.C., 1910–59.
GI Admissions	*Register of Admissions to Gray's Inn 1521–1889*, ed. J. Foster, 1889.
Gleason	J. H. Gleason, *The Justices of the Peace in England 1558–1640*, Oxford, 1969.
HLRO	House of Lords Record Office.
HLQ	*Huntington Library Quarterly.*
HMC Gawdy	*Report on the Manuscripts of the Family of Gawdy* (Historical Manuscripts Commission, Tenth Report, Appendix II), 1885.
HMC Salisbury	*Calendar of the Manuscripts of the Marquis of Salisbury* (Historical Manuscripts Commission, Series 9), Vols I–XXII, 1883–1971.
Harl. Soc.	Harleian Society Publications.
Hughes & Larkin	*Tudor Royal Proclamations*, ed. P. L. Hughes & J. F. Larkin, 3 vols, 1964–9.
IHR	Institute of Historical Research.
IT Records	*A Calendar of the Inner Temple Records 1505–1603*, ed. F. A. Inderwick, 1896.
Jeayes	*Letters of Philip Gawdy. 1579–1616*, ed. I. H. Jeayes, Roxburghe Club, 1906.
KL	King's Lynn.
L & P H VIII	*Letters and Papers of Henry VIII.*
LI Admissions	*Lincoln's Inn. Admissions from 1420 to 1799*, 1896.
LI Black Books	*Lincoln's Inn. The Black Books*, 2 vols, 1897–8.
NA	*Norfolk Archaeology.*
NAM	*Norfolk Antiquarian Miscellany.*

NNRO	Norfolk and Norwich Record Office.
NOL	H. Le Strange, *Norfolk Official Lists, from the Earliest Period to the Present Day*, Norwich, 1890.
NRS	*Norfolk Record Society.*
Neale, *Commons*	J. E. Neale, *The Elizabethan House of Commons*, 1949.
Neale, *Parliaments 1559–1581*	J. E. Neale, *Elizabeth I and her Parliaments 1559–1581*, 1953.
Neale, *Parliaments 1584–1601*	J. E. Neale, *Elizabeth I and her Parliaments 1584–1601*, 1957.
P & P	*Past & Present.*
PCC	Prerogative Court of Canterbury.
PRO	Public Record Office.
PRO ASSI 35	Clerks of Assize, S.E. Circuit, Indictments.
PRO C 66	Chancery, Patent Rolls.
PRO C 192	Chancery, Miscellaneous Fiats (Crown Office).
PRO C 193	Chancery, Miscellaneous Books (Crown Office).
PRO C 219	Chancery, Writs and Returns of Members to Parliament.
PRO C 227	Chancery, Sheriffs' Rolls, Petty Bag Office.
PRO E 123	Exchequer, King's Remembrancer, Entry Books of Decrees and Orders, Series I.
PRO E 137	Exchequer, King's Remembrancer, Estreats.
PRO E 163	Exchequer, King's Remembrancer, Miscellanea of the Exchequer.
PRO E 178	Exchequer, Special Commissions of Inquiry.
PRO E 179	Exchequer, King's Remembrancer, Lay Subsidy Rolls.
PRO E 372	Exchequer, Lord Treasurer's Remembrancer's and Pipe Office, Pipe Rolls.
PRO SC 6	Special Collections, Ministers' and Receivers' Accounts.
PRO SP 11	State Papers, Domestic, Mary.

PRO SP 12	State Papers, Domestic, Elizabeth.
PRO SP 15	State Papers, Domestic, Addenda, Edw. VI to Jas. I.
PRO St. Ch. 5	Star Chamber Proceedings, Elizabeth I.
Procs.SIA	*Proceedings of the Suffolk Institute of Archaeology.*
Smith, 'Norf. Gentry'	A. H. Smith, 'The Elizabethan Gentry of Norfolk: Office-Holding and Faction' (London PhD thesis 1957).
Stiffkey Papers	*The Official Papers of Sir Nathaniel Bacon of Stiffkey, Norfolk, As a Justice of the Peace 1580–1620*, ed. H. W. Saunders (Camden Soc. 3rd series xxvi), 1915.
Stone, *Crisis*	L. Stone, *The Crisis of the Aristocracy 1558–1641*, Oxford, 1965.
Strype, *Annals*	J. Strype, *Annals of the Reformation and Establishment of Religion . . . in the Church of England during Queen Elizabeth's happy reign*, 4 vols, 1824.
TED	*Tudor Economic Documents*, ed. R. H. Tawney & E. E. Power, 3 vols, 1924.
Trans.RHS	*Transactions of the Royal Historical Society.*
VCH	*Victoria County History.*
Venn, *Al. Cant.*	J. & J. A. Venn, *Alumni Cantabrigienses. A Biographical List of all known Students, Graduates and Holders of Office at the University of Cambridge . . . from the Earliest Times to 1900*, part 1 (4 vols), Cambridge, 1922–7.
Visit. of Norf.	*The Visitation of Norfolk in the Year 1563*, ed. G. H. Dashwood & W. E. G. L. Bulwer, 2 vols, 1878–95.
WRS	*Wiltshire Record Society* (formerly the *Wiltshire Archaeological and Natural History Society, Records Branch*).
Williams	N. Williams, *Thomas Howard Fourth Duke of Norfolk*, 1964.
Williams, 'Maritime Trade'	N. J. Williams, 'The Maritime Trade of the East Anglian Ports 1550–1590' (Oxford DPhil thesis 1952).

Woodworth	Allegra Woodworth, *Purveyance for the Royal Household in the Reign of Queen Elizabeth*, Philadelphia, 1945.
YBESR	*Yorkshire Bulletin of Economic and Social Research.*

Note on Transcription

In quoting from contemporary documents I have revised punctuation and capitalization but kept the original spelling.

PART I

NORFOLK AFFAIRS 1558–1572

CHAPTER I

Elizabethan Norfolk

DURING the late Middle Ages Norfolk had ranked among the wealthiest and most densely populated counties in England, a fact still reflected in its landscape of magnificent perpendicular churches. By the early sixteenth century its prosperity, founded on the manufacture of worsted cloth and the production of grain and wool, had declined in relation to other areas, but it remained a rich and populous shire.[1]

An open society went with wealth. Norfolk had a higher proportion of freeholders than most other English counties, while a fragmented manorial structure, where one lord rarely controlled the social and economic life of an entire community, tended to weaken landlord domination. These factors undoubtedly contributed to the litigious character of Norfolk people, which had become proverbial long before the sixteenth century. 'That it may please Thee to preserve us from all Norfolk barrators, we beseech Thee to hear us', responded some of the monks at Bury St. Edmunds on hearing that the Norfolk-born Samson might be their new Abbot. 'The Inhabitants . . . are so well skilled in matters of the law', boasted an early seventeenth-century topographical writer 'as many times even the baser sort at the plough-tail will argue *pro et contra* cases in law, whose cunning and subtiltie hath replenished the shire with more lawyers than any shire whatsover though far greater, and made themselves suspected of most shires of the realm & given the beginning unto the common word Norfolk wyles many a man beguiles.' The excessive number of attorneys in the county caused comment in fifteenth and sixteenth-century parliaments; one Bill, introduced in 1589, stipulated that the number of attorneys in Norfolk should be limited to fourteen.[2]

[1] *Econ.HR* 2nd ser. ii, 1950, p. 254; xviii, 1965, pp. 504–6.

[2] R. H. Tawney, *The Agrarian Problem in the Sixteenth Century*, 1912, p. 25. *The Chronicle of Jocelin of Brakelond*, ed. H. E. Butler, 1949, p. 12. *The Chorography of Norfolk*, ed. C. M. Hood, Norwich, 1938, p. 68. BM MS. Lansd. 55, f. 185.

Physically the county can be divided into three regions: the Fenlands, occupying the extreme west and a narrow coastal strip from King's Lynn almost to Cromer; an extensive area of light and medium soils covering the western and northern parts of the county and in the sixteenth century given over almost entirely to a sheep and corn husbandry; and a less extensive area of heavy boulder clay in south and central Norfolk 'sustayned cheefelye by graseinge, by dayries and rearinge of cattell'.[3]

Then, as now, the light soils of north and west Norfolk were renowned for their barley and other grain crops; but, unlike today, fertility could be maintained only by constant dunging and treading by sheep.[4] In order to accommodate large flocks within a basically arable system Norfolk farmers had developed the 'fold course'—an area of land containing sufficient arable, pasture, and waste to provide grazing throughout the year for up to 1,500 sheep. From September to March the flock grazed over the stubbles and winter-sown corn; during spring and summer it was either folded on the fallows or allowed to graze over the waste and meadows. These flocks were invariably owned by manorial lords, some of whom ranked among the great sheep-owners of England. The fourth Duke of Norfolk,[5] Sir Henry Farmer, and Sir Richard Southwell all owned sheep in excess of the 13,000–14,000 grazed by that great Northamptonshire flockmaster Robert Spencer of Althorp, while many landlords numbered their sheep in thousands rather than hundreds.

In most cases these lords were not heavily involved in arable farming, grain production being largely the concern of freehold and tenant farmers who usually owned few sheep. This differentiation between the farming activities of lords and their tenants should not, however, be too rigidly drawn; when one substantial landowner—Sir Bassingbourne Gawdy—died in 1606 he had at least 240 acres of standing corn besides flocks totalling over 5,000 sheep. Whatever the role of lord and tenant in the complementary activities of grain and wool growing, there is no doubt about the large quantity of

[3] For the farming regions of Norfolk, see *The Agrarian History of England and Wales*, iv, ed. J. Thirsk, Cambridge, 1967, pp. 40–9. W. Rye, *Musters Beacons and Ship Money*, Norwich, 1907, p. 181.

[4] For a detailed study of the sheep-corn husbandry, see Allison, 'Wool Supply', pt. I; *AHR* v, 1957, pp. 12–30; *Econ.HR* 2nd ser. xi, 1958, pp. 98–112.

[5] Stone, *Crisis*, pp. 298–9.

barley and wheat produced on these light soils of Norfolk. One early-seventeenth-century writer claimed that after local demand had been satisfied the region could still annually 'serve out of the countie by sea to other places forraine or within the realm 40,000 quarters of barley & the lyke quantitie of wheat & rye'.[6] The regulation of these corn exports, as will be shown, became an important issue in the political controversies of Elizabethan Norfolk.

This region contrasted markedly with the heavy soils of central and southern Norfolk where cattle rearing and dairy production predominated. Whereas the light soils had remained unenclosed and devoid of woodland, these heavy soils had long been enclosed, largely by a process of gradual reclamation from natural forest, creating the familiar landscape of broken woodland and irregular fields. The ownership of land was also more widely based than in the sheep–corn region; farms tended to be small or medium in size and to this day the area abounds in distinctive timber-framed houses built by prosperous yeomen during the late sixteenth and early seventeenth centuries.[7] As befitted an essentially pastoral economy, these houses were widely scattered, giving rise to dispersed villages rather than the nucleated settlements of north and west Norfolk. Also in contrast with the light-soil region, rural industries flourished. The manufacture of worsted cloth predominated, but other industries included linen weaving in the Waveney valley and wood turning and the manufacture of other forest products around Wymondham.

However great the contrast between the wood–pasture and sheep–corn regions, the Fenlands differed even more strikingly from both. There, prior to the great seventeenth-century drainage schemes, regular flooding gave rise to very distinctive topographical features and agricultural practices. Villages like Terrington, Walpole, and Tilney clustered along a ridge of silt running parallel to the coast while their lands stretched out, ribbon-like, into the seaward marshes on one side and the inland fens on the other where a great deal of reclamation had already taken place. In this region pasture farming predominated; once the fens and marshes had dried out they provided excellent grazing for sheep, cattle, and horses, while in the winter they yielded a rich harvest to the fisherman and wildfowler.[8]

[6] BM MS. Add. Ch. 16549. NNRO MS. 2641 (3A2).

[7] J. Spratt, 'Agrarian Conditions in Norfolk and Suffolk 1600–1650' (London MA thesis 1935), esp. pp. 189–99.

[8] For the economy of the Lincolnshire Fenlands, see J. Thirsk, *Fenland Farming in the*

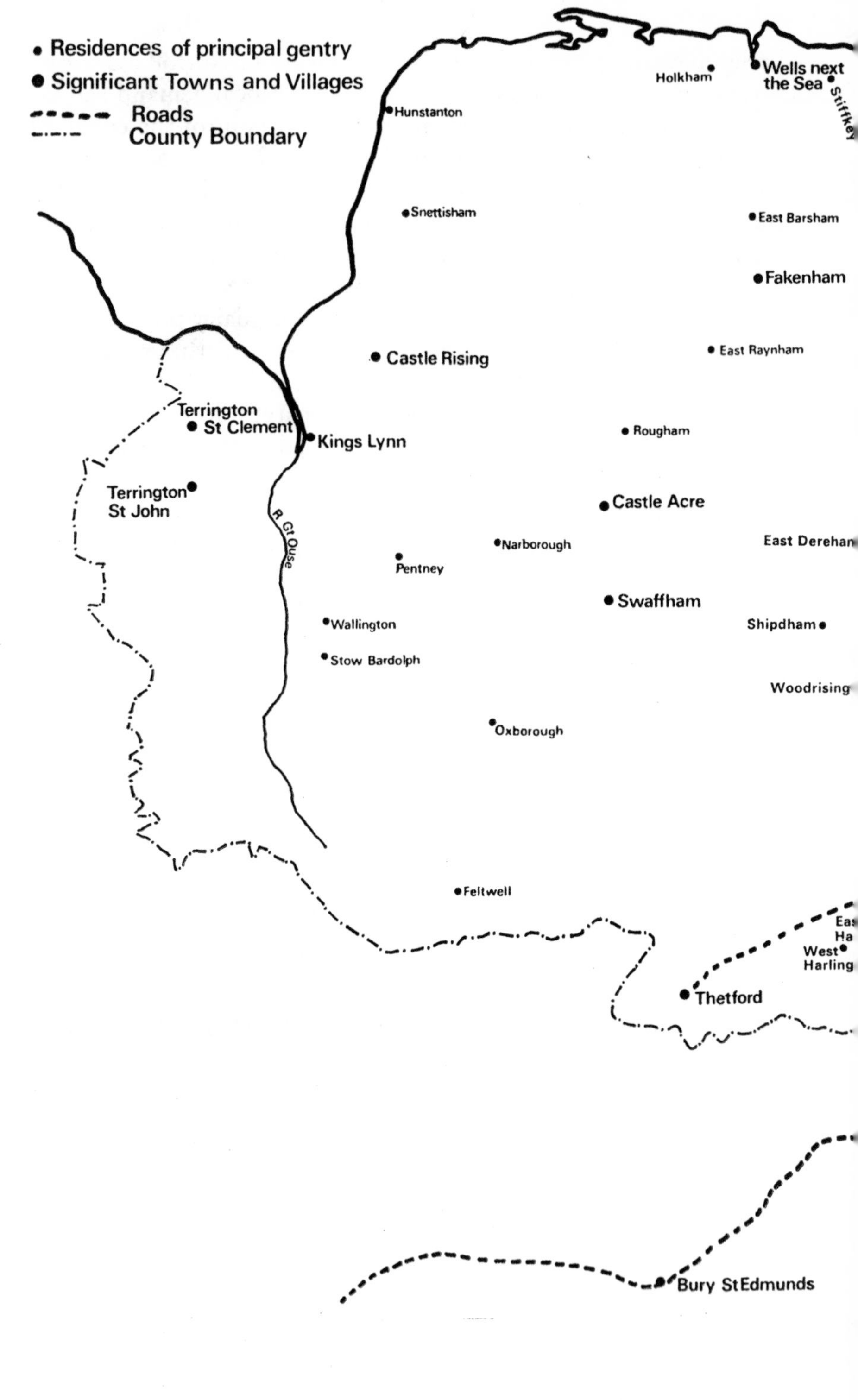

Residences of principal gentry
Significant Towns and Villages
Roads
County Boundary
Holkham
Wells next the Sea
Stiffkey
Hunstanton
Snettisham
East Barsham
Fakenham
East Raynham
Castle Rising
Terrington St Clement
Kings Lynn
Rougham
Terrington St John
Castle Acre
R. Gt Ouse
Narborough
East Derehan
Pentney
Swaffham
Wallington
Shipdham
Stow Bardolph
Woodrising
Oxborough
Feltwell
West Harling
Thetford
Bury St Edmunds

Map I. Places mentioned in text

In each region the inhabitants developed their own identity and community of interests. Fenmen, engaged in ceaseless combat with the sea, experienced a very different pattern of life from that of people elsewhere in the county. Their activities were dominated, indeed their personalities moulded, by the necessity to guard 'against the encroachments of sea and river flood'. Although they were prosperous and their wealth widely distributed, when confronted with the heavy cost of sea defences they had no qualms about seeking support from the body of the county.[9] For the 'tilth-masters' in the sheep-corn region, with a vast surplus of grain in their barns and a lucrative market in the Low Countries, the sea was no enemy; it offered a highway to prosperity, and they worried lest their corn exports should be impeded by war, piracy, or, most commonly, by Council embargoes.[10] The graziers and dairy farmers of the heavy soils, for their part, cared little about corn embargoes or sea defences their economic interests lay with their fellow dairy farmers in central and north Suffolk. Norwich and London provided their chief markets, large quantities of cheese and butter being carted to Southwold and other north Suffolk creeks for shipment to the Thames.[11]

Representatives of these divergent interests, meeting at quarter sessions, rarely agreed about how best to deploy county rates for public works. Fenmen wanted financial help in repairing sea banks; corn growers and merchants wanted resources directed to harbour repairs and the protection of shipping from piracy; while inhabitants of the wood–pasture region wanted impassable highways improved. Such conflicting interests underlay much of the county politics described in part III.

Like these farming regions, the towns of Norwich, Lynn, and Yarmouth also had their independence and economic interests to safeguard. Norwich had achieved administrative autonomy in two early fifteenth-century charters which granted it county status under the government of a mayor, twenty-four aldermen, and sixty common

Sixteenth Century (Dept. of English Local History Occasional Papers No. 3), Leicester, 1953.

[9] Below, pp. 98–9. [10] Below, pp. 19, 99–100.

[11] Williams, 'Maritime Trade', pp. 188–92.

councillors; thereafter it appointed its own J.P.s and sheriffs who administered the law and executed justice in a series of courts which paralleled those for the county.[12] For much of the sixteenth century, as in the county, the Dukes of Norfolk had dominated its affairs, but after the fourth Duke's execution in 1572 the citizens reasserted their separate identity. Through their high stewardship they secured the patronage of influential courtiers; they consistently chose Norwich citizens rather than county magnates to represent them in parliament, and as militia training developed they insisted upon holding their own musters rather than joining with the county.

Prosperity stimulated this civic assertiveness. After a recession in the worsted industry during the early sixteenth century, the city's economy recovered and expanded rapidly under Elizabeth. Undoubtedly the revival of cloth manufacture under the stimulus of Dutch and Walloon craftsmen contributed most to this resurgence.[13] In 1565 the Queen had granted a licence for thirty families from the Low Countries, not exceeding 300 people in all, to settle in the city, but this community expanded so rapidly that by 1583 it exceeded 4,000 persons. These 'strangers' introduced the manufacture of New Draperies so successfully that within a decade they were producing an average of 30,000 cloths annually. After some initial hostility, they rapidly became integrated with the citizens, teaching them the requisite skills to participate in this profitable manufacture, so that by the end of the century Norwich had become 'the greatest centre in the Kingdom for the New Draperies'.[14]

This new prosperity did not depend entirely upon the revival of cloth manufacturing. The increase in the number and wealth of gentlemen, coupled with their propensity for large-scale building and lavish hospitality, created a demand for high-quality furnishings, food, and clothing to which Norwich merchants and craftsmen quickly responded. Thus, when Sir Thomas Knyvett of Ashwellthorpe died in 1617 he owed the Norwich draper Thomas Pettus £228 for cloth; while Nathaniel Bacon of Stiffkey hired a cook and a

[12] W. Hudson & J. C. Tingey, *The Records of the City of Norwich*, Norwich, 1906, pp. lx–lxxi.

[13] For the Dutch and Walloon settlement, see R. W. Ketton-Cremer, *Norfolk Assembly*, 1957, pp. 113–30. D. L. Rickwood, 'The Origin and Decline of the Stranger Community of Norwich 1565–1700' (East Anglia MA thesis 1967). W. J. C. Moens, *The Walloons and their Church at Norwich: Their History and Registers 1565–1832* (Publications of the Huguenot Society of London, vol. 1), 1887–8. *TBESR* 13, 1961, pp. 61–77.

[14] Williams, 'Maritime Trade', p. 87.

banqueting service from the city on the occasion of his daughter's marriage, as well as making large purchases of currants, spices, marzipan, caviar, sugar, and wine. This development of Norwich as a regional centre catering for 'conspicuous consumption' was reflected in its changing trade structure. Between 1525 and 1569 the number of freemen engaged in the distributive and clothing trades, especially those of grocer, haberdasher, tailor, and cordwainer, nearly quadrupled whereas the numbers employed in textile manufacturing remained fairly static.[15]

The revival of Elizabethan Norwich also brought prosperity to its merchants. Since the city was a port with access to the sea via Yarmouth, the commercial activities of one community complemented those of the other, with Norwich merchants chartering ships which were owned by Yarmouth burgesses. By the early sixteenth century, however, shifting sands had blocked the northern entrance to Yarmouth haven and jeopardized the livelihood of merchant and shipowner alike. Only the successful cutting of a new harbour entrance in 1567 enabled Norwich merchants like Roger Weld, Ellis Bate, and Henry Barker to become prominent in international trade during the latter part of Elizabeth's reign.[16]

By then, Norwich had once more become a thriving and prosperous city—probably the foremost in England outside London.[17] Its population, after remaining fairly static for a century or more, increased phenomenally from about 10,000 people in 1582 to 32,000 in 1622.[18] Early seventeenth-century commentators sang the city's praises. Sir Thomas Wilson wrote that he had known twenty-four Norwich aldermen 'which were esteemed to be worth £20,000 a peece, some much more, and the better sort of cittizens the halfe'. Sir John Harrington judged the city 'to be another Utopia, the people live so orderly, the streets kept so cleanly, the tradesmen, young & old, so industrious, the better sort so provident and withall so charitable that it is as rare to meet a beggar there, as it is common to find them in Westminster'.[19]

[15] Ibid., p. 76. NNRO MS. Bradfer-Lawrence, VIIb, household account book 1592–6, entry for 21 Sept.–2 Oct. 1592. J. F. Pound, 'The Elizabethan Corporation of Norwich 1558–1603' (Birmingham MA thesis 1962), pp. 131–6. *P & P* 34, 1966, pp. 49–64.

[16] Williams, 'Maritime Trade', pp. 216–17.

[17] W. G. Hoskins, *Local History in England*, 1959, pp. 176–7.

[18] Population estimates vary. I have followed K. Allison here.

[19] 'The State of England 1600', ed. F. J. Fisher, p. 20, *Camden Miscellany XVI* (Camden Soc. 3rd ser. lii), 1936. *Econ.HR* 2nd ser. iii, 1951, p. 371.

King's Lynn and Yarmouth had also ranked among the foremost towns and ports of medieval England. Like Norwich, they both declined in the late medieval period and then enjoyed a period of economic resurgence during Elizabeth's reign. Lynn's prosperity depended upon its unique location at the head of a river network whose 'various streams ran through the counties of Warwick, Leicester, Northampton, Rutland, Bedford, Buckingham, Huntingdon and Cambridge', as well as Norfolk. It dominated the water-borne trade of one of England's richest industrial regions and her principal corn-growing lands, so that 'The town of Lynne whose haven and ryver reacheth farre into dyverse shyres out of Norfolk apt & plentyfull for grayne hath allwayes in readynesse great store of grayne for transportation'. As Dr. Neville Williams has written, 'the fortunes of Lynn merchants were founded on corn'.[20]

The renewed prosperity of Lynn and Yarmouth arose from a growing demand in England for grain and coal. In times of dearth London imported grain from Lynn, but the largest and most regular demand for corn came from the coal-mining and salt-manufacturing areas of north-east England—a demand which was fully met by the merchants of Lynn. Their grain ships returned with cargoes of coal, totalling thousands of tons annually, some of which was discharged at Lynn and Yarmouth for shipment up river into seven or eight counties, the rest being carried to the Thames where these merchants held a large stake in the provision of London's coal supplies. The complementary trade in grain and coal proved so profitable to East Anglian merchants that they began to invest heavily in new ships.[21]

This new shipping enabled them to displace the Dutch merchants when war with Spain disrupted Dutch domination of the carrying trade between the Low Countries and East Anglia and impaired Antwerp as a great entrepôt. When trade with the Netherlands resumed after 1574 neither Antwerp nor the Dutch merchants regained their former pre-eminence. Instead, their rivals at Lynn and Yarmouth continued to send ships in increasing numbers to the Low Countries with grain, to Iceland for fish, to Norway and the Baltic with cargoes of cloth, leather, tin and lead, returning with timber, rope, pitch, tar, and other naval supplies, to the Atlantic

[20] *Medieval Archaeology*, 6–7, 1962–3, pp. 194–201. NNRO MS. 2641 (3 A2). Williams, 'Maritime Trade', p. 175.

[21] Williams, 'Maritime Trade', pp. 67–8, 162–73, 175–81.

Map II. Administrative towns and cities

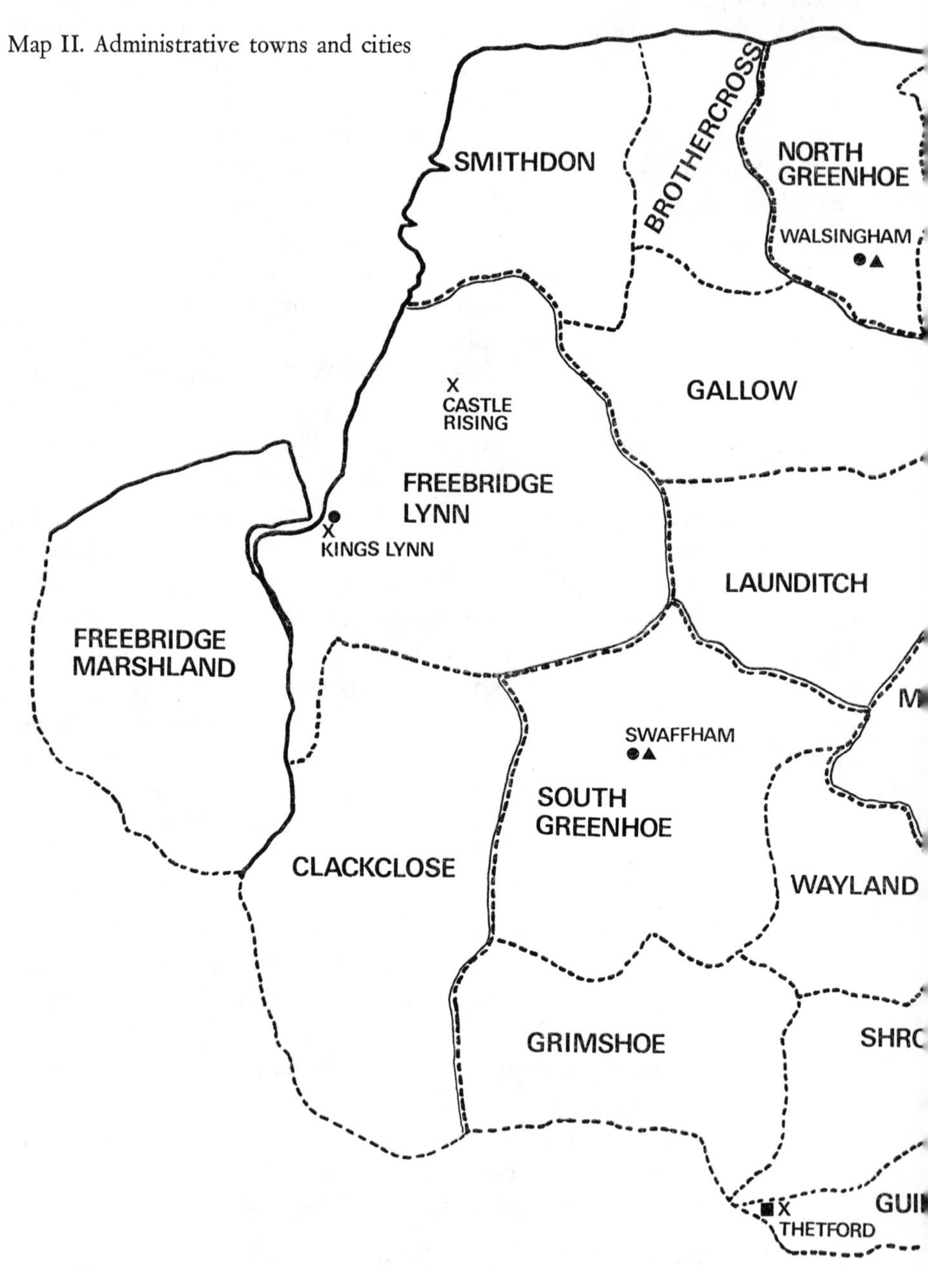

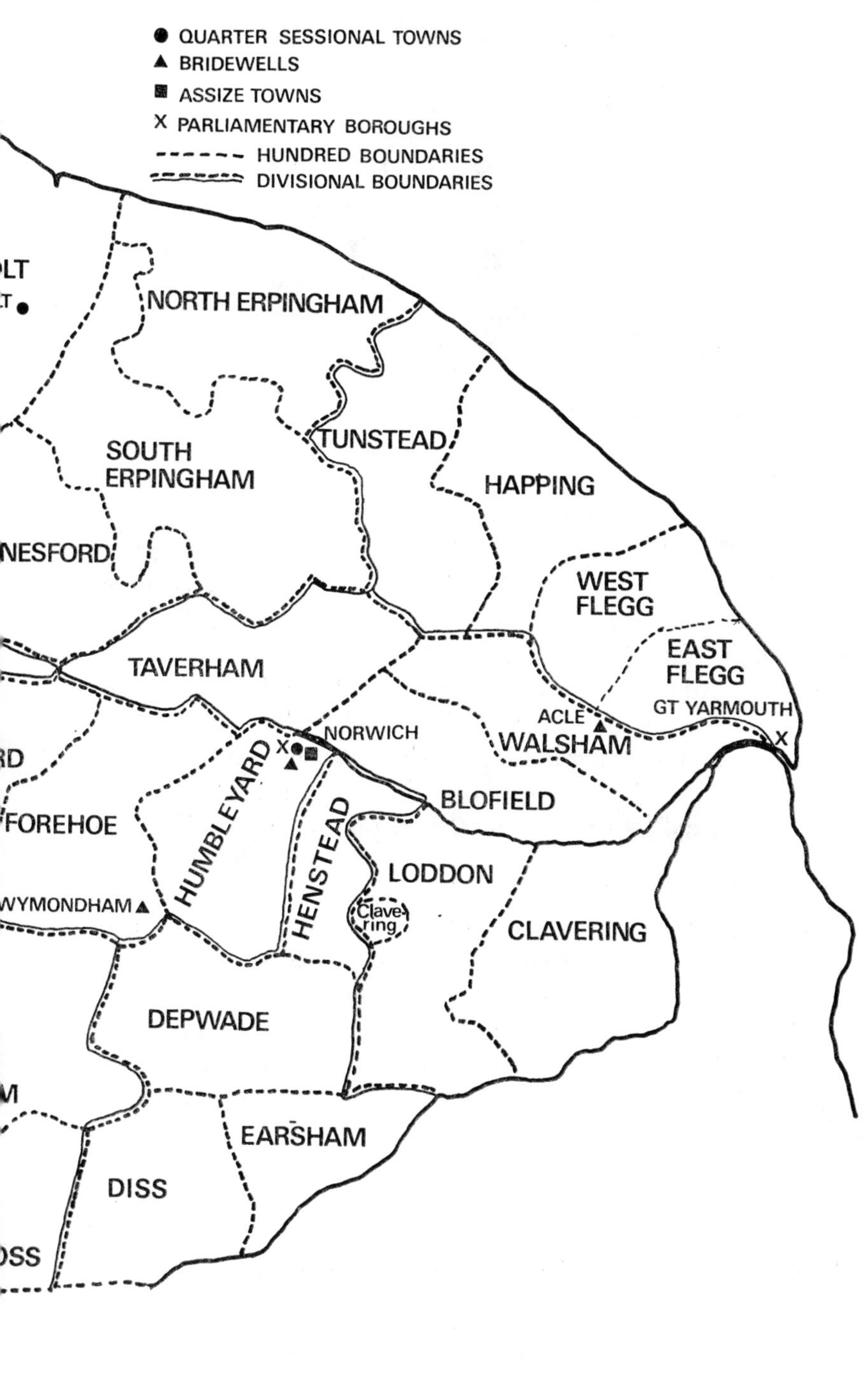

QUARTER SESSIONAL TOWNS
BRIDEWELLS
ASSIZE TOWNS
PARLIAMENTARY BOROUGHS
HUNDRED BOUNDARIES
DIVISIONAL BOUNDARIES
NORTH ERPINGHAM
SOUTH ERPINGHAM
TUNSTEAD
HAPPING
WEST FLEGG
EAST FLEGG
GT YARMOUTH
ACLE
WALSHAM
TAVERHAM
NORWICH
BLOFIELD
FOREHOE
HUMBLEYARD
HENSTEAD
LODDON
Clavering
CLAVERING
WYMONDHAM
DEPWADE
EARSHAM
DISS

ports of France and Spain with cargoes of herring, cloth and grain, returning annually with 2,000 tons of Bay salt for Yarmouth, wine for Lynn, and quantities of dyestuffs and other produce from the East for both ports.[22]

Lynn and Yarmouth quickly regained something of their former glory. Great merchants like Thomas Grave and Thomas Clayborne, wealthy from overseas ventures and coastwise trade in grain, salt, and coal, continued to expand their fleets and began to rebuild their warehouses. Between 1565 and 1587 the number of Lynn-owned ships registered in the port-books more than trebled (from 17 to 60) while the tonnage quadrupled. The situation was similar at Yarmouth, with the result that by 1582 Norfolk ports provided a greater tonnage of shipping than those of any other maritime county. Similarly, 'between 1550 and 1700 practically every warehouse along the Ouse bank was rebuilt' and spacious new ones added alongside. The Lynn merchants' demand for specialized warehousing had become so great that during the 1580s the corporation began to build a complex of sixteen warehouses between the common staithe and the Tuesday Market.[23]

The prosperity of Lynn and Yarmouth depended so completely upon commerce that their burgesses developed a keener sense of their community of interests with other regions both in England and overseas than did landowners in inland areas. Moreover, constantly threatened by the elements, war, piracy, and trading embargoes, they expected financial assistance in times of crisis from inland areas of the county which clearly benefited from their risky, albeit profitable, operations. For example, when their shipping became threatened by the marauding activities of Dunkirk pirates they demanded that their fleets be 'wafted' either at the Crown's or the county's expense. Similarly by the 1590s they had become insistent that their outlay for the provision of ships during the war with Spain should be shared by the entire county—a claim resisted by all inland areas.

Although the agricultural regions and principal towns of Norfolk

[22] Ibid., pp. 79–90, 109–58.

[23] Ibid., pp. 213–16, 251–60. V. Parker, *The Making of King's Lynn*, 1961, pp. 119, 122–3.

developed separate and sometimes divergent interests they had sufficient in common to bind them together into a powerful county community. The prosperity of Norwich, for example, greatly depended upon a flourishing textile industry; but that industry was widely dispersed throughout east Norfolk where a large number of craftsmen combined cloth manufacture with farming. These rural craftsmen and their counterparts in Norwich in turn depended upon the wool-growers of western and central Norfolk and particularly upon the wool-broggers of Mattishall and district who supplied them with the small quantities of wool appropriate to the scale of their operations.[24]

Besides industrial interdependence, strong social ties had developed between county magnates and the principal citizens of Norwich. Many of the latter were immediate descendants of yeomen and minor gentry who had moved into the city and prospered in commerce. After one or two generations members of this new city élite frequently married into county families, purchased estates, and aspired to leading positions in county government. Moreover, during Elizabeth's reign at least a third of the county magistrates owned or rented houses in Norwich where they regularly resided and participated in the city's social activities.[25] They were drawn to Norwich by the increasing importance of quarter sessions and assizes as administrative assemblies for the entire county. These courts, each lasting several days, also provided occasions for the transaction of a great deal of informal political, social, and business activity.

A similar interrelationship probably developed between gentry of the sheep–corn region and the burgesses of Lynn and Yarmouth, since they all depended for prosperity upon the shipment of corn both coastwise and overseas. As they were at pains to inform the Council, if these shipments were in any way hampered, merchants would buy less at lower prices and 'by that means the fermor must be first undone by the greatnesse of his farme & lowe prices of his grayne, so the lords and owners of the lands so greatlie abused muste soone followe in their decaye whereby it will shortlie come to passe

[24] *YBESR* 12, 1960, pp. 73–82. B. H. Allen, 'The Administrative and Social Structure of the Norwich Merchant Class 1485–1660' (Harvard PhD thesis 1951).

[25] NNRO MSS. City Records 18d, Landgable Books 3, 4; 3e Docket Book of Enrolled Deeds 1509–1776; 18a Chamberlain's Account Books 1551–67, 1580–9, 1589–1602.

that neyther lord nor tenant in those parts shall be able in anie good measure to defraye their own charges'.[26]

In a sense it is unrealistic to distinguish between landowners or corn-growers of the county and merchants of the ports since a landowner might well be 'something of a corn-merchant himself'. Thomas Sidney, a great corn-grower around Walsingham who became 'customer' of Lynn, was deeply involved in the corn export business. Gentry who lived near the coast had every incentive to take the extra profits which accrued from exporting local grain. Sir Thomas Woodhouse of Waxham, 'charged with the duty of preventing the export of corn during the lean year of 1565, [loaded] cargoes of his own for shipment to the continent', while Nathaniel Bacon improved the creek at Morston, built his own quay, and engaged in merchandising on a considerable scale. Gentry in the vicinity of Lynn and Yarmouth often operated as merchants and shipowners alongside the burgesses. At least eleven gentry from north-west Norfolk owned merchant property at Lynn and most participated in trading;[27] about six were similarly involved at Yarmouth.[28]

Whatever part this interdependence played in overcoming regional particularism, it is likely that reaction against interference from London and Court interests proved the greatest single factor in developing cohesion within the county. Merchants from Norwich, Lynn, and Yarmouth became united in their struggle against the strangling tentacles of the chartered companies. By 1509 Norwich members of the Merchant Adventurers' Company were objecting to the growing control of London over the Company abroad. Subsequently they tended to ignore the Company altogether: 'in succeeding years there were only about twelve Norwich merchants who styled themselves "merchant adventurers", and the term becomes even less common as the century continues despite the rise of Nor-

[26] NNRO MS. 2641 (3A2).

[27] Williams, 'Maritime Trade', p. 42. V. Parker, *The Making of King's Lynn*, 1971, p. 42.

[28] They were: Sir Wm. Paston, Sir Thos. Woodhouse, Edw. Spany, Edw. Clere, Henry Woodhouse, and possibly Thos. Godsalve and Chas. Clere; see Yarmouth muniments AGYC C4/256–262, *passim*. I am indebted to Mr. David Kirby for these references.

wich to the position of second city in the kingdom'. At Lynn and Yarmouth very few, if any, of the merchants joined the Company. In 1565 the mayor and burgesses of Lynn complained to the Council that whereas 'in tyme past they had free libertie to trafique with there clothes & other merchaundise into Flaunders and the Lowe Contreys without any impechement whereof, nowe they be inhibited by reason of the company of the merchaunt venturers who restrayneth all men excepte suche as be of the said company, or at least all other be dryven to seke suche corners and lyve in suche feare of there streight orders as few have pleasure to trafique of the seas'. Pleasure or not, their search for 'corners' in which to sell their goods was undertaken vigorously and brought immense rewards. It was as 'interlopers', regularly boycotting the official mart towns, that the merchants of Norfolk conducted an expanding international trade.[29]

They apparently adopted an equally independent attitude towards the Eastland and Spanish companies. After the incorporation of the Eastland Company in 1579 Lynn and Yarmouth merchants deliberately ignored the staple at Elbing and used Danzig instead. As soon as the Spanish Company had been incorporated in 1577 Yarmouth merchants petitioned the Council that 'the late corporacion of merchantes of Spaine, nor any restraint in the charter to them granted, may extende to take from us or to empeache our former libertie of traficking into those partes'. Having stated their position these merchants then proceeded to act as if the Spanish company did not exist. Although its membership was open to all who had traded to Spain and Portugal since 1568, they made no attempt to join it, simply continuing to trade in their previous 'disorderly fashion'. Even after the outbreak of war with Spain and the dissolution of the Spanish Company, Norfolk merchants continued to carry grain to Spain.[30]

Norwich cloth merchants were engaged in a similar struggle to prevent a London take-over of the marketing of worsted cloths and New Draperies. Because these cloths had been manufactured from Norfolk-grown wool which had not been a staple commodity, they had been exempt from aulnage and export duties; Norwich merchants had therefore had a free hand in their disposal. They had exported them through Yarmouth and sold them at local fairs and markets, taking only a few to London where they then sold them

[29] Williams, 'Maritime Trade', pp. 221–5.

[30] Ibid., p. 227.

'in close chambers & corners' rather than at the Worsted and Bay Halls. As early as 1477 the London mercers had framed a Bill against the 'worstetmen of Norwiche' who sold 'worstettes, coverleddes & other wares in theyr innes as well to forreyners & more than to freemen'. Down to 1577, however, London interests had made little headway in these efforts to control the marketing of Norwich cloths. A report on the state of Worsted Hall in that year stated that only 4,000 Norwich cloths were entered whereas 30,000 'should come' each year.[31]

Having avoided the payment of aulnage and prevented the channelling of their sales through the London Halls, in 1578 Norwich merchants suddenly found themselves at the mercy of two courtiers—Delves and Fitzwilliam—who had been granted a patent for seven years to collect both aulnage and subsidy on all New Draperies. The city challenged the legality of this patent, in the event unsuccessfully; but it subsequently managed to get the courtiers' 'rights in the letters patent . . . transferred to two Norwich aldermen' who, in turn, vested the right in the city. In 1585, however, the patent was regranted to Delves and Fitzwilliam whereupon the burgesses once more contested its validity and resisted any aulnage payments. But by this time the city's opposition had become merged in a county-wide protest against the implementation of other patents and when, in 1604, the aulnage grant was transferred to the Duke of Lennox, the city's case was taken up in parliament, not only by its own burgesses, but by the knights of the shire as well.[32]

Similarly, the merchants of Lynn and Yarmouth united with landowners in opposition to government embargoes upon the coastwise and overseas shipments of grain. The Tudors tried to regulate grain exports from areas of high production in order to ensure an adequate supply of reasonably priced corn in urban areas and in regions less well suited to corn growing. To this end parliament had passed a series of corn laws which forbade any overseas shipment of grain whenever prices rose above a certain ceiling. These were never entirely effective since no law could prevent coastwise shipments from mysteriously being blown off course and landing up in continental markets. In any case by Elizabeth's reign corn regulation had become

[31] Ibid., pp. 76, 231–3. Allison, 'Wool Supply', p. 400. *Econ.HR* 2nd ser. xxv, 1972, pp. 575–6.

[32] Allison, 'Wool Supply', pp. 613–32. NNRO MS. Sotheby 28/12/67, MS. endorsed 'a note touching the Worsted Weavers'.

a fiscal device which the Crown used to support public works or to reward courtiers. A clause in the statutes of 1571 and 1593 had acknowledged the Queen's right to prohibit the export of grain at any time no matter how abundant the harvest. In the event she issued embargoes with increasing frequency, permitting shipments overseas or coastwise only under special licence. These licences, frequently for the export of 10,000 or 20,000 quarters of grain, she then granted to courtiers or to port-towns seeking to repair their harbour defences. Such grantees in turn sold off their licences to merchants with surplus grain at a rate of up to £7 for a licence to export 100 quarters. Although a licence usually served as cover for shipping grain far in excess of the quantity stipulated, its high price underlines the huge profits which could be made in the European markets and which were denied to the merchants of Lynn and Yarmouth, and indirectly to corn-growers throughout the extensive sheep–corn region of Norfolk, whenever the Council restricted exports. Nothing was better calculated to unite gentry, justices, and merchants in strong protest both in parliament and at the Council Board.[33]

Nothing, that is, except the increasing tendency for the Crown to grant administrative, dispensing, or monopoly patents which suitors could then implement to their own profit and the detriment of various county interests. The patent granted in 1586 to Thomas Wilkes, Clerk of the Council, for the manufacture and sale of white salt at King's Lynn, Boston, and Hull provides an excellent example. Wilkes sold this patent to a group of merchants which included John Smith, searcher in the Lynn customs office. He and his fellow patentees proceeded to obtain their supply of salt by compulsorily purchasing every shipload that was brought into the above ports. At Lynn their activities broke the near-monopoly of three influential merchants—Clayborne, Grave, and Shaxton—who had previously either imported or bought up nearly all the salt at Lynn and then shipped it up river to sell at great profit in Mildenhall, Cambridge, and many other inland towns. Besides damaging the fortunes of these influential burgesses, the patentees, so it was claimed, almost doubled the quayside price of salt at Lynn and its creeks, thereby doubling its price throughout the large hinterland supplied from Lynn. The patentees also compelled manufacturers of salt along the Norfolk coast to compound with them and used the Admiralty

[33] Below, pp. 99–100, 234–6.

administration to arrest shipowners who brought in salt on their own account, imprisoning them until they paid fines of up to £6. For fifteen years, until its repeal in 1601, Lynn burgesses campaigned against this patent; their efforts were strongly supported by gentry and justices throughout the county who organized a concerted protest through the quarter sessions.[34] Nor was such united opposition an isolated occurrence. As will be shown later, it was frequently stimulated by the unpopular activities of a few courtiers and county figures who implemented patents and other conciliar demands to the detriment of the county community.

[34] 'Supplementary Stiffkey Papers', ed. F. W. Brooks, pp. 1–3, *Camden Miscellany XVI* (Camden Soc. 3rd ser. lii), 1936. NNRO MS. 1620 (1C9). E. Hughes, *Studies in Administration and Finance 1558–1825*, Manchester, 1934, pp. 45–66. *TED* ii. 254–62. KL Muniments, Congregation Books, 5, ff. 348, 368v; 6, ff. 149v, 164, 171, 173v, 175v, 186v, 187v.

CHAPTER II

'The Right Noble Prince Thomas Duke of Norfolk'

THOMAS Howard was born on 10 March 1538 at Kenninghall Palace. His father, Henry Earl of Surrey, soldier-poet and Renaissance scholar, was the eldest son of the third Duke of Norfolk, Henry VIII's Lord Treasurer, who had built the great mansion at Kenninghall (alas, long since vanished) to rival Wolsey's palace at Hampton Court. An Italian astrologer, who cast the young Thomas's horoscope, predicted that his father would meet with an untimely death and that the youth would be doomed to a life of sorrow and misfortune. It was a sound prediction since before Thomas was nine years old his family had been broken in the struggle for power during the closing years of Henry VIII's reign. His father was executed on Tower Hill for treason, and his grandfather, to whom he had probably been closest, suffered imprisonment in the Tower throughout the reign of Edward VI. He lost the last vestige of intimate family life when he was taken from his mother to live for nearly six years in the household of his aunt the Duchess of Richmond, where he was tutored by John Foxe the Protestant martyrologist. Mary's accession in 1553 brought a respite from family misfortune. His grandfather was released from the Tower and restored to lands and title, but by now an old man of nearly eighty, he died a year later, thus having no time, even if he had the will, to reassert the Howard pre-eminence in national and local affairs.[1]

This task fell to sixteen-year-old Thomas, who succeeded his grandfather as fourth Duke. But before discussing his part in local affairs it is worth tracing how his ill-fated career accorded with the astrologer's prediction. Domestic affairs certainly caused him much unhappiness, for he lost three wives in childbirth before he was thirty. Meanwhile he gained little satisfaction from his career at Court, never achieving that influence among Elizabeth's councillors which befitted the premier peer of the realm. At first his youthfulness may have precluded him from the Council, but he was appointed

[1] This chapter relies heavily upon Neville Williams's *Thomas Howard Fourth Duke of Norfolk*, 1964. Unless otherwise stated I have drawn information from this source.

to its board in 1562 when still only 24. Unfortunately his aloofness and outspoken manner, especially over the question of Elizabeth's marriage, did not commend him to his sovereign; nor did his opposition to the ambitions of her favourite Robert Dudley, Earl of Leicester. No doubt his tendency to shun the Court—he rarely, if ever, went on progress with the Queen and often withdrew for long periods to his estates in Norfolk—also contributed to his failure as a councillor. Sometimes ill health or bereavement occasioned these withdrawals, but it is difficult to avoid the conclusion that he lacked the constant application to intrigue, negotiation, and courtly behaviour which made for success in sixteenth-century politics.[2]

Eventually grief at the death of his third wife Elizabeth, in 1567, and despair at his declining position at Court combined to distort his judgement and start him upon the path which led to his execution in 1572. He listened readily to suggestions that he should marry Mary Queen of Scots who had recently fled to England. At first the proposal appeared attractive to some councillors, including the Earl of Leicester, since such a marriage might help to secure Mary's restoration to the Scottish throne and to solve the succession problem in England should Elizabeth die childless. Mary had strong claims to the English crown, and her marriage to an English nobleman might help allay those fears aroused by her Roman religion and French upbringing. Unfortunately, as Thomas's enthusiasm for the marriage grew, no doubt nourished by his desire for that prestige at Court which had so far eluded him, the project began to attract support from those Catholics at home and abroad who were eager to depose Elizabeth in favour of a Catholic ruler. The sequel was the Ridolphi plot which aimed to release Mary from captivity, marry her to the Duke, proclaim her Queen, and drive Elizabeth from the kingdom with the help of Spanish troops. Almost unwittingly the Duke allowed himself to become the centre of a Catholic deposition plot. He was arrested, charged with high treason, found guilty, and executed on Tower Hill.

His death ended the hegemony of the Howards in Norfolk. The dukedom remained in abeyance for nearly 100 years, and although many of the estates were restored to Thomas's son, Philip Howard Earl of Arundel, he resided in Sussex and had little impact on the East Anglian scene. Until 1572, however, the fourth Duke domi-

[2] For an assessment of the Duke of Norfolk's political ability see W. MacCaffrey, *The Shaping of the Elizabethan Regime*, 1969, pp. 239–42.

nated that scene and it is with his impact upon society, politics and administration in Norfolk that this chapter is concerned.

In January 1567 he married Elizabeth, widow of Thomas Lord Dacre. Since she was his third wife their marriage was quietly solemnized in London. In contrast, the citizens of Norwich prepared a magnificent reception for the new Duchess. The county's ordnance had been manhandled from its storehouse in Yarmouth and shipped up river to Norwich, where the citizens welcomed the Duke and his new bride with a salute which, to judge from the quantity of powder purchased, must have resembled a cannonade. The mayor then presented Elizabeth with a 'nutte of sylver doble gylte weying 45 ounces' and costing the city £16, together with spicebread and wafers and two gallons of ypocras wine. In return the Duke and Duchess entertained the mayor and aldermen to a great banquet at their palace in Norwich.[3]

This welcome reflected the young Duke's power and status in the eyes of the Norfolk gentry and the citizens of Norwich. They styled him their 'Right Noble' or their 'high and mightye Prynce Thomas Duke of Norfolk'. His palace in Norwich which his grandfather had built beside the Wensum in the parish of St. John Maddermarket—'the greatest mansion to be found outside London and Westminster'—had been designed for lavish entertainment, with its fine furnishings, great 'bowling alley', and tennis court. The administrative centre of the Howard lands, however, was at his second great palace at Kenninghall, which the third Duke had built early in the sixteenth century to replace Framlingham Castle as the principal Howard residence. The maintenance of these palaces, together with establishments at Framlingham, Castle Rising, Thetford, Castle Acre, and two great mansions in London, suggests that the premier nobleman of the realm was also numbered among the richest. In 1559 his estimated gross annual income from rent (£6,000) surpassed that of any other nobleman, and it was greatly augmented by the profits from commerce, industrial investment, and extensive demesne farming. The Duke has been described as 'the greatest sheepmaster of the Elizabethan age', owning flocks of sheep which totalled in basic

[3] NNRO MSS. City Records, Chamberlains' Accounts 1551–67, ff. 359–359v.

stock over 16,000 animals. Judicious marriages also helped to improve his income. He gained £300 or £400 a year from the Audley lands which came to him on his second marriage, and a further £700 when the Dacre estate came under his control after his marriage to the widow of Lord Dacre of Gilsand and Graystoke in 1567. In this way the Duke ensured that in an inflationary age, when many noblemen were driven to sell property, his finances remained buoyant; Dr. Neville Williams has estimated his net income from land and stipends in the late 1560s at over £4,500. Not without reason he once boasted to Queen Elizabeth, 'I count myself, by your Majesty's favour, as good a prince at home in my bowling-alley at Norwich as . . . [Mary Stuart] is, though she were in the midst of Scotland.'[4]

Wealth and conspicuous consumption may have been ingredients of power, but the Duke's pre-eminence in East Anglia rested principally upon widespread loyalty which was fostered in many ways. It stemmed, in part at least, from his all-pervasive authority throughout his liberty which comprised the Hundreds of Launditch, South Greenhoe, Earsham, and Guiltcross, as well as fourteen other manors.

> None of the royal officials, whether sheriff, escheator, coroner, clerk of the market, steward or marshal of the Queen's household . . . could enter this extensive private franchise. . . . Instead, the duke appointed his own coroner, clerk of the market and other officials. To the duke's bailiffs belonged the right of returning and executing all writs and precepts, whether from the Crown or from its judges and commissioners. The duke kept for himself all fines imposed in any court in the kingdom on men residing in his liberty, and also enjoyed the goods and chattels of all felons, fugitives and outlaws. He had his own gaol at Lopham. His tenants could not be summoned in the sheriffs' court for debts under 40/– or for trespasses in which the damages were less than that sum, nor could they be attached for appearance in court.

It is impossible to assess how far, if at all, the Duke's bailiffs and stewards mitigated the harshness of royal administration for those who dwelt within his liberty, but undoubtedly many of these people knew little of law and administration beyond that implemented by the Duke's officials. In a very real sense he was their prince.

Bonds of loyalty could also burgeon between lord and tenant, especially under the stimulus of benevolent estate management such as appears to have been traditional throughout the Howard domain for much of the sixteenth century. This loyalty could become a

[4] NNRO MSS. City Records, Assembly Minute Book 1553–83, ff. 121, 124. Stone, *Crisis*, pp. 232, 298–9, 346, 368, 760. J. E. Neale, *Queen Elizabeth*, 1934, p. 185.

significant political factor whenever a magnate owned extensive property which was concentrated in one county rather than being scattered across several. Although a detailed study of the Howard estates is still awaited, evidence so far available suggests that, while they were far-flung in the early sixteenth century, the third and fourth Dukes deliberately consolidated and extended their holdings in East Anglia, particularly in Norfolk. As early as 1531 the third Duke had been selling land in Bedfordshire, Warwickshire, Staffordshire, and Shropshire while acquiring it in Suffolk; he also exchanged lands in Northamptonshire and Oxfordshire for estates in Norfolk and readily seized the opportunity provided by the fluid post-Dissolution land market to mortgage or sell estates in the Midlands and south-eastern England in order to purchase ex-monastic lands throughout Norfolk and Suffolk. He further increased his Norfolk holdings when Henry VIII granted him extensive confiscated lands as a reward for political services. By his death in 1554 he had concentrated the bulk of his estates into Norfolk and Suffolk; his only substantial holdings outside East Anglia being in Sussex, Surrey, and Kent. The fourth Duke continued this policy of consolidation; in 1562, when faced with debts of over £5,000 to the Crown, he devised an ingenious scheme whereby he surrendered to the Queen afforested lands in Sussex in exchange for arable land in Norfolk. In this way he paid off his debts with the timber, while at the same time acquiring further estates in Norfolk.[5]

The solidarity between the Dukes and their growing body of East Anglian tenantry may well have been strengthened by a tradition of long service among the Howard household officials. Successive generations of Blennerhassetts, Fulmerstons, Tolemaches, Timperleys, Hollands, and Cantrells became key figures in the ducal administrative hierarchy. Such continuity undoubtedly betokened their loyalty and in turn instilled a sense of loyalty among the tenantry.[6]

[5] *L & P H VIII*, iv(2), no. 5132; v, nos. 220, 1207; xii(1), no. 1330(26); xii(2), no. 1311(24); xiv(1), no. 651(31); xv, nos. 498, 942(42 & 44); xx(2), no. 496(18). *Rot. Parl.* 25 H VIII, c. 24; 31 H VIII, c. 13; 21 H VIII, c. 22. I owe these refs. to Mr. F. R. Grace. See also his thesis, 'The Life and Career of Thomas Howard, Third Duke of Norfolk' (Nottingham MA thesis 1961), Appendix I. *NA* xxxiv, 1966, pp. 21–2. T. H. Swales, 'The Sequestration of Religious Property in Norfolk at the Reformation' (Sheffield PhD thesis 1965), p. 227. NNRO MS. NRS 27260 (361 X 3). *CPR, 1558–60*, pp. 260, 393; *1560–3*, pp. 563, 597; *1563–6*, p. 496; *1566–9*, pp. 238, 302; *1569–72*, pp. 126–7.

[6] R. J. W. Swales, 'Local Politics and the Parliamentary Representation of Sussex 1529–1558' (Bristol PhD thesis 1964), Appendix, pp. 36, 174–5, 460–1. G. H. Ryan &

The bonds of personal loyalty are elusive factors, but the Duke's pre-eminence in his county rested upon more than sentiment or allegiance dictated by economic necessity. There is no doubt that he was intimately involved in local affairs. His responsibilities as Earl Marshal of England, and after 1562, as a privy councillor, rarely prevented him from spending as much time in Norfolk as at Court. Invariably he celebrated Christmas at his palace in Norwich or Kenninghall and usually he slipped away from Court in the early summer, seldom returning to London till Michaelmas had passed. By temperament he seems to have preferred the exercise of his untrammelled authority in Norfolk to the intrigues and compromises of national affairs. In the long run this aloofness from the Court weakened his ability to attract clients and opened the way for magnates like the Earl of Leicester and Sir Nicholas Bacon to begin to challenge his near-monopoly of patronage in the county.[7]

There was much to attract and flatter him in Norwich where merchants, whose vaults encompassed his palace, entertained him lavishly. In 1563 they elected him to St. George's Company, successor to the great medieval merchant guild, and in subsequent years admitted over forty of his followers and household officials. For a brief period this once great civic company resembled a club for county gentry. The Duke attended its annual feast with such a large entourage that extra plate had to be purchased and supplementary funds provided. Indeed, so great was the merchants' esteem for their 'prince' that they even entertained the array of notabilities from other shires who frequently gathered at the palace in Norwich to partake of his grace's sumptuous hospitality. In 1568, anticipating the Duke's attendance with 'dyvers . . . strangers' at the forthcoming feast, congregation voted its feastmakers '100/– owt of the stock . . . over and besides the £4 before given' to cover their extra purchases of wine. Even before the Company had elected the Duke to its membership it feasted a distinguished gathering of his friends and relatives which included his two young sons—the Earl of Surrey and Lord Thomas Howard—the Earls of Northumberland and Huntingdon, Thomas Howard Viscount Bindon, the Lords Willoughby, Neville, Scrope, Wentworth, Berkeley, and Sheffield,

---

L. J. Redstone, *Timperley of Hintlesham*, 1931, ch. I. PRO SC 6/6305. I am indebted to Mr. F. R. Grace for this reference.

[7] Below, pp. 29–30, 33, 35, 38, 42, 66.

together with sixty knights and esquires as well as 'dyvers and many other'. Such an assembly of noblemen and knights in Norwich must have been surpassed only by that which attended the feast, reputedly held in the Cathedral cloisters, in honour of the Queen when on progress into Norfolk in 1578.[8]

Certainly the Duke ruled in his country. His name headed the commissions of the peace for Norfolk and Suffolk, and when resident in Norfolk he attended quarter sessions at Norwich. He was also steward of the Duchy of Lancaster's lands in Norfolk, Suffolk, and Cambridgeshire, steward of the Liberty of St. Edmunds, feodary of Norfolk and Suffolk, and high steward of at least one borough. Perhaps surprisingly, he was never *custos rotulorum*[9] for Norfolk or Suffolk and held the lord lieutenancy of these counties for only a few months, simply because during his lifetime the Queen rarely appointed a lieutenant. But his power was not the product of the offices he held: his authority rested largely upon the influence he could exert and the patronage he could dispense on behalf of client gentry and borough corporations.[10] He owed his unrivalled position at the centre of a great patronage network, in part at least, to the absence of any other influential East Anglian nobleman round whom clients could gather. Down to 1545 Charles Brandon, second Duke of Suffolk, had attracted an extensive clientage, but the tragic death of his two young sons Charles and Henry in 1551 and the execution of Henry Grey in 1554 extinguished the Suffolk dukedom. The only other nobleman in Norfolk was Henry Lord Cromwell, grandson of Thomas Cromwell, who resided at North Elmham. He appears to have been impecunious and commanded little political influence, while his son Edward, 'an impoverished Baron of no consequence', staked all on Essex's abortive uprising at the end of the century, subsequently selling his English property to settle in Ireland.[11]

The Duke jealously guarded his patronage. 'I wold have bene sorye', he once told Cecil, 'that my cuntrye mene schuld have hade

[8] NNRO MSS. City Records, Book of St. George's Co. 1452–1602, pp. 1, 9, 255, 229–30, 233; Norfolk Sessions Minute Book 1562–7, *passim*. Below, p. 218.

[9] For *custodes rotulorum* in Norf. see Appendix I.

[10] R. Somerville, *History of the Duchy of Lancaster*, i, 1953, p. 595. NNRO MS. NRS 27260 (361 X 3). Yarmouth Assembly Book 1550–9, f. 118.

[11] GEC xii(1), 461–2. Stone, *Crisis*, pp. 266, 457, 485. Neale, *Commons*, p. 56. *DNB*, s.v. Brandon, Charles and Cromwell, Edward.

cawse to have judged that enye matter concernyng the Quenes Majestyes sarvys in Norfolke or Suffolke shulde rather have bene committyd off first to others than to me.'[12] Aldermen, justices of the peace, even Dutch 'strangers' appreciated the importance of his assistance in expediting their business; while Norwich merchants enmeshed him in their guild activities, their fellows at Yarmouth took the precaution to elect him high steward of their borough. They had no reason to regret their choice, since his powerful backing was a significant factor in the revival of this once-prosperous port and constituted one of the Duke's great services to his county.

Throughout the Duke's childhood the townsmen of Yarmouth had struggled to improve the navigability of their harbour. In the early Middle Ages its two entrances, one to the north of the town and the other well to the south, had facilitated the arrival and departure of shipping. But for several centuries the efficiency of the haven had been seriously impaired because the northern and most convenient channel had been blocked by sand and shingle banks, leaving only the southern outlet which, being at the end of a long shingle spit, presented serious navigational hazards. For over 200 years Yarmouth men had tried unsuccessfully to cut through the spit at a point nearer their wharves and warehouses. In their sixth attempt, begun in 1549, they had blocked the southern entrance with sunken vessels hoping to divert the stream so that it would scour their new and more convenient cut. The attempt failed, so that with the remaining entrance blocked and the new one unnavigable, the harbour seemed doomed. The situation was critical both for the inhabitants of Yarmouth, whose livelihood depended entirely upon trade and fishing, and for the merchants of Norwich whose ships reached open waters through the haven. Eventually, in 1567, with advice from the skilled Dutch engineer Joyce Johnson, the present channel was successfully cut and protected by huge piers—an enterprise which required finances on a scale beyond the means of a declining sea-port.[13]

In their ceaseless endeavours to raise money the bailiffs and corporation of Yarmouth had constant recourse to the Duke's patron-

[12] PRO SP 15/13/52.

[13] For the rebuilding of Yarmouth haven see esp. T. Damet, *A Booke of the Foundacion & Antiquitye of . . . Greate Yarmouthe*, ed. C. J. Palmer, 1847; H. Manship, *History of Great Yarmouth*, ed. C. J. Palmer, Yarmouth, 1854.

age.[14] In April 1565 they sent two of their number to London 'to wayte uppon the Ducke his grace of Norfolk for the delyvery of serten bokys concernyng the decaye of the towne . . . and, yf yt shalbe thowght good by the Ducke his grace furder to travayle and to exhibit a supplycacon to the Quene's Majestie for the same, that they to travayle therin'. The subsequent appointment of a commission to inquire into the state of the haven suggests that his grace decided to plead their case at the Council Board, if not with the Queen as well. The inquiry resulted in the successful completion of the work under Johnson—an operation which required immense labour as well as feverish fund-raising activities. The bailiffs once more turned to their patron who undoubtedly supported their petition to the Queen for a licence to export corn. In April 1568 they were granted a patent which empowered them to export 6,000 quarters of grain annually for three years, at a time when shipments of corn overseas were forbidden or rigorously controlled. Since they quickly sold the first year's licence to two Yarmouth merchants for £666.13*s*.4*d*., the entire proceeds from this licence cannot have fallen far short of £2,000. Appropriately, the Duke was appointed to oversee the expenditure of this new income.[15]

His patronage is evident at every stage of this struggle to save the haven. He supplied timber from his own estates, contributed generously to the special harbour fund (although his steward sometimes found it difficult to honour his promises), secured a remission from subsidies for the townsmen of Yarmouth, and even prevailed upon the Norwich aldermen to vote 200 marks towards the haven's repair. The Duke's power and influence are evident in the city's prompt response to this request which may be contrasted with its unwillingness to make any contribution towards financing other sea defence works later in Elizabeth's reign.[16]

Although there is no doubt about the primacy of his patronage in the affairs of Yarmouth, it would be an oversimplification of the Elizabethan political scene to represent him as having an outright monopoly there. On several occasions 'Mr. Secretary Cecil' received gifts of ling, which betoken either payment for favours

[14] NNRO MS. Yarmouth Assembly Book 1559–70, ff. 68, 78, 81, 81v, 88, 88v, 128, 136v, 142, 147v.

[15] *CPR, 1566–9*, p. 160. Thomas Damet states that the licence was sold for £1,407 (op. cit., p. 30).

[16] NNRO MS. City Records, Assembly Minute Book 1553–82, f. 79v. Below, pp. 98–9.

received or investment in what the burgesses deemed to be future high-yielding political stock. Nor did they restrict their clientage to a single patron: at the height of their campaign for a corn licence they sent the Earl of Leicester, the Lord Admiral, the Lord Keeper, and the Master of the Rolls fifty 'great lyng' each; they even chartered a special boat for this cargo and appointed one of their brethren to 'se the same lyng delyveryd accordyng to hys instruccons'.[17]

Nor did Yarmouth have any special claim upon the Duke's patronage. King's Lynn Congregation books reveal the extent to which it too depended upon the Duke, although its relations with him were not entirely cordial.[18] The Lynn burgesses disliked his interference in their choice of M.P.s and deliberately delayed appointing a high steward until immediately after his death, although their counterparts at Yarmouth had bestowed this honour upon him in 1555. Their coolness may account for his apparent failure to visit the town despite the proximity of Rising Chase. None the less such was the Duke's primacy in East Anglia that aldermanic deputations frequently waited on him: they asked him to mediate in their dispute with Thomas Johns over ownership of St. James's Chapel, and in their conflict with fishermen from Wolferton over rights to mussel-beds at the mouth of the Ouse; they solicited his backing at the Council Board in their campaign for reduced military rates and for licences to permit 'strangers' to settle at Lynn, to allow the manufacture of tapestries and bays, and, most profitable of all, to enable transportation of corn after the manner of the Yarmouth licence. Sometimes, too, the Duke intervened of his own accord as when he compelled the townsmen to sell their goods according to the standard bushel, instead of a reduced measure which they had instituted. On another occasion he summoned their leaders to Norwich in order to mediate in their dispute with his chamberlain, Sir Nicholas L'Estrange. As at Yarmouth, however, there are signs that during the 1560s Lynn burgesses were turning to patrons who commanded greater favour and esteem at Court. For some years the town had given the Lord Treasurer an annual fee, and when they sought their corn licence in 1567, besides approaching the Duke, the mayor journeyed to the Court to solicit the Earl of Leicester to whom they subsequently presented a piece of plate.[19]

[17] NNRO MS. Yarmouth Assembly Book 1559–70, ff. 90, 107v, 112v.

[18] Below, pp. 37–8.

[19] KL Muniments, Congregation Books 1544–69, ff. 326, 330, 359, 379, 381v, 419v,

Norwich, also, was much in the Duke's debt. In 1564, when its industry and trade were extremely depressed, he bestowed £30 'in rewards and alms to the poor'. The citizens must have been particularly grateful to him for his part in persuading the Queen to permit 300 Dutch and Walloon refugees to settle in Norwich, since the city's subsequent resurgence largely depended upon the skills introduced by these 'strangers'. The Duke seems to have taken a personal interest in these settlers who, in turn, were quick to appreciate the importance of his patronage. Gille de Vinch described how he was daily in the mansion of the Duke 'who is the one nearest the Queen', and as soon as Howard had returned from Court to keep the Christmas of 1565 in Norwich a deputation sought his help to obtain a church 'where they may resort to heare the word of God according to their former manner'.[20] The city duly gave them the chancel of the former Blackfriars Church, now St. Andrew's Hall, which it had acquired at the Reformation and where memorials to some of their early pastors may still be seen.

The Duke's influence upon county government can be detected in the appointment of J.P.s, although inadequate sources prevent a thorough assessment of this aspect of his patronage.[21] When he succeeded to the title in 1554 Howard influence was at a low ebb. The aged third Duke, who died within a year of his release from imprisonment under Edward VI, had not even managed to secure the restoration to the Bench of his friends and household officials who had been dismissed during his imprisonment.[22] Initially the fourth Duke made no greater impact upon the administrative scene. In 1554 he was still a minor of sixteen and he does not appear to have had any close associations with the six justices known to have been appointed between 1555 and 1557.[23] A similar decline of Howard

---

424, 436, 452, 455v, 457, 466v, 474, 474v, 483, 483v, 484, 495, 496, 507, 519v; 1569–90, ff. 13, 73.

[20] W. J. C. Moens, *The Walloons and their Church at Norwich 1565–1832*, Lymington, 1888, pp. 221, 253.

[21] The difficulty of obtaining an accurate chronology of the appointment of J.P.s is discussed more fully below, pp. 73–4. See also *HLQ* xxii, 1959, pp. 301–12.

[22] Sir Nicholas Hare, Richard Fulmerston, Sir Nicholas L'Estrange, and Sir John Clere.

[23] Robt. Barney, Thos. Ragland, John Jenny, Anthony Thwaytes, James Brown, and Wm. Brampton. cf. PRO SP 11/5/6 with the reconstructed list of justices for 1557/8 in Smith, 'Norf. Gentry'. pp. 412–13.

influence in Sussex, albeit in electoral affairs, has been detected during the period 1553–8.[24]

With Elizabeth's accession, however, Thomas Howard's influence becomes paramount. The return to Protestantism necessitated a careful scrutiny of the loyalty of all magistrates and led to some drastic changes in the Norfolk Bench. At least 44 per cent of the late Marian justices lost their places. Out of eleven new justices, excluding *ex officio* members, who were appointed to replace those of doubtful loyalty, six had close associations with the Duke and may well have been his nominees.[25] There can be little doubt about his influence in the appointment of his chamberlain Sir Nicholas L'Estrange, his treasurer Richard Fulmerston, and his stepfather Thomas Steynings; he may also have played a part in the appointment of his friend Thomas Gawdy (for whom he subsequently procured the keepership of the Marshalsea and King's Bench prison), and of John Appleyard and William Paston who were both Howard dependants.[26]

Moreover, during the first decade of the Queen's reign he appears steadily to have packed the Norfolk Bench with his own clients. In 1561 one of his principal household officers, John Blennerhassett, and his clients Thomas Lovell and Edward Clere appeared in commission as did another of his officials, Thomas Hogan, and at least three more Howard clients some time between 1564 and 1569.[27] By 1564, excluding *ex officio* members of the commission, at least eleven out of the eighteen magistrates in Norfolk could well have been appointed through ducal patronage or, to present the statistics differently, out of thirty-two justices who were appointed or re-

[24] R. J. W. Swales, 'Local Politics and the Parliamentary Representation of Sussex 1529–1558' (Bristol PhD thesis 1964), pp. 78–84.

[25] *HLQ* xxii, 1959, pp. 301–12. Smith, 'Norf. Gentry', pp. 412–13.

[26] Thos. Gawdy was eldest son of Thos. Gawdy of Shottesham, serjeant at law, who had been high steward of all the 3rd Duke's lands in Norfolk, see NNRO MS. NRS 27260 (361 X 3). *CPR, 1569–72*, p. 450. For John Appleyard, see NNRO MS. NAS Frere, box K12a, bundle marked Humbleyard Hundred, letter from Appleyard to Edw. Flowerdew, dated 3 Oct. 1564. Appleyard subsequently lost the Duke's favour and was left out of the commission of the peace in 1560.

[27] Robt. Balam, Thos. Southwell, Roger Woodhouse, and possibly Edw. Warner. For Balam, see Norah M. Fuidge, 'The Personnel of the House of Commons of 1563–7' (London MA thesis 1950), p. 19. Balam was also appointed a J.P. in the Isle of Ely when the Duke was Bailiff (*CPR, 1563–6*, p. 29; *1566–9*, p. 405). For Thos. Southwell, see PCC 13 Babington. For Roger Woodhouse, see *NA* xv, 1904, p. 100; xxiv, 1930, p. 74. For Edw. Warner, see PCC 12 Crymes and below, p. 41.

appointed between 1558 and 1572 seventeen are likely to have received his backing.

Although the Duke seems to have had extensive influence on the appointment of magistrates in Norfolk, here again he had no monopoly. The commissions of the peace, like the records of King's Lynn and Yarmouth, testify to the influence of other patrons. The Earl of Leicester could equally well have had a hand in John Appleyard's appointment to the Bench in 1558. Leicester had married Appleyard's half-sister, Amy Robsart, and claimed responsibility for securing his appointment to the shrievalty of Norfolk in 1559 and the portership of Berwick in 1565. The odds are that Leicester also expedited the appointment of Edward Flowerdew in the late 1560s. Flowerdew's brother William was steward to the Earl who clearly relied heavily upon the family for his business in Norfolk. In return he requited them well as Flowerdew acknowledged when he bequeathed a silver cup to 'my very good Lord Leycester' with the request that the Earl should 'continue his goodness to my nephew Anthony'.[28]

Most likely Lord Keeper Nicholas Bacon also had a hand in the appointment of magistrates; his servant John Eyer joined the Norfolk Bench in 1558, and he had close family ties, not to mention radical religious affinities, with Sir William Butts and Thomas Barrow, both of whom appeared in commission early in Elizabeth's reign. Sir Nicholas Bacon's influence is not surprising since he resided at Redgrave, a Suffolk village close to the Norfolk border, and had a town house in Norwich. In any case the procedure for appointing justices was such that the Lord Keeper's influence might easily obtrude.[29]

Despite these indications that other influential courtiers extended their clientage into Norfolk, there is little doubt about the superiority of the Duke's patronage which was both extensive and constant. Its constancy emerges from an examination of the tenure of various magistrates. As is shown in chapter IV, the dependence of clients upon a patron did not end with their appointment as justices; their names might well be omitted from a succeeding commission unless someone at Court constantly spoke up for them. In the provision of

[28] *NAM* iii, 1887, pp. 306, 310. W. Rye, *Norfolk Families*, Norwich, 1913, p. 221. PCC 23 Windsor. For Leicester's connection with Norfolk, see below, pp. 39–40.

[29] PCC 22 Loftes. *NA* xxix, 1946, p. 200 (geneal. table). Blomefield, iv. 136. For their religious views see below, p. 207.

such unremitting attention the Duke's patronage outclassed that of his rivals. Few of his client justices were subsequently dismissed, whereas many, indeed most others lost their places a year or two after appointment.[30] On the rare occasions when his clients were omitted from the commission, usually on account of conservative religious views, he seems to have procured their speedy restoration.[31]

His influence is also apparent in the actual size of the Norfolk commission. Early in Elizabeth's reign the Council, at Cecil's instigation, had decided that quiet and godly government could best be achieved through the work and influence of a few high-minded justices in each county.[32] In pursuit of this policy the Lord Keeper dismissed large numbers of magistrates; between 1558 and 1562 the Bench in Norfolk was reduced from 37 to 24, in Sussex from 45 to 31, and in Essex from 60 to 45. In nearly all counties, however, numbers in commission soon increased again despite a further 'purge' in 1564, so that in less than a decade they stood at least as high as in 1558. But not so in Norfolk where numbers remained steady at between 24 and 29. This suggests that the Duke not only agreed with Cecil's conservative policy, but also had the authority to implement it in Norfolk. This surmise is supported by the immediate proliferation of justices in Norfolk after his death in 1572 when numbers almost doubled in less than a decade, rising from 28 in 1574 to 46 in 1579.[33]

But he did not always play the Council's game. In 1564 their lordships, anxious that all justices should be in sympathy with the religious settlement, decided to dismiss any who were 'backward' in religion and to appoint reliable Protestants in their stead. They therefore requested the bishops, in consultation with a few well-affected leaders in their dioceses, to report on the religious views of all magistrates and others in authority and to recommend replacements for those with popish inclinations. Most bishops, after con-

[30] Appendix I; cf. the career-lines of such justices as John Blennerhassett, Richard Fulmerston, Wm. Paston, Thos. Steynings, Nich. L'Estrange, and Roger Woodhouse (jun) with those of Thos. Barrow, Thos. Brampton, Wm. Brampton, Wm. Cocket, Martin Hastings and Henry Reppes.

[31] e.g. Thos. Lovell (sen) and Thos. Knyvett (sen). But John Appleyard and Edw. Clere were Howard clients who were dismissed and not restored; there is, however, evidence that both lost the Duke's favour.

[32] Below, pp. 76–80.

[33] Appendix I.

sultation with their chancellors, commissaries, and neighbouring magnates, submitted a detailed schedule on the religious views held by magistrates in their dioceses, especially recommending good Protestants worthy of being promoted to the local Benches. The Bishop of Norwich,[34] however, submitted a return for Norfolk which was oddly out of keeping both with those of his fellow bishops and with his own radical religious persuasions. Alone among the episcopate, he saw fit to consult with a nobleman—inevitably the Duke. He alone made no specific report upon the religious views of each magistrate, merely naming four who were 'not thought by common fame to be so well bent as the other'. Even in their case his report was unique in that he neither advocated their dismissal nor suggested the names of any devout Protestants who might be appointed in their stead. In fact he specifically recommended that no new justices be appointed, 'the shire being alredie in so good quiet . . . I thinke the number sufficient for this shire'. This reticent report, with its thinly-veiled resentment against the Council's attempt to displace the religious conservatives on the Norfolk Bench, was submitted by one of the most radical early-Elizabethan bishops who, when left to himself after 1572, packed the Norfolk commission with zealous Puritans. All this suggests that for Parkhurst the Duke's dictates mattered more than Protestant principles.[35]

The Duke's patronage is also evident in appointments to the shrievalty. Most early Elizabethan sheriffs of Norfolk and Suffolk (the two counties shared the same sheriff until 1575) wore his livery. Lionel Tolemache (1566–7) had been a member of the third Duke's council and came of a family which had long served the Howards. Similarly Robert Wingfield (1560–1) was son of an official of the Howard household, while Thomas Tyndale (1561–2), Owen Hopton (1564–5), William Paston (1565–6), Edward Clere (1567–8), and Ralph Shelton (1571–2) were all tenants, friends, or followers of the Duke.[36] None the less, as in the case of the commission of the peace, it is possible to exaggerate his influence upon these appointments, since Leicester's hand is once more evident in the selection of John Appleyard (1559–60), and perhaps the Lord Keeper's in that of Sir William Butts (1562–3). The Duke's word

[34] John Parkhurst.

[35] 'A Collection of Original Letters from the Bishops to the Privy Council 1564', ed. Mary Bateson, pp. 58–9, *Camden Miscellany IX* (Camden Soc. N.S. liii), 1895.

[36] PRO SC 6/6305. *HMC Salisbury*, i. 438.

could, however, be mandatory in the appointment of under-sheriffs. In 1565 William Paston, the incoming sheriff, had hoped to bestow the under-shrievalty for his 'further benefit', but such aspirations were dashed when Mr. Ashfield arrived bearing a letter from the Duke requesting his appointment to the office. Paston, himself a Howard man, automatically 'granted [him] the certen gift therof'.[37]

The Duke's influence can be detected in appointments to the whole range of county offices. The commission for sewers contained at least seven of his household officials as well as several friends and followers whose religious views were too avowedly popish for even the Duke to be able to procure them a place on the Bench. At least five of the escheators for Norfolk and Suffolk appointed between 1555 and 1566 had close associations with the Duke. He sometimes intervened in appointments to militia captaincies, while members of his household invariably acted as tax collectors and receivers of Norfolk and Suffolk. His influence is also clearly discernible in the appointment of the *custos rotulorum* and vice-admiral for the county.[38]

Thomas Howard's princely status in Norfolk rested largely upon his ability to help an array of clients drawn from all strata of society to fulfil their diverse economic, social, and political aspirations. Power still depended upon a feudal following even if, in the less turbulent Tudor age, it was more frequently deployed in the dutiful voting of freeholders at elections, the partial verdicts of jurymen at assizes and quarter sessions, or the partisan activities of commissioners engaged in innumerable tasks of local government. Nowhere is the Duke's concern and ability to oblige clients more evident than in his electoral patronage; and here it is possible to return from conjecture to established fact, thanks to the researches of Sir John Neale and the numerous scholars who have assisted in his study of Elizabethan parliaments.

Between 1558 and 1572 five Norfolk boroughs—Norwich, King's Lynn, Yarmouth, Castle Rising, and Thetford—each returned two burgesses to parliament and at almost every election they all chose

[37] BM MS. Add. 27447, f. 110.

[38] *CPR, 1569–72*, pp. 217–18. *APC, 1558–70*, p. 21. Sir Jas. Boleyn (*custos* 1558–60), Sir Wm. Woodhouse (*custos* 1562) and Sir Chris. Heydon (*custos* 1564–79) were all close associates of the Duke. The *custos* is usually indicated in the *Libri Pacis*. The vice-admirals of Norfolk and Suffolk during the period 1558–72 were Sir Wm. Woodhouse, Sir Thos. Woodhouse, and Henry Woodhouse; all were closely associated with the Duke. *EHR* xxiii, 1908, p. 747. *CSPD, 1547–80*, pp. 22, 388.

at least one ducal nominee. Thetford and Castle Rising presented no problem; they were Howard pocket boroughs. Thetford was a Duchy of Lancaster borough, but by the beginning of Elizabeth's reign the Duke had become its unchallenged patron by virtue of being lord of the manor and the most important Duchy official in the county. Besides this, his trusted servant Sir Richard Fulmerston was the principal landowner in and around the borough. The Duke's interest can be detected most clearly in 1563 when Thetford returned his client Edward Clere and Sir Richard Fulmerston. He probably had no need to interfere directly since both candidates had strong local influence. As late as 1571 his influence is still apparent in the election of his protégé Thomas Hogan and of Philip Appleyard, a squire whose family had been closely connected with the Howards. Only in the 1559 election, when the townsmen returned their mayor, Edmund Gascoign, and Thomas Poley, is the evidence less than conclusive. On this occasion Sir Richard Fulmerston was probably influential in the return of Gascoign, to whom he had leased land, while the likelihood of ducal influence provides the only plausible explanation for Poley's return for the second seat. Poley does not appear to have been a burgess—he probably hailed from Little Saxham in Suffolk—and there is no evidence that he had any personal connection with the borough.[39]

Castle Rising, enfranchised in 1558, probably at the Duke's request, regularly returned his chamberlain Sir Nicholas L'Estrange. It was, however, slightly less constant in its choice of a second member: in 1559 the burgesses chose his stepfather Thomas Steynings and in 1563 they returned Francis Carew, an outsider from Surrey whom Howard may have put in at the instigation of his friend Nicholas Throgmorton, but in 1571 they elected George Dacre[40] who had no apparent connections with either the county or the Duke.

At King's Lynn the aldermen appear to have accepted the Duke's intervention with some reluctance. On 27 December 1559 they convened an extraordinary council meeting to consider the Duke's request for the nomination of one of their burgesses to the forthcoming parliament. At this meeting they 'condiscended that my Lord of Norfolk shall at his request have the nomination of oon of

39 Unless otherwise stated, the account of the Duke's role in elections is based upon information from the History of Parliament Trust. The interpretation is mine.

40 Of Cheshunt, Herts. Not to be confused with the Dacres of the North.

the burgesses of the next parliament'; then, early in January, they elected the Duke's client Thomas Hogan, together with Thomas Waters. Their behaviour at the 1563 election strongly suggests disapproval of the Duke's interference. On this occasion they chose their recorder Robert Bell, but omitted to elect a second burgess, merely minuting 'that a burgess of the town shalbe another'; meanwhile they hastily admitted to the freedom of the borough Richard L'Estrange, younger brother of the Duke's chamberlain, and then reconvened to elect him to this parliament. The evidence suggests that they had refused to elect the Duke's nominee until he became a burgess. Such a gesture may have been encouraged by Robert Bell who so disliked this sort of electoral interference that in a subsequent parliament he proposed the imposition of a £40 penalty upon every borough electing a nobleman's nominee.[41]

Yarmouth was in no position to resist the Duke's dictates; indeed it had every reason to strengthen its association with him by choosing his clients. In 1558 and 1559 it elected William Barker, 'present servant to my Lord of Norfolk', and Sir Thomas Woodhouse who, so the clerk noted, was to inform the Duke of Norfolk—an entry which could indicate that he had been elected in deference to his grace's wishes.[42] In 1563 the town dutifully returned Thomas Timperley, comptroller of the Duke's household, but gave the other seat to William Le Grice, one of its principal citizens. The latter's election suggests either that Yarmouth had made a gesture to assert its independence, or that the Earl of Leicester's patronage had obtruded, for by the 1570s Le Grice was a client and Puritan associate of the Earl. By 1571 the town again returned Le Grice, this time with William Barker who by then had become the Duke's secretary.

The citizens of Norwich had little difficulty in reconciling the Duke's wishes with their own choice of burgesses, since in a sense his servants and followers ranked as citizens. Most of them were members of St. George's Company and a few, like Sir Nicholas L'Estrange, owned property in the city. The career of John Blennerhassett, who was elected burgess to the second session of the 1563 parliament as well as to that for 1571, illustrates the interrelationship between the city and the ducal household. His father had served the

[41] KL Muniments, Congregation Book 1544–69, ff. 324v, 325, 385v.–387v.

[42] NNRO MSS. Yarmouth Assembly Book 1550–59, f. 203; 1559–70, f. 36. C. J. Palmer, . . . *Continuation of Manship*, 1856, p. 198.

Howards, and he had long been one of their chief legal advisers; then in 1562 he was elected Steward of Norwich, continuing in that office until 1567 when he returned to full-time service with the Duke as treasurer of the household in succession to Sir Richard Fulmerston. In the same way Sir William Woodhouse, elected a burgess in 1559, was one of the Duke's clients and most substantial tenants as well as being sufficiently prominent in St. George's Company to bequeath it 'a crimson satin doublet striped with gold . . . for him to wear that shall yearly play the George at Saint George's feast in Norwich'.

The evidence for Howard's influence on county elections is less conclusive, and only in the 1566 by-election is it clear that his word was mandatory. This election was caused by the death of both knights of the shire before the parliament elected in 1563 met for its second session in 1566. In the ensuing by-election Thomas Howard instructed the sheriff, William Paston, to 'nominate' Roger Townshend and Clement Paston, with the proviso that should his treasurer Sir Richard Fulmerston, then burgess for Thetford, wish to have the second county seat Clement Paston should stand down and accept nomination for Thetford in Fulmerston's stead. Perhaps Fulmerston was already failing in health; at any rate he declined the honour, and the county court, under William Paston's guidance, dutifully proceeded to execute the unmodified Howard plan by returning Townshend and Paston.[43]

Such positive evidence of the Duke's electoral influence must weigh in any consideration of the more circumstantial evidence for his influence in the elections of 1559 and 1563. At the former the freeholders elected Robert Dudley, subsequently royal favourite and contender for Elizabeth's hand in marriage, as first knight of the shire. The second seat they gave to Sir Edmund Wyndham, aged, politic, respected through years of service to his county, rich with monastic spoils, in precedence yielding place to none but the Duke himself. Although distantly related to the Howards, he had strong claims in his own right to end his public service in the county, as indeed he had begun it, with the honour of election as knight of the shire.

By contrast Robert Dudley, fifth son of the ill-starred Duke of Northumberland, was a 'foreigner' of barely ten years' standing in the county. Such property as he held came through his wife Amy

[43] Bodl. MS. Douce 393, f. 94.

Robsart, daughter of Sir John Robsart of Sidestrand and Wymondham. It has been suggested that he first met Amy when campaigning with his father against Ket and his followers in 1549. Be that as it may, the couple were married in 1550 and Robert, a youth of about eighteen, settled in Norfolk, rapidly assuming a prominence in local affairs far beyond that normally accorded to a newcomer of such tender years and experience. His name figured high in various commissions, including those for the peace, subsidy, and gaol delivery; he was appointed joint lieutenant of Norfolk in 1552 and 1553; at a by-election in 1552, occasioned by the death of Sir Edmund Knyvett, he was returned as knight of the shire, and he sat for the county again in March 1553. Only his father's intervention can explain the virtually unprecedented appointment of a twenty-year-old newcomer to these coveted positions, and inevitably Northumberland's execution in 1553 impaired his career as a county magnate.

Why, then, did the Norfolk gentry and freeholders again elect him in 1559 as their first knight of the shire? Could it be that already the county deferred to the dictates of its young Duke, as was certainly the case in 1566? The notion is not entirely fanciful. The antipathy between Norfolk and Dudley, can too easily be ante-dated. It has been suggested that at first everything had pointed to friendship between them—a friendship which may well have been fostered by the Duke's marriage in 1558 to Dudley's sister-in-law Lady Margaret, widow of his brother Lord Henry Dudley. Moreover, during the first uncertain months of the new reign, none of the issues had emerged which were subsequently to cloud their relationship. It seems that Dudley had not begun his flirtation with the Queen, with all its attendant political consequences, nor had he unequivocally assumed his title as 'cherisher and patron-general' of the Puritans. Lacking that security which he subsequently gained as a result of the Queen's favour, 'as yet he had taken up no ideological stance or policy position'.[44]

The Duke of Norfolk, for his part, not yet twenty-one and faced with rebuilding the Howard interest in central and local government, may never have been as reactionary in his religion as has sometimes been supposed. Whatever his convictions, he subordinated them to his sense of loyalty, as when he found a place in his household for his former tutor, John Foxe the martyrologist. Robert Dudley, too, had

[44] Williams, p. 49. Collinson, p. 53. W. MacCaffrey, *The Shaping of the Elizabethan Regime*, 1969, p. 85.

grounds for expecting Howard patronage: his father-in-law Sir John Robsart had been receiver of the third Duke's estates in Norfolk, and after Robsart's death in 1553 Thomas Howard may well have felt some responsibility for the latter's heiress Amy Robsart. But the association did not end here. After the third Duke's attainder for treason, while the Howard lands were escheated to the Crown, Sir John Robsart and his son-in-law had been appointed joint 'steward of the lordship, constable of the castle, and master of the hunt of deer or ranger of the chace of Rising'.[45] Thus, when the third Duke was restored to his lands and Castle Rising again became Howard property, Robert Dudley may have been a Howard official.

The Duke's role in the 1563 county election is equally enigmatic. On this occasion Sir William Woodhouse and Sir Edward Warner were chosen as knights of the shire. Woodhouse had already represented the county in 1558 but had been ousted in 1559 when he had sat instead for Norwich. He was a distinguished naval commander who had greatly extended his properties through royal grants and judicious purchases, so that it is perhaps surprising that after retiring to Waxham in the early 1550s he was not elected to represent the county during Mary's first four parliaments. It may well be that as a tenant of the Duke and head of a family which had close Howard associations, Woodhouse's parliamentary career developed in step with the restoration of Howard influence under the fourth Duke. Sir Edward Warner, on the other hand, was not a great county figure; he was the son of a minor gentleman, had spent most of his career in royal service, and when elected in 1563 he was serving a second term as Lieutenant of the Tower; at that time he was a J.P. in Middlesex but had not figured in the Norfolk commission of the peace. Such status as he had in Norfolk derived largely from his marriage to the widow of Thomas Hobart of Plumstead. His election as second knight of the shire could only have been at the behest of a patron, and who more likely than the Duke in view of his commanding role in the ensuing 1566 by-election? The only indication of any relationship between the two comes from Warner's will where he mentions the Duke owing him £100.

The fourth Duke was undeniably a prince in his county—frequently

[45] *CPR, 1549–51*, p. 402.

in residence at Norwich or Kenninghall, he dominated local society, largely dictating the personnel of local government, influencing administrative decisions, mediating in local disputes, and supporting local interests at Court, in the Council, and even before the Queen. However, he never attained that complete mastery within the county which he would undoubtedly have liked, and certainly claimed. There are signs of rival patronage, especially in the late 1560s; by then his failure to consolidate his position at Court was causing ambitious gentry to attach themselves to patrons who seemed more influential with the Queen and Council. As early as 1565 he complained that 'her Hyenes hardlye thynkes enye thynge well bestowyd apon me, be yt never so small.'[46]

Despite this inability to make his mark at Court, the fourth Duke had gone a long way towards restoring the Howard hegemony in Norfolk. His immense power derived partly from the great Howard liberty, partly from his personal participation in local affairs, and partly from that great concentration of estates in East Anglia which he and his grandfather had deliberately built up. These estates yielded an income greater than the lands of any other peer; they ensured a large following of loyal tenants; their administration necessitated the great ducal household at Kenninghall as well as lesser establishments at Framlingham and Castle Rising; they supplied the provisions for that sumptuous hospitality which the Duke dispensed, particularly from his palace in Norwich. These factors, in turn, ensured immense electoral influence and in the last resort an array of retainers, tenants, and servants which could be weaponed swiftly from the store at Kenninghall.

The Duke's essentially locally based power contrasted with that of the new *noblesse de la robe*, whose influence and wealth derived from service to the Crown and whose local roots were frequently extremely shallow. For example, Robert Dudley, Earl of Leicester, who acquired great estates by a series of grants from Edward VI and Elizabeth, lacked a substantial compact territorial holding even around his great castle at Kenilworth. He had to pick up land where he could, with the result that he received small parcels widely scattered throughout England. In consequence he commanded no great regional loyalty and had no substantial body of tenants to wield the weapons he accumulated in the great armoury at Kenilworth. This rootlessness is particularly apparent in his electoral patronage

[46] Stone, *Crisis*, p. 268.

where Sir John Neale has described him as 'promiscuous'; he had little or no influence upon county elections and no consistent control over borough returns.[47] For noblemen in this position the loss of office or favour at Court could have dire consequences, as the career of the Earl of Essex subsequently displayed; it lessened their ability to secure place and patronage for clients, thereby depriving them of gratuities and, far more important, of followers; it cut them off from access to the fount of royal bounty, depriving them of grants of lands, licences, and patents. Such dependence contrasted markedly with the independence of great territorial magnates like the Howards; a fact which no doubt helps to explain that haughtiness which characterized the fourth Duke and his father and which led both of them to underrate the significance of the Court as a source of local power and prestige.

But even among those noblemen whose power was firmly based in great regional estates, the Duke stood in a class of his own. By Elizabeth's reign he alone combined all the prerequisites of the potential overmighty subject—a place in the counsels of the realm; immense wealth; a peer amongst his peers; vast compact estates; a neo-feudal loyalty from a tenantry which included many East Anglian gentry; great electoral influence and potential military strength. His fellow territorial magnates—George Talbot, sixth Earl of Shrewsbury, William Herbert, first Earl of Pembroke, Edward Stanley, third Earl of Derby, and Thomas Percy, seventh Earl of Northumberland—all failed to qualify on one or more of these counts. The Earls of Shrewsbury, Derby, and Northumberland lacked sufficient influence at Court to maintain unchallenged local pre-eminence in the face of rival magnates who were deliberately building their own gentry clientele. The Earl of Shrewsbury's position was further weakened because his estates were scattered across five midland counties where other powerful figures held sway. The Earl of Pembroke, who was in any case an *arriviste*, had augmented his income from estates in Glamorgan by gaining extensive lands and crown offices in Wales, but he lived as an absentee lord at Wilton in Wiltshire and made little effort to command the loyalty of tenants. Indeed, as a man who had recently acquired his wealth and power through the Court, he stood closer to the new men like the Earl of Leicester.[48]

[47] *DNB*, s.v. Dudley, Robt. Neale, *Commons*, p. 210–12.

[48] Stone, *Crisis, passim*. *BIHR* xxxiii, 1960, p. 74; xxviii, 1955, p. 18. MacCaffrey, op. cit., pp. 31, 32, 226.

In fact the Duke of Norfolk can perhaps best be compared with that great nobleman of an earlier generation—Edward Stafford, third Duke of Buckingham, who was also executed for treason. This 'man of towering strength, the like of which', wrote Professor Stone, 'was never to be seen again', derived his power from 'his strategically located castles, his masses of retainers, his widespread territorial possessions, his carefully cultivated patronage of the local gentry (over 130 of whom were entertained to dinner at Thornbury on feast days), his huge rent-roll, his powerful connexions by marriage, [and] his royal lineage'. Almost identical words could have been written of Thomas Howard, fourth Duke of Norfolk. Indeed a nobleman who, in the summer of 1562 when the new regime was still 'terrifyingly fragile', could entertain two earls, seven barons, sixty knights and esquires, together 'with dyverse and many other', and could divert this gathering with 'shooting and other martial exercises', might well rival Buckingham for the epithet 'last of the great overmighty subjects'.[49]

[49] Stone, *Crisis*, pp. 253–4. Blomefield, iii. 279–80. NNRO MSS. City Records, Book of St. George's Co. 1452–1602, pp. 229–30.

PART II

OFFICE-HOLDING: ITS SIGNIFICANCE IN COUNTY POLITICS 1572–1603

CHAPTER III

Introductory

THE execution of the Duke of Norfolk in 1572 signalled the end of an era in Norfolk's administrative, social, and political affairs. Since the late fifteenth century the Howards had dominated East Anglian society and government, but the impact of the fourth Duke had been particularly marked in Norfolk: his will had been paramount in decisions relating to the size and composition of the commission of the peace; he had greatly influenced county and borough elections; the list of sheriffs read like a roll-call of his tenants and followers; his patronage had been a prerequisite for any person or corporation hoping to tap the flow of royal bounty; his fiat had settled disputes; his favour had been essential for any gentleman aspiring to the front ranks of county society.

The Duke's death created a hiatus in all aspects of county life since the only remaining nobleman in the county lacked sufficient status to assume his princely mantle. In administrative and political affairs Norfolk gentry were compelled to find new patrons and to establish fresh channels of communication with the Court; they were forced to think constructively about procedures which they had taken for granted under the Howards. On whose advice and by what mechanism, for instance, were justices to be selected after 1572? What persons or factors would henceforth dominate the electoral scene? Through what patronage channels could the burgesses of Norwich, Lynn, or Yarmouth seek their export licences or promote their particular economic interests?

Social consequences were no less profound. Demand for precedence, hitherto curbed by the Duke's dominant position, immediately increased; the foremost gentry began to vie with each other for pre-eminence while those in the second rank jostled to improve their status. In these circumstances an unstable situation developed as gentlemen clamoured for the principal offices in Norfolk in order to assert their prestige: elections were contested; keen competition developed for the deputy lieutenancies; demand for a place on the Bench caused a rapid expansion of the commission of the peace. Moreover, success in these matters depended so greatly upon a patron that clientage developed apace. Lesser gentry were drawn into the ambit of county magnates who, in turn, sought out patrons at Court; in this way the tensions and divisions between the leading councillors exacerbated relationships in the county while local rivalries and quarrels heightened tension at Court.

There were many issues in late-sixteenth-century Norfolk which enabled the gentry to clothe jealousy and personal animosity with righteous indignation. Conflict between Catholics and Protestants intensified during the 1570s, particularly in East Anglia where Puritanism appears to have flourished. Then, too, the fragmented structure of Norfolk manors meant that neighbouring estates were so intermingled that disputes over boundaries, common rights, and damage caused by straying cattle provided rival gentry with ample opportunities for complaint and litigation.[1] Magnates even disagreed as to how readily the county should respond to the increased administrative and financial burdens imposed upon it by the Council. In short, the situation encouraged personal quarrels and factional disputes. But before examining these it is necessary in this part to establish some of the mechanics of local administration upon which rivalry and conflict thrived.

There is an extensive literature on the administrative and legal activities of local officials—more especially about the work of the justices, upon whose shoulders rested the burden of keeping the peace.[2] Conscientious justices were probably involved almost daily in the procedures for detecting and bringing to trial those suspected of committing crimes and misdemeanours—work now undertaken by the police force. Then, at quarter sessions, they changed their role and assumed responsibility for the trial and punishment of offenders. In order to ensure a measure of legal competence on the Bench, those justices who had some legal training were designated as members of the *quorum* and at least one of them had to be present at each session. As well as being responsible for keeping the peace, Elizabethan justices were the principal administrative officers in the counties, being called upon to supervise the implementation of a

[1] Below, pp. 182, 187, 194, 197.

[2] See esp. Barnes, *Somerset*. *Wiltshire County Records*, *Minutes of Proceedings in Sessions 1563 and 1574 to 1592*, ed. H. C. Johnson (*WRS* iv, Devizes, 1949). E. P. Cheyney, *A History of England from the Defeat of the Armada to the Death of Elizabeth . . .*, New York, 1926, part VIII. J. Hurstfield, 'County Government 1530–1660', *VCH Wilts.* v, 1957, pp. 80–110. J. H. Gleason, *The Justices of the Peace in England 1558–1640*, Oxford, 1969.

multitude of statutes and proclamations by which the Tudors sought to regulate society.

These aspects of their work have been documented in great detail by others and are only incidentally touched upon below. The principal purpose of chapters IV and V is to examine the social and political potential of a place on the Bench; to see in what ways and to what extent opportunity existed for magistracy to be harnessed in the service of private, factional, or political ends, and what aspects of a justice's work gave rise to controversy and dispute. Was it possible, for instance, for justices to be appointed and dismissed with such ease that rival gentry deliberately tried to manipulate appointments to the Bench for factious ends or pack it for political ones? This, in turn, raises the question of how justices were selected and, once appointed, what security of tenure they had.

The shrievalty will also be examined with similar questions in mind. Its official place in county government need only be briefly stated here. Sheriffs were appointed annually, invariably being chosen from among the leading gentry of a county. At one time, as their title suggests, they had been the Crown's chief representatives in the counties, but by the late sixteenth century their duties had become essentially ministerial; they were little more than the executants of other crown officials. They discharged a variety of duties within the legal system, serving writs, empanelling juries, and executing the processes for both quarter sessions and the courts at Westminster; they arranged lodgings for the judges on circuit and acted as chief executive officers of the assizes; they also kept the county gaols, whipped the rogues and hanged the felons. They had lost most of their judicial functions to the expanding quarter sessions: their Hundred Tournes had virtually expired and the county court lingered on only for minor civil cases and as a gathering of freeholders for holding elections and promulgating proclamations. In the administration of revenue they had retained responsibility for collecting and paying into the Exchequer all profits arising from royal estates, grants of franchises, and the administration of justice, but by the sixteenth century these had become relatively minor items in the composition of the royal budget. In short, sheriffs were officially everybody's servant and nobody's master. As a result historians have suggested that the office was unpopular among Elizabethan gentry and that many tried to avoid it.

What is said about the sheriff in chapter VII does not retraverse this ground, but looks instead at the unofficial aspect of his work, and attempts to assess the extent to which his ministerial role provided opportunities to influence the conduct of disputes. Professor Neale has already shown how sheriffs could manipulate elections, but the manner in which their partiality could intrude into other aspects of county affairs has never been thoroughly examined.[3]

The lords lieutenants and their deputies comprised the third and newest element in Elizabethan local administration. As the name suggests, they were essentially military administrators with responsibility for mustering and training the county militia, particularly the élite 'trained bands'.[4] Lords lieutenants were usually selected from among the nobility or, since powerful Court connections were a prerequisite of office, from those commoners who were members of the Privy Council. By the 1580s they worked through deputies chosen from the principal gentry in each county; these deputy lieutenants became very influential figures by virtue of their direct access to a privy councillor, and of their authority to appoint militia captains, to undertake militia training, and to stipulate the amount of taxation needed to meet this and other military requirements. After 1572 no magnate in East Anglia had sufficient status to undertake the lieutenancy of Norfolk and Suffolk, with the result that in 1585 Lord Hunsdon, a cousin to the Queen, Lord Chamberlain and a privy councillor, was appointed to this office. Since he was a stranger to both counties his deputies effectively wielded the lieutenant's power—a situation which was likely to add edge to the competition for these prestigious and influential positions.

As will be shown, the lieutenancy had immense potential for factional intrigue. But it also had profound significance for Elizabethan and Stuart constitutional developments. It is one of the principal themes in this study that by the 1590s the lieutenancy's development had engendered a major constitutional conflict among the gentry of Norfolk; a conflict which subsumed all other private quarrels and factional disputes, gaining thereby in intensity and bitterness. As an introduction to this controversy chapter VI will examine the role of the lieutenancy in relation to other developments in county administration.

[3] Neale, *Commons*, pp. 77–98.

[4] The best general study remains G. Scott Thomson's *Lords Lieutenants in the Sixteenth Century*, 1923, but there is also a great deal of material in L. Boynton's *The Elizabethan Militia 1558–1638*, 1967.

CHAPTER IV

A Place on the Bench

A. SOCIAL ANALYSIS

THE *Statutes of the Realm* and *Acts of the Privy Council* have left historians in no doubt that Elizabethan England was a much governed country and that the day-to-day burden of this government fell heavily upon the J.P.s. Besides their peace-keeping functions they were charged with implementing an array of statutes regulating economic, social, and military affairs. Then, too, they had responsibility for supervising parish officials as well as for an increased oversight of the activities of high and petty constables. Indeed, the enforcement of almost all Elizabethan statutes, proclamations and Council orders depended upon the assiduity and co-operation of the magistracy. It is therefore pertinent to enquire who undertook this onerous office in Norfolk, whether they did so willingly, and by what means they were selected. Too little attention has so far been given to these questions because historians have tended to assume that the gentry named in each commission of the peace were 'identical with the list of landed and well-born families in the county'; and that these gentlemen 'by reason of the background and the landed wealth it afforded them . . . alone possessed the social distinction which made them the natural rulers of their society'. An analysis of society in Elizabethan Norfolk, however, suggests that the equation between supply and demand was less simple.[1]

There is little doubt that Elizabeth and her councillors would have liked to confine magistracy to a few of the principal gentry in each county. Council letters and memoranda furnish considerable information about the qualifications deemed necessary for office: a justice should be wealthy, have good Court connections, keep hospitality, and be sufficiently well-born to stand pre-eminent in his locality; he should rule by precept and with an authority which

[1] E. P. Cheyney, *A History of England from the Defeat of the Armada to the Death of Elizabeth*, ii, New York, 1926, p. 314. A similar view is implicit in Gleason, pp. 66, 81–2, and W. J. Jones, 'Ellesmere and Politics, 1603–17', *Early Stuart Studies*, ed. H. S. Reinmuth, Minneapolis, 1970, p. 21.

stemmed from respect for his family's long-standing service in the neighbourhood.[2] Such was the ideal. What of the reality?

In 1558 there were fourteen such established magnate families in Norfolk. These were the Townshends of Raynham, Bedingfelds of Oxborough, Heydons of Baconsthorpe, Woodhouses of Kimberley, Pastons of Oxnead, L'Estranges of Hunstanton, Lovells of Harling, Spelmans of Narborough, Southwells of Woodrising, Yelvertons of Rougham, Knyvetts of Buckenham and later of Ashwellthorpe, Hobarts of Loddon, Cleres of Ormesby and Stokesby, and the Wyndhams of Felbrigg. For several generations these families had furnished the county with J.P.s and sheriffs; they had provided the *dramatis personae* of the *Paston Letters* and since then had been steadily expanding their estates and consolidating local power. Under Elizabeth recusancy thinned their ranks; it accounted for the total exclusion of the Bedingfelds and branches of the Knyvett and Hobart families, as well as the virtual suspension for many years of the Lovells and Southwells. Others, notably the Heydons, were suffering serious economic stresses which eventually lowered their magnate status.[3] Consequently by the late 1570s there were less than a dozen of these families to provide justices for a commission which usually included upwards of thirty local gentry.

In the late sixteenth century this small group of magnate families was afforced by such rising gentry as the Gawdys of Harling and Claxton, and the Bacons of Redgrave and Stiffkey, together with the Heveninghams who had recently shifted their centre of power from Suffolk into Norfolk. But simultaneously the number of justices rose dramatically from 34 in 1577 to 61 in 1602. Clearly, therefore, throughout Elizabeth's reign, and more especially towards its end, the Lord Chancellor had to appoint many magistrates from lesser magnate families. This prompts the question whether there was an identifiable group of second-rank gentry which by virtue of land,

[2] Below, pp. 79–80.

[3] Smith, 'Norf. Gentry', pp. 2–3. Blomefield, i. 378–9; ii. 540–59; v. 153–62; vi. 150–65, 477–95, 504–12; vii. 130–7; viii. 112–18; x. 29–35, 273–9, 312–21; xi. 234–8. *NA* iv, 1855, pp. 1–55; ix, 1884, pp. 226–39; xii, 1895, pp. 158–63; xviii, 1914, pp. 46–77; xxiii, 1929, pp. 93–105. K. Bedingfeld, *The Bedingfelds of Oxburgh*, 1912. *NAM* (2nd ser.) i, 1906, pp. 143–61. *NRS* xx, 1949. H. A. Wyndham, *A Family History 1410–1688*, Oxford, 1939. For the Recusancy of certain of these families, see PRO SP 12/117/27i, /142/43, /170/49, f. 1, /185/3i, /188/9ii, /191/22, f. 1v, /208/16, f. 1, /251/53, f. 2v. *HMC Salisbury*, ii. 194; iv. 269. A. Jessopp. *One Generation of a Norfolk House*, 1879, pp. 69, 79, 81.

wealth, and birth automatically filled these extra places.

This question can only be answered by establishing the extent and composition of the gentry class in Norfolk. For this purpose no sources are entirely satisfactory, but it is possible to make a reasonable estimate of its size in about 1580 by augmenting a list of Norfolk gentry in 1578 with names derived from the Heralds' visitation records for 1563 and from a smaller list drawn up in 1585. Since it is important to discover the number of gentry who might constitute a potential pool of magistrates, and since two generations of the same family rarely sat concurrently on the Bench, wherever a father and son both figure in the lists they have been counted as a single unit. Calculating on this basis there appear to have been at least 424 gentlemen in Norfolk in about 1580.[4] Yet new justices appointed between 1578 and 1603 numbered only 84, so that obviously the entire gentry class did not constitute a ready-made commission of the peace.

Within this class, however, there existed a clearly defined social hierarchy of gentlemen, esquires, and knights. Is it possible that only those who were styled esquires and knights provided, as of right, the necessary recruits for the Bench? Earlier in the sixteenth century Garter King at Arms considered that the title 'esquire' belonged to '. . . the heires male or [those] descended from the heire male of a nobleman's younger son, or from the heires male of a knight, or that by long prescription they can shew that their lineall auncestors were soe stiled . . . alsoe divers of the Kings servants which have the title Esquire by reason of the offices they beare'.[5] What more likely than that magistrates should have been drawn from families which had already distinguished themselves in public service? Elizabethan councillors undoubtedly intended this, and statistics suggest that they achieved their aim. During the entire period 1578–1603 only two magistrates were appointed from the 300-strong group styled 'gent',[6] whereas 84 of the 130 knights and esquires became justices. Since at least 23 of these knights and esquires were disqualified from magistracy by virtue of their papist sympathies, and allowing for a few families which for any number of reasons failed to figure in the commission, it would seem that the number of esquires and knights in the county coincided closely with

[4] Smith, 'Norf. Gentry', pp. 333–64.

[5] A. R. Wagner, *Heralds and Heraldry in the Middle Ages*, Oxford, 1936, p. 5.

[6] The Everards of Gillingham and the Pratts of Riston.

the number of new justices appointed; that a clearly defined county group did fill, almost as of right, the places on the Bench.[7]

But it would be wrong to draw this conclusion from such a statistical correlation. When the names of the esquires and knights are compared with those in the commission of the peace it is evident that considerably less than half of the former appear in the latter.[8] Thus, although esquires and knights furnished a substantial number of new justices, they by no means provided a ready-made commission. Moreover, as the commission expanded, their contribution to it seems to have diminished. Between 1578 and 1603 membership of the Bench almost doubled; as a result, the Lord Chancellor frequently had to select justices from families which had not previously been represented on the bench. In fact 47 out of the 84 new magistrates appointed in this period came from such families. An examination of the social background of these 47 justices reveals that substantially less than half of them were recruited from the knights and esquires of the county; indeed, 27 came not only from outside the esquire group of families, but also from outside the entire gentry class of Norfolk.[9]

These outsiders were an interesting, if somewhat transient element, in Norfolk politics. Several were lawyers who had recently settled in the county, the most notable among them being Nicholas Hare of Stow Bardolph. The son of a London mercer who had purchased monastic lands in Norfolk, and nephew of Sir Nicholas Hare, a former judge and Speaker of the Commons, Nicholas prospered as a lawyer and invested his profits in land around Stow, where he built a stately mansion from which he and his descendants governed extensive tracts of bleak fenland. Other lawyers who appeared in the commission had a less enduring impact upon the county; they purchased no extensive estates and founded no magisterial families; indeed, none of their sons succeeded them on the Bench. Edward Bartlett, probably an official of the Earl of Sussex, appeared in the commission in 1593, soon after he had moved into the Earl's manor-house at Attleborough; he participated in county government throughout the last decade of the century and then faded from the picture.[10] So, too, did Anthony Death, a barrister who hailed from

[7] Smith, 'Norf. Gentry', pp. 333–64. I have revised the figures.

[8] 52 out of 130.

[9] Smith, 'Norf. Gentry', pp. 11–12. I have revised the figures.

[10] PCC 1 Stafford. Blomefield, i. 518–19, 533. *LI Black Books*, ii. 31 et seq. *Harl. Soc.* lxv, 1914, p. 69.

Lincolnshire, settled at Gimingham, and became a J.P. in 1593.[11] Richard Gwynn, a Welshman and a distinguished lawyer from the Inner Temple who purchased a manor at Fakenham, gained a place on the Bench in 1601 and subsequently became recorder of Norwich and Yarmouth. Although he held his place as a J.P. until his death in 1630 he was always regarded as an outsider by his neighbours. He described them as 'unrulie and evill disposed people, not regardinge [him] or anie thinge [he] did or could do for them'.[12] The civil law accounts for the appointment of at least three other non-county men to the Norfolk Bench: Dr. Robert Redmayne, chancellor of the diocese, and Dr. Thomas Talbott, judge in the vice-admiral's court, both of whom hailed from Lancashire, and John Hunt, a master in Chancery, who may have come from Suffolk.[13]

A few lawyers who obtained a place on the Norfolk Bench came from old-established local families which had never ranked among the gentry. Foremost in this category comes Robert Houghton of Gunthorpe, a judge of the King's Bench under James I. Despite a distinguished legal career he appears to have owned little property in the county, since soon after his appointment to the commission in 1593 he was assessed for subsidy at only '£11 coins'. When he died in 1624 none of his sons succeeded him on the Bench and his family faded from county government until the Interregnum.[14] No doubt legal prowess also explains how Thomas Oxborough, successively town clerk and recorder of King's Lynn, Robert Tilney of East Tuddenham, and John Jay of Holverston climbed from humble origins into the county's magisterial ranks.[15]

Marriage, like the law, provided opportunities for outsiders to

[11] NNRO MS. CCN, 1612, no. 67. *LI Black Books*, ii. 14, 22, 26, 52. *LI Admissions*, i. 77.

[12] *NA* xiv, 1901, pp. 341–2. PCC 51 Scroope. *IT Records*, ii. 98–104. *NOL*, pp. 127, 170. J. Haydn, *Book of Dignities*, 1894, p. 409. See sources cited in Appendix III.

[13] *NOL*, p. 68. Blomefield, ii. 53; iii. 634. BM MS. Harl. 6822, f. 293v. *Harl. Soc.* xxxii, 1891, p. 279. *APC, 1588–9*, p. 78. *Select Pleas in the Court of Admiralty*, ed. R. G. Marsden (Selden Soc. xi), ii. liii. PCC 15 Barrington; 56 Scroope. J. Haydn, *Book of Dignities*, 1894, p. 395. C. Monro, *Acta Cancellariae*, 1847, pp. 24–5.

[14] *DNB*, s.v. Houghton, Robt. *Harl. Soc.* xxxii, 1891, pp. 160–1. *LI Black Books*, ii. 11, 17, 43, 57. *NOL*, p. 127–8. BM MS. Harl. 6822, f. 293v. PCC 28 Byrde. Appendix III.

[15] *Harl. Soc.* xxxii, 1891, pp. 211, 289. *LI Black Books*, i. 422. *NOL*, pp. 200, 202. PCC 3 Byrde; 69 Woodhall. *GI Admissions*, p. 56. W. Rye, *Norfolk Families*, Norwich, 1913, p. 400.

appear on the Bench alongside the county's natural rulers. In 1592 Robert Mansell, fourth son of Sir Edward Mansell of Glamorganshire, married Sir Nicholas Bacon's daughter Elizabeth, widow of Francis Wyndham, a judge of the Common Pleas. Mansell, having settled on the latter's estates at Pentney, soon appeared in the Norfolk commission of the peace (1593) and for some years played a prominent part in local affairs; then, when Elizabeth died he just as suddenly returned to Glamorganshire. Sir William Hatton flitted on and off the Norfolk Bench in similar fashion. A nephew of Elizabeth's Lord Chancellor, Sir Christopher Hatton, in 1588/9 he married the daughter of Sir Francis Gawdy, justice of the Queen's Bench and one of the foremost magistrates in north-west Norfolk; four years later he appeared in the Norfolk commission of the peace, but by this time his wife had died and he soon remarried and left the county. By contrast, Richard Jenkinson made a more lasting impression upon the local scene. Of merchant stock, he had recently settled at Tunstall when, in 1596, his son married Anne, daughter of Sir Henry Gawdy, a notable figure in south Norfolk who was also well connected at Court. A year later Jenkinson appeared in commission and continued to participate in county government until his death. Unlike many of these newcomers his heirs remained members of the Bench well into the seventeenth century.[16] William Hungate, a Yorkshireman, and Le Strange Mordaunt from Essex also came into the county through marriage into influential Norfolk families and subsequently became magistrates. Both remained in commission until their deaths, but thereafter their families took no further part in county administration.[17]

Ecclesiastical connections may account for the appearance of James Scambler and Thomas Dove in the commission of the peace. Scambler, who settled at Hickling while his father was Bishop of Norwich, was appointed a justice in 1593; after his father's death he continued to live in Norfolk and remained on the Bench for many years. Although he died childless, his brothers had also settled in Norfolk and his relatives appeared regularly in seventeenth-century commissions of the peace. In contrast, Thomas Dove, a Londoner who appeared in the commission shortly after his appointment as Dean of Norwich in 1589, had no further connection with

[16] Rye, *Norfolk Families*, pp. 402–3. P. Millican, *The Gawdys of Norfolk and Suffolk*, Norwich, 1939, p. 69. *PRO Lists & Indexes*, ix. 88. Appendix III.

[17] Smith, 'Norf. Gentry', pp. 22–3. Appendix III.

Norfolk after he became Bishop of Peterborough in 1601.[18]

Finally there is left a group of justices whose appointment to the Norfolk Bench remains inexplicable. With one exception they are shadowy figures who appeared but briefly in commission, rarely resided for long, if at all, in the county, and whose descendants scarcely figured as magistrates. Such were John Steward of Marham, fourth son of a Suffolk squire and a man of considerable wealth with land in several counties; Richard Frestone, son of a London merchant and married into a Suffolk family; Clement Higham, son and heir of Sir John Higham of Barrow in Suffolk; and Bartholomew Cotton of Starston who hailed from Toft in Cambridgeshire.[19] Furthermore Henry Clere, Thomas Bennett, and William Lewis—all of whom appeared only briefly on the Norfolk Bench—are difficult to trace at all. Sir Arthur Heveningham is the one exception in this otherwise undistinguished group. The Heveninghams were an old-established Suffolk family; even after Thomas Heveningham had inherited Ketteringham manor near Wymondham in 1525 their interest and influence remained in Suffolk. None of them appeared on the Norfolk Bench until Sir Arthur succeeded to the family property in 1575 and thereafter made Ketteringham his principal seat. Although it is difficult to explain adequately why he moved from Heveningham in Suffolk to Ketteringham in Norfolk, there can be no doubt about the impact of this irascible and unpopular newcomer who, as will be shown later, acted as a catalyst for strife and discontent throughout late Elizabethan and early Stuart Norfolk.[20]

Clearly many justices appointed to the Norfolk Bench between 1578 and 1603 were newcomers to the county, often residing there for only a few years and rarely founding county families. Their appearance in the commission is further proof that the county's established esquire-class families did not provide the Council with a ready-made commission of the peace. Most of these strangers, however, were either thrusting lawyers, perhaps with influential contacts at Court, or transient members of the Bench who appear to have

[18] *NRS* v, 1934, p. 192. PCC 38 Sadler. Appendix III. *DNB*, s.v. Scambler, Edm.

[19] Blomefield, vii. 384. PCC 37 Hayes; 12 Weldon. *Harl. Soc.* xxxii, 1891, p. 121. E. E. Trafford, 'Personnel of the Parliament of 1593' (London MA thesis 1948), p. 238. BM MS. Add. 38139, ff. 144v–146. *HMC Salisbury*, xi. 183. *Harl. Soc.* xli, 1897, p. 23. Appendix III.

[20] W. A. Copinger, *The Manors of Suffolk*, ii, Manchester, 1908, 93–4. *NA* iii, 1852, pp. 281–3. Below, pp. 157–9.

been slightly regarded by their fellows. Consequently it is still possible that the essential and stable element of the Norfolk Bench was recruited from a group of families at once larger than the magnate class but smaller than the esquire class, and yet clearly defined in that a hereditary place on the Bench had become its special preserve. According to at least one historian, 'so customary was it, in those families rooted in the county, for son to succeed father on the commission of the peace that the absence of the next generation indicates failure of the line, disgrace—personal or political—or failure of fortune.' How often, then, did a place on the Norfolk Bench remain the preserve of a family for several successive generations?[21]

One hundred and fourteen families provided justices in the period 1558–1603 but only 16 of these were represented on the Bench for three consecutive generations while no less than 54 provided only a single representative and then disappeared from the magisterial ranks.[22] Failure in the male line explains why some of these families ceased to be represented on the Bench, but at least 20 (and probably considerably more) had heirs who could have succeeded to their fathers' places but in fact did not. These figures suggest that old-established magisterial families who virtually pre-empted a place in the commission were less common than has been assumed—a conclusion which is reinforced by a closer examination of the apparent continuity of tenure among that minority of 16 families which did provide justices for at least three consecutive generations.

This reveals that throughout Elizabeth's reign only 9 sons immediately succeeded their fathers in commission,[23] whereas 14 had to wait anything from 6 to 32 years.[24] This delay must have been tantamount to a break in family continuity since in the meantime new magistrates would have assumed responsibility for government in

[21] Davies, *Enforcement*, p. 180. Gleason, p. 57.

[22] The figures in the following paras. are based on Appendix III. Where a younger brother founded a separate branch, living often in a different part of the county, he and his heirs have been counted as a separate family. The 15 families represented on the Bench for three generations were : Bacon, Bell, Corbett, Guybon, Heydon, Holdich, Knyvett, Lovell, Moundford, Reppes, Southwell, Spelman, Woodhouse of Kimberly, Woodhouse of Waxham, and Yelverton.

[23] Nath. Bacon, Nich. Bacon, Thos. Guybon, Chris. Heydon, Wm. Heydon, Philip Woodhouse, Wm. Woodhouse, Henry and Wm. Yelverton.

[24] Edm. Bell, Miles Corbett, Humphrey Guybon, Henry Holdich, John Holdich, Thos. Knyvett of Buckenham, Thos. Lovell, Francis Moundford, John Reppes, Robt. Southwell, Thos. Southwell, John Spelman, Clement Spelman, Roger Woodhouse.

their localities. It is possible, however, that these 14 heirs were not old enough at their fathers' deaths and succeeded as justices immediately they had acquired sufficient years and experience; that for all practical purposes they did inherit their fathers' places on the Bench but, pending their maturity (it was quite common for justices to be appointed in their mid and late twenties)[25] 'caretaker' magistrates took over. Facts do not support this supposition, since only 6 were disqualified by age when their fathers died[26] and 3 of these did not even succeed to a place when they reached maturity, but had to wait until they were about 36, 38, and 54 respectively before their appointment.[27] Clearly minority is not a sufficient explanation for the delay in their promotion. Similarly, the pattern of frequent and often inexplicable delay before a son succeeded to his father's place on the Bench also emerges from an examination of the 44 families which provided justices for two generations. Although there is insufficient evidence for an exhaustive analysis of this group, on at least 19 occasions the heir had to wait anything from 10 to 40 years before his appointment as a J.P.

Since nearly half the magisterial families in Elizabethan Norfolk provided a justice for only one generation, and since many of the others experienced an unusually long delay between a father's death and his son's appointment, it is necessary to modify the view that there existed a core of magisterial families whose heirs 'succeeded [to the Bench] almost as automatically as they succeeded to their patrimonies'. No doubt strict succession took place in a few families, but in most cases the heir appeared in commission only if he had gained sufficient status and reputation in the county and, perhaps even more important, sufficient influential contacts at Court to bring his name to the Lord Chancellor's attention. In fact whether or not he eventually appeared in the commission depended upon his own efforts; he had to make his own way into the commission and sometimes it took years to do this. Intent, not inheritance, usually explains his appointment.[28]

[25] Smith, 'Norf. Gentry', p. 57.

[26] Miles Corbett (*LI Admissions*, i. 61); Henry Holdich (PCC 90 Flack); John Reppes (PCC 1 Stonarde. *Visit. of Norf.* i. 196–7); Clement Spelman (PCC 37 Darcy); Edm. Bell (Outwell Parish Register); Thomas Knyvett of Buckenham (R. J. W. Swales, 'Local Politics and the Parliamentary Representation of Sussex 1529–1558' [Bristol PhD thesis 1964], ii. 283).

[27] Edm. Bell, Henry Holdich, and Miles Corbett.

[28] Dr. J. T. Cliffe, in his *Yorkshire Gentry from the Reformation to the Civil War*, 1969,

If magistracy was not essentially the preserve of a well-defined group of gentry, if it was not simply accepted as a duty which went with family inheritance, then several new questions demand answers. Did any gentleman, for instance, so desire to undertake these burdensome administrative and legal responsibilities that he went out of his way to gain a place on the Bench? Or, as might be inferred from this analysis, were many of the county's natural rulers opting out? While there is no evidence to support the latter suggestion, there is evidence of keen competition for the office. As will be shown later in this chapter, the Council's repeated attempts to reduce the number of justices in commission were utterly defeated by the pressure from gentry seeking appointment to it.[29]

At first sight it is difficult to see what gentry had to gain from a place on the Bench. They received no payment beyond an allowance of two shillings for each day's attendance at quarter sessions; nor is there any evidence that they could expect to collect the sort of fees and gratuities which went with some offices under the Crown. But the office had many attractions which, albeit less tangible, were none the less real. In the first place it provided one of the principal means whereby a gentleman, ever anxious about prestige and precedence, could raise his status; a place on the Bench established his pre-eminence in his locality and at every quarter sessions publicly displayed to the assembled county that he had been numbered among its principal officers. Numbered, too, in a literal sense since each justice sat on the Bench according to a strict order of precedence governed by his 'placing' in the commission of the peace.[30]

Then, too, in a litigious and quarrelsome age magistracy might be used as an instrument of faction.[31] Just as a sheriff could influence an election, so a justice could indict his opponent's tenants and ignore the unlawful activities of his own; he could influence the choice of constables, both high and petty; as a commissioner for

---

pp. 232–50, suggests that there were considerable changes in the personnel of the early Stuart Yorkshire commissions of the peace, and that appointments were by no means the automatic preserve of certain families. See also A. D. Wall, 'The Wiltshire Commission of the Peace 1590–1620. A Study of its Social Structure' (Melbourne MA thesis 1966), pp. 24–7, and H. Aveling, *Northern Catholics, the Catholic Recusants of the North Riding of Yorkshire 1558–1790*, 1966, pp. 202–5. The situation seems to have been more stable in Somerset, see Barnes, *Somerset*, p. 304.

[29] Below, p. 86. See also Barnes, *Somerset*, p. 43.

[30] Below, pp. 71–2.

[31] Below, esp. ch. IX. Barnes, *Somerset*, pp. 43–4.

musters he could over-assess his rival for military rates and press the latter's tenants for overseas service; he could influence the licensing of alehouses or the appointment of bridewell keepers; in a great variety of ways he could harass an enemy or help a friend. It would, however, be misleading to imply that Norfolk gentry were unduly preoccupied with petty and spiteful rivalries. As will be shown in part III, they were also deeply concerned about methods of government. They regarded their county as a political entity and held differing opinions about the aims and methods of administration. In these circumstances magistracy clearly had great potential, since it was the principal means by which policies could be implemented.

But the factional and political potential of magistracy could only be realized if there was a reasonable chance that factious or politically minded gentry could get into the commission or, when occasion demanded, could get their opponents dismissed. It is, therefore, important to consider how magistrates were selected and, once appointed, how vulnerable they were to dismissal.

B. APPOINTMENT

Justices of the peace were appointed by the Crown and usually chosen by the Lord Chancellor. During the sixteenth century the necessity for more justices to implement Tudor paternalist policies, coupled with an expansion of the gentry class from which these justices had to be selected, meant that the Lord Chancellor had to take advice about these appointments. The scale of the problem can be illustrated statistically: whereas down to 1462 a commission of the peace for Norfolk rarely numbered more than ten or fifteen justices, by the late sixteenth century it invariably contained between fifty and sixty names. Those best qualified and most readily available to advise the Lord Chancellor were the judges, each of whom, through his assize circuit, had contact with the gentry in a group of counties. They were certainly being consulted by 1562 when Cecil compiled lists of gentry 'thought mete by the Justices of Assize to be put into the commission of the peace and some omitted out'. But during Elizabeth's reign their advice increasingly proved inadequate. Because they rarely resided in their circuits, they had to rely upon information gleaned from local magnates who, in factious counties like Norfolk, frequently proffered conflicting advice. In such circumstances the judges might have to choose between rival aspirants or, more likely, would see their recommendations completely ignored as powerful county interests found other ways of acquainting the Lord Chancellor with the virtues of particular candidates. Indeed, by the late sixteenth century a gentleman who aspired to be a magistrate had various methods by which to bring his name to the Lord Chancellor's attention.[32]

The recommendation of his bishop provided one of the most effective channels. Periodically the Council asked each bishop to report upon the religious loyalties of all magistrates in his diocese and to recommend 'well affected' gentry who might replace those whose opinions were in doubt. Such a survey was ordered in 1564. Before replying Bishop Parkhurst of Norwich felt obliged to consult the Duke of Norfolk with the consequence that the advice he finally tendered reflected the Duke's views rather than his own.[33] In 1587 Burghley commissioned another episcopal enquiry in which Bishop Scambler reported that ten Norfolk justices were 'suspected and reputed backwards in religion'. On this occasion Burghley particularly desired to rid county benches of several categories of unsatisfactory justices who were 'as drones among bees', and he had consulted the bishops precisely because he suspected the inadequacy of reports he had already received from the justices of assize.[34]

In addition to submitting these reports and recommendations to the Council, bishops frequently requested the Lord Chancellor to place their own nominees in the commission of the peace. In 1571 John Parkhurst asked Lord Keeper Bacon to appoint three new justices in Norfolk 'because the number of justices here do dymyneshe'. He recommended William Blennerhassett as much for 'his earnest and godlye zeale to the trueth as for his experience and depe wisdome', together with Robert Kemp and Thomas Barrow. Apparently the Lord Keeper ignored his solicitations, since a year later he wrote again 'on the behalfe of Mr. William Blennerhassett of Little Plumstede, latelye maryed to the Ladye Warner, who for his wisdome and godlye zeale beside many other vertues deserveth greate favour and preferment'. This time, instead of Kemp and Barrow, he recommended Edward Spanye from near Lowestoft,

[32] R. Virgoe, 'East Anglia under Richard II', *The Reign of Richard II*, ed. F. R. H. Du Boulay & C. M. Barron, 1971, p. 241. BM MS. Lansd. 1218, f. 90.

[33] 'A Collection of Original Letters from the Bishops to the Privy Council 1564', ed. Mary Bateson, pp. 1–83, *Camden Miscellany IX* (Camden Soc. N.S. liii), 1895. Above, p. 35.

[34] BM MSS. Lansd. 52, ff. 199–201; 103, ff. 85–86v. Below, p. 84.

explaining that there was no justice resident in the Hundred of Lothingland 'where are many stubborne people neither religious nor otherwies well disposed'. Parkhurst's second letter achieved moderate success; Bacon appointed William Blennerhassett, but passed over Edward Spanye who never figured on the Norfolk Bench.[35]

Bishops did not always make impartial recommendations or proffer unbiased opinions about the personnel in commission. On at least two occasions bishops of Norwich used their patronage to pack the Norfolk Bench with friends and supporters. In the late 1570s Edmund Freake, unduly influenced by a group of gentry with papist sympathies, procured places in commission for several of his friends in an effort to counter resourceful Puritan attacks upon his authority. Subsequently, when Edmund Scambler became involved in defending ecclesiastical property against concealment patentees in the early 1590s, he may well have tried to sway the Bench by bringing in several of the outsiders mentioned in the previous section.[36]

Lords lieutenants could also recommend candidates for the Bench. As early as 1559 they had been entrusted with a general oversight of the magistracy, being instructed to inform the Lord Keeper of any shortage of justices in their shires, to recommend anyone 'founde meete for his residencie and other qualities for suche place', and to ensure that all J.P.s 'accordinge to the lawes of the realme do take a corporall othe therefore provided'.[37] Since Elizabeth appointed a lieutenant in Norfolk only intermittently, and for no more than fifteen years throughout her entire reign, this potential patronage was never fully realized. Even so, Lord Hunsdon, the sole lieutenant in Norfolk to hold office for a long period (1585–96), may well have been influential in the appointment of several new justices. He became deeply involved in local faction and certainly expedited Thomas Farmer's dismissal in 1586.

Law officers also had special opportunities to influence the Lord Chancellor's selection of justices. Norfolk, noted for its litigiousness in the fifteenth century, boasted a long and illustrious succession of judges in the late sixteenth century: Edward Coke, Solicitor General (1592), chief justice of Common Pleas (1606) and of King's Bench (1613); Sir Thomas Gawdy, judge of the Queen's Bench (1574) and his half-brother, Francis Gawdy, who succeeded him in 1589; Francis Wyndham, judge of the Common Pleas (1579); Edward

35 CUL MS. Ee. II. 34, ff. 68v, 102v.

36 Below, chap. X and pp. 265–75, 309.

37 PRO SP 12/93, f. 100v.

Flowerdew, third Baron of the Exchequer (1584); Sir Robert Bell, Chief Baron of the Exchequer (1577); Sir Robert Houghton, serjeant at law (1603) and judge of the King's Bench (1613); Sir Henry Hobart, serjeant at law (1603) and chief justice of Common Pleas (1613); and Sir Christopher Yelverton, serjeant at law (1589) and justice of the Queen's Bench (1602). Their eminence in the county secured them places in the commissions of the peace, while their eminence in the legal hierarchy afforded many opportunities to confer with the Lord Chancellor and privy councillors. Thus, strategically poised between Court and county, they undoubtedly had many opportunities to procure places on the Bench for friends and clients. Edward Coke, for example, used his influence to ensure that Sir John Townshend was made 'of the quorum' in 1600, and that Henry Windham and Anthony Browne were named in the commissions for 1599 and 1601 respectively. Similarly Francis Gawdy secured places for Humphrey Guybon and Dr. Thomas Talbott.[38]

In addition to the patronage of bishops, lords lieutenants, and law officers, there appear to have been almost as many ways into the commission of the peace as there were magistrates. Professor Neale has stressed the fundamental role of Court patronage in Elizabethan political life, but its significance in county government and local politics, where many justices owed their appointment to the influence of a kinsman or patron at Court, has received less attention.[39] It can be seen in the negotiations which preceded Thomas Lovell's appointment to the Norfolk commission of the peace in 1599. For many years Lovell had been at loggerheads with his neighbour Bassingbourne Gawdy, who in 1592 had managed to procure his dismissal from the Bench on the pretext of suspected Recusancy.[40] But in 1599 Lovell had succeeded in getting himself restored, much to the consternation of Philip Gawdy, half-brother to Bassingbourne, who wrote in alarm from the Court describing Lovell's tactics:

The meanes that he camm in [to the commission of the peace] by was my Lord Northe.[41] For after he had missed of his knighting for which he flewe such a

[38] PRO Index Room 4208, pp. 142, 157, 175. Jeayes, p. 96. BM MS. Eg. 2804, ff. 129, 133.

[39] The role of the Earl of Essex in appointments to local office in S.W. Wales is described in H. A. Lloyd, *The Gentry of South-West Wales 1540–1640* Cardiff, 1968, pp. 112–18.

[40] Below, pp. 181–92.

[41] Roger North, Treasurer of the Queen's Household and a privy councillor (*DNB*).

pitche . . . he was contented at last of his meare humilitye to be made a justisse of the peace . . . He made such a speache at my Lord Northe's boorde how he had long lyved in blindness and that now God had opened his eyes so that he sawe his errors wherin he had lyved so long . . . His speache in the ende tended to the good he ment to do his contry. Whereuppon my Lord upon meere zeale procured him to be in commyssion. And Sir Henry Northe,[42] for mere affection, was content to take £200 of him, and Mr. Powell was more reasonable to take but bare forty pounde for restoring him to his former place.[43]

The vicissitudes of the Southwells of Woodrising demonstrate how closely office and power in the county could depend upon influence at Court. Until Elizabeth's accession this family had ranked among the foremost in both national and local affairs. The brothers Richard and Robert Southwell had both held important positions in Thomas Cromwell's reformed administration, Sir Richard as Receiver of the Court of Augmentations, Sir Robert as Solicitor and subsequently Attorney of the court. The latter became Master of the Rolls in 1541, while Sir Richard was a privy councillor to Edward VI and Mary and also held the Mastership of the Ordnance from 1554 to 1559. His influential position at Court had been mirrored in the county where for many years he headed the Norfolk Bench as *custos rotulorum*.[44] Loyalty to Mary, however, rendered him suspect to Elizabeth and she did not appoint him to her Privy Council. His eclipse in the county was as total as at Court: he was left out of the commission of the peace and therefore lost his post as *custos*. His nephew Thomas, who succeeded him in 1566, managed to gain a place in the commission of the peace for a brief period before he died in 1568, but the latter's son Robert was too young to succeed him on the Bench; since the boy grew up as a suspected Recusant, the eclipse of the family seemed final and complete. But in 1585 the young Robert, still not twenty-five, was suddenly knighted, appointed vice-admiral of Norfolk (Sir William Heydon being dismissed to make way for him) and placed on the Bench high in order of precedence. This unexpected resurgence of Southwell power was undoubtedly occasioned by Robert's marriage to Elizabeth, daughter of Lord Howard of Effingham, Lord Chamberlain in 1584 and Lord Admiral of England in 1585. While Southwell had such backing at Court no office in the county lay

[42] Younger son of Roger, Lord North (*DNB*).

[43] Jeayes, p. 111. This letter is incorrectly ascribed to 1600.

[44] PRO E 372/401–3; SP 11/5/6, ff. 42v–43v; C 193/12.

beyond his grasp, as he proved in 1594 by his appointment to a deputy lieutenancy.[45]

No doubt similar connections with leading courtiers enabled several other quite undistinguished Norfolk gentry to achieve the honour of a place on the Bench. Wimond Carey, a 'stranger' from Essex who appeared in commission shortly after settling in Norfolk, was half-brother to Sir Francis Walsingham and cousin to Lord Hunsdon, lord lieutenant of Norfolk.[46] Isaac Astley, the first member of his family to be appointed to the Bench, was nephew to John Astley, master of the Queen's jewel house, 'cousin of Queen Elizabeth and husband of her dear friend and woman of the Bed Chamber, Mistress Katherine Astley'.[47] John Appleyard, half-brother to Amy Robsart, almost certainly owed his brief appearance on the Bench to his brother-in-law Robert Dudley, Master of the Queen's Horse and later Earl of Leicester. No doubt, too, the Earl secured a place in commission for his client Edward Flowerdew, junior member of a 'mere gentry' family which had never before attained this position. Flowerdew subsequently became an eminent lawyer, but his appointment as a J.P. occurred at least ten years before he achieved legal distinction.[48] John Eyer, a staunch Protestant who appeared in Elizabeth's first commission for Norfolk, was a servant of Lord Keeper Sir Nicholas Bacon;[49] while William Lewis, recorder of King's Lynn and a county magistrate in 1590, probably had the backing of Burghley himself.[50] Finally, Thomas Sidney, customer of King's Lynn and the first in his family to serve as a magistrate, almost certainly owed his appointment to friendship with Sir Francis Walsingham and Sir Walter Mildmay.[51]

Not all newcomers to the Bench had relatives or friends in high places; many had secured appointment through less direct channels of patronage. They employed the services of minor courtiers, frequently younger sons, who sought excitement and fortune on the fringes of

[45] Williams, p. 14. PCC 13 Babington. *Visit of Norf.* i. 126–7. BM MSS. Lansd. 52, f. 201; 157, f. 419; Harl. 6996, f. 126.

[46] *DNB*, s.v. Walsingham, Francis. *The Visitations of the County of Devon*, ed. J. L. Vivian, Exeter, 1895, p. 154. PCC 28 Fenner. PRO St. Ch. 5, C 28/14.

[47] C. H. Garrett, *The Marian Exiles*, Cambridge, 1938, p. 73. Delaval Astley, *Astley of Melton Constable*, 1936.

[48] Above, p. 33; Below, p. 192.

[49] PCC 25 Loftes.

[50] FSL MS. Bacon–Townshend L.d. 202.

[51] PCC 17 Brudenell.

the Court rather than accept their humble status at home. These men provided that contact, so vital to Elizabethan administration, between courtiers who were anxious to enhance their prestige by dispensing patronage and ambitious gentry whose success depended upon receiving it. Philip Gawdy exemplifies these lesser figures at Court. While his elder brother Bassingbourne ran the family estates and cut a figure in the county, Philip made a career as a soldier and the family agent at Court. Here he mingled with influential administrators and cultivated their goodwill in anticipation of their assistance in expediting family business sent up by his brother. He gave them presents; he dined with them at the Inns of Court; he even hob-nobbed with privy councillors at weekend house and hunting parties.[52]

In 1603 Philip needed all the contacts he could establish when rumours spread that the King intended to revive the Norfolk lieutenancy after it had been in abeyance for seven years. The news aroused great rivalry among the leading gentry who were anxious to get themselves appointed to prestigious deputy lieutenancies. Philip wrote confidently from the Court about Bassingbourne's prospects:

> I spake with my Lord Thomas [Howard?] my Lord Henry [Howard?] and my Lord of Northumberland, and besydes I have now an especyall frend of the Councell: my Lord Souche, by whom I dare undertake at all tymes to do you a good turne. I acquaynted him particularly with the matter whensoever ther shall be any matter brought in question . . . So that assure your self all is safe and well, as yow can wishe.

In fact James delayed until November 1605 before appointing Henry Howard, Earl of Northampton, to the lieutenancy and naming Bassingbourne Gawdy as one of his deputies.[53]

Between such phases of intensive patron-hunting Philip had to watch assiduously that his brother was named and correctly placed in the numerous commissions which issued from Chancery. For instance, when Bassingbourne was knighted Philip had to negotiate his promotion in the commission of the peace to a position commensurate with his increased status *vis-à-vis* his fellow gentry. Also, after Bassingbourne had been omitted from the subsidy commission during his shrievalty in 1601, Philip worked hard not only to get

[52] BM MSS. Egerton 2804 and Add. 27395. The majority of these letters have been edited by I. H. Jeayes in *Letters of Philip Gawdy of West Harling* . . ., (Roxburghe Club, 1906).

[53] Jeayes, p. 131. Letter Book of Philip Woodhouse, *penes* the Earl of Kimberley.

him reappointed but also placed above his rival Thomas Lovell. Similarly, when Lovell tried to appoint biased subsidy assessors in south-west Norfolk, Philip intrigued successfully in Chancery to get him dismissed from the subsidy commission.[54]

The Knyvetts of Ashwellthorpe had a similar arrangement, with Henry acting as agent at Court for his brother Sir Thomas in the county. Henry appears to have had a close relationship with Sir Thomas Bromley, Lord Chancellor from 1579 to 1587, but otherwise he had little success at patronage hunting. He complained in May 1587 that Bromley's death 'hathe made a greate meanye whiche spake me faire and shewd me good countenance, eyther to offer me wronge measure for some thinges that I have or to seeme strangers unto me when I have occassion to use their frendshippes'. He had good reason for this lament since within months his brother Sir Thomas had been dismissed from the commission of the peace and from his deputy lieutenancy in Norfolk. Henry continued to live in London throughout the 1590s trying to eke out a living as deputy receiver of Norfolk and Huntingdonshire and doing what he could to further his brother's legal affairs in the county by working through his brother-in-law Robert Bowyer, who during the 1590s became secretary to Lord Buckhurst. But his own affairs and his brother's status in the county never recovered and in a desperate bid to re-tap the stream of patronage he offered to serve with Essex in Ireland.[55]

The Gawdys and Knyvetts were in no way exceptional in having a relative at Court who acted as a resident agent. Both the Woodhouses and the Pastons had a similar arrangement. Sir Henry Woodhouse maintained the family estates and cut a figure in the county as a J.P. and vice-admiral, while his younger brother Sir William sought fame and fortune as a soldier and minor courtier.[56] Clement Paston, also a soldier-courtier, looked after the interests of his nephew William Paston and of neighbours like Christopher Heydon, for whom he secured the office of *custos rotulorum* in 1564.[57]

[54] Jeayes, pp. 93–4, 116–17. For the importance of 'placing' in these commissions, see below, pp. 71–2.

[55] This para. is based upon a fine series of letters from Henry Knyvett to Sir Thos. Knyvett (NNRO MSS. KNY 372 X 5).

[56] Jeayes, pp. 81, 89, 95, 112. *HMC Salisbury*, ix. 78. *CSPD Add. 1566–79*, p. 542; *Letters of John Chamberlain*, ed. N. E. McClure, i, Philadelphia, 1939, pp. 62, 69–70, 79.

[57] *NA* iv, 1855, pp. 42–3. BM MS. Add. 27447, ff. 104, 141. PCC 27 and 28 Lewyn.

Although few families can have been as well organized as these, many Norfolk gentry had easy access to the Court. Sir Dru Drury, *custos* in Norfolk from 1583 until at least 1604, was a gentleman usher of the privy chamber throughout Elizabeth's reign as well as being Lieutenant of the Tower in 1595–6. Although his papers have not survived, there is evidence that he used his position to help both Bassingbourne Gawdy and Nathaniel Bacon; moreover, since he was a zealous Puritan it would be surprising if he did not exert influence to secure the appointment of religious radicals to positions in county government.[58] Sir John Peyton provided another link between county and Court. In 1588 he held a deputy lieutenancy in Norfolk while serving as colonel of the Queen's bodyguard; then, at the turn of the century, he was a muster commissioner in the county and also Lieutenant of the Tower—a fact which no doubt explains how he procured John Reppes's reappointment as a justice in 1600.[59] Sir Thomas Knyvett of Buckenham (d. 1569) and his son Thomas, both gentry with Catholic sympathies, possibly owed their appearances in the commission of the peace to Sir Thomas's brother, also named Thomas, who was a gentleman of the privy chamber. In fact they had many sources of patronage, being well connected among the peerage.[60] Nathaniel Bacon, another influential Norfolk magistrate, also had close associations with the Court although he held no official appointment there. He was a son of Lord Keeper Sir Nicholas Bacon, and brother-in-law of Sir William Peryam, judge of the Common Pleas, while his daughter Elizabeth became a gentlewoman of the Queen's privy chamber.[61] Bacon's opponent Sir Arthur Heveningham likewise established firm links with the Court, his visits to London invariably coinciding with the most bitter conflicts in the county. Like Bacon he held no Court office, but he had considerable influence with Lord Hunsdon. As well as this, Heveningham's sister Lady Abigail Digby was at Court—probably as a gentlewoman of the Queen's privy chamber. She may well have been responsible for

---

L & P H VIII, xix(1), p. 161. J. F. Pound, 'The Elizabethan Corporation of Norwich 1558–1603' (Birmingham MA thesis 1962), pp. 303–4.

[58] FSL MS. Bacon–Townshend L.d. 272. Appendix I. Jeayes, p. 6. Bodl. MS. Eng. Misc. C20, ff. 42, 43, 49. PCC 39 Weldon.

[59] *DNB*, s.v. Peyton, Sir John. *APC, 1587–8*, p. 38; *1596–7*, p. 388; *1597–8*, p. 484. PRO Index Room 4208, p. 188.

[60] Swales, op. cit., ii. 282–3. NNRO MS. KNY 785 (372 X 6).

[61] *NRS* xx, 1949, p. 19.

getting his undistinguished relative Edward Everard into the commission of the peace.[62]

Despite the intricacies of the Elizabethan patronage system the Lord Chancellor continued to rely upon advice from the judges when he appointed new justices. In June 1592 the assize judges for Norfolk informed the Lord Chancellor that 'ther is greate wante of men learned in the lawe in the commyssion of peace. . . . We have therfore thoughte good for her majesties better service . . . to recommend unto your lords Mr. Nicholas Hare of the Inner Temple, Mr. Robert Haughton of Lincolne's Inne and Mr. Henrye Hubberde of Lincolne's Inne'. Then in 1599 Sir Nicholas Bacon and Sir Bassingbourne Gawdy asked the assize judges to recommend that 'Henry Holdiche esquire be in the commission of peace, there being none other within eight miles of his residence'. By 1605 Lord Chancellor Ellesmere was attempting to cut through the patronage network by announcing that thereafter he would appoint J.P.s only on the recommendation of two assize judges. In the event his intentions were overwhelmed by the pressure of Court patronage, but initially his announcement caused consternation to an assiduous patronage broker like Philip Gawdy who was rebuffed in his endeavours to get his 'cousin Colby' appointed to the Suffolk Bench. Philip complained bitterly that, whereas in the 1590s he could have done so 'without commendacions of any, or any other troble', now 'my lord chancelor hathe taken order that none shall comme in [to the commission of the peace] but by meanes of the justice of assyses and they to receyve commendacion from two justices of peace out of the country'.[63]

So far attention has been focused upon the means by which a would-be justice could gain the Lord Chancellor's warrant for his placing in the commission of the peace. But his problems did not end with this achievement; in fact they had barely begun since he still had to transact some delicate business at the Crown Office in Chancery. Before taking his place on the Bench he needed two documents: first a writ of *dedimus potestatem* empowering three trusted gentry to administer to him the oath of supremacy; secondly, a new commission

[62] Jeayes, pp. 76, 78, 104, 107, 143. *DNB* s.v. Digby, George.

[63] *HMC Gawdy*, p. 67. BM MS. Harl. 286, f. 197. Jeayes, pp. 156–7.

of the peace which, when proclaimed at quarter sessions, officially announced his appointment. Sueing out this commission could present problems, since, unless a justice appeared in person or sent his agent to pay the engrossment fee, the commission might lie for months in the Crown Office. Even worse, having obtained it he might find himself wrongly named or entitled, since the clerks did the engrossing cheaply and carelessly. This meant that he could not take his place on the Bench until the mistake had been rectified in a new commission, as apparently happened to Thomas Lovell when he was incorrectly styled 'esquire' instead of 'knight'.[64]

Above all a new justice needed to ensure that the Crown Office clerks 'placed' his name correctly in the new commission, for he was not simply appointed to the Bench but to a special place on it. At quarter sessions and assizes all J.P.s sat in an order of precedence which was regulated by the ordering of names in the commission. After being knighted in 1597 Bassingbourne Gawdy waited anxiously for the new commission which would register his enhanced prestige by placing him higher on the Bench. He knew only too well that if it did not arrive in time for the forthcoming assizes he would have to suffer the indignity of sitting in his old place among the esquires. When he implored his courtier-brother to expedite its delivery, Philip replied reassuringly: 'you neade not to make any doubte of it for your right placing, for Mr. Powell is a most honest carefull man . . . my lord chief justice . . . ment to have a neue comission for Norfolke so that that way you shall be suere to be altered. . . . The assyses for Suffolke and Norfolk beginnes at Cambridge the 28th of August so that ther will be tyme enoughe for the alteration.' This sensitivity about seniority on the Bench cannot be too strongly stressed. Sometimes it led to unseemly disputes, as at Thetford quarter sessions in 1582 when the mayor had to intervene and order 'the said three persons to take their places and sit as they come, until advice be taken of those that be learned for the determining of the said contention.'[65]

A justice's precise placing in the commission depended upon some intricate negotiations in the Crown Office. The familiar ordering of society dictated a rough placing. First came those great officers of state like the Lord Chancellor and Principal Secretary whose official duties warranted their inclusion in most commissions; then followed,

[64] PRO Index Room 4208. *BIHR* xxxii, 1959, pp. 222–7. Below, p. 191. Jeayes, p. 110.
[65] Jeayes, pp. 93–4. *HMC Var. Coll.* vii. 136.

in descending order, peers, judges, knights, esquires, and occasionally gentlemen. The precedence of officers of state and peers, who were usually *ex officio* members, presented no problem; but placing a newly appointed justice among his fellow knights, esquires, or gentlemen appears to have been an extremely subtle business. He did not necessarily start at the bottom of the commission and gradually rise in seniority. Nor was he usually placed at the bottom of his social group within the commission. Instead, his name was inserted at a point which supposedly reflected his status in relation to his fellows. Robert Buxton, for instance, first sat on the Bench seven places above the last of the esquires. Even when a son followed his father into the commission he rarely succeeded to the latter's place. Thus Thomas Guybon, who was appointed to the Bench within a year of his father's death, sat sixteen places lower than had his father, but still thirteen places above the last member of the esquire group. A new justice's place in the commission mattered as much to those already appointed as it did to himself; his gain was their loss, so that ambitious gentry, intent upon maintaining if not improving their seniority, found it necessary to retain someone at Court constantly to watch over these 'placings'.[66]

Once more Philip Gawdy provides graphic details. As soon as he heard in 1601 that his brother's rival Thomas Lovell had been knighted, he negotiated at the Crown Office to ensure that Lovell's name was not set down above Bassingbourne's in the new commission. 'I was withe Mr. Powell', he told his brother, 'and . . . can assure you of my faythe that Mr. Lovell made sute not only to be above you in comyssion, but above iii more in the countrey as I will shortly tell you more at large.' It would be interesting to know if Lovell employed tactics similar to those he had used in 1598 when he paid £40 'to be restored to his former position in the commission' of the peace. This time, whatever his tactics, he failed, his name appearing in the commission immediately after Gawdy's.[67]

Unless a justice ensured that his interests were watched with this degree of attention, he might well lose precedence; but even worse, he might be left out of the commission altogether. Shortly after Henry Windham had been appointed a magistrate, Philip Gawdy remarked that he 'is lyke to be lefte out in this commission . . . for there is no body followes the matter for him'. Windham's name was

[66] *BIHR* xxxii, 1959, pp. 222–32. Appendix I.
[67] Jeayes, p. 168. Appendix I.

in fact omitted and then restored a few months later. If his predicament was at all typical it underlines the necessity for unremitting vigilance at Court and in Chancery if a justice wished to maintain his position on the Bench.[68]

Dismissal was especially humiliating because of the public manner in which it was done. A magistrate received no private notification: his name was simply left out of the commission and he might arrive at quarter sessions only to find that the clerk reading over the new commission did not summon him to take his place on the Bench. Apparently Sir Arthur Heveningham suffered this disgrace when he arrived at the epiphany sessions for 1583, there 'to have servyd her Majesty . . . beinge, as he then thought, one of her Majesty's justices of peace . . . and yet . . . at his being at the same sessions, fynding he was not [?on the commission] of the peace he had not anything there to do'.[69]

C. SECURITY OF TENURE

The experience of Henry Windham and Sir Arthur Heveningham suggests that magistrates laboured under threat of being left out of the commission. But how typical were these cases? What degree of security had a justice? Did he, as has been claimed, enjoy 'long and in most cases continuous service, usually ended only by death', or did he ride to quarter sessions and assizes anxiously wondering whether his name was still included in the most recent commission brought down from Chancery?[70]

It is difficult to discover how frequently justices were dismissed. In order to obtain a precise chronology of a justice's career it is necessary to know the composition of every commission of the peace for his county throughout his adult life. Unfortunately hardly any original Norfolk commissions have survived. However, during the periods 1558–64 and 1594–1603 one commission for each county was enrolled annually on the dorse of the patent rolls and these are extant. They could make possible a precise chronology, at least for the early and later Elizabethan periods, provided that the commission which the clerk enrolled was the sole one issued during that year. This, however, seems improbable since a new commission was necessary to register every justice's appointment, promotion, or dismissal. These doubts are confirmed by the entries in the first extant

[68] BM MS. Eg. 2804, f. 133. Appendix I. PRO Index Room 4208, p. 156.

[69] PRO St. Ch. 5, F 8/32, f. 50.

[70] Davies, *Enforcement*, p. 179. Gleason, p. 65.

Crown Office docquet book—one of the administrative records produced as part of the procedure for issuing new commissions. Its role in this procedure makes it an authoritative source: whenever the Lord Chancellor appointed or dismissed a justice he directed a warrant to the clerk of the Crown in Chancery authorizing the engrossing of a new commission; in due course the clerk returned this commission to the Lord Chancellor, briefly indicating on an attached docquet the changes he had made and also registering these in the Crown Office docquet books, one of which has fortunately survived for the period 1595–1603. This reveals that at least six commissions of the peace were engrossed annually for Norfolk.[71]

Clearly the single commission enrolled each year on the patent roll dorse will give an inadequate picture of a justice's career on the Bench. For instance, according to the patent rolls, James Scambler had been appointed to the Bench in 1593, dismissed in 1596, reappointed by July 1598, and thereafter remained in commission until at least 1603. The docquet book, however, reveals his restoration to the commission in July 1595 as well as in December 1597. He must, therefore, have been dismissed at least once more than is indicated by the patent rolls. To take one other example: the patent rolls indicate Wimond Carey's uninterrupted membership of the Norfolk Bench from 1593 until 1603, whereas the docquet book and other sources reveal that he was dismissed early in 1595 and then, in July, restored to the very commission which the Chancery clerk enrolled for that year.[72] These, and many similar cases, leave no doubt that justices were appointed and dismissed so frequently that the annual enrolment of a single commission on the patent rolls provides only a rough guide to their careers on the Bench.

But for most of Elizabeth's reign even annual lists have not survived. Between 1564 and 1594 no commissions of the peace for Norfolk were enrolled on the patent rolls, and our only sources are *libri pacis*. These 'books of the peace' comprise lists of all justices in England and Wales, and must have been compiled as official departmental reference books. Many are undated and most have been unsystematically amended in an effort to keep officials up to date with the numerous changes embodied in a constant stream of new commissions. Hence it is virtually impossible to obtain from them

[71] PRO Index Room 4208. *BIHR* xxxii, 1959, pp. 224–8.

[72] Cf. Appendix I with Salisbury MS. 278, ff. 65v–68v and PRO Index Room 4208, pp. 3, 84.

a precise list of justices at any one time. To make matters worse, there are no *libri pacis* for the period 1564–73 and thereafter their coverage is patchy.[73]

Such defective sources will provide a very conservative guide to the number of dismissals and the frequency with which a justice may have suffered this disgrace. It is therefore all the more significant that an analysis of these sources reveals that half the justices of Elizabethan Norfolk—75 out of a total of 149—were put out of the commission at least once.[74] Some were appointed and dismissed two or three times. Thomas Farmer, for instance, was appointed in 1579, lost his place about 1588, regained it in 1593 only to lose it once more in 1595—this time for good, although he lived until 1623. Thomas Barney had an equally chequered career: he was appointed in 1592, dismissed in 1595, reappointed in 1596, dismissed again in 1603, and finally reappointed in 1608, thereafter managing to keep his place until he died in 1618. It would be tedious to accumulate instances, but the bare statistics suggest that insecurity and uncertainty must have dogged many justices. Few of them can have been sure of their inclusion in the next commission—certainly far fewer than the figures suggest.[75]

So far it has been assumed that a J.P. whose name had been omitted from a commission had been dismissed rather than that he had voluntarily withdrawn from an onerous and thankless task. Clearly there must have been cases of resignation, but probably infrequently. There is no evidence from Norfolk of anyone seeking retirement during Elizabeth's reign and little from other counties.[76] Indeed all the indications are that justices wished to remain in the commission. Social pressures kept them there: great prestige derived from a place on the Bench; conversely dismissal was commonly regarded as a mark of disgrace. Altogether the weight of evidence suggests that there was considerable demand to get into the commission and, generally speaking, to stay in. The cause of instability has to be sought elsewhere.

One explanation for the insecurity of tenure which many justices experienced is to be found in county faction and politics. As will be

[73] *BIHR* xxxii, 1959, pp. 237–40.

[74] Between 1590 and 1620 a third of the Wiltshire justices were left out of the commission at least once. See Wall, op. cit., p. 9.

[75] Appendix II.

[76] Gleason, p. 52.

shown in later chapters, controversy in quarter sessions about methods of local administration gave rise to frequent attempts to influence the decisions of the Bench by getting rid of opponents and bringing in friends. So, too, did the common practice of using public office in the conduct of private quarrels. But an explanation in terms of county affairs is not, in itself, adequate. Magistrates were appointed and dismissed by the Lord Chancellor, frequently after extensive discussion at Court and at the Council board. Hence the councillors could, if they were so minded, withstand local demand for frequent changes in personnel; equally they could encourage it by their willingness to dismiss justices on the slightest pretext. It is therefore important to investigate the Council's attitude towards tenure in the commission of the peace.

During Elizabeth's reign privy councillors frequently voiced dissatisfaction with the conduct of local administration. In parliament and Star Chamber they reiterated complaints about inefficiency and slackness: 'whatsoever care is taken for the devising, penning and publishing of good and fitt lawes, yet litle heede and lesse travayle is bestowed in promoting thexecution of theim'.[77] It is tempting to dismiss such outbursts as the platitudinous utterances of those in authority whose task was either to cajole or coerce unpaid amateurs into becoming their efficient agents. There is, however, extensive evidence to suggest that Elizabeth's councillors went beyond these generalized complaints and attempted to implement reforms in order to rectify some of the deficiencies in local administration.

They disagreed, however, about how best to do this. Two conflicting diagnoses of the basic defects in local administration resulted in some councillors pleading for the appointment of more justices, while others advocated a reduction in numbers, thereby leaving a small core of county magnates to shoulder the entire burden of administration and law enforcement. William Lambarde, antiquary, lawyer, magistrate and author of a best-selling manual for justices, knew of this debate when he wrily commented that 'to dispute where it bee now better to have many or fewe justices of the peace in each shire is a noble question and worthie of a higher considera-

[77] BM MSS. Harl. 5176, ff. 112v–114; 6846, f. 226. For similar complaints, see Neale, *Parliaments 1559–1581*, pp. 238–9. J. Hawarde, *Les Reportes del Cases in Camera Stellata*, ed. W. P. Baildon, 1894, pp. 20–1. *CSPD, 1598–1601*, pp. 347, 441. *HMC Salisbury*, x. 182–4. BM MS. Add. 48041, ff. 167–70 (Yelverton 46). FSL MS. 89.2, pp. 69–70, 72–6. Corpus Christi College, Camb. MS. 543, speech by Sir Nich. Bacon in the parl. of 1571.

tion: and therefore it becometh not me to enter into it.' Sir Thomas Smith, a privy councillor relatively detached from local administration by virtue of his training as a civil lawyer and his ambassadorial service in France, voiced the common-sense view that more justices were required in order to prevent the creaking machinery of local administration from utter collapse under the weight of Tudor paternalistic legislation. In 1563 he argued that although there were as many as thirty or forty justices in each shire, 'so manie more beeing founde, which have either will, or power, or both, are not too manie to handle the affaires of the commonwealth in this behalfe'. In opposition to this view Cecil led a powerful group of councillors who wanted to reduce numbers in the commissions of the peace. He advocated a select group of justices in each county who might then 'exercise justice with a herculean courage'.[78]

Cecil based these apparently impractical suggestions upon a shrewd appraisal of some of the basic factors which led to unrest in mid-Tudor England—a matter which much concerned the Council since it feared that local disturbances might be fused into rebellion by Catholic enemies who plotted the Queen's overthrow. Cecil maintained that factious local gentry did much to promote riots and rural disorders. Had not a private feud between John Flowerdew and the Kets of Wymondham transformed a local riot into the 1549 rebellion? There is extensive evidence that rivalry and conflict between the gentry was reflected in the behaviour of their servants and tenants, giving rise to the sort of rural unrest so vividly depicted in the *Paston Letters* and usually associated only with the fifteenth century. There is no doubt that 'bastard feudalism', with all its tendencies towards instability, continued unabated in late-sixteenth-century Norfolk. The phenomenon, if not the name, was familiar enough to sixteenth-century rulers. Their great problem was how to curb it; how to destroy the roots through which it fed.

It was at this point that Cecil and other councillors perceptively related the gentry's quarrelsome propensities to what they considered to be the inflated size of the commission of the peace. Both Cecil and Sir Nicholas Bacon argued that many of the gentry became magistrates in order to use their power and authority for factious ends, 'more to serve the pryvate affeccon of them selves and frends as in overthrowing an enymy or mayntinge a frende, a servante or

[78] W. Lambarde, *Eirenarcha*, 1599, p. 35. Sir Thos. Smith, *De Republica Anglorum*, ed. L. Alston, Cambridge, 1906, p. 85. J. Hawarde, op. cit., p. 21.

tennaunt, then to maynteyne the comon goode of there countrye, respecting more the persons than the matters'. An anonymous Star Chamber speaker was even more outspoken: he declared that 'a great sorte doe seek for the place [of J.P.] inordinately, not of any mynde to bring good to theire countrie, but of a desyre eyther to beare rule and swaye . . . or to be avenged upon theire private offendors'. Lord Keeper Egerton spoke in the same vein when he asserted that 'many justices of peace were made who only came to the assizes to maintain and bear out causes, and did nothing all the year before nor after'.[79]

This appears to have been the reasoning which led Cecil to conclude that in the interest of good government he should 'abridge the multitude of justices of the peace which doe soe swarme that they trouble and moleste the Benche'. He spoke with admiration of a past age when 'our progenitors, having grete care to see to the preservation of the peace amongst there subiects did authorise . . . 5 or 6 but not much above, to be preservators and justices of peace wherby grete quietnes grew in the contrees, and more authorite and reverence [ex]isted in the same justicees than if a gretar nomber [had] bene therto appoynted.' Similar views were expressed by the Earl of Leicester and Lord Keepers Bacon and Puckering. The latter, addressing the justices in Star Chamber, demanded 'that special enquirie bee made of al unable, turbulent and remissive justices of the peace, to thend that, the commissions being purged of all suche as eyther do harme or cannot or will not do good, the number may upon iust cause be diminished'.[80]

The argument that many justices used their power for factious purposes was only one of several which culminated in this demand for a smaller commission of the peace. Some privy councillors attributed slack administration to an excess of inferior justices, arguing that bad justices drove out good. As early as 1561 Cecil observed that

> . . . it is dayly seene that with the increase of nomber of justices of peace . . . the conservation of peace hath decreased . . . by reason that the better sort of the justicees being of gravite and creditt have forborne to intermedle in exercise of those officeas as thynking them selves associated with a nomber of unmeet [persons] ether for wysdom, vertue, lerning or other qualite of creditt.

[79] FSL MS. 89.2, pp. 69–70. BM MS. Harl. 6846, ff. 226v. *HMC Salisbury*, x. 182.
[80] BM MSS. Add. 48041, f. 169v (Yelverton 46); Harl. 6846, ff. 226v–227. PRO SP 12/17, f. 100.

Thirty years on he was still complaining about the large number of unsuitable justices which caused those best suited to rule to 'be ashamed to sit with such companions as some of them be'. In 1582 the Earl of Leicester welcomed the news that 'nombers of base men shuld be left owt' of the commission of the peace with the observation that '. . . every where ther ys no so very a doger nor pelter at the lawe, yea even comon attorneys and no better, but ar by heapes putt into the comyssyon and remayn . . . God forbyd yt shud be'. The Archbishop of York propounded a variation on this when he requested that

as fewe inferior and meane persons be in the comission of the peace as may be ffor that the gentlemen and people disdayne to be subiecte unto them, and therfore will doe their best to disgrace and crosse their proceedings, nether will they . . . attend to doe any service, their inferiors sytting on the benche, everye man desyring or thinking him self as worthy to syt ther as they.[81]

Such arguments determined the categories of justices who ought to be dismissed. Since justices needed to be respected figures who were of such integrity that they would refuse to subvert to private ends the special powers entrusted to them, any who were 'base' and 'subservient' should be put out of commission. Baseness was generally taken to mean those who were 'of so meane lyvyng and countenance as they doe not answere in subsedie . . . as a persone of £20 landes or some better value in goodes'. It was less easy to decide what constituted subservience, but on several occasions the Council attempted to rid the commission of any justices known to 'weare the lyvery of any person, or to take wages for service in howshold with any man, or that be reteyning to any person otherwise than by the lawes of the realme is permitted'.[82]

Further, since the Council wished to confine magistracy to a few substantial gentry, it had to ensure that these gentry resided regularly in their counties and kept hospitality there. It therefore ordered the dismissal of justices who had 'noe dwelling howse' in the counties in which they served, or who lived there for less than ninety days each year. As well as insisting upon residence it also endeavoured to secure a reasonable geographical distribution of magistrates. In 1575 it asked the *custodes rotulorum* to certify the names of justices according to the Hundreds and Divisions in which they dwelt, while

[81] PRO SP 12/17, f. 100; /155/42, f. 2. BM MS. Lansd. 53, f. 174.
[82] BM MS. Lansd. 53, f. 187. PRO SP 12/17, f. 101.

by 1583 Burghley had begun to plot the seats of principal gentry in a beautiful volume of county maps now preserved in the British Museum. Desire to avoid concentrations of justices and to prevent the undue influence of one family no doubt underlay the Council's directives against father and son sitting concurrently on the Bench.[83]

All councillors, whatever their views as to the desirability of a large or small commission, laboured constantly to exclude Recusants from the commission of the peace. A statute of 1563 obliged every justice to take an oath acknowledging the Queen's ecclesiastical supremacy before they could undertake their duties. But gentlemen of papist persuasion could frequently avoid this by procuring 'commissions of *Dedimus Potestatem* to particulare frends to receave the othes, who . . . [did] not accordinge to the truste reposed in them . . . [see] the parties sworne'. Privy councillors knew all about such stratagems and ordered a justice's dismissal at the slightest hint of popish practices.[84] They frequently tried to discover any ill-affected persons in the commission, sometimes ordering every justice to take an oath of allegiance before the *custos* or justices of assize,[85] sometimes, as has been shown, calling for special reports from the bishops and justices of assize.

The view that there were too many justices, many of them unsuitable to govern, appears to have prevailed in the Council. On at least seven occasions the Lord Chancellor dismissed so many justices throughout England and Wales that it is justifiable to speak of his 'purging' the commissions. Whether such drastic measures necessarily produced the ideal county Bench envisaged by Burghley can best be seen by an examination of their effects upon the Norfolk magistracy.

The first and possibly the most extensive change of personnel occurred a few weeks after Elizabeth's accession. Its precise extent is difficult to ascertain because there is no complete list of late Marian justices against which to compare the first Elizabethan commission. Yet sufficient evidence survives to make feasible a reconstitution of the Norfolk commission at the end of Mary's reign. A comparison of this with Elizabeth's first commission, issued in December 1558 or January 1559, reveals that 22 out of its 42 mem-

[83] BM MSS. Lansd. 53, f. 166; Royal 18 DIII. PRO SP 12/104. *APC, 1571–5*, p. 398.

[84] 5 Eliz. c. 1. BM MS. Eg. 3048, f. 78v. *APC, 1575–7*, p. 238.

[85] e.g. in 1568, 1579, and 1592, see *APC, 1578–80*, p. 178; *1592*, pp. 253–61; PRO SP 12/48, f. 179; /60, f. 2; /133/13.

bers lost their places. Death accounted for 6, but the remaining 16 must have been summarily dismissed. They were replaced by at least 17 new justices, bringing the total in commission up to 37. These figures indicate virtually a 50 per cent change in the personnel of the Norfolk Bench at Elizabeth's accession. A similar analysis of the commissions for Sussex and Northamptonshire reveals equally extensive changes in those counties.[86]

Undoubtedly political and religious considerations weighed heavily in this purge. The accession of Elizabeth meant a return to Protestantism as the official form of religion in England. In nurturing this new faith magistrates had a crucial role to play both by example and by enforcement of statutory sanctions. Consequently, in reforming the ranks of the Norfolk magistracy, the Lord Keeper and his fellow councillors were bound to dismiss prominent Marian supporters like Sir Richard Southwell and Sir Henry Bedingfeld. No doubt similar considerations caused them to dismiss six other justices who came from families subsequently noted for their Recusancy, and to bring in at least two new justices who held radical religious views.

But however strongly councillors would have liked this reconstitution of the Norfolk Bench to be guided by religious and political considerations, in the event other factors obtruded. By no means all Catholic sympathizers were dismissed, and the one common factor among the new justices appointed in Norfolk in 1559 was their commitment, not to the Protestant faith, but to Thomas Howard, fourth Duke of Norfolk. His influence upon the composition of the early Elizabethan commission of the peace for Norfolk has already been examined and undoubtedly the 1559 purge served to provide the young Duke with a timely opportunity to reassert Howard influence.

In June 1561 the Council made its first attempt to curtail the number of justices in each county, or, as Cecil put it, to reduce 'the former great nomber to a less'.[87] It is difficult to calculate the exact reduction in numbers on the Norfolk Bench by the end of the year because, as in 1559, there is no record of those in commission for the previous year with which to make comparison. But once more it is possible to reconstruct the commission as it stood on the eve of the Council's purge. There is evidence that 8 of the magistrates named

86 *HLQ* xxii, 1959, pp. 301–12. I have revised the figures.

87 PRO SP 12/17, f. 101.

in 1559 had died by 1561 and that 8 new ones had been appointed, so that the total number in commission probably still stood at 37. On this basis at least 14 justices were dismissed, the number in commission thereby being reduced by at least a third.[88] The pattern was similar in Sussex where numbers rose slightly during 1559 and 1560 and then fell abruptly from 45 to 29.[89]

'Last in first out' seems to have been the formula used to decide which justices should be dismissed. Since it could be applied mechanically and did not depend upon any subjective judgements, it seems to have been satisfactorily implemented. Out of the 14 justices who were dismissed from the Norfolk Bench no fewer than 6 had been members for less than a year; 4 others had served for barely two; only Sir Richard Fulmerston and Sir Thomas Knyvett could be regarded as well-established justices, the latter no doubt losing his place because of his suspect religious views.[90] It is surprising that the Council did not try to dismiss justices whom it deemed either unsatisfactory or unworthy, but in fact Cecil particularly asked the judges at the assizes to reassure any who felt aggrieved by loss of office that it did not signify reproof, but had been dictated by the necessity 'to reduce the order and governance of the contrye to a smaller numbre'.[91]

Barely three years later conciliar interference caused further insecurity among members of the Bench. By 1564 the Council had become so alarmed by reports of lukewarm support for the Anglican settlement among the magistracy that it called upon the bishops to examine the religious sympathies of every justice throughout England, to suggest any who ought to be dismissed, and also to nominate gentry who, as 'favourers of godly proceedings', might be appointed in their stead. As has been shown, John Parkhurst's report on the Norfolk magistracy was not representative of the episcopal returns, since it seems to have been dictated by the Duke of Norfolk. The

[88] Appendix I. The following justices were dismissed: Wm. Cockett, Edw. Clere, Wm. Brampton, Thos. Barrow, Thos. Brampton, John Appleyard, Martin Hastings, Thos. Knyvett of Buckenham, Thos. Thrower, Thos. Gawdy, Henry Reppes, George Hogard, Francis Thoresby, and Richard Fulmerston.

[89] I am indebted to Dr. Joyce E. Mousley for the Sussex figures. They are considerably more reliable than those for Norfolk since they are based on the lists of justices contained in the Assize rolls for the Home Circuit (PRO, ASSI. 35/1–4).

[90] Appendix I; also cf. the list of justices for 1 Eliz. with the reconstructed list of late Marian justices in Smith, 'Norf. Gentry', pp. 412–13.

[91] PRO SP 12/17, f. 101.

Bishop, although renowned for his radical views, did not recommend any zealous Protestants and only half-heartedly named four justices who 'by common fame' were less well affected than the others. As a result the Norfolk commission remained virtually unchanged; but the threat of dismisal had been real enough, and in many counties extensive changes in personnel actually occurred. In Sussex, for instance, nine justices—a quarter of the entire magistracy—were dismissed and seven others appointed in their stead.[92]

Justices again faced the prospect of loss of office in 1572, 1580, and 1582. On the first occasion Burghley proposed that 'the commissions of the peace in all shyres . . . be viewed and the unmete persons removed, and their roomes supplyed with more trusty and hable persons'; in 1580 he jotted down for conciliar consideration: 'excess of justices of peace'. Since there are few reliably dated lists of justices for this decade, it is difficult to assess the consequences, but in 1582 the Council certainly undertook 'a reformation . . . in the commission of the peace'. According to the Earl of Leicester, the Queen had commanded it and had ordered the dismissal of 'notorius papists' and 'nombers of base men'. What happened in Norfolk is not clear but in Sussex seven justices were dismissed; whether any of them were papists or 'base men' is another matter. The Earl of Leicester had his doubts, since he remarked sceptically that 'in the last reformacion I know the best protestants be putt owt in sondry shires and the very ancyentest justices'.[93]

Leicester knew only too well that whenever the Council attempted to dismiss unsuitable magistrates its intentions were thwarted in the process of implementation. This can be illustrated from what happened during the purge of 1587. Apparently in the spring the Queen had commanded 'the Lord Chancellor and others the Lords of her privie counsell to peruse the numbres of the justyces for the peace in the realm and to deminish the great nombre therof for that it was . . . excessyve and rather a hyndrance than furthrance to the peace'.[94] The Lord Chancellor immediately asked the assize judges to advise him which justices he should dismiss, urging them to reply quickly so that he could send out new commissions in time for the

[92] 'A Collection of Original Letters from the Bishops to the Privy Council 1564', ed. Mary Bateson, *Camden Miscellany IV* (Camden Soc. N.S. lii), 1895. PRO, ASSI. 35/4–7.

[93] BM MSS. Lansd. 104, f. 27; 103, f. 20. PRO SP 12/155/42, f. 2.

[94] This and the succeeding paras. are based upon BM MSS. Lansd. 103, f. 85; 52, ff. 200v–201; 53, ff. 165–94; 121, ff. 65–65v. Smith, 'Norf. Gentry', p. 77.

summer assizes. He specifically mentioned four classes of magistrates which ought to be eliminated from the Bench: those who could be spared because of an 'overgreat number' in their neighbourhood; those who were unable to perform their duties because of non-residence; those who were ill-suited to the task through ignorance or inadequate status; and finally those whose faith prevented them from executing the 'laws established for advancement of religion'. Since the judges had little time to make a first-hand appraisal of the magistracy in their circuits, their reports seriously misled the Lord Chancellor. For example, out of nine justices he dismissed from the Norfolk Bench only one appears to have had papist sympathies and none fell within any of the other categories he had enumerated.

Too late Burghley realized that in many factious counties the judges had relied upon biased reports, with the result that 'some [justices] almost in every shyre that war displaced war more mete to have remayned than others that war suffered to contynew, in that many of them that war displaced are known well affectid in religion and many of them for the place of ther habitations necessarily to be contynued'. Although Burghley admitted that this attempt to purge the commission had misfired because it had been carried out with 'more spede . . . than for such a cause was requisit', he decided to try again immediately. By August 1587 he had asked the bishops for advice about which justices ought to have been removed and which of those who had been dismissed ought to be reinstated. He gave them the same guidance about unsuitable justices as he had given the judges except that he added a further category: 'that none be in commission . . . whose fathers are in commission and be resident in the same countye'.

The Bishop of Norwich failed to make a very thorough report because, so he complained, 'the commicion of peace is so often altered and dailie renewed' that he did not know precisely who was and who was not a justice at that time. He noted that out of the nine who had just been dismissed only one was popish while three others could well be dispensed with, although he gave no reasons. He then listed ten justices who were still in commission although they were 'suspected and reputed to be backwardes in religion', as well as two others who were 'young justices whose fathers are in commission of peace'. Deficient sources conceal the extent to which Burghley acted on this report, but they suggest that he followed it closely. If such were the case, then nearly half the justices in Norfolk suffered dismissal at one time or another during the year 1587–8. Moreover, even if Burghley and the Lord Chancellor did not display the same naive trust in the bishops' recommendations as they had in those of the judges, the news of further impending dismissals must have caused many justices to wonder who would next be dismissed.

In 1595 the Elizabethan Council made its last attempt to reduce numbers in the commissions of the peace, this time dismissing nearly a quarter of the Norfolk Bench. A list of J.P.s amended in Burghley's hand and preserved at Hatfield House makes it possible to deduce the categories of justices which the Council hoped to displace:[95] those who were servants to other people, those assessed for subsidy at under £20, and those suspected of Recusancy. What happened, however, was very different. Three Recusant suspects were certainly removed from the Norfolk commission,[96] but out of seven justices whose subsidy assessment fell below the Council's minimum requirement,[97] only two lost their places on the Bench.[98] With them, however, went nine other justices who seem to have been well qualified on all counts to remain.[99] There is little doubt that, as in 1587, the Lord Chancellor dismissed many of the fittest justices and left in commission many whom their lordships deemed unsuitable. This conclusion is supported by the speed with which several of the justices who had been dismissed were restored to the Bench. Over the scored-out name of Sir Henry Woodhouse Burghley wrote 'stet', and although this purge is unlikely to have taken place before May 1595,[100] a new commission for Woodhouse's restoration was issued on 21 July 1595. Wimond Carey and James Scambler had been restored even more quickly, a commission to that end being issued on 18 July.[101]

Privy councillors undoubtedly intended to improve the quality and efficiency of local government by reducing the number of

95 Salisbury MS. 278, ff. 65v–68v.

96 Thos. Knyvett of Buckenham, Martin Barney, and Henry Yelverton (PRO SP 12/208/16. BM MS. Lansd. 52, f. 201).

97 John Hunt, Robt. Redmayne, Wm. Blennerhassett, Robt. Houghton, Richard Kemp, Anthony Death, and Jas. Scambler.

98 John Hunt and Jas. Scambler.

99 Henry Woodhouse, Thos. Farmer, Wm. Gresham, Wimond Carey, John Reppes, Thos. Barney, Gregory Pratt, Thos. Clere, and Richard Frestone.

100 In May 1595 Burghley wrote a 'Memorial' on the categories of justices to be removed from the commission (PRO SP 12/252, no. 42).

101 PRO Index Room 4208, p. 3.

justices and appointing only those best qualified for magistracy. But although they made at least seven attempts to reform and reduce the commissions of the peace, they never managed entirely to rid them of those categories of magistrates whom they deemed unsuitable; nor did they succeed in reducing the number of justices on the county Benches. Indeed, during Elizabeth's reign the size of the Norfolk commission increased steadily until in 1603 it contained twice as many names as it had forty years earlier.[102] The Council's well-intentioned purges merely provided factious gentry with further opportunities to manipulate the Bench for their own particular purposes.

[102] Appendix I.

CHAPTER V

County Administration: the Quarter Sessions

COUNTY government centred on the biannual assizes and quarterly sessions of the peace. On these six occasions each year the principal gentry and many men of more humble origin assembled to uphold the law and settle administrative problems. No doubt many people found that these gatherings provided convenient occasions to meet friends, transact private business, or lobby the justices over public or private issues; but most of those who attended had an essential role in the conduct of the court's business. Participants included 15 or 20 magistrates (more at assizes where attendance was virtually compulsory), several private clerks employed by the foremost magistrates,[1] the sheriff, the clerk of the peace, all high constables (32), members of the grand (23), petty (12), and Hundred juries, and of course prisoners and those bound by recognizance to appear.[2] To these must be added the alehouse keepers and corn dealers seeking new licences, the maimed soldiers and other distressed people—all hoping for relief out of county funds—as well as petitioners, informers, and no doubt a host of attorneys. Quarter-sessional and assize towns were thronged with people for several days; rumours spread, bargains were struck, decisions made or shelved, Council orders promulgated, grievances voiced. No doubt many gentry, riding home after the hubbub and excitement, found it difficult to differentiate between the official and unofficial business which had been transacted.

A statute of 2 Henry V required J.P.s annually to hold general sessions of the peace during the week following the feasts of Epiphany, the Close of Easter, St. Thomas the Martyr (7 July), and

[1] From draft letters and letter-books it appears that at least 12 Norfolk magistrates employed private clerks who spent a great deal of time on official business. Prof. T. G. Barnes has identified 22 in early-seventeenth-century Somerset (Barnes, *Somerset*, p. 75). See also B. W. Quintrell, 'The Government of the County of Essex 1603–1642' (London PhD thesis 1965), p. 47.

[2] *WRS* iv, 1949, pp. 23, 45, 46, 88. W. Lambarde, *Eirenarcha*, 1599, pp. 370–89. Some lists of high constables, marked as if names had been called over, are extant among the sixteenth-century Norfolk quarter sessions rolls.

St. Michael the Archangel (29 September). In some counties the magistrates held all these sessions at the county town, in others they held each quarterly session at a different town. In Wiltshire, for example, they usually assembled for their Epiphany, Easter, Summer, and Michaelmas sessions respectively at Salisbury, Warminster, Devizes, and Marlborough or Chippenham. Possibly the Wiltshire justices developed this system in order to share the business brought by quarter-sessional crowds among as many market-town traders as possible. To some extent it may also have reduced people's travelling time and hostelry expenses by taking the sessions to them; but for most participants any saving in time and money at their nearby sessions was offset by the inconvenience of attending subsequent sessions at the other side of the county.[3]

The Norfolk justices operated a quarter-sessional system which, although complicated, brought extra trade to a number of market towns and made for good administration by genuinely reducing travelling time and expenses for everyone except themselves. Whereas the Wiltshire justices annually held each sessions in a different town, their Norfolk counterparts by means of adjournments, held each sessions in three different towns, so that nobody ever needed to travel outside his 'division' to attend quarter sessions. This system took shape during the fourteenth century when the justices began to meet at King's Lynn to deal with affairs in north-west Norfolk before adjourning to Norwich where they presided over the business of the rest of the county. By the sixteenth century they had divided the county into three quarter-sessional areas, assembling every quarter in each: at King's Lynn or Swaffham for the western division; at Walsingham, Holt, or East Dereham for he northern division; and at Norwich for the south-eastern division. The justices' itinerary varied with the seasons. They commenced their so-called Epiphany sessions during mid-December at King's Lynn, adjourning, with a day's interval, to Walsingham or Holt, and then, after a second adjournment over Christmas and the New Year, they completed their business at Norwich during Epiphany week. Easter sessions opened at Norwich somewhat prematurely during the first week in Lent and were then adjourned successively to King's Lynn and Walsingham where the justices always met during the last week in Lent or Easter week. Summer sessions, like those at Epiphany, opened in the western division, but at Swaffham

[3] *WRS* iv, 1949, pp. xxi, 45–54. *VCH Wilts.* v. 88.

instead of King's Lynn. Here the justices met early in the week preceding Trinity Sunday; two days later they reassembled either at East Dereham or Holt, and so to Norwich immediately after Trinity Sunday. Occasionally they started the summer sessions at Norwich during the first week in Trinity, in which case they adjourned for five weeks before meeting in the western and northern divisions during July. Michaelmas sessions were less prone to variation. Once more the justices assembled in the western division, usually at King's Lynn, in mid-September, adjourned to Walsingham, and then to Norwich where they always met immediately following the feast of St. Michael.

This quarter-sessional programme made strenuous demands upon the magistrates. Early Elizabethan sessions at King's Lynn, Swaffham, Walsingham, and Holt usually occupied a day each; those at Norwich frequently lasted two or three days. By the 1590s most divisional sessions lasted for two days, while the Norwich Bench often deliberated for four. This meant, for instance, that during 1598 assiduous justices could have spent up to 35 days on the Bench. They could obviously lighten this burden by attending only their divisional sessions, thereby splitting the county into three exclusive quarter-sessional regions. Certainly those in the northern division had little direct contact with their western counterparts, but the magnetism of Norwich sessions prevented excessive localism. Here, since the Bench dealt with administrative matters relating to the entire county, justices attended from far and wide; in 1599, for example, at least seven magistrates from the northern and western divisions also assembled at Norwich. In fact, far from dividing the county, this system enabled justices to dispose of half their routine legal business at King's Lynn and Walsingham so that they gained more time at Norwich to discuss the county's multifarious administrative problems.[4]

Administration usually involved taxation and so tended to stimulate interest in quarter sessions. There is little evidence that the Norfolk commission contained many of those idle justices who haunted the imaginations of parliamentary speakers—justices who, according to Sir Nicholas Bacon, kept 'the name and place of a justyce more for reputacon's sake then for any care they have to performe their offyce and othe and be in effect but as drones among

[4] *NRS* viii, 1936, p. 3. NNRO MSS. Norfolk Sessions Minute Books 1562–86.

bees'.[5] Records of quarter-sessional attendances suggest that Norfolk justices were not merely conscientious, but even enthusiastic: late Elizabethan sessions at King's Lynn, Swaffham, Walsingham, and Holt regularly attracted 6 or 8 justices; those at Norwich rarely less than 15. Out of 38 J.P.s who could have attended quarter sessions in 1595, no less than 30 were present for at least two days, while 16 had attendances varying from eight to twenty days. Similarly, out of 70 justices resident in Norfolk between 1590 and 1600 only 5 failed to attend quarter sessions for at least a few days during most years. It is noteworthy that justices who sat low in the order of precedence were among the most assiduous in their attendance.[6]

The *custos rotulorum* presided at quarter sessions; in his absence the senior barrister on the Bench deputized for him. Early Elizabethan *custodes* in Norfolk regularly took the chair at every quarter-sessional meeting, but their successors were less conscientious. Indeed, for the last twenty years of the century there was no regular chairman: Sir Christopher Heydon (*custos* 1564–80) never attended the sessions at King's Lynn or Swaffham where Francis Gawdy frequently deputized for him; his successor, Sir Dru Drury (*custos* 1580–*c.* 1604), was a gentleman usher of the Queen's chamber and presided only intermittently at any Norfolk sessions.[7]

Sessions opened with some formal preliminaries. First the sheriff made his return of the precept and the processes directed to him, together with the calendar of persons summoned to attend the court and the prisoners to be tried. Next the crier called the court, noting

[5] FSL MS. 89.2, p. 69.

[6] Appendix I. These figures are based upon three sources: (a) NNRO MSS. Norfolk Sessions Minute Books 1562–86. These do not provide a complete record of all justices who attended each sessions, since the clerk sometimes wrote '*et alii*' when listing the justices present. This happened most frequently at the Norwich sessions and probably indicated that extra justices had attended on the second and third days when the clerk had no space to record their names. (b) PRO E 137/33/3 (Estreats of Fines at quarter sessions for 4 and 37 Eliz.). These record the justices who attended each sessional adjournment and confirm that the Q/S minute books do not always list all justices who attended. (c) PRO E 372/404–447 *sub* Norfolk (enrolments of justices' wage claims on the Pipe Rolls). In some counties, by the early seventeenth century, these enrolments had become formalized (see *VCH Wilts.* v. 90–1), but there is no doubt, from the nature of the Norfolk entries, that except in the case of the *custos* these represent claims for genuine attendances.

[7] The *custos rotulorum* is named in commissions and invariably indicated in the *Libri pacis*. See Appendix I.

the absence of any officials who should have been present. Then, while the justices handed the clerk of the peace their records of recent inquisitions and recognizances, members of the grand, petty, and Hundred juries took their oath. The grand jury had two functions: first, to examine indictments preferred by the justices and to decide whether or not there were reasonable grounds for trial; secondly, by presentments to draw the court's attention to unrepaired highways, misconduct among minor officials, decayed bridges, and other matters which might be detrimental to the entire county. The sheriff selected twenty-three of the most substantial freeholders for this jury. The petty jury of twelve freeholders decided upon the innocence or guilt of those indicted by the grand jury, while the Hundred juries did for the localities what the grand jury did for the county.

Preliminaries over, the chairman delivered his 'charge' to the jurors—an oration which sometimes lasted for over two hours. It comprised two parts: an introductory exhortation varying in quality and length with different chairmen, followed by a summary of the laws appertaining to quarter sessions. Many 'charges' probably echoed the Council's opinions about matters which needed urgent attention; these the chairman may have gleaned from speeches in Star Chamber, where, from time to time, Lord Chancellors or Lord Keepers berated justices and jurors for their slackness. Sometimes, however, chairmen must have expounded their personal views on matters of moment as did Edward Flowerdew in 1573 when he caused 'great question . . . what bread ought to be used at the communion' by making 'mention of common breade to be used by authoritie of the statute'. Occasionally, when the Council wished to commend or justify its policy, it sent down a special 'charge' for the chairman to deliver. Robert Buxton received one on the eve of the Michaelmas sessions in 1592. For two hours he delivered a polished, learned exposition of the relationship between Church and State. It was intended to galvanize the county into a concerted campaign against Jesuit missionaries and their recusant supporters:

> if there bee any putrified branch or member, if there bee any in whome there is no suretie of allegiance, by suspition of rebellious or treacherous practizes or seditious behaviour, it is proper and belonging to all the rest of the members of this civile and pollitique body to joyne in common aide to committ that branche and member to the censure of cyvile justice least it infecteth and corrupteth the whole bodie.

Thus the solemn words rolled from the lips of Robert Buxton, faithful servant to Philip Howard, Earl of Arundel, who was already in the Tower under suspicion 'of rebellious and treacherous practizes'.[8]

Occasionally, no doubt, a luckless justice suffered the fate of the Surrey magistrate who arrived at quarter sessions to find the regular chairman unexpectedly absent and his colleagues proposing that he should deputize. He managed to deliver an extempore 'exhortacon to the juryes of betwene a quarter and halfe an houre and then caused the clarke of the peace to reade the lawes'—the formal part of the 'charge' which set forth the statutes under which quarter sessions operated. All but the most experienced chairmen would read from a prepared classification available in an up-to-date procedural handbook like Lambarde's *Eirenarcha*. This exposition frequently took an hour or more and, exceptional circumstances apart, comprised the bulk of the 'charge'.[9]

After this the court turned to business. The grand jury examined all criminal bills and decided which presented a *prima facie* case for trial. The sheriff then arraigned prisoners against whom the grand jury had found a 'true bill', each in turn pleaded either 'guilty' or 'not guilty', or refused to plead. Refusal to plead was tantamount to a plea of 'guilty'; in both cases the court merely awarded punishment; only defendants pleading 'not guilty' received trial before a petty jury. By the late sixteenth century quarter sessions no longer heard felonies which involved the death penalty or cases of grand larceny, any *casus difficultatis* being reserved for assizes. Occasionally Norfolk justices exceeded their jurisdiction, but not for long. When, for instance, in 1597 Chief Justice Popham heard that 'divers very notorious offendors being convicted were by some few of the justices reprived', he instructed the Bench that 'from hensforth you doe forbeare at your quarter sessions to deale with anie offendors in case of murther, manslaughter, burglaryes, rapes, robberies upon the high way and horse-stealing as matters fittest to be tried at the Assizes'. No doubt magistrates dealt as summarily as possible with minor

[8] *William Lambarde and local government: his Emphemeris and twenty nine charges to juries and commissioners*, ed. Conyers Read, New York, 1962. CUL MSS. Ee. II. 34, f. 145v; Buxton Box 96, a small vol. with parchment covers, entitled 'The Recognition of the High & Sacred authority of the supremacie invested in our most gratious Soveraigne Ladie Elizabeth . . .', f. 5.

[9] *Surrey Arch. Collections*, ix, 1888, p. 184. W. Lambarde, *Eirenarcha*, 1599, pp. 389–467. *Wilts. Arch. & Nat. Hist. Mag.* xiv, 1874, pp. 208–16.

felonies, larcenies, and misdemeanours so that they could hurry on to more challenging administrative business; but one procedural innovation—the travers—militated against this rapid completion of criminal proceedings. Anyone charged with misdemeanours (minor offences such as trespass, battery, vagrancy, bastardy or petty thefts) could travers the indictment, provided he came to the court of his own volition rather than under compulsion of a bail bond. In this way a defendant could plead his exception to the charge, but the pleading resembled that in civil suits, with pleas and counter-pleas, each occupying a considerable time. Sometimes the charge was quashed; if not, hearing and determining the case took up more time at the next sessions.[10]

Particularly at the Norwich sessions justices had also to deal with a variety of administrative matters—business which involved them all because it had financial and political implications. It is important to remember that quarter sessions had become 'not merely a criminal court for the county, but also a governmental assembly, a board with governmental and administrative powers'.[11] Within the framework of parliamentary statutes, justices in quarter sessions had many delegated powers whose implementation frequently necessitated decisions of a political nature. Some were straightforward and routine; others were reached only after acrimonious discussions followed by voting, which, in a factious county, could cause large attendances at quarter sessions. Little is known about such proceedings because the clerks who kept the sessional minute books merely recorded the court's decisions without any reference to the deliberations by which they were reached. Voting is, however, implicit in much sessional business and occasionally a document refers to it. The most explicit account appears in a late-seventeenth-century diary kept by Sir Roger Hill of Buckinghamshire. The story is best told in his own words:

> the 28th of March, 1693 I received a letter from Mr. Thomas Smith, clerke of the peace for the county of Bucks., (dated the same day) by which he gave me notice that I was left out of the commission of the peace; which was noe unwelcome news to me, the rather because I was turned out for doeing my duty, viz. because att last Easter sessions I opposed Mr. Thomas Wharton's turning out of Henry Munday from his place as Master of the house of correction unless

[10] NNRO MS. NAS Safe II.28, f. 12. For procedures at Q/S see esp. Barnes, *Somerset*, ch. III.

[11] F. W. Maitland, *Constitutional History of England*, Cambridge, 1908, p. 233.

he were proved guilty of those crimes which Mr. Wharton accused him of, viz. of his being an enemy of the government, and his being a drunkard, whore master and swearer. I moved that he might have leave to clear himself, or else till he was proved guilty I must think him innocent, but upon conviction of any one of those crimes I was ready to remove him or any other that was in my power. *nota*: att Mr. Whartons directions it was put to the vote; not half the company voted against Munday but noe one except Captain Salter haveing courage to second me (though the same day they severall of them thanked me for what I sayd), Munday was declared out, and one Read was att Mr. Wharton's nomination declared his successor. *Nota*: alsoe all this proceeding was extra-judiciall, it being done out of sessions; it was done in the chamber after diner, the sessions haveing been adjorned att the rising of the court to be holden again att the public hall after dinner. Att Midsummer Sessions Munday moved to be restored [but] all Mr. Wharton's ffriends suspecting it, appeared on the bench though severall of them new parliament men and the Parliament was then sitting. However, they fearing it would goe against them, Mr. Beake moved to adjourne it till Michaelmas sessions because Mr. Wharton, who he sayd was concerned, was not present, neither did he spare to reflect upon me for opposing him behind his backe, alledging I durst not doe it before his face, though severall of the justices then present affirmed I sayd much more when he was by att the former sessions; att length it was put to the vote and Mr. William Busby (the chaire man) and Sergeant Thurbarn refuseing to give any votes and Mr. John Shall Cross, who, though he had alwaise been Munday's acquaintance and ffriend, (haveing as supposed by some things he had done made himselfe obnoxious and fearing he should hear thereof if he disobliged some more) voteing against him, his vote cast Munday out; *nota*; Munday was wholy a stranger to me but I could not agree to an arbitrary punishment of anyone without proofe and from the Easter Sessions aforesaid Mr. Wharton would never speak to me, and as I heare he and Mr. Hamden have reported I should be turned out of commission, and accordingly this last Assizes I was left out and four new ones put in . . . which confirmes me in the belief that if Henry Munday was guilty of whoremongering and swearing and drinking he was not turned out for those crimes.[12]

It is possible to discern occasions when justices meeting at Norwich must have discussed, disputed, and finally resorted to voting after this fashion. Tension and disagreement could just as easily arise over a high constable's appointment as over a Bridewell keeper's. Until the sixteenth century high constables had been appointed in the Hundred courts; but as these courts declined and the constables increasingly assumed the role of administrative assistants to the

[12] J. L. Stern, 'His Brother's Keeper. The Buckinghamshire Justice of the Peace 1678–1689' (Princeton PhD thesis 1960), pp. 124–6.

justices, their appointment and good bearing became a quarter-sessional matter. Careful selection provided the best safeguard against corrupt and inefficient constables, but justices might well differ as to a candidate's merit. In 1603 Nathaniel Bacon expected discussion, perhaps even dispute, when the Bench had to appoint a new constable for Launditch Hundred. In preparation he noted 'that a chief constable be appointed. . . . Mr. Ferrar's . . . sonne in lawe . . . is thought very fitt for the place and desired by Mr. Gooch [the remaining constable] to be his partener. Mr. Utbert is not thought so fitt because he is a greate brewer and maie become a freind to the alehousekeepers whereof ther are great store in that Hundred.' However carefully justices selected these constables, upon occasion they had to indict and even dismiss an inefficient or corrupt one, a procedure which could result in scenes similar to those depicted by Sir Roger Hill of Buckinghamshire.[13]

Rating assessments gave rise to frequent debates and disputes since counties financed all their local government from *ad hoc* levies. Some of these rates were raised to pay for particular projects: to repair a bridge; to assist the port-towns in providing ships for war; to reconstruct local harbours; to relieve distress after a disastrous fire such as occurred at North Walsham in 1600; to repair an important highway like the main Norwich–London thoroughfare between Wymondham and Attleborough; to strengthen sea-banks; or to provide 'coat and conduct' money for the latest levies. Others were an annual charge to meet recurrent expenses: maimed soldiers' pensions; the King's Bench and Marshalsea fund; muster-masters' salaries; purveyance for the royal household; or maintenance of houses of correction. Each year the justices re-estimated and re-granted these recurrent rates, as well as sanctioning others as occasion demanded, so that few sessions passed without discussion over both the amount of a particular rate and each Hundred's contribution towards it.[14]

[13] NNRO MS. Bradfer–Lawrence Xd, memoranda book 1602–6, p. 21. *Stiffkey Papers*, p. 26. *WRS* iv, 1949, p. x. Davies, *Enforcement*, p. 170. W. B. Willcox, *Gloucestershire 1590–1640*, New Haven, 1940, pp. 49–50. BM MS. Add. 41140, f. 64.

[14] BM MSS. Add. 23007, ff. 37v, 39v; 48591, ff. 20v, 51v, 148; 41656, f. 1; King's 265, ff. 226–8. NNRO MSS. NAS Safe II.28, ff. 26, 26v, 31, 36, 58, 73, 112; Frere Box K.12(A), Tunstead bundle, letter dated 30 July 1600. Bodl. MS. Tanner 95, f. 20a. *APC, 1571–5*, pp. 106, 194; *1595–6*, p. 328; *1596–7*, pp. 64–5, 461. *NA* xxvi, 1938, pp. 287–95. H. Swinden, *History and Antiquities of . . . Yarmouth*, Norwich, 1772, pp. 102–3, 413, 421–2.

Dissension could arise at either stage: in Norfolk, for instance, justices from inland areas usually protested against the estimates for sea defences or harbour repairs, while those from near the coast complained about excessive rates for improving inland highways.[15] Even if they compromised about the total rate, they would almost certainly disagree again over the assessment of each Hundred's contribution. There appears to have been no accepted formula for calculating this, so that whenever a rate had to be apportioned between Hundreds the justices were likely to argue about the relative wealth of their localities, and frequently they adjusted contributions. In Wiltshire, for instance, they raised one 'division's' contribution towards gaol repairs from £6.10*s*.0*d*. to £7.10*s*.0*d*. and reduced another's from £9.0*s*.0*d*. to £7.10*s*.0*d*. These may be paltry sums, but when, as in Norfolk, at least fourteen rates were levied in one year, it behoved a justice to secure as low a rate as possible for the Hundreds in his neighbourhood. By 1600 Norfolk magistrates spent so much time arguing about these assessments that Nathaniel Bacon put forward a scheme whereby each Hundred could be rated without discussion. It must have been rejected since the Norfolk Bench was contemplating the adoption of a similar scheme in 1628.[16]

Debate did not end with approval of the rate; the processes of assessment and collection frequently gave rise to further disputes at quarter sessions. These usually arose as a result of complaints either against high constables for over-assessment when they apportioned the rate between townships in their respective Hundreds, or against petty constables when they assessed individual parishioners. In the ensuing discussions the justices usually disagreed about an equitable system for assessing the rate in each parish. Even if they devised one it was almost invariably disregarded. In 1598 Nathaniel Bacon became so incensed by the failure to implement a scheme which he and his fellow magistrates had hammered out that he complained bitterly to the Council:

It maie please your Lordships further to be advertised that by occasion of some differences in this country about the equall rating of money towards her majesty's diett, the setting forth of soldiers, the muster maisters' wages and such like, there was in Lent last at a general sessions of the peace holden for the

[15] Below, pp. 98–9, 256, 261.

[16] *WRS* iv, 1949, 153. BM MS. Add. 48591, f. 51v. Holkham MS. General Estate Deeds, misc. bundle A, no. 3. *Musters, Beacons and Ship Money*, ed. W. Rye, Norwich, 1907, pp. 131, 161–2.

countie a conference had thereabout by the justices of peace there meeting. And by their generall consent with some direction had before from the Lord Chief Justice of England this rule was then sett downe: viz. that the levies and taxacons of all extraordinary kynds should be guided principally by the value of lands in every man's occupation. And yet regard should be also had to raise or abate every person charged according to his substance in the said parish beside his land. This was and is thought to be a rule very indifferent bicause the richer sort did occupie lands in sundrie parrishes and did contribute onely in the parishes where their dwelling was and thereby the poorer sort was forced to beare part of their burthen. The equity of this rule is partly approved by the last Statute made for the relief of the poore. Now there be manie of the better sort of persons some dwelling in the countrey, some out of the countrey, who do refuse in the setting forth of the late soldiers for Ireland to be contributory by the former rule, whereby wee shalbe inforced to alter that which we have agreed upon unless we may be aided by your Lordships' authority.[17]

Dissension deepened when justices disagreed, not about the methods of rating or the amount to be levied, but about whether to sanction a tax at all. A major dispute arose in Norfolk in 1588–9 when many justices refused to authorize a rate which Sir Arthur Heveningham demanded, under cover of letters patent, for repairing two important highways. This incident became a *cause cèlebre* with both parties arguing their case on constitutional grounds. Then, in 1596, these same justices challenged attempts by the burgesses of King's Lynn and Yarmouth to extract a contribution from the county towards the cost of providing two ships for the Earl of Essex's impending expedition to Cadiz. The rate was not approved until 1597, and even then by no means unanimously. The argument and indecision among the justices was reflected throughout the county: some chief constables refused to levy the rate, while others were forbidden to do so by their neighbouring justices. The outcome of the controversy is unknown, but while it lasted it must have engendered debates which raised legal and constitutional principles. Justices who were prepared to instruct constables to disregard Council letters and quarter-sessional warrants must have grounded their opposition in something more than expediency. Indeed, one suspects that in these Norfolk rating disputes many arguments were first formulated which were to be stated with growing vehemence and conviction during the first three decades of the seventeenth century.[18]

[17] NNRO MS. Bradfer-Lawrence VII b(2), draft letter to Council in hand of Bacon's clerk, 20 Dec. 1598. Amended in Bacon's hand.

[18] Below, pp. 253–65, 281–4.

Other rating problems led to similar quarter-sessional disputes. In October 1600 north-westerly gales, coinciding with spring tides, whipped up heavy seas which breached the sea-banks at Terrington and caused widespread flooding. The Marshland commissioners of sewers estimated that reconstruction would cost at least £2,000 but stressed the urgency of temporary repairs in order to prevent further inundation during the winter. The Terrington members of the commission therefore proposed that £400 should be raised immediately by rating their own township at £200 while the seven other Marshland towns which sheltered behind Terrington's banks should provide the rest. Customarily each township repaired its own banks so that it is not surprising that the other Marshland commissioners 'withstood this proposal'. The defeated minority, led by Nathaniel Bacon, then persuaded the Council to order an enquiry into the arrangements for Marshland's sea defences; in due course a special commission reported that £5,000 would be needed to protect the area from flooding—clearly a sum beyond Marshland's means, let alone Terrington's. A parochial rating dispute had revealed the necessity for repairs on a scale which could only be undertaken with county financial support—or so Bacon pleaded at the Easter sessions for 1601. Inevitably the Bench demurred since justices from the rest of the county considered that they had far more urgent claims upon their resources. Indeed several justices from south-east Norfolk retaliated by seeking Council backing for a county rate to repair similar sea-breaches at Waxham.

Meanwhile Marshland supporters had procured two letters from the Council which recommended the justices to sanction a county-wide contribution towards repairing Terrington's banks. Although the sheriff (Richard Jenkinson) received the first letter several days before the summer sessions opened, and the second one during these sessions, he deliberately withheld both while the Bench again rejected outright Marshland's request. Then, immediately sessions had ended and magistrates dispersed to their estates, he convened a special meeting to answer the Council's letters. As he had anticipated, few justices attended—none at all from distant Marshland—so that he had reasonable justification for postponing any reply until the assizes on 15 July. Here the justices rejected the proposal for a county rate, a majority agreeing to inform the Council that 'the ruynes of the common banck there . . . maie be repaired and set in good state for lesse than £700 which the principall follower of the cause being present cannot much gaynsaie. Which some, wee are credibly informed maie be easily borne by the land occupiers of the said towne'. As an additional safeguard they appointed commissioners—all justices from south Norfolk—who inspected the damaged banks and reported favourably upon Marshland's ability to sustain the expenditure. So ended another quarter-sessional wrangle. Terrington was rated at £500, the other Marshland towns together contributed £500, and in due course the banks were inadequately repaired, only to be breached again in 1607 and 1613.[19]

Despite these controversies, a county could act as a community, especially when its justices united to protest against, and even obstruct, unpopular Council orders. The campaign waged in Norfolk against the embargo on corn exports aptly illustrates this aspect of quarter-sessional business. For a variety of reasons the Elizabethan government frequently forbade the shipment of grain coastwise and overseas except under royal licence. As has been shown, this suited neither Norfolk corn-masters whose production regularly exceeded local demands, nor merchants at King's Lynn and Yarmouth who were shipping grain from five agricultural counties.[20] Their complaints received a ready ear at quarter sessions where the justices, many of them corn growers if not exporters, concerted how best to secure free transportation. At the Epiphany sessions for 1600 they drafted a persuasive letter to Lord Treasurer Buckhurst which resulted in a temporary repeal of the export embargo. A few months later he reimposed it, but after receiving further lengthy entreaties from the justices at their summer sessions, Buckhurst made some concessions. He agreed to allow free transportation coastwise, provided that he received a monthly report, prepared by at least six justices, on the county's grain supplies. The Norfolk Bench responded with alacrity and at its Michaelmas sessions assured Buckhurst that supplies were plentiful. For a few weeks Norfolk merchants freely shipped their corn to less well-stocked regions, but by December 1600 the restraint had been reimposed. After prolonged discussions at their Epiphany sessions the justices drafted another plea for free transportation. It was of no avail, and at the Easter

[19] *Stiffkey Papers*, pp. 102–23. 'Supplementary Stiffkey Papers', ed. F. W. Brooks, p. 24, *Camden Miscellany XVI* (Camden Soc. 3rd ser. lii), 1936. NNRO MSS. NAS Safe II.28, ff. 57v–58, 63v–65, 68v–69; C3/2/8, justices of Norfolk to Privy Council, 7 May 1601.

[20] Above, pp. 18–19.

sessions they agreed upon a more strongly worded letter. It is not clear whether this led to a temporary lifting of the embargo, but certainly by autumn 1601 merchants were again forbidden to ship unlicensed grain coastwise or overseas. Buckhurst, meanwhile, had received so many petitions from Norfolk against the 'tyrannous' restraint that in November he promised to allow coastwise shipments for an indefinite period provided that at each of its sessions the Bench would certify to him 'the plenty and severall prizes of grain'. Once more the concession was short-lived, so that the justices' pleas continued, with occasional limited success, well into the seventeenth century; indeed, as long as the county continued its struggle for unrestricted grain exports, quarter sessions provided the rallying point for opposition.[21]

Nor was this an isolated instance. During Elizabeth's reign justices meeting at quarter sessions and assizes regularly acted as the champions of what they regarded as the community's interests. For instance, when the Council made efforts to improve the standard of militia training and equipment during the period 1560–80, it frequently became involved in protracted correspondence with justices and commissioners for musters who were adept at making counter-proposals or excuses for inactivity in order to reduce their county's financial liability. The procedure can be illustrated from Essex. In 1580 the Council appointed special commissioners to ensure that each county improved the quantity and quality of its horse-bands. Essex certified that it had 73 lances and 227 light horse; the Council demanded 110 lances and 386 light horse; presumably the county riposted unfavourably since the Council reduced its demand to 89 lances and 344 light horse; the county again demurred, perhaps more than once, until compromise was eventually reached at 76 and 249 respectively—figures which were much closer to the county's original offer than to the Council's demands. In 1569 Yorkshire justices had responded in a similar manner when they had been instructed to replace the militia harquebuses with calivers. To offset the increased cost they decreased their assessments from 1,500 harquebuses and 500 corslets to 1,200 and 400 respectively, 'abating the overplus', as they put it, 'in respect of the greatnes of the charge of the caliver'. In Norfolk, when the Council, at rather short notice, increased the number of days' training and stipulated in some detail when these should take place, the justices cut short the Whitsun

[21] *Stiffkey Papers*, pp. 130–59. *HMC Salisbury*, xii. 637. BM MS. Eg. 2714, f. 61. NNRO MS. NAS Safe II.28, ff. 28–9, 40v–41, 74, 114–15.

training on the pretext that quarter sessions were imminent.[22]

The administration of purveyance for the royal household down to 1591 also placed responsibility on the justices for deciding whether their county should compound for the supply of some or all provisions, or continue to suffer the depredations of purveyors. A decision to compound frequently gave rise to protracted negotiations with councillors or household officials. 'When Northamptonshire compounded in 1563', writes Miss Woodworth,

> 'the terms were arrived at by interchange of letters. Sir William Cecil opened the proceedings by sending down a preliminary draft which stated the number of sheep and oxen which he thought the county should furnish. But the justices of the peace, after having consulted "the worshipful & others of the shire", replied that, though they were obliged to reject the suggested quota, they would make two offers, the one preferred, the other the maximum to which the county could agree. How many letters had to be exchanged before a settlement was reached is not known since the records stop short at this point.

Even when the justices had finally signed an agreement they could, and sometimes did, break it after a year, subsequently renegotiating a new one.[23]

Norfolk justices not only voiced the community's grievances; they even offered councillors gratuitous advice on matters which affected their county. At the Michaelmas sessions for 1602 they discussed the appointment of a successor to Bishop Redman, apparently reaching sufficient unanimity to present their views to Sir Robert Cecil. 'We are bould to comend unto your honor's consideracon the preferment of Doctor Dove, our late Deane . . . we cannot think of a man more fyt or whome we doe more wishe to be preferred to the place both for the increase of the glorye of God and the quyet government of the country.'[24] This was perhaps taking themselves too seriously and it is hardly surprising that Dove was passed over in favour of John Jegon who had recently been appointed Dean of Norwich.

The development of such a county-orientated view of government can be better understood when one realizes how engrossed many justices were in the busy routine of day-to-day county administration. However frequently they may have engaged in debate, discussion, or controversy, and however extensive may have been their

22 Boynton, pp. 74, 82–3, 116.

23 Woodworth, p. 42.

24 NNRO MS. WALS XVII/I, pt. ii, f. 155.

bargaining with, or passive resistance towards, the Council, it is necessary to remember that their attention at quarter sessions was mainly occupied with routine business which rarely provoked dissent or controversy. Poor-law administration, although substantially an out-of-sessions activity, usually figured on their agenda, principally because disputed settlement cases went on appeal to quarter sessions. Here too, after 1592, the justices annually chose one of their number to administer the fund for relief of maimed soldiers; they also frequently adjudicated upon veterans' claims, and chivied the constables into collecting the necessary rate. Similarly, at every sessions after 1599 they dealt with petitions for assistance out of the fund for poor prisoners in the Queen's Bench and Marshalsea, usually, oddly enough, on behalf of people who had suffered grievous loss by fire.[25]

The administration of laws regulating economic and social affairs provided quarter sessions with plenty of business. Although two justices acting out of sessions usually granted alehouse licences, applications for these were sometimes heard in sessions. Also at quarter sessions the magistrates renewed or granted corn-badgers' annual licences and throughout the period 1571–93 regularly discussed whether grain supplies were sufficiently plentiful for them to allow unrestricted shipment overseas.[26] Indeed matters relating to corn supplies sometimes prolonged their business. This was because the Council, always fearful lest high corn prices should cause social unrest, frequently instructed justices to take special care to ensure that markets were well stocked with reasonably priced grain. To this end many of them worked conscientiously out of sessions, but they still spent long hours in sessions co-ordinating their efforts and compiling detailed reports for the Council.[27] The success of much

[25] BM MSS. Add 27401, f. 22; 8840, f. 265. Pembroke Coll. Camb. MS. L.C.II.230, ff. 31, 33, 34, 67, 79. Bodl. MS. Gough Norf. 34, f. 26. Photostats of MSS. at Raynham Hall, *penes* T. S. Blakeney, vol. 33, no. 30. NNRO MSS. Frere Box K.12(A), bundles marked 'N. Greenhoe, Walsingham etc.', letter to Nath. Bacon 20 May 1602, and 'Earsham, Earsham Parish etc.', letter to Sir A. Heveningham 25 March 1604; Box K.7(B), Lopham bundle, petition to justices 11 Jan. 1602; Garboldisham bundle, petition of justices 2 Oct. 1604.

[26] *Stiffkey Papers*, p. 54. *WRS* iv, 1949, p. xvii. 13 Eliz. c. 13.

[27] BM MS. Add. 41655, ff. 226v–227. *APC, 1597–8*, pp. 42–4; *1597*, pp. 88–9. NNRO MS. NAS Safe II.28, ff. 9, 34v. E. M. Leonard, *The Early History of English Poor Relief*, Cambridge, 1900, p. 88. *Stiffkey Papers*, pp. 140–1. 'Supplementary Stiffkey Papers', op. cit., pp. 5–6. W. J. Ashley, *The Bread of our Forefathers*, Oxford, 1928, pp. 37, 182–3.

of this paternalistic administration depended upon close co-operation with the high constables who, in turn, needed to command respect within their Hundreds. It is not surprising, therefore, that the Bench spent a considerable amount of time and energy over the selection and supervision of these constables. During the 1590s this supervision particularly took the form of an annual audit of constables' accounts, since these officers, who were responsible for collecting the increasing number of local rates, were sometimes accused of embezzlement or other corrupt practices.[28]

This activity at quarter sessions was merely the tip of the iceberg: it arose out of numerous out-of-sessions tasks which necessitated their own administrative structure; a structure largely hidden from the historian because so few records have survived. None the less it is worth trying to penetrate beneath the surface in order to glimpse this administrative sub-structure.

Keeping the peace and enforcing the mass of Tudor statutes involved justices, either singly or in pairs, in such extensive out-of-sessions work that they developed two new institutional devices to facilitate their labours—the 'division' and divisional sessions. A statute of 1530 instituted the first tentative steps towards both. It ordained that each county should be subdivided into four, six, or eight areas in which local justices should meet once every six weeks. The act cannot have been popular since parliament repealed it in 1545 on the pretext that 'the Kinges most lovinge subjects are muche trayvaled and otherwise encombred in commynge and keepinge of the saide sixe weekes sessions'. Whether or not Norfolk magistrates had found these extra sessions burdensome, they apparently needed an administrative unit larger than the Hundred, for in 1546 the subsidy commissioners divided the county into eight 'divisions' instead of the thirty-two Hundreds upon which they had formerly based their supervision of local collectors and assessors. By 1570, after experimenting with various Hundred groupings, these eight 'divisions' had been clearly delineated and henceforth they superseded the Hundreds as the basic units for magisterial authority throughout the county. The 1572 poor-law, for instance, instructed justices to allocate themselves to 'divisions' and make 'enquierye of all aged poore ympotent and decayed persons borne within their said divisions'; similarly, when the county compounded

[28] *Stiffkey Papers*, pp. 10, 13. FSL MSS. Bacon–Townshend L.d.951, 981.

for purveyance in 1596 justices in their 'several divisions' collected the composition money; by this time, too, the militia was being mustered and trained by 'divisions'.[29]

Although parliament had repealed the statute which instituted six-weekly sessions, Norfolk justices found it administratively convenient to hold frequent *ad hoc* divisional meetings which gradually assumed a regular pattern. Their concern to grapple with the problems of poverty and unemployment particularly stimulated this development. As early as 1574 justices in south-east Norfolk had established a bridewell at Acle and in 1598 others were set up, with statutory encouragement, at Wymondham, Swaffham, and Walsingham. In order to ensure adequate supervision of these bridewells, justices met monthly and, once assembled, no doubt found it convenient to deal with other divisional affairs. An account of proceedings at Acle reveals them groping towards a petty-sessional system.

> Upon the Wednesday, beinge market day ther, the Byshoppe, with certan gentlemen and chief yomen therabouts do mete once in thre wekes or a moneth, at ix of the clocke, when they firste repare to the church ther and spend one howre in prayer and preachinge, the chief effect wherrof is to perswade love, obedience, amitie, concorde, etc. That done they returne to ther inne, wher they dyne together at ther own charges, observinge the lawe for Wednesday. In the meanewhile, betweene sermone ended and dynner, they go to the said howse of Bridwell to consider and examyne howe all things ther ar provided and ordered as well for ther due punishment and reasonable worke as for ther meate and necessaryes, without which often sight and overseinge the said howse and orders wold come quicklie to nothing. After dynner, if any chief constable ther prove of any disorder or misdemenor within ther hundreds, redresse wherof belongeth to the justices of peace, which els wold require the said constables further travile to some justice's howse, if he will complaine of it ther, the offender is eyther openly punished or other order taken as the cawse requireth. And if besides all this, ther be anye private controversies betwene pore neighbours, wherof the hundred courte had wonte to be full, they bestowe the rest of the day in intreatinge them to peace one with another by accorde betweene themselves or by arbytrament of ther neareste neighbours.

Emphasis upon preaching suggests that Puritans were prominent in initiating these early bridewell sessions. Godly magistrates certainly held sway at Acle, where the pro-Puritan Bishop Parkhurst presided over the deliberations of such zealots as William Blennerhassett and

[29] 22 H VIII, c. 12, 37 H VIII, c. 7, 14 Eliz. c. 5. PRO E/179/281 (subsidy comms. for 14 and 37 H VIII). BM MS. Lansd. 82, f. 218. *HMC Gawdy*, p. 68.

William Butts, and where, on more than one occasion, John More, the Puritan 'Apostle of Norwich', preached the sermon which preceded their business meeting.[30]

Besides these monthly bridewell assemblies, late Elizabethan justices were meeting in their respective 'divisions' at least once between quarter sessions. It is impossible to say precisely when divisional as opposed to bridewell sessions started but they are evident by the turn of the century. In February 1600 justices gathered at Watton and in September 1603 William Rugg attended 'Wymondham sessions'; in neither case could these have been quarter sessions since both time and place were wrong. At least as early as 1602 justices in north-east Norfolk met every six weeks at Holt, while in August 1604 the Norfolk Bench approved a county-wide system of monthly divisional assemblies in order 'to take knowledge and informacon how the lawes and other orders towching . . . alehowses are kept and observed'. When a Council order of 1605 directed magistrates in every county to allocate themselves to 'divisions' and 'assemble them selves together once betweene everye quarter session', it can have caused little stir in Norfolk; it merely confirmed an established procedure.[31]

Petty sessions, to use the seventeenth-century name, emerged as a response to the administrative challenge created by the Elizabethan propensity for economic and social regulations. But the successful enforcement of these regulations depended much more upon a justice's daily attention to a host of minor matters than upon his attendance at either monthly or quarterly sessions. The administration of Tudor poor laws made heavy demands upon his time. Although their implementation ultimately depended upon the intimate knowledge and assiduous work of parish officials, the latter would have achieved little without oversight by magistrates. In principle each parish vestry had sole responsibility for appointing annually two overseers of the poor, but in practice local justices had

[30] NNRO MSS. NAS Safe II.28, ff. 23, 36, 36v; C3/2/12, memo. dated 1602. *NA* ii, 1849, pp. 95–6. N. Bownde, *Three Godly and Faithful Sermons*, 1594. According to Bownde these sermons were preached by More at the Q/S at Acle and were written at the justices' request. Q/S were never held at Acle. I am indebted to Professor P. Collinson for this reference.

[31] *HMC Gawdy*, p. 89. NNRO MSS. NAS Safe II.28, f. 51v; C3/1/9, orders sent by Council to justices of assize, 23 June 1605; Bradfer-Lawrence Xd, memoranda book, 1602–6. BM MS. Add. 23007, f. 38. FSL MS. Bacon-Townshend L.d. 1033.

to approve the candidates and frequently nominated them as well. Supervision followed; notably the tedious task of checking annually these overseers' accounts. Besides this supervisory role, justices had precise duties in the administration of the poor laws, frequently becoming involved in lengthy investigations and extensive correspondence over disputed settlement orders and cases of bastardy. Meanwhile their warrant was necessary to commit sturdy beggars, rogues and vagabonds to the bridewell.[32]

Even alehouse licensing could be a troublesome business. Each year justices had to review and regrant alehouse keepers' licences; they usually did this out of sessions, since effective decisions depended upon intimate knowledge of local conditions. Sometimes the granting or refusal of a licence could engender such strong feeling that a justice might find himself caught between rival factions. The situation could be further complicated by the machinations of local patronage, as Edward Moundford discovered when Sir William Paston, a county magnate, compelled him to license an alehouse keeper whom he had previously committed to prison for keeping unlicensed premises.

The intrigues which beset Bassingbourne Gawdy when he suppressed an alehouse can scarcely be typical, but they illustrate the ramifications of this apparently straightforward task. In 1600 townsmen from New Buckenham and Wymondham had petitioned the justices to suppress Richard Howse's alehouse on the pretext that he encouraged gaming, lewd words, and similar unlawful behaviour. Presumably other inhabitants counter-petitioned for the renewal of Howse's licence, since the justices at quarter sessions reached deadlock and referred the case to the assizes, where Chief Justice Popham ordered that the alehouse be closed. Before Bassingbourne Gawdy and his neighbour Sir Nicholas Bacon could implement Popham's decree Howse rode off to solicit assistance from his former master Sir John Fortescue, Chancellor of the Exchequer. He returned flourishing a letter over the signature of Robert Clarke, Baron of the

[32] W. B. Willcox, *Gloucestershire 1590–1640*, New Haven, 1940, p. 247. *Stiffkey Papers*, pp. 18–23, 59. Bacon MS. *penes* B. Cozens-Hardy, 'the account of Thos. King & John Poundiche overseers'. NNRO MSS. Frere Box K.7(A), Happing Hundred, sheet 8; Box K.12(A), Diss, Shelfhanger bundle, letter to Bass. Gawdy 15 June 1598. *History Teachers' Miscellany*, ed. H. W. Saunders, i, 1922–3, pp. 37–8. There is a large number of overseers' annual statements of account scattered throughout the Bacon and Gawdy MSS.

Exchequer and Popham's fellow judge on the Norfolk circuit, which instructed Gawdy to relicense the alehouse. For the time being, therefore, the ale continued to flow; but Gawdy, suspecting that the letter had been forged, wrote to Popham and Clarke who confirmed his suspicions and ordered the alehouse's immediate suppression. By the time constables arrived to remove the sign and take bonds for Howse's good behaviour he had again disappeared, this time to solicit support from his magnate neighbour Thomas Knyvett.[33] Apparently he succeeded, since subsequently Knyvett complained bitterly to Gawdy about the defacement of his family crest which had been emblazoned upon Howse's sign and which the constables had removed when they closed the alehouse.

Howse seems to have been an accomplished patronage hunter, since, hard on Knyvett's complaints, Gawdy received a letter from Sir John Fortescue accusing him of injustice towards Howse. The case was reopened at the assizes in 1601 but Chief Justice Popham upheld his previous decision. Even so, Howse remained obdurate and resourceful. By 1602 his patron Sir John Fortescue had written to Gawdy's opponents on the Norfolk Bench asking that the 'said Howse . . . maye be by your meanes and permission suffred to use his trade untill next tearme at which tyme my Lord Chieffe Justice and I maye meete'. At this point the records fail, but they suffice to illustrate the hazards which could beset a justice engaged upon routine alehouse business.[34]

The oversight of alehouses can rarely have been as complicated and troublesome as this, but the picture it presents of Gawdy's constant involvement may be fairly typical of his entire career in local government. His propensity for record keeping enables the historian to glimpse him at work during the winter of 1600. On 8 January he rode from Harling to Norwich for a Recusancy commissioners' conference. Two days later he returned to Norwich for quarter sessions which lasted four days. Then, on the 18th and 24th he conferred there with his fellow muster commissioners, but still managed to attend a bridewell meeting at Swaffham on the 25th. February brought no respite: muster-commission meetings on 1st, 10th, and 13th; quarter sessions in Norwich from 15th to 19th; finally, on 28th, militia business at Thetford, where he stayed to

[33] Thos. Knyvett of Buckenham. Not to be confused with Sir Thos. Knyvett of Ashwellthorpe.

[34] NNRO MS. NAS Safe II.28, ff. 37, 37v, 42v–44, 50v–51, 62v–63, 95.

join with other justices in protest against the new system of compounding for purveyance.[35]

A similar picture of earnest daily endeavour emerges from the voluminous papers of Nathaniel Bacon. But it would be unwise to assume that all justices involved themselves so fully in the affairs of their county, or that such dedicated involvement made for efficient administration if by efficiency is meant the thorough implementation of statutes and conciliar orders. Personal and local factors usually obtruded; justices who favoured a measure no doubt prosecuted it with vigour while those who disliked it might lapse into inactivity or attempt deliberate obstruction. However, if recognizance-taking be an index of endeavour, then most justices were busy men who governed their localities vigorously. Indeed they could scarcely do otherwise since their prestige depended upon local respect.[36]

There is considerable evidence to suggest that in late Tudor and early Stuart England most people who could think politically regarded themselves as members of a county community which had its own economic, social, and political character, and which stood apart from, sometimes even in opposition to, the greater but remoter community of the nation, of which—and let there be no mistake about this—they were none the less also conscious. They referred to their county as their 'country'; those who lived beyond its boundaries were 'foreigners' and 'strangers'. This is hardly surprising since the shire was their effective unit of government; its hierarchy of offices, ranging from those of bailiff and high constable through sheriff and justice of the peace to deputy lieutenant, provided fulfilment for the political aspirations of all but the greatest; it, or even its sub-units, defined the area of regular social intercourse and provided a meaningful, subtly graded society within which everyone's position could be identified and through which anyone's social progress could be carefully charted. There is nothing new about this. 'To describe the England of those days as a federation of counties', Sir John Neale has written, 'would be legally ridiculous, yet such a misnomer con-

[35] Ibid., ff. 23, 28, 29, 31, 32, 36. Holkham MS. General Estate Deeds, misc. bundle A, no. 7, ff. 14, 15. BM MS. Add. 48591, ff. 13, 15v, 18v, 19, 20v.

[36] NNRO MSS. Norfolk Q/S rolls for 15, 23, 31 and 35 Eliz.

veys a valuable truth'.[37] As both he and Professor Everitt have conclusively demonstrated, the political history of Tudor and Stuart England can be more fully understood by studying the interaction between county and national affairs.

The foregoing account of justices' activities in quarter sessions reveals the way in which these sessions had begun to provide the institutional framework for this interaction; the way in which they had developed as a forum and debating chamber for the formulation of a county viewpoint—a prerequisite of any meaningful interaction with central government. On these occasions the justices reached many routine administrative decisions about such matters as the location of houses of correction, the repair of bridges, the export of corn, the appointment of constables and bridewell keepers, or the examination of churchwardens' accounts. They also dealt with petitions for relief from those in distress through the ravages of fire, tempest, or war; with petitions from moralists who wanted fewer alehouses in their townships, and counter-petitions from the more gregarious elements in these communities; with petitions from the coast towns seeking protection for their ships against pirates; with petitions against informers and patentees: in short, the sessions had become the focal point for the expectations and grievances of the entire community. Here, too, the justices received letters and instructions from the Council on all aspects of local administration: some they implemented with alacrity; others, however, gave rise to prolonged debate and controversy which frequently resulted in the drafting and submission of counter-proposals. This was especially so when the implementation of Council orders involved the provision of county finances. As will be shown, determination to protect their county from what they regarded as burdensome taxation caused many justices, especially those trained in the law, to formulate powerful legal arguments against participating in administrative developments which implied extensive financial commitments.

Such opposition should not, however, be taken to imply unanimity among the justices. They regarded quarter sessions as essentially an occasion for conducting, if not resolving, conflict and dispute *within* the county. Clashes of personality, faction, and the divergent interests of the county's sub-regions ensured that the sessions rarely became routine and perfunctory meetings, and that county-wide opposition to government policy never became unanimous.

[37] Neale, *Commons*, p. 21.

The emergence of quarter sessions at Norwich as a focus for county political activity may have been both reflected in and assisted by the justices' acquisition of a purpose-built sessions chamber and records repository. During the fifteenth and early sixteenth centuries justices appear to have held their sessions in a building located in the castle bailey, but as their numbers grew this building became inadequate. The new shire-house, probably completed in 1579, was given a more elevated position, actually abutting the north face of the castle. It was completely destroyed by fire in 1746 but a late-seventeenth-century artist depicted it in the style of a gentleman's house, and it is tempting to see it as the embodiment of gentry politics within the county.[38]

Here, too, the assizes were held.[39] Although this chapter has focused upon quarter sessions, it must be remembered that assizes provided two further opportunities annually for the discussion of county administrative problems.[40] All justices were expected to attend assizes; so, too, were all high constables and bailiffs, together with an array of freeholders summoned for jury service. Elections apart, these occasions undoubtedly attracted the greatest number of gentry and freeholders, so that important issues were frequently reserved for discussion after legal business had been completed. Assizes also provided convenient occasions for communication between central government and the counties. The Privy Council briefed the judges upon the content and tenor of their 'charge' and it expected them to report back on the state of the counties within their circuits. The significance of the circuit judges in county politics is reflected in the scale of entertainment and feasting which accompanied these occasions, despite government efforts to maintain judicial impartiality by providing the judges with expense allowances.

Historians have, as yet, given insufficient attention to this development of quarter sessions and assizes as focuses for a county's aspirations, as congresses and forums for the formulation of its views, and as institutions through which these views could be communicated to the Council. The eventual political consequences can be seen in the facility and frequency with which the justices and

[38] *NA* xxxv, 1973, pp. 145–8.

[39] Assizes were sometimes held at Thetford. In the absence of records for the Norfolk Circuit it is impossible to ascertain how regularly Thetford was used.

[40] Above, p. 107. Below, pp. 258, 259, 302. Prof. J. S. Cockburn's book, *A History of English Assizes 1558–1714*, appeared too late to be used in this text.

gentry from many parts of England dispatched petitions to the Short and Long Parliaments in the period 1640–2.[41] Their finesse implies a group of magistrates who, over several decades, had acquired great experience in debating an issue, formulating an opinion, and communicating it to parliament, Council, or minister. The circumstances under which justices gained this experience and the significance of such quarter-sessional political activity will be shown in part III of this study.

[41] A. Everitt, *The Community of Kent and the Great Rebellion*, Leicester, 1966, ch. iv. J. K. Gruenfelder, 'The Election to the Short Parliament', *Early Stuart Studies*, ed. H. S. Reinmuth, Minneapolis, 1970, pp. 225–8.

CHAPTER VI

County Administration: A Challenge to the Quarter Sessions

THE tendency for many justices to act as guardians of their county's interests against outside interference appears to coincide with the emergence of paternalistic central government during the mid and late Tudor period; it may therefore not be too fanciful to suggest that justices in quarter sessions assumed this leadership of the county community deliberately to resist those dictates of central government which threatened the well-being, particularly the economic well-being, of a county's articulate members—the gentry and substantial yeomen. Busy though justices may have been, it was a busyness geared to their own concerns and not necessarily to the dictates of central government. When statutes required the enforcement of a policy which might be detrimental to those interests, the justices ignored them; when conciliar demands appeared excessive, they made counter-offers or propounded an endless succession of excuses to justify their inactivity. In her study of the enforcement of apprenticeship legislation Mrs. Gay Davies concluded that the implementation of 'new statute law was effectively taken up into the mass of pre-existing obligatory duties [of local magistrates] only when it met an urgent need of the local community or was in harmony with strong public sentiment'.[1] Justices were prepared to implement the entire array of penal statutes when they needed them to safeguard the well-being of their 'commonwealth', but otherwise they paid scant attention to them.

The facility with which justices in quarter sessions distorted the dictates of parliament and Council was matched by a similar ability among their subordinates. High and petty constables and juries of presentment performed their duties with vigour or indifference as circumstances dictated, and often these called for inactivity. The petty constables, chosen annually from among the more articulate parishioners, were reluctant to implement orders which ran counter to the interests of friend and neighbour; juries of presentment found

[1] Davies, *Enforcement*, p. 162.

equal difficulty in denouncing their fellows. A similar clash of loyalties confronted the subsidy assessors when making their assessments or the churchwardens when presenting Recusants; undoubtedly the importunities of their neighbours were often more compelling than magisterial and statutory requirements.

The entire system creaked badly and criticism was widely voiced. Churchwardens, high and petty constables, jurors, and justices were all unpaid; their sole reward rested in the power and status conferred by their position. For churchwardens, constables, and jurors, there was little of either; torn between loyalty to the community in which they lived and their obligation to implement the dictates of superior officials, many would have endorsed the sentiment: 'damned if I do, damned if I don't.' But there were degrees of damnation and on the whole they preferred rebukes from their superiors to ostracism and threats from their neighbours. Justices were particularly vociferous about the failure of juries to present. In 1591 William Lambarde, author of the first manual for justices and chairman of Kent quarter sessions, devoted his entire 'charge' to belabouring the constables and jurors: 'what is the service of our country like to be advanced by all the juries that be summoned hither? Take away the matters that we of the bench do bring hither with us and, in a manner, the sessions may be shut up so soon as the charge that we give you is at an end.'[2] It may be that he was prompted to make these criticisms out of fear that quarter sessions, and with them the local autonomy for which they stood, might be displaced by a more centralized system of local administration; but many justices were inclined to chastise their subordinates for no better reason than that they in turn were being constantly chastised for slackness by the Council. This is scarcely surprising since one of the most crucial problems confronting Elizabeth and her councillors was how to ensure that local administrators implemented policies which bore some resemblance to those embodied in statute, proclamation, and conciliar instruction. It was a challenge which they accepted, but their efforts to find a solution have so far not received much attention from historians.

Government attempts to deal with this problem appear to have been guided by the maxim that efficient administration was inversely proportional to the number of administrators; that it was 'prejudiciall to the successe of all causes to leave them to the care of many . . . [since] those deuties which concerne all men are neclected of every

[2] *William Lambarde and Local Government*, ed. Conyers Read, New York, 1962, p. 106.

man'. It has already been shown that Burghley and other Elizabethan statesmen tried to apply this proposition to the commission of the peace, but that they had clearly failed; the dictates of the patronage system coupled with the shortcomings of chancery administration caused numbers in the commission of the peace to rise, despite conciliar efforts to reduce them. In these circumstances ministers did the next best thing: they tried to create an élite within the total body of magistrates in each county by instructing the Bench 'to select by mutuall consent . . . some three or fower or more of your nomber . . . to whose peculier care you maye at the begeninge of every yeare commend the execution and dispach' of proclamations, letters, and commissions.[3]

This tendency to entrust a small number of magnates with specific administrative tasks can be detected in developments within various offices of local government—particularly in that of commissioner for musters. Down to about 1573 justices of the peace doubled in this role, but thereafter muster commissions named a select group of justices—usually about one-third of the total magistracy—to 'take a prencipale care of the execucion of this commission'. Initially the special responsibilities entrusted to these justices did not necessarily preclude the rest from assisting in military administration. As the Council was at pains to make clear, 'it is not ment that by naminge of some to take the speciall care, . . . you, or any of you of the rest being in commission and having authoritie, should think your selves discharged [from militia responsibilities]'. However, when lords lieutenants superseded the muster commissioners during the 1580s, they delegated the entire responsibility for militia administration to three, four, or five deputies unassisted by any magistrates. Although many lieutenancies were allowed to lapse during the 1590s the revived muster commissions were much smaller than those of the 1570s, usually comprising only the ex-deputy lieutenants together with the sheriff. Thus, during Elizabeth's reign management and control of each county's militia had passed from its entire magistracy to a small committee of not more than six or eight justices headed by the sheriff.[4]

The emergence of a magisterial élite is also evident in the development of the subsidy commission. For much of the sixteenth century

[3] *Stiffkey Papers*, pp. 24–5.

[4] CUL MS. Mm. v. 7. BM MS. Cotton Titus B. v, ff. 59–79. PRO SP 12/114, f. 92; /136/52, f. 2v; /133/14. *APC, 1596–7*, pp. 51–3.

the commission for Norfolk numbered forty or fifty persons; it included most of the justices afforced by other gentry as well. Such a large commission was no doubt justified by the amount of administration involved in the assessment and collection of a subsidy. First, all commissioners met to share out their duties on a divisional basis; then they met divisionally to appoint assessors from among the lesser gentry, subsequently calling these assessors together to deliver a conciliar exhortation against corruption. Next, the assessors, working in close co-operation with Hundred constables, compiled the subsidy books—a parish by parish valuation of all landholders. This done, the commissioners met once more to examine these books and, if necessary, to adjust individual assessments. Finally, they met to appoint collectors and take bonds for safe delivery of the money at the Exchequer. A large commission may well have been necessary to ensure supervision of such elaborate administration, but its size may also have reflected demand for the job, since a commissioner had ample opportunity to tax himself or his friends lightly and his enemies heavily either by carefully selecting the assessors or by altering the assessments they made. In these circumstances many gentlemen, particularly in a factious county, endeavoured to safeguard their own and clients' interests by procuring appointment to the commission. There is no doubt that as the subsidy commission grew, so income from subsidies fell. Consequently, by the 1580s the Council may well have decided to see whether a smaller commission might result in less corruption and increased yields. Such a policy was in line with that adopted towards the commission of the peace. Moreover it was successfully applied to the subsidy commission; that for Norfolk, for instance, being reduced by half to 20 or 25 members at the very time when the Bench of justices had expanded to 40 or 50.[5]

Developments in the system of composition for purveyance also culminated in special commissioners being appointed in each county to supervise the provision of supplies for the royal Household. Down to 1591, as has already been shown, the entire Bench decided whether to negotiate a composition agreement; if it did so it then assumed responsibility for implementing the agreement. After 1591,

[5] *Stiffkey Papers*, pp. 75–95. PRO E 179/281; SP 12/197/33. NNRO MSS. NAS Safe II.28, ff. 38–39v; NAS Frere Box K.11(A), Wayland Hundred, sheet 7; Box K.8(A) Humbleyard Hundred, sheets 6–9. Letter Book of Philip Woodhouse, *penes* Earl of Kimberley. Bodl. MS. Tanner 241, ff. 31–2. BM MS. Add. 38508, ff. 15–19. *HMC Gawdy*, p. 66.

however, the Council made strenuous efforts to compel every county to compound for all provisions. To facilitate this policy councillors preferred to deal directly with a small group of county representatives. They therefore instructed each county to empower three or four justices both to negotiate with the Board of Green Cloth and, once an agreement had been ratified, to organize the delivery of their county's quota of provisions.[6]

In each instance cited above, a few magistrates were appointed to supervise an important aspect of administration, largely to the exclusion of their fellows. But provided each administrative task was entrusted to different justices all of them might have remained equally involved. In fact this did not happen. In the majority of cases the same magnates were appointed to each commission, so that there emerged an élite of ten or fifteen justices differentiated from the others by virtue of their experience and the trust reposed in them.

The Council's inclination to commission a select group of justices to undertake important administrative tasks inevitably meant that the quarter-sessional Bench was deprived of a measure of initiative and authority, although it usually retained responsibility for approving any rate needed to implement the commissioners' decisions —a sure formula for conflict, as will be shown in part III. The circumstances in which these commissioners usually met might also rouse jealousy and resentment among their fellow justices. Since their business could most conveniently be despatched at the time of quarter sessions, they frequently met just before the Bench assembled or after it had adjourned, thereby confirming suspicions among their fellows that government by an élite was beginning to replace the corporate decisions of the entire Bench.[7]

Other administrative developments presented an even more serious threat to quarter-sessional autonomy. These arose particularly from governmental attempts to grapple with problems of security. In the uncertain atmosphere of Elizabeth's early years her councillors particularly wished to ensure widespread enforcement of statutes designed to prevent social unrest and to safeguard the realm against rebellion and foreign attack—statutes relating to usury, tillage, regrators, forestallers, apparel, retainers and liveries, clerical

[6] Woodworth, pp. 41–3. Below, p. 297.

[7] See esp. the fine series of letter-books concerning county government kept by Bassingbourne Gawdy senior and junior: Bodl. MS. Tanner 241. BM MS. Add. 48591. NNRO MSS. NAS Safe II.28, WALS. XVII/I; parts 1, 2.

non-residence, non-lawful games, horse armour and weapons, vagabonds, and the export of corn. Such considerations compelled the Council to confront the vexatious problem of how best to enforce penal statutes.[8]

Hitherto enforcement procedures had proved totally inadequate. As has been indicated, constables and juries had been reluctant to present law-breakers; consequently Tudor legislators had increasingly relied upon the activities of common informers. Most penal statutes made provision for private persons to lay information against suspected offenders and, in the event of conviction, to receive one-third or half of the fine. Thus, in contrast to members of presenting juries, informers were encouraged by the lure of profit to risk their neighbours' wrath. Even so there is little evidence that informing was a particularly lucrative business or that it attracted many recruits. Professor Elton's account of the career of George Whelplay shows the comparatively small return which that busybody obtained for his efforts, although he was a Londoner running an extensive informing agency. All too frequently his efforts were thwarted by the 'stubborn local loyalties of assize juries who rated perjury very much lower in the scale of crime than the conviction of a local man on the word of a Londoner'. Such evidence as exists about informers in Norfolk suggests that they were equally unpopular and probably no more successful.[9] They aroused hostility from all sections of the community partly because they attempted to enforce economic legislation which their neighbours found inconvenient, but more particularly, one suspects, because they indulged in intimidation and extortion by threatening to inform against innocent and guilty alike and then compounding with them out of court. Their universal unpopularity was apparent in almost every Elizabethan parliament where a succession of Bills was introduced to curb their abuses, and where violent demonstrations against informers took place outside the commons during debates on these Bills. It would seem that at no

[8] PRO SP 12/19, ff. 84–6. *Elizabethan Government and Society*, ed. Bindoff, Hurstfield, and Williams, 1961, p. 85. NNRO MS. City Records, Mayor's Court Book 1555–62, pp. 513–15.

[9] G. R. Elton, *Star Chamber Stories*, 1958, pp. 112–13. Davies, *Enforcement*, pp. 42–3. Photostats of MSS. at Raynham Hall, *penes* T. Blakeney, vol. 27, no. 71; Letters of Nath. Bacon, *penes* B. Cozens-Hardy, copy of letter from Bacon to Sir Robt. Mansell, 20 Mar. 1599/1600, and Bacon to Thos. Farmer, 23 Sept. 1583. W. J. C. Moens, *The Walloons and their Church at Norwich*, Lymington, 1888, ii. 270. PRO SP 12/160/37. Allison, 'Wool Supply', pp. 315–18.

time during the sixteenth century did private informers provide a coherent and satisfactory mechanism for the enforcement of penal laws.[10]

Frustated by inadequate machinery for the thoroughgoing enforcement of statutes, Elizabethan councillors canvassed various reforms in local administration. Cecil advocated a smaller number of carefully selected justices. Others, notably Sir Thomas Smith, considered that many more justices were needed before the welter of statutes could be adequately enforced.[11] Most, however, would probably have agreed that the problem was essentially one of supervision and organization. Lord Keeper Bacon, for instance, suggested that magisterial endeavour could best be kept in line with government intent by a series of visitations similar to those undertaken by bishops. 'For the banishing of sloth there would bee through out the Realme a tryennuall or byennual visitacion . . . of all temporall officers and ministers.' This would be undertaken by a commission which would 'try out and examine by all good meanes and waies the offences of all such as have not seen to the due execucion of the lawes accordinge to the offences so founde and certified'.[12] The view that better supervision would ensure a more thorough enforcement of statutes was frequently expressed in mid-sixteenth-century England by political commentators like Thomas Starkey.

By 1566 the Council, probably at Cecil's instigation, had made supervision an essential feature of a scheme devised both to improve presentment of offenders against the statutes mentioned above, and to relieve 'subiectes from the . . . wronges to them daily don by common promoters'. In this scheme, specially appointed parish and Hundred teams were to present offenders at quarter sessions before a jury which had been empanelled 'besides the ordynary jury'. These presentment teams were to be supervised by a small group of carefully chosen justices who, in turn, were to be judged by results, the clerk of the peace submitting to the Council biannually a role of all persons convicted or indicted at the sessions so 'that their Lordships may understand . . . where diligence is used for the execution of these laws, and where not, in order that negligent or remiss justices

[10] Davies, *Enforcement*, pp. 64–70. Hughes & Larkin, ii. 288–9. Neale, *Parliaments 1559–1581*, pp. 218, 224. 18 Eliz. c. 5; 27 Eliz. c. 10; 31 Eliz. c. 5.

[11] Above, pp. 76–9.

[12] Corpus Christi Coll. Camb. MS. 543, speech by Sir Nich. Bacon in parliament of 1571.

may be removed out of the commission and others put in their place, and those that do well have thanks'. Realism prevailed throughout these proposals. All members of presentment teams were to be paid one shilling for each day's attendance at Hundredal or quarter sessions; they were also to be 'comforted in their well-doing & not to be made afrayed by the parties that shalbe charged nor their frindes'. Conversely, if the supervisory justices thought that presentment teams were concealing information they could examine them under oath at quarter sessions.[13]

The scheme was probably embodied in a Lords' Bill in the 1566 parliament. A 'memorial of things fit to be considered of against parliament', annotated in Cecil's hand, proposed 'to prefer unto the parliament some such device for the execution of penal statutes as the subjects of this realm may in no such sort be greved by promoters as presently they are'. On its first day of business the Lords read a Bill 'for the better execution of certain statutes, & for the reformation of certain disorders used in the law'. After only one reading the House submitted it to a committee which included a Lord Chief Justice, the Chief Baron of the Exchequer, and a justice of Queen's Bench. Six weeks later a Bill of similar title was given a second reading and again committed, the committee once more including law officers. This Bill was passed by the Lords, but it made no headway in the Commons where another Bill 'touching informers for execution of penal laws' had already been passed.[14]

If, as is suggested, this Bill embodied the scheme outlined above it is not surprising that the Commons rejected it—at least not if that House had any regard for its electorate. Upon those substantial freeholders who comprised the parish presentment teams it bestowed the mantle of the hated informer; for the justices it meant the further entrenchment of an élite, the provision of a yardstick against which to assess their efficiency, and the prospect of dismissal for those who fell short in this assessment.

Its rejection disappointed Cecil who immediately consulted the judges as to whether these reforms in the system of presentment could be authorized by commission and 'if not to show the reason why & how it is to be remedied'. Unfortunately the judges' advice

[13] *CSPD, Add. 1566–79*, pp. 20–2. BM MS. Harl. 589. This MS. is incorrectly ascribed to 1561; it clearly relates closely to PRO SP 15/13/42.

[14] Conyers Read, *Mr. Secretary Cecil and Queen Elizabeth*, 1955, p. 356. D'Ewes, pp. 99, 109–10, 122–3, 126–8, 132–4. *Lords Journals* i. 655.

has not survived, but a commission embodying the points set out above was drafted and amended by Cecil. A few commissions may even have been issued, as is suggested by an outburst of angry criticism in the Commons in December about 'a commission for execution of penal laws'.[15] As might be expected, Cecil was filled with gloom because his efforts to galvanize into efficiency the existing machinery of local administration had been thwarted. Although this was by no means his only disappointment in this parliament it may well have prompted two of the 'lamentations' he jotted down towards the end of the session:

> 'The oppression of the informers not amended'
> 'The commission of inquisitors: to unmeet persons'.[16]

The collapse of this scheme for improving the established system of law enforcement may well have been a turning-point in Elizabethan local administration. Thereafter the Crown tended to entrust specific administrative tasks to *ad hoc* agencies rather than to the general body of J.P.s. This development caused concern among many justices, but whether it be deemed to have presented a serious challenge to the supremacy of quarter sessions depends upon its extent and scope.

The use of licensed informers was one aspect of this development. Undoubtedly failure to revitalize the existing system of law enforcement made the Crown more receptive to proposals that courtiers should be licensed to inform upon breaches of particular statutes within a county or group of counties. A systematic implementation of such proposals would have been tantamount to the establishment of a nation-wide network of royal agents financially committed to law enforcement. The idea was not new: it was extensively discussed by the 'commonweal' men of the 1540s, and as early as the 1530s proposals had been circulated within the Cromwellian circle for greater central control over local administration. A draft poor law Bill of 1535 had proposed the creation of a 'Councell to avoide vacabundes' which would have appointed its own officers to supervise schemes of public work in the localities. Another Bill, probably drafted privately and submitted to Cromwell in 1534, had made provision for a special court which was to ensure the systematic

[15] *CSPD Add. 1566–79*, pp. 20–2. BM MS. Harl. 589; incorrectly ascribed to 1561. *Commons Journal*, i. 81. Neale, *Parliaments 1559–81*, p. 170.

[16] Conyers Read, *Mr. Secretary Cecil and Queen Elizabeth*, p. 370.

enforcement of all penal statutes by appointing its own local officers in each county—sergeants of the commonweal as they were called. Since these sergeants were to receive such portion of the fine as each statute awarded the private informers, the scheme was tantamount to institutionalizing the common informer. Further proposals of this sort were discussed under Mary and early in Elizabeth's reign, but with little consequence until the failure of the Council's attempts to reform the system of local presentments in 1566.[17] Thereafter the Crown quite frequently granted one or more courtiers the right, within a county, a region, or even throughout the entire country, to lay informations under one or more penal statutes.

In August 1566 William King, a yeoman of the chamber, was licensed 'to put in execution the statute [of] 33 Henry VIII for the maintenance of artillery and debarring of unlawful games' throughout the counties of Essex, Hertfordshire, Kent, Sussex, Suffolk, and Lincolnshire. In the following year a consortium of four courtiers received a similar commission for Wiltshire. In April 1570 Edward Horsey was licensed 'to search out offences against a statute of 7 Edward VI and other laws concerning the keeping of taverns and sale of wines' committed between September 1566 and Michaelmas 1570. In June 1571 the Crown granted Humphrey Gilbert sole right during a seven-year period to compound with offenders against the Marian statute 'for having horse armour and weapons'. In July two gentlemen pensioners, Henry Macwilliam and Robert Colshill, were empowered for a period of seven years to 'inquire and try out all offences concerning usury, wool, woolfells, yarn, felts, pelts . . . transportation of leather, boots, shoes, buskins . . . and transportation of wood and other victuals'. They, too, received powers to compound. Barely a year later a further grant extended their enforcement activities by authorizing them to inquire into breaches of statutes relating to usury, preservation of woods, the assize of fuel, the making of leather, export of corn, extortion, perjury, and sheep grazing. Also in 1572 Henry Middlemore received a patent to inquire into offences against several statutes for the encouragement of archery.[18]

This small but expanding group of patentees presented a challenge to the system of law enforcement and administration by justices

[17] *Econ.HR*, 2nd ser. vi, no. 1, 1953, pp. 55–63. *Trans.RHS*, 4th ser. xix, 1936, pp. 119–44. *BIHR* xxv, 1952, pp. 117–31. *Econ.HR*, 2nd ser. x, no. 2, 1957, pp. 232–3.

[18] *CPR, 1563–6*, p. 494; *1569–72*, pp. 14–15, 165, 279–80, 325–7, 328–9, 359–60.

in quarter sessions. Part of this challenge stemmed from the fact that both licensed and unlicensed informers chose to ignore quarter sessions, laying the majority of their informations in the Exchequer court at Westminster.[19] No doubt they calculated that the deterrent of a journey to London and the high fees involved would encourage defendants to compound. But they also knew that informations laid at quarter sessions upon statutes which ran counter to particular local interests would be likely to receive short shrift from local jurors. It may not be too wide of the mark to suggest that their activities centred principally on the courts at Westminster precisely because of a general quarter-sessional hostility towards the activities of men who for the sake of private gain were prepared to enforce policies which appeared detrimental to the local community.

But licensed informers threatened the justices in an even more direct manner. If they frequently enforced statutes which many justices preferred to ignore they also usurped functions which the latter were keen to exercise. For instance, the licensing of taverns, with its implication for law and order, was a matter about which many justices, Puritans especially, held strong views; upon occasions it gave rise to acute local controversy. Moreover, since patentees were usually empowered to compound with offenders, magistrates might well find themselves barred from proceeding at law against notorious offenders when the local situation demanded such action.[20]

Then, too, licences to inform tended to detract from a justice's prestige, frequently designating him as a subordinate of the patentee. William King's patent for implementing the statute for maintenance of artillery and debarring of unlawful games empowered him 'to require the justices and other officers of the Crown . . . to make search within their jurisdictions for persons using unlawful games' and to hold musters for viewing weapons and even to deliver to him 'written in parchment under their hands and seals the names of offenders'. A proclamation which commanded 'justices & other our officers to be aiding, helping & assisting our said commissioners' underlined this subordination.[21] The patent granted to Henry

[19] *Econ.HR*, 2nd ser. x, no. 2, 1957, p. 225.

[20] Above, p. 106. NNRO MS. 21508/8 (368 X 5), undated notes for parl. business. Such complaints were rife in the early seventeenth century. See *Commons Debates 1621*, ed. W. Notestein, F. H. Relf, and H. Simpson, iv, New Haven, 1935, pp. 85, 244; vi. 150, 252, 256, 378.

[21] Hughes & Larkin, ii. 362. The editors follow Steele in dating this proclamation

Macwilliam and Robert Colshill for inquiring into breaches of a wide variety of statutes instructed 'the Queen's officers throughout the realm diligently to execute' the grantees' precepts. Patentees were on the way to becoming the justices' taskmasters—a view which was forcibly expressed in the 1621 House of Commons when members were discussing Sir Giles Mompesson's patent for inns. 'Never hath anything bene ever graunted under the Great Seale which did derogate so much from the authoritie of the justices of peace', declared one speaker; while Edward Coke described the patent as 'a great dishonour to the justices of peace and a great indignitie'.[22]

While some patents subordinated the justices to the patentee, others ignored them altogether, providing alternative machinery for law enforcement which resembled that outlined in the draft Henrician statutes mentioned above. Such patents empowered the informer to operate through the agency of local commissioners who were 'appointed under the hands of the Privy Council' on the patentee's nomination, just as the proposed council to avoid vagabonds was to have appointed its own officers in each locality. In this way each patentee was officially provided with his own agents, thereby rendering unnecessary any assistance from the justices and their subordinates.[23]

How extensively justices were either superseded by, or subordinated to, patentees depends upon the extent to which administrative patents proliferated during Elizabeth's reign. Unfortunately this cannot easily be ascertained in the absence of the *Calendar of Patent Rolls* after 1572. There is considerable evidence of other administrative patents being issued in the 1580s and 1590s, and, as will be shown later, they became a feature of Norfolk administration, but it is impossible to say what proportion of the total these represent.[24] At present, therefore, there is insufficient evidence to suggest that the government consistently licensed informers to act as agents in local administration. It seems more likely that the Crown issued patents in response to demand from individual courtiers who exploited the

---

to March 1572. Internal evidence suggests that it was issued to accompany these early reforming patents in 1566/7.

[22] *Commons Debates 1621*, vi. 252, 257.

[23] *CPR, 1569–72*, pp. 279–80, 325–6.

[24] Below, chaps. XI, XII. *Econ.HR*, 2nd. ser. x, no. 2, 1957, pp. 230, 233. *Camb.H.J.* xiii, 1957, pp. 116–30. *APC, 1571–5*, p. 370. BM MS. Add. Ch. 67530.

government's concern for efficient local administration in order to provide against the Crown's inability to recompense them for their services. Even so, enough patents may have been granted to convince many justices that they constituted a serious threat to the magistracy and to a local community's economic well-being.

Complaints in parliament particularly stressed the second of these threats—an emphasis which undoubtedly reflected county opinion. As one Norfolk man put it to Nathaniel Bacon after his election to parliament in 1593:

> The good subiects speciallie of the meaner sorte are prayed upon as kytes praye upon karyon and not to her Majisties use nor for defence of the Realme, but by others (comonlie the worst of all others) by patentes penall lawes and many other practyses to make themselves riche and all the Realme poore . . yf anie such patentes or penaltyes of lawes maye be lawfullye and well taken, yt were much better to be ymployed towardes the chardges of the warres then on such caterpillars.[25]

Opposition to licensed informers had become sufficiently vociferous by 1575 to cause the Council to rescind at least seven patents. The degree of concern they aroused among magistrates can also be gauged from the Lord Keeper's closing speech to parliament in 1576. He was giving the justices one of his regular exhortations to greater efficiency and on this occasion saw fit to warn them that if they persisted in their parochial attitude towards law enforcement the Queen would be 'driven cleane contrarie to her most gratious nature and inclinacion to appoint and assigne private men for profitt and gaines sake, to see her penall lawes to bee executed'. In his determination to send the justices back to their counties less intent upon safeguarding their particular interests and more concerned about implementing government policies, Sir Nicholas Bacon deliberately set out to jar a sensitive nerve. The threat was real enough; nor was it to be diminished by the Crown rescinding a few patents. Indeed the issues raised were widened by subsequent developments in militia administration.[26]

Undoubtedly the greatest challenge to the pre-eminence of J.P.s in local administration arose from developments in militia organization

[25] NNRO MS. 21508/8 (368 X 5).

[26] *APC, 1571–5*, pp. 370–1. Corpus Christi Coll. Camb. MS. 545, f. 27v.

during Elizabeth's reign. The acts passed in Mary's last parliament for 'having of horse armour & weapons' and 'for taking of the musters' had been designed to so arm and train every able-bodied Englishman that his obligations to military service could be enforced in a meaningful manner. The administration of these statutes rested with the J.P.s. They were to be responsible for the 'appointing and lymiting of the harness and weapons'; they were also 'to make searche and vewe of and for the said furniture of horses geldings armour and weapons . . . and to heare and determyne at their quarter sessions all and every the defaultes committed or done contrary to the Acte'.[27] Unfortunately, in view of the rapid continental developments in military science and tactics, these statutes made inadequate provision for training and weapons. Since, however, parliament failed to revise them, the Council had no means of improving militia standards except by requiring county muster commissioners both to provide weapons and training over and above the statutory requirements and to meet the extra cost by levying higher rates on those best able to pay. This meant that the burden of financing these reforms fell most heavily upon those who were to implement them—the justices and muster commissioners—or upon their social equals over whom they had least influence. Consequently conciliar demands encountered in many counties that masterly inactivity which was one of the characteristics of Elizabethan local government.

A few examples must suffice. In 1569 the Council proposed to establish a corps of about 4,000 highly trained harquebusiers. Its cost was to fall chiefly upon J.P.s, officials holding posts in the Queen's gift worth 50 marks a year, and clergy, particularly nonresident ones, who were each to provide and maintain one harquebusier, while their fellow gentry were to finance the expensive training of these soldiers. The proposal received short shrift from the muster commissioners who denounced it as very 'overburdenous' imposing 'importunate' and 'unwonted charges'. Confronted with widespread opposition from those meant to carry out this scheme, the Council backed down and directed its efforts towards improving the quality and quantity of weapons which each county supplied to its militiamen. Here, too, success depended upon ability to persuade the wealthier elements of society to contribute more substantially to the supply of arms and armour; to contribute 'according to their

[27] 4 and 5 Philip and Mary cc. 2, 3.

landed income and not by the fictional undervalues of the subsidy-books'. The muster commissioners presented the government's case with varying degrees of enthusiasm, but there is little evidence that they managed to exact substantially increased contributions from those best able to pay. Their inability to overcome the tardiness of their fellow gentry became even more apparent when the Council ordered them to procure improved mounts and equipment for the county horse-bands. Reaction ranged from 'plausible procrastination' to the precise constitutional stand taken by some Nottinghamshire gentry: 'we doe not knowe that we are chargeable by anie lawe to so great a burthen as by your Lordship hath bene geven us severally in note for to furnish, touchinge demilances and light horsemen. And it is farre more then we and oure livinges proporconally for eche one was able to perfourme.' By 1580 the horse-bands remained so ill equipped and under strength that Elizabeth appointed privy councillors or leading courtiers to supervise recruitment and training by the muster commissioners.[28]

As the Council's military requirements became more demanding, more urgent, and invariably less acceptable to the counties, it became clear that muster commissioners and J.P.s (usually the same person held both offices) were too closely integrated with county society to act as effective agents of reform and reorganization. All too often the dictates of central government ran counter to the interests of these county leaders. Increased taxation was, of course, a continual source of friction, but it was only one among many: the Council wanted the large militia companies divided into smaller units to facilitate better training, but smaller companies meant diminished prestige and influence for the established captains as well as providing opportunities for their inferior neighbours to gain equal commands; the Council wanted militia training to be directed by professional muster-masters, but such men, often strangers to the county, cared little about the heavy expense of prolonged and frequent musters; the Council, faced with defending a long and vulnerable coastline, wanted trained bands in one county to march to the assistance of those in another, but militia captains and muster commissioners, obsessively concerned about the safety of their own county, were extremely reluctant to comply.[29]

In 1585 the Crown took decisive steps to overcome this county

[28] Boynton, pp. 59–62, 63–4, 76–80, 81.
[29] Below, pp. 277–89.

particularism by appointing lords lieutenants in nearly all counties. In one sense there was nothing new about this since during the previous three decades most counties had, on more than one occasion, been placed under a military lieutenant. But in another sense these appointments in 1585 represented a significant departure. Hitherto lieutenants had been appointed on an *ad hoc* basis during periods of actual or threatened unrest; for example, Elizabeth appointed the Duke of Norfolk as lieutenant of Norfolk and Suffolk during the summer of 1559; but at the onset of winter, 'wherein is nothinge to be douted anye like insolence of disordered people as before', she relieved him of office. In the following spring she again commissioned a lieutenant, and since the Duke of Norfolk was leading the English forces against Scotland, Sir Edmund Wyndham and Sir Christopher Heydon jointly held office in his stead; but they too were relieved of their responsibilities during the autumn. Thereafter the lieutenancy appears to have lapsed until the unrest of 1569 when Lord Wentworth was appointed to Norfolk and Suffolk. But by November 1570 the crisis had passed and the Queen, as earlier, revoked his commission, leaving the lieutenancy of these counties in abeyance until 1585, when she appointed Lord Hunsdon. His appointment, and that of his fellow lieutenants throughout England, marked a new phase in the development of the lieutenancy since in most cases they continued in office for life.[30] The difference is crucial. The brief tenure of early lords lieutenants had masked their latent challenge to magisterial supremacy since they had not had time to consolidate their position. There is no evidence that before 1569 they appointed deputies to assist them, and even during the 1570s justices acting as muster commissioners remained the key figures. But once lieutenants held office for long periods they were able to appoint amenable deputies and to establish a system of military administration which was independent of, and perhaps a challenge to, the indulgent proceedings of justices in quarter sessions.[31]

For in every respect lords lieutenants were agents of the central

[30] GEC ix. 622. PRO SP 12/12, f. 14; /18, ff. 154–5; /59, f. 190; /74, f. 91. G. Scott Thomson, *Lords Lieutenants in the Sixteenth Century*, 1923, p. 50. J. C. Sainty, *Lieutenants of Counties 1585–1642*, (*BIHR* Special Supplement no. 8, 1970), pp. 1–3.

[31] During the sixteenth century deputy lieuts. seem to have been appointed by the Lord Chancellor on the recommendation of six privy councillors. Since lords lieut. were usually privy councillors their views undoubtedly carried great weight. See: BM MS. Harl. 6996, f. 126; J. T. Cliffe, *The Yorkshire Gentry*, 1969, pp. 236–7; below, pp. 242–3.

government. Both the circumstances of their appointment and their social position ensured them an especially close relationship with Crown and Council. The majority, like Lord Hunsdon, were privy councillors, and all were great magnates with intimate court connections.[32] As such, they responded more readily to central government dictates than did the justices in quarter sessions with their endless deliberations and delaying tactics. Working directly through three or four deputies, usually chosen from among the justices, lords lieutenants assumed responsibility for implementing the Council's extensive programme of militia training and reorganization. The justices and muster commissioners whom they displaced inevitably forfeited the opportunity to influence a variety of decisions which bore directly upon their social and economic well-being. These included such matters as the number of men to be trained in their county, the frequency and duration of musters, the appointment of captains and muster-masters, the size of companies, the provision of powder and shot for training, and the question of whether arms should be kept locally or in county arsenals. All that remained for the justices was the formidable and unwelcome task of providing adequate funds to finance schemes which the Council propounded in its pursuit of an improved militia and the lieutenancy readily put into effect.

Inevitably tension arose between J.P.s and the lieutenancy in the closing years of the Queen's reign. But to depict this clash too starkly does less than justice to a very complicated situation. Lords lieutenants, for instance, had dual loyalties; as well as being privy councillors and courtiers they, too, were members of county communities and on occasion they spoke out against over-zealous government measures. Similarly deputy lieutenants were drawn from the ranks of county gentry. They had been, and almost invariably remained, justices of the peace, displaying varying degrees of zeal for their new office. Some undoubtedly continued to see matters from the county viewpoint. When all this is admitted, however, it is possible to detect a change of tempo after 1585. A more professional approach prevails; record-keeping develops apace, leading to the frequent compilation of lieutenancy journals and letter books;[33] ord-

[32] Scott Thomson, op. cit. In 1585 18 out of 20 lords lieutenants were either privy councillors or Presidents of the Councils of Wales and the North. By 1587 the figures were 28 out of 37.

[33] Boynton, pp. 300–1. Other letter books for Norfolk are: NNRO MS. WALS.

nance depots are established; better transport facilities are provided; there is greater professionalism in training and, so the lieutenancy's detractors claimed, in the perpetration of corrupt practices as well; professional captains begin to replace local squires; experienced muster-masters are regularly appointed; members of trained bands are extensively recruited for overseas service and elaborate arrangements made for one county to send its men to defend another. Above all, the majority of justices, denied any opportunity to influence these developments and to cushion their impact upon the county, increasingly resented them.[34]

That lords lieutenants had deprived the justices of control over administrative decisions which affected their prestige and which imposed heavy financial burdens on their county, was cause enough for concern on the Bench. But this challenge to the justices'autonomy was even more far-reaching since lords lieutenants rapidly assumed the role of overlords. Their responsibility for preventing internal unrest as well as for defence against invasion inevitably implied extensive powers of a non-military nature. The Crown's instructions in 1559 authorized them to ensure the proper enforcement of laws for conformity in religion and for the punishment of vagabonds and seditious tale-tellers; they were also 'often times to take accomptes of the justices doings . . . and not to spare the punishment of any princypal officer'. Where necessary lieutenants were even to recommend new candidates for appointment to the Bench. To exercise such widespread powers during the uncertain months of Elizabeth's accession was one thing; to do so during the 1580s and 1590s, when lieutenants usually held office for life, was another. None the less the Crown continued to empower lieutenants and their deputies to oversee the justices and even upon occasion to act in their stead. They invariably supervised the supply of victuals for the navy; in 1586 Lord Hunsdon severely reproved the Norfolk justices for failing to provide the stores he demanded. He informed them in no uncertain manner that the days were past when they could bargain over the

XVII/I Philip Woodhouse letter book, *penes* Earl of Kimberley. BM MSS. Add. 23007, 48591. Holkham MS. General Estate Deeds, misc. bundle A, no. 3 (an index of a milit. letter book covering last two decades of sixteenth century). One of the reasons for this proliferation of letter books relating to militia affairs may have been the constitutional wrangles which accompanied much militia administration; see below, pp. 410–25, and *Archives*, ix, 1969–70, pp. 216–18.

[34] Boynton, *passim*. Below, pp. 410–25.

amount of these impositions, this he had already done for them, their job was simply to deliver the goods.[35]

The lieutenancy also supervised the collection of loans and tendentious levies like ship-money. In 1588 deputy lieutenants drew up lists of loan-worthy gentry in the counties, selected a few justices 'whome thei [thought] meet for their credytte and good disposition' to extract maximum contributions from their neighbours, personally interviewed recalcitrants, and, if the latter remained obdurate, sent them before the Council in London. The voluminous evidence for all this activity strongly suggests that justices had become little more than assistants to the lieutenancy, with little scope for protecting themselves and their fellow gentry against burdensome exactions. There is also evidence that the lieutenancy assumed a positive role both in the drive against Recusants during the early 1590s and in enforcing a variety of economic regulations ranging from the enforcement of lenten observances to the planting of mulberry trees.[36]

Perhaps the justices' greatest concern arose over the extensive and ill-defined power of deputy lieutenants. They derived this power from their ability to summon before the lord lieutenant and even the Council Board anyone who flouted their authority. Since their victim rarely knew whether they were acting in their capacity as justices or as deputy lieutenants they could and did invoke their special authority as deputy lieutenants to assist them in many of their non-lieutenancy functions. In Norfolk, for instance, Sir Arthur Heveningham frequently used his lieutenancy powers to overcome opposition to his conduct as a patentee.[37] Moreover once super-administrators had emerged in this way, their power tended to increase under its own momentum. Inevitably they were appointed to special commissions on account of the authority they wielded. Thus in Sussex, all four deputy lieutenants were named in the commissions for searching out Recusants, and in 1592 they were given a general warrant to search for suspected Recusants.[38]

In one aspect of local administration the lieutenancy particularly

[35] PRO SP/12/93/18, f. 52. Bodl. MS. Tanner 241, ff. 26–9. G. Scott Thomson, op. cit., p. 139.

[36] *Stiffkey Papers*, p. 95. R. B. Manning, *Religion and Society in Elizabethan Sussex*, Leicester, 1969, *passim*. J. J. N. McGurk, 'Lieutenancy in Kent c. 1580–1620' (London MPhil thesis 1971), pp. 154–99. W. B. Willcox, *Gloucestershire, 1590–1640*, New Haven, 1940, pp. 75–6, 110. E. P. Cheyney, *A History of England . . .*, ii, 1926, pp. 221, 368–9.

[37] Below, pp. 244, 249, 259–262, 268.

[38] Manning, op. cit., p. 148.

challenged the legal processes of quarter sessions; it appointed its own officials—provost-marshals—to deal with rogues and vagabonds by martial law. The origins of provost-marshals in England are obscure, but in the early sixteenth century they were responsible for the enforcement of martial law within the army during military campaigns. By this time, however, their counterparts in France had also developed civil jurisdiction, working with the local gentry 'to control disbanded troops, vagabonds and all highway criminals'. It is easy to see how the disbanding of an army could cast upon society large numbers of poverty-stricken unemployed who might swell the number of rogues and vagabonds to the point at which they began to threaten civil disorder. Faced with this situation a government might be tempted to extend military jurisdiction to these wandering ex-soldiers, which almost inevitably meant extending it to the riff-raff of Tudor society from whom they were virtually indistinguishable. The crisis came in 1589 with the return of the Portugal fleet and Lord Willoughby's expedition from France. On 13 November the Crown, fearful of disturbances, empowered lords lieutenants to appoint provost-marshals in every county to execute martial law not only on all wandering disbanded soldiers but also on all 'vagrant and ill-disposed persons'. This 'astonishing extension' of the provost-marshal's powers into civilian administration was to last 'for the space of three monethes only . . . except new occacion be geven'. Except new occasion be given; but who decided exactly what constituted 'new occasion'? In fact the extraordinary circumstances of 1589 became the normal pattern of events in the 1590s. Fear of invasion, failure of harvests with consequent food riots, the constant levying and disbanding of military units—all served to provide the Council with an unending series of 'new occasions'. In consequence, provost-marshals with their summary jurisdiction became a semi-permanent feature of county government which some justices regarded as a threat to the statutory procedures for dealing with rogues and vagabonds, as well as being a vote of no-confidence in those empowered to implement these procedures.[39]

This, at least, was the view expressed by William Lambarde in his charge to the Kent grand jury in September 1591. First, he extolled the common law system: 'The law or policy of this realm of England, as it is a peculiar government, not borrowed of the imperial or Roman law (as be the laws of the most part of other

[39] *EHR* lxxvii, 1962, pp. 437–55.

Christian nations) but standing upon the highest reason, selected even for itself; so doth it in one special thing above any other most apparently vary from the usage of other countries: I mean in the manner of proceeding that we have by jurors.' He then complained that 'by the only default of jurors and inquests the native liberty and ancient pre eminence of the English policy is already by little and little exceedingly shred off and diminished'. The principal threat to this 'native liberty' came from 'this new invention of provost marshal' which the 'Queen's Majesty and her Council now presently brought in amongst us (to our no less shame than charge) . . . to rake our rogues together'. Lambarde, bent upon exhorting the juries to greater efficiency, may have overstated the consequence of their slackness, but it is interesting to note that a leading justice and common lawyer chose to beat them with this particular stick.[40]

Nor was Lambarde alone in his expressions of concern. In 1598 the Earl of Essex advised that officials akin to provost-marshals should continue to scour highways, but, in order to avoid summary executions by provost-marshals, those arrested should be dealt with at a twice-weekly court martial held by warrant under the Great Seal. He thought it necessary to provide such safeguards for three reasons: first, it was contrary to 'her Majesty's merciful and excellent government . . . to let her subjects die *sans replique*, as the Frenchman terms it, while her kingdom is free both from invasion and rebellion'; second, a 'Marshal Court' would avoid the arbitrary decisions of provost-marshals—'there is like to be better justice done and discretion used in the taking of men's lives'; third, since 'it carries with it a form of civil justice as well as martial, whereby it will be thought less hard, so it will as fully and effectually meet with the inconvenience as if the provost-marshal had authority to hang them upon first sight'.[41]

Although these proposals were never put into practice, there is some evidence that provost-marshals did tend to work within the legal framework; apparently justices sometimes held special sessions for the indictment of vagabonds rather than such men being summarily executed by the marshals who had rounded them up. But it would seem unwarranted to argue, as does Dr. Boynton, that the

[40] *William Lambarde and Local Government*, ed. Conyers Read, New York, 1962, pp. 104–7.

[41] *EHR* lxxvii, 1962, p. 446.

justices welcomed the marshals' activities. The latter remained agents of the lieutenancy and as such intruded upon the normal peacekeeping operations of local justices. In a crisis the Bench might be grateful for their assistance, but their continued presence represented one more challenge to the existing system. It may not be too fanciful to regard Lambarde's expostulations and Essex's doubts as an early formulation of the complaints against martial law which figured in the Petition of Right in 1628. Boynton explains the complaints 'as a sudden upsurge of hate against the pernicious influence of the lieutenancy', but it would seem more likely, as he himself admits, that 'this storm had been long a-brewing'.[42]

Justices' fears that their indulgent county administration was threatened by a proliferation of licensed informers and the consolidation of the lieutenancy may have been further increased by their failure to win a dominant role in the enforcement of two important statutes—those concerning Recusants and the export of grain. The Act of Uniformity in 1559 placed responsibility for its enforcement in the hands of either diocesan officials or the justices of assize. It empowered churchwardens to levy a fine of one shilling on everyone who failed to attend divine service on Sundays or holy days; if their authority was flouted they could present the Recusants in the church courts or at the assizes. J.P.s and their subordinates had little part in implementing this statute, although they were ordered to be 'aiding and assisting' to the court of High Commission.[43]

The increase of Recusancy during the 1570s underlined the inadequacies of this enforcement machinery, despite the Council's efforts in 1577 to make it more efficient. When parliament met in January 1581, anti-Catholic feeling had become so intense that Lords and Commons between them introduced no less than four Bills designed to procure more stringent measures against Recusants.[44] The story behind these Bills is one of conflict: conflict

[42] *EHR* lxxix, 1964, p. 279.

[43] 1 Eliz. c. 2.

[44] The succeeding paragraphs are based upon Neale, *Parliaments 1559–1581*, pp. 385–92, and F. X. Walker, 'The Implementation of the Elizabethan Statutes against Recusants 1581–1603' (London PhD thesis 1961), pp. 43, 121–33. This account is only concerned with the enforcement clauses of these Bills.

between the Queen and those radicals in both Council and parliament who wanted draconian measures against Recusants; conflict between J.P.s, extensively represented in the Commons, and bishops, entrenched in the Lords, as to whether magistrates or ecclesiastical officials should be responsible for enforcing these new anti-Recusant measures. The first Bill 'For obedience to the Queen's Majesty against the see of Rome' was framed by a Commons committee and introduced into that House on 8 February 1581. It was a harsh measure imposing a series of heavy fines, culminating in imprisonment, for absence from church. Its significance in the present context is that it proposed to remove the enforcement of this new code from the ecclesiastical hierarchy and to entrust it entirely to the J.P.s and justices of assize. It was quite uncompromising on this issue, making no provision for the ecclesiastical courts to retain even their former powers under the 1559 statute.

By contrast, a second Bill, introduced in the Lords, gave augmented power to ecclesiastical courts. It provided less severe penalties but proposed a very thorough procedure for detection, employing parish officials and the diocesan hierarchy and vesting responsibility for the imposition of its still substantial penalties with the ecclesiastical High Commission. After a series of conferences between representatives of both Houses, a new Bill, which appears to have had the backing of the temporal lords, was introduced into the Commons. This Bill, which never got beyond a first reading, made slight concessions to the bishops' views by allowing the ecclesiastical hierarchy to retain its 1559 powers, but maintained harsh penalties and again provided for Recusancy cases to be determined at quarter sessions and assizes.

One of the principal differences between Lords and Commons in their approach to the Recusant problem was over jurisdiction: whether the detection and punishment of Recusants should rest with the ecclesiastical administrators and church courts or with the civil magistrates and common law courts, particularly with the justices in quarter sessions. The importance which both sides attached to this issue is evident from Thomas Norton's comments on the conferences between Lords and Commons which he had attended as a member of the Commons' delegation. He claimed that 'the bishops spake most or onely for jurisdiction, in so much that one great Bishop said that rather than he wold yeld that private scholemasters should acknowledge their conformitie in religion before justices of peace in open sessions, he would say nay to the whole Bill of religion'. To which Norton apparently riposted that 'the bishops had filled the Church with unlearned and unfitt ministers . . . that the number of papestes . . . had increased under them by their remissnesse in executing their aucthorities, being yet both bishops, justices of peace and hye commissioners'.[45]

In this struggle over jurisdiction victory went to the temporal magistrates. In March 1581 Sir Francis Knollys introduced a fourth Bill, which eventually became law, imposing a £20 fine for each month's Recusancy and enacting that only assize judges and J.P.s in open sessions could inquire, hear, and determine Recusancy offences; diocesan courts and the High Commission were totally excluded from any jurisdiction in these matters. 'It was a major defeat for the ecclesiastical courts and the end of the bishops' long struggle for increased jurisdiction against recusants.' Conversely it was a major triumph for the justices.[46]

Their success was short lived. During the 1580s Recusancy had too many political ramifications, both national and international, for its detection and suppression to be left entirely in the hands of justices and their subordinates. As Professor Manning has shown for Sussex, complete control over the Bench's religious composition was something which eluded Elizabethan statesmen, who soon realized that justices could be as slack and ineffective in detecting and punishing Recusants as had been the ecclesiastical hierarchy. Consequently, as in military affairs, there were tendencies towards imposing greater central control over the administration of Recusancy laws, inevitably at the expense of the justices' newly acquired authority in these matters. In 1587 parliament passed an 'Acte for the more speedie and due execucon of certeyne braunches of the statute made in the xxiiird yere of the Quenes . . . Raigne' which took away from quarter sessions the responsibility to convict for Recusancy, leaving it vested in Queen's Bench and assizes. The new Act made no provision for discovering and presenting suspected cases of Recusancy, but presumably it intended that juries should continue to present at quarter sessions, or informers to lay informations in the appropriate court. The tendency for centralized control to intrude is particularly apparent in one aspect of this legislation. Whereas the 1582 Act had allowed the justices to apply one-third of all Recusancy

45 *Archaeologia*, xxxvi, 1855, p. 112.

46 23 Eliz. c. 1. F. X. Walker, op. cit., p. 133.

fines to local poor-relief, the new provisions stipulated that they should use some of this income for 'impotent and maymed soldiers' and the maintenance of houses of correction, but—and the sting was in the tail—only as 'the Lord Treasurer, Chancellor and Chief Baron . . . shall order and appoynte'. 'As with the operation of the law', concludes one student of Recusant history, 'so with the fruits of it, the tendency was away from local control and concerns.'[47]

Barely four years later, central government still further tightened its control over the administration of anti-Recusancy measures when, in October 1591, the Crown appointed by proclamation special commissioners in each county to search out priests and those who concealed them. The commissioners were empowered to organize a committee of eight people in each parish who were to visit every house at least once weekly and question the occupiers. Those who did not answer satisfactorily were to be sent before the county commissioners for further interrogation. The details of this commission 'show that the government felt impelled to organize a system over and above the existing county administration'. In Norfolk, as in Sussex, the commission included the deputy lieutenants together with the Bishop and several justices well known for their anti-Catholic views. They acted with vigour and by the spring of 1592 had held special sessions at which Recusants were presented prior to indictment at the assizes. Clearly, initially at least, this machinery worked well, and the Council greased the wheels by authorizing the sheriff to pay every commissioner 5*s*. and the presenting jury 13*s*. 4*d*. for each day's sitting.[48]

This streamlined machinery, which appears to have functioned quite independently of quarter sessions, did not for long operate unchallenged. In the 1601 parliament there were unsuccessful attempts to introduce new legislation against Recusants which included proposals to reinstate the J.P.s as linchpins in its enforcement. The debates provided occasion for some trenchant criticisms of justices and in the end the Bills were narrowly defeated. Even so the tenor of these debates leaves no doubt that the method of enforcement was

[47] Manning, op. cit., pp. 238–46. 29 Eliz. c. 6. F. X. Walker, op. cit., p. 246.

[48] Hughes & Larkin, iii. 86–92. *HMC Salisbury*, iv. 148. F. X. Walker, op. cit., p. 307. NNRO MS. Aylsham, bundle 176, Privy Council to the comms. for Recusants and seminaries, 13 Aug. 1592. *History Teachers' Miscellany*, ed. W. H. Saunders, ii, 1923–4, pp. 157–60. NNRO MS. NAS C3/2/3, letter to Bass. Gawdy, 25 Jan. 1591. *Stiffkey Papers*, pp. 170–81. *APC, 1591–2*, pp. 159, 336, 365–6. NNRO MS. WALS. XVII/I, f. 17–17v.

as much an issue for members as was the anti-Recusant content of the Bills.[49]

It was during the second half of Elizabeth's reign that the justices also lost responsibility for administering the laws regulating exportation of grain. Freedom to ship their corn was a matter of great concern to justices and gentry alike, particularly in an agrarian and maritime county like Norfolk where farmers, landowners, and merchants could be vitally affected by export restrictions. An act of 1563 had laid down that grain could be freely transported overseas provided prices did not exceed specified rates per quarter—10*s*. for wheat, 8*s*. for rye, peas, and beans, and 6*s*. 8*d*. for barley and malt. Undoubtedly these regulations, made to keep markets well stocked at reasonable prices, worked to the advantage of areas of high grain consumption like London and the North-East, but to the detriment of farmers and landowners in areas of high grain production whose interests would best be served if they could decide when markets were denuded of supplies to the point where exports should be stopped. Such flexibility of control was accorded to the counties in the 1571 statute 'for the increase of tillage'. This authorized export to all countries in amity with England so long as prices in the exporting county remained 'reasonable and moderate'. The decision as to when shipment overseas should be prohibited was vested in the justices meeting in quarter sessions, with the proviso that they informed the Council of their proceedings.[50]

This victory for county autonomy over central control was short-lived for two reasons. First, the statute on which it rested was repealed in 1593 and grain exports were once more prohibited when prices rose above a stated level. Secondly, and more importantly, throughout the 1590s the Crown repeatedly exercised its right, safeguarded in both the 1571 and 1593 statutes, to prohibit the export of grain at any time. These embargoes seem to have been fiscal in intent since they were accompanied by the sale of licences, frequently to particular merchants. But whether by embargo, or through the operation of the statute, control of corn exports passed out of local hands. The justices meeting at Norwich constantly protested about these restraints, demanding that they should be consulted before embargoes were imposed and that, if licences must be granted, the Bench should be allowed to nominate the licensees. The evidence suggests that as

[49] Neale, *Parliaments 1584–1601*, pp. 396–406. F. X. Walker, op. cit., pp. 418–19.
[50] 5 Eliz. c. 5; 13 Eliz. c. 13.

Elizabeth's reign drew to a close this issue continued to sour relations between the Council and Norfolk justices.[51]

It would be stretching the evidence too far to argue that local administration by the justices in quarter sessions was under deliberate and concerted attack; the developments described above may not even have constituted a serious challenge, but they do indicate that there was a central government view of administration as well as a county view, and that these two views frequently diverged. Their development, and the degree of conflict between them, will be made clear in part III of this book.

[51] 35 Eliz. c. 7. Above, pp. 18–19, 99–100.

CHAPTER VII

The Shrievalty

SHERIFFS held office for only one year and could not be reappointed until a further two had elapsed. The Queen chose them during November by placing the time-honoured stylus prick beside one of the three names normally included for each county in a short list—the 'bill' as it was called. This had previously been compiled in the Exchequer by the Lord Chancellor, the Lord Treasurer, privy councillors and some of the judges. They usually selected candidates from among the magisterial class, frequently renominating those who had not been pricked in the previous year. Undoubtedly their choice was also influenced by representations, made through the usual channels of sixteenth-century patronage, from gentry seeking to gain or avoid appointment to the office. Occasionally the 'bill' bears marks of last-minute intrigues; for instance, after it had been compiled in 1601 Bassingbourne Gawdy's name was inserted among those for Norfolk and then the Queen's hand was guided to 'prick' him.[1]

If, as seems likely, Gawdy campaigned for the shrievalty, his enthusiasm for the office is surprising, since by Elizabeth's reign sheriffs had been shorn of much of their former power. Their duties relating to the administration and supervision of Crown lands and feudal rights had passed to the escheators, feodaries, and receivers; their judicial power in criminal matters had passed to the justices of the peace, as had responsibility for the enforcement of penal statutes. As the Crown's chief local revenue officers they had been eclipsed early in the sixteenth century, when special commissioners had been empowered to collect the new parliamentary subsidy. Then, in the middle of the century, radical changes in the methods of training and recruiting an army had resulted, first, in sheriffs sharing responsibility for county military organization with muster commissioners, and then in their losing it entirely to the newly created lords lieutenants.

This diminution of power was not necessarily accompanied by

[1] *EHR* xlvii, 1932, pp. 31–45. PRO C 227/19.

fewer duties and responsibilities.[2] It is important to remember that the sheriff continued to act as executive agent or minister of those to whom his power had passed. Though shorn of his former glory, he was burdened with the detailed administrative routine attendant upon the decisions, orders, and judgements of J.P.s, muster commissioners, and deputy lieutenants. As the principal officer of quarter sessions he had to arrange when and where the court should meet—no easy business in Norfolk since each quarter sessions adjourned to three different towns and not necessarily to the same ones each time. He had then to empanel the grand, petty, and Hundred juries, and was expected to attend each session. Long after official proceedings had ended, his staff remained heavily involved levying fines, whipping rogues, branding thieves, and distraining upon jurors and witnesses for non-attendance. He also provided the principal channel for communication between local magistrates and the Privy Council. Their lordships usually dispatched letters about county affairs to his office and he then had to decide whether the business could wait until the justices assembled at the next quarter sessions or whether urgency demanded that he convene an extraordinary meeting at one of the Norwich inns.[3] His executive role in relation to the justices increased proportionally with the development of their administrative responsibilities throughout the sixteenth century, and in order to emphasize this role he was banned from membership of the Bench during the year of his shrievalty.

Besides his responsibilities to the justices, a sheriff also undertook the extensive clerical work and administration arising from deliberations of the muster commissioners; but in this case he was named in the commission and attended meetings in the capacity of a commissioner as well as of an executive officer.[4] Meanwhile he continued to hold the monthly county and Hundred courts which involved considerable administrative work, and, since knights of the shire were elected in the county court, occasionally thrust him into the forefront of county politics.

[2] In this and succeeding paragraphs I have relied heavily upon Barnes, *Somerset*, ch. v, and Michael Dalton, *Officium Vicecomitum*, 1623.

[3] NNRO MS. NAS Safe II.28, ff. 63v, 117. *HMC Gawdy*, pp. 18, 81.

[4] In this connection it is interesting that several of the letter-books concerned with militia affairs (above, p. 128 n.o.) were started by sheriffs during their year on the muster commission (see NNRO MSS. NAS Safe II.28; WALS XVII/I. BM MS. Add. 23007). *APC, 1596–7*, pp. 51–3. *HMC Gawdy*, p. 73. BM MS. Add. 23007, f. 17v.

He also had administrative responsibilities to the courts at Westminster, responsibilities which grew more onerous as the business of these courts increased in the late sixteenth century. Besides executing writs and processes, empanelling juries, summoning witnesses, collecting fines, and keeping the gaol, he had to arrange the venue of assizes and provide lodgings and hospitality for the judges. This was always a costly business and could sometimes prove troublesome, as Bassingbourne Gawdy discovered in 1594 when he arranged to hold the assizes at Thetford. Since he lived nearby at Harling this was no doubt more convenient for him and profitable to the neighbouring innkeepers, but the townsmen had less accommodation to offer than their counterparts at Norwich and inevitably there were difficulties. Having arranged to lodge the judges at a house belonging to Edward Eden, Gawdy discovered at the last minute that Eden had made no preparation for their arrival because, apparently, he had received no payment for the use of his property. Gawdy's efforts to disentangle this muddle added yet more work during one of the busiest periods of his shrievalty. But no doubt his chief concern was with the expense of feasting and entertaining the judges. Down to 1575 this responsibility was particularly onerous in Norfolk and Suffolk since the two counties were joined in a single shrievalty so that the sheriff had to entertain the judges at four assizes. In 1563, for instance, Sir William Butts laid out £92 on entertainment at Bury as well as £75 at Thetford.[5]

Each sheriff recruited an extensive staff to undertake these time-consuming and frequently unpopular administrative duties. Headed by an under-sheriff, it comprised clerks to the under-sheriff, bailiffs, deputies for replevin, stewards of Hundred courts, and gaolers. The key figure was the under-sheriff who took charge of all routine legal and financial administration. In London he accounted at the Exchequer for revenues due from the county; in the county his office provided a clearing house for the receipt, execution, and return of all writs, commissions, and Council letters. He also kept the list of freeholders from which juries were empanelled.

In every Hundred the sheriff and his deputy were assisted by a bailiff who provided the final administrative link between government and subject. His responsibilities are clearly set forth in a bond made in 1601 between William Bruning, bailiff of Diss Hundred,

[5] NNRO MS. NAS Safe II.28, loose letter, Edward Eden to Bass. Gawdy, 6 Feb. 1593/4. BM MS. Add. 27404, f. 33.

and his sheriff Bassingbourne Gawdy. Bruning undertook to make a just account of all issues, fines, revenues, and profits of the Queen's tournes, leets, and courts within his Hundred; to account for all goods of felons and persons outlawed, and for escheats and forfeitures; to execute all warrants directed from the sheriff or any other of the Queen's officers; to make arrests, either taking bail or delivering his charge to the sheriff's prison; to levy Exchequer estreats; and, finally, to compile a list for the under-sheriff's office of all freeholders in his Hundred. A small group of bailiffs-arrant were attached to the under-sheriff's office with specific responsibility for communication with the bailiffs in their respective Hundreds.[6]

Broadly speaking, in Elizabethan Norfolk each sheriff appointed his own bailiffs. This represented a reversal of the late medieval trend when monarchs had granted away the lordships of most Hundreds in Norfolk and with them the right to appoint bailiffs. During the sixteenth century the Crown had resumed many of these private franchises through either escheat or confiscation at the Dissolution. There are indications, too, that even where these lordships had not reverted to the Crown the rights which they conferred were being whittled away by the sheriffs. This was certainly so in Clackclose and Freebridge Lynn Hundreds where, despite Sir Nicholas Hare's lordship, sheriffs interfered on several occasions during the 1560s and 1570s. Thus, by resumption or usurpation the sheriff's patronage gradually expanded, until by the late sixteenth century he was appointing bailiffs in the majority of Norfolk's thirty-three Hundreds. By then few liberties remained, apart from those of the Duchy of Lancaster and the Dukes of Norfolk—the latter having passed to Philip Howard, Earl of Arundel.[7]

Moreover, even within these liberties the sheriff frequently retained some influence over the bailiffs. Just how much depended upon the terms of the charter under which the lordship had been granted away. Often, for instance, the return of writs had not been included, and in such a case the lord's bailiff could not undertake this task until he had been authorized by the sheriff. Edward Coke

[6] NNRO MS. NAS Frere Box K.13(A), Diss Hundred bundle, MS. endorsed 'Wm. Bruninge Balyff of Dysse his Bond'.

[7] G. E. Morey, 'The Administration of Norfolk and Suffolk under Henry IV' (London MA thesis 1941), p. 35. *HMC Gawdy*, pp. 7, 14. BM MSS. Add. 27959, f. 12; 27447, f. 110. The Gawdy MSS. in particular, contain a large number of letters from suitors for bailiwicks. See esp. *HMC Gawdy*, pp. 7, 14, 39, 71, 76.

annually had to request the sheriff to grant his bailiff a 'general warrant for the breaking up of all processes and writs to be executed within my said liberty'. Similarly, in 1602 the deputy steward of the Duchy estates in Norfolk sought 'general warrants' for Mr. Bunting, bailiff of two Duchy Hundreds there. Presumably the sheriff could, if he wished, withhold such warrants and appoint his own bailiffs to execute writs in these Hundreds, as indeed became common practice in the eighteenth century.[8]

The sheriff also appointed a steward of each Hundred court. Although these courts had long been losing their powers to quarter sessions, they continued to function for the settlement of petty disputes and the appointment of minor officials. Their business must still have been sufficient to provide some income from fees, since attorneys were willing to pay small gratuities to secure this office.[9]

The bestowal of these stewardships, together with the appointment of the under-sheriff, bailiffs, and keepers of gaols, provided the sheriff with an extensive range of minor patronage. He might not always care to use it, preferring rather to reappoint those officials who had served his predecessor; in doing this he would at least ensure the discharge of business by experienced administrators. But as will be shown later, in the event of faction and dispute within a county, the bestowal of these posts could be of considerable significance, since the empanelling of a partial jury or the delay of a writ could be tactically important. There is considerable evidence from Norfolk to suggest that many sheriffs appointed new under-sheriffs as required by statute, and frequently brought in a large number of new bailiffs as well.[10]

Regrettably, little is known about the sort of people whom the sheriff recruited for his service. Under-sheriffs, according to one early-seventeenth-century authority, were 'most commonly men of small worth'.[11] But there is evidence to the contrary: several minor gentry held the under-shrievalty in Norfolk,[12] and Professor Barnes,

[8] Pembroke Coll. Camb. MS. volume of letters presented by the Rev. Charles Parkin, ff. 26, 72. MS. *penes* Captain A. Hamond, Sir John Townshend to Sir Bass. Gawdy, 1602.

[9] *HMC Gawdy*, pp. 75, 76. BM MS. Add. 33597, f. 16.

[10] Barnes, *Somerset*, pp. 136–8. Below, pp. 151–2. 23 H VI c.7.

[11] Michael Dalton, *Officium Vicecomitum*, 1623, f. 135v.

[12] e.g. Edmund Knyvett (1597/8), Richard Curtis (1594/5), Philip Lewgar (1591/2), and John Ferrour (1589/90), see PRO, *Deputy Keeper's Report*, xxxviii, 1887, p. 424. PRO E 123/16, f. 179v. *HMC Gawdy*, p. 51.

writing of Somerset in the early seventeenth century, suggests that there, too, the office attracted men who were but a 'peg below the social status of their masters'. A few Norfolk under-sheriffs appear to have attended one of the Inns and most were attorneys with extensive legal experience. Hundred bailiffs in Norfolk generally came from a slightly lower social stratum, but were still a cut above the 'yeomen, petty townsmen and husbandmen' who appear to have filled the office in Somerset a few years later. Occasionally a bailiff graduated to the under-shrievalty or a former under-sheriff had to be content with a bailiwick, which suggests that both officials had similar backgrounds; indeed such evidence as exists indicates that many bailiffs were also recruited from among the county attorneys.[13]

The sheriff's staff received no direct payment. Instead each officer was empowered to collect statutory fees from anyone upon whom he served a writ or warrant. If the degree of competition for an office reflects the return it yielded, then the Norfolk under-shrievalty and bailiwicks must have provided substantial profit, since as soon as a gentleman was rumoured to be in the 'Bill' for sheriff he was beset by eager attorneys soliciting appointment to his staff. Once the sheriff had been pricked these place-seekers intensified their efforts; indeed, such was the demand for the under-shrievalty in the mid-1570s that at least three contenders enlisted the backing of influential courtiers.[14] There is also plenty of evidence for similar competition for the bailiwicks:[15] 'one Mr. Guybon and Mr. Henrye Vallenger . . . desiered me to move you to bestowe the ballywick of Freebridge beside Lynne on them . . . and Mr. Nicholas Mynn and William Mynne the receyvor ar likewise sutors to you for the same Hundred', wrote Thomas Jermy to the incoming sheriff in 1565. When Mr. Crofts, one of three contenders for the bailiwick of Tunstead Hundred, offered the sheriff £5 'rather than he should go without it' he was taking no more than due precautions since it was common for suitors to offer gratuities ranging from £2 to £5 for such an office. There is no evidence that the Norfolk bailiwicks yielded sufficient profit 'to make the office a form of investment', as appears

13 Barnes, *Somerset*, pp. 137, 138.

14 Bodl. MSS. Tanner 241, ff. 1–3; 238, f. 189.

15 See, for example, when Bass. Gawdy was appointed sheriff in 1601: *HMC Gawdy*, pp. 75–6. NNRO MSS. NAS Safe II.28, ff. 75v–77; WALS XVII/I, part ii, f. 122. MS. *penes* Captain A. Hamond, Sir John Townshend to Sir Bass. Gawdy, endorsed 1602. Pembroke Coll. Camb. MS. volume of letters presented by the Rev. Charles Parkin, ff. 72, 74.

to have happened in Gloucestershire, but apparently the Norfolk under-shrievalty was lucrative enough to attract at least one speculator who intended 'not to execute the office hym self, but onlye seketh a porcion of monye', paying a deputy to do the work.[16]

What proportion of these profits came from statutory fees and what proportion from extortion is another matter. It is certainly not difficult to find complaints about the corrupt dealings of bailiffs, and although none in Norfolk appears to have suffered the fate of William Marshall of Somerset who, after ten years of extortion, was shot dead by a householder whom he was trying to arrest, Arthur Futter, bailiff in Mitford Hundred, must surely have come near to it. A list of allegations against him, compiled in 1597, provides a glimpse of his nefarious practices although it is only fair to say that some of his activities may have been directed by others.[17] He arrested people without warrant, taking fees before releasing them, and when he did have a warrant for arrest, he refused to take sureties, clapping his victims into East Dereham prison where he charged heavy gaol fees 'whereas never any were paid before'. He sent his under-bailiffs into nearby Hundreds to drive men's cattle into Mitford and then compelled the owners to regain them by replevin. He even took bribes from men anxious to avoid jury service at assizes and quarter sessions and gave out that he would exempt anyone who dealt at his mother's shop in Dereham.[18]

Bailiffs had no monopoly in corruption and harsh dealings. John Ferrour, under-sheriff in 1590, was noted for usury, extortion, and oppression; despite complaints to the Council and several inquiries into his dubious activities, he seems to have gone his way intimidating, threatening, extorting, and even acting as an informer.[19] He once sent Henry Spelman certain maxims which, although he disclaimed authorship, could well have guided his own conduct:

Love no man but theyselfe, or if any man, doe it for thyselfe.

[16] BM MS. Add. 27447, f. 110. W. B. Willcox, *Gloucestershire 1590–1640*, New Haven, 1940, p. 47. BM MS. Add. 27447, f. 110.

[17] Below, p. 149.

[18] Barnes, *Somerset*, p. 140. NNRO MS. 12872 (31 F 2). See also C. W. James, *Chief Justice Coke his Family and Descendants*, 1929, pp. 307–9.

[19] BM MS. Add. 41306, ff. 3–8. PRO SP 12/155/65, ff. 1–2. NNRO MS. Aylsham, bundle 176, letter from Privy Council to Nath. Bacon and other justices, 12 May 1580. F. W. Brooks, 'Supplementary Stiffkey Papers', pp. 7–9, *Camden Miscellany XVI* (Camden Soc. 3rd ser. lii).

> Trust no man so shalt thou never be deceaved.
> Be ritch in promise to all, thoughe in performance to fewe.
> Above all thinges make not thy servant to rich for then you shall want hym when you neede him. Let hym neyther syncke nor swyme.
> Whatsoever your adversary sayed, oppose it how true soever it bee, bycause hee sayed it.
> You must be as carefull to breake his faction as to strengthen your owne; to break it divyde it.
> With the heade of the contrary faction neyther have friendship nor seme to have enmytye.
> Whatsoever you doe agaynst hym pretende the prynce's good and common wealth's; by this slye course you shall soner cutt his throate . . .[20]

At first glance it would seem that the prospect of the shrievalty must have daunted even the most public-spirited sixteenth-century gentleman. Confined to his county for a year, he ministered to justices, judges, and Exchequer barons; in the performance of his onerous duties he had to rely upon a staff of self-seeking subordinates over whom he frequently had little control; in the final reckoning he would almost certainly be heavily out of pocket, since whatever profits remained after under-sheriff and bailiffs had taken their cut would be more than offset by heavy expenses—fees for entering and leaving office, the outlay for entertainment at the assizes, and expenditure on accoutrements. The latter were not obligatory but, since his office had declined in power, a sheriff frequently clung to its trappings; he felt bound to ride to assizes and quarter sessions with a substantial liveried following, and at least one sheriff-elect spared no expense to attire himself in the latest court fashions with a saddle such as 'my Lord of Essex, Sir Charles Blunt, Sir Roger Williams and suche other cavilleros at this hower do use' and a footcloth 'garded not after the old fashion but the newest'. Moreover, while in office a sheriff was barred from taking his place on the Bench, thereby yielding to a neighbour initiative and influence in the day-to-day affairs of his district. With much to lose and little to gain men must have shunned this dubious honour. Such was the case in Somerset and Gloucestershire, where no gentleman actively sought the office and many tried to avoid it. Nobody 'undertook the office with any delight and all were very happy to relinquish it when their year was up'; it was 'a curse imposed, not a benefit desired'.[21]

[20] BM MS. Add. 34599, f. 8.

[21] Jeayes, p. 77. Barnes, *Somerset*, p. 133. Willcox, op. cit., pp. 39–40.

In Norfolk, however, the situation was by no means so clear-cut. There is some evidence that during the first half of Elizabeth's reign gentlemen may have contemplated the prospect of the shrievalty with the same gloom, if not positive alarm, as did their counterparts in south-west England. None of them sought the position, and a few took positive steps to avoid it. Bassingbourne Gawdy (sen.) managed to do so for three consecutive years, but eventually had to undertake the 'troublesome office'; while Sir Roger Woodhouse, using more direct tactics, 'by his owne earenest sute [got] . . . him selfe struckne oute of the Bill'. But in contrast to this reluctance during the first half of Elizabeth's reign, there is abundant evidence of vigorous competition for the shrievalty during the latter part. Four of the principal gentry—Nathaniel Bacon, Arthur Heveningham, Henry Gawdy, and Bassingbourne Gawdy—each held it twice during the period 1581–1607, and there is no doubt that they, and others, used all the devices of Court intrigue to ensure that they were pricked.[22]

In 1593, for example Bassingbourne Gawdy had to conduct a lively campaign against three rival candidates before the Queen's stylus finally ensured his triumph. His chief opponent, Sir Arthur Heveningham, went to Court and 'made great suit to preferr himself', while Gawdy stayed at home and entrusted his suit to the care of his courtier-brother Philip. In this appointment Lord Hunsdon was a key figure since he held the lord lieutenancy of Norfolk as well as being Lord Chamberlain and a privy councillor; no candidate was likely to succeed without his backing. Heveningham, already one of his deputy lieutenants, made strenuous efforts to ingratiate himself by giving him a 'very big flying tassell'[23] and becoming 'the most importunate sutor to be shreife that ever was', but he made little headway against a professional courtier like Philip Gawdy who claimed to have persuaded the Lord Keeper and the Lord Admiral, as well as Lord Hunsdon, to advocate the appointment of his brother, although subsequently he assured Bassingbourne that 'thine own credit made thee sheriff'. Meanwhile, once Heveningham realized that he had no chance of succeeding in his own suit, he changed tactics and campaigned to get either Philip Woodhouse or 'Mr. Knyvett'[24] pricked in preference to Gawdy. Philip Woodhouse

[22] NNRO MS. NAS C3/1/9, John Brett to Bass. Gawdy, 15 Nov. 1576. BM MS. Add. 36989, f. 5. Jeayes, *passim*.

[23] A tiercel—a male hawk used in falconry.

[24] Probably Thomas Knyvett of Buckenham.

achieved his ambition in 1594, but Sir Arthur Heveningham had still not been chosen by 1600. In that year his sister, Lady Digby, a gentlewoman of the bed-chamber, 'tooke great pains for him, but he missed the [oc]cashion, which put him in a great chafe', especially since the appointment went to Richard Jenkinson, a newcomer to county politics. Demand for the shrievalty continued into the seventeenth century; in 1607 Framlingham Gawdy hoped 'by the assystance of allmighty God to be heigh shreife of the county of Norfolk' before he died. It is also significant that during these years of intense competition there is no hint of anyone trying to avoid the office.[25]

This competition in late Elizabethan Norfolk could be explained in straightforward administrative terms. Strictly speaking, until 1575 Norfolk had no sheriff of its own since the office was shared with Suffolk. Joint shrievalties of this kind had been common in medieval times, but most of them had been abolished by statute in 1567 'forsomuche as the service and charges of that office [in two counties] is more then in tymes past hath ben, and is nowe commonly greater then one sheryffe is able to serve and supplie'.[26] For some reason Norfolk and Suffolk were omitted from this Act and had to wait until 1575–6 before each was given its own sheriff. Once this reorganization had relieved the shrievalty of excessive expense and responsibility, county magnates may well have sought it for the prestige it conferred.

A more likely explanation is to be found in the changes brought about in Norfolk society by Thomas Howard's execution in 1572. While he lived he had so dominated every aspect of life in the county that no gentlemen could aspire to excessive power and prestige; they lived within an ordered cosmos in which all change depended upon his fiat. His fall left a principality without a prince, since the county had no nobleman worthy to assume his mantle. In these unstable conditions lesser men aspired to leadership, and the Duke's autocratic rule gave way to rivalry, jealousy, and faction. For a time, as will be shown later, Norfolk society once more displayed that turbulence so familiar in the pages of the *Paston Letters*. Under these conditions the shrievalty, despite its apparent unattractiveness, could be an office of extreme significance, a major weapon of faction.

Litigation provided one of the principal instruments of faction and one over which the sheriff could exercise considerable control

[25] Jeayes, pp. 76, 78, 107. BM MSS. Add. 23007, f. 9v; 36990, f. 20.
[26] 8 Eliz. c. 16.

since he held a commanding position in the administration of legal processes.[27] Through the agency of his bailiffs, writs could be delayed or wrongfully served and innocent persons even be arrested and imprisoned without warrant. Viewed in this light Arthur Futter's extortionate practices may not have been motivated entirely by economic self-interest. Indeed almost certainly they were not. He exercised his bailiwick as a deputy to Sir Edward Clere, one of the richest and most quarrelsome magnate-gentry in Norfolk, and he frequently acted under Clere's direction.[28] One of the complaints against Futter was that he 'arrested five poor men at the suit of Sir Edward Clere, they not knowing of any process taken out for them'. There are also other indications that Futter's unscrupulous activities, far from being indiscriminate, were deliberately directed, possibly at Clere's instigation, against a small group of persons. For instance, three times he arrested 'a godly minister named William Holby' whose sureties on each occasion—George Clements and Adam Bozum—had also been victims of Futter's nefarious activities.

The direction which Sir Edward Clere gave to Arthur Futter's activities was in no way unique. An amenable bailiff could be of such significance in the conduct of local disputes that many gentry sought to place a friend or servant in this office. When Sir Francis Gawdy and Sir Nicholas Hare quarrelled, each resorting to litigation against the other's tenants, both tried to nominate the bailiff of Clackclose Hundred. In 1578, with his nephew as sheriff, Gawdy secured the appointment of his servant Stephen Carrow, with predictably unpleasant consequences for Hare's tenants. Two years later each was still anxious to ensure control of the bailiff's activities: as soon as Gawdy heard that Sir Edward Clere had been tipped for the shrievalty he wrote seeking the bailiwick for his man 'before Mr. Hare can move for it', as he unashamedly admitted.[29]

Even under normal circumstances gentry endeavoured to safeguard their positions by securing the appointment of friendly bailiffs. As soon as Sir Christopher Heydon, Francis Gawdy, and John Nonne heard that Bassingbourne Gawdy had been appointed sheriff in 1578, they wrote asking him to appoint their servants or clients to their local bailiwicks. Indeed some gentry appear to have been so

[27] Below, esp. pp. 271–2.

[28] Below, pp. 160–3.

[29] *HMC Gawdy*, pp. 7–10, 14. NNRO MSS. Hare 137, 144, 146 (185 X 2). BM MS. Add. 27959, f. 12.

anxious to forestall their neighbours that, instead of waiting for the sheriff to be chosen, they wrote commending their candidates to all the gentry named in the 'Bill'. Others acted upon 'leaks' from Court. Thus as soon as Sir Arthur Heveningham heard that Gawdy was likely to be pricked in 1578 he wrote asking to be allowed to nominate the bailiff of Humbleyard Hundred.[30]

The sheriff's duty to empanel juries also provided him with opportunities for manipulating the law in the interest of friend and faction. In Tudor England an impartial jury was rarely empanelled and everything militated against such an occurrence: the closely knit structure of county society, the relatively small number of persons eligible for jury service, the tenurial relationship which still bound one man to another all combined to produce a situation in which juries could be easily swayed and became very aware of the innuendoes of an apparently innocent piece of litigation. 'A truly indifferent jury', Professor Hurstfield has written, 'was as hard to obtain as indifferent commissioners. Sometimes it was known that a great lord, for example, the Earl of Worcester, was "able to command most in Monmouthshire from whence the jury must come"; sometimes it was thought that the jury was simply "hired thereunto" by the great landowners. . . . What kind of jury could a wretched sheriff be expected to assemble, torn as he was between warring factions or, more likely, himself an active partisan of one of them?'[31]

In such circumstances both plaintiff and defendant became suitors to the sheriff for a jury partial to their cause or at least one which was not partial to their opponent—an 'indifferent' or 'upright' jury as they called it. Nicholas Hare wrote begging that none of the 'Pratts, Butts, Morrises or Drapers' be returned; he thought the panel would be indifferent if it came from Marshland and Wells, but feared Mr. Yelverton and other 'bearers in the cause if it were laid on this side of Norfolk'. Michael Stanhope asked for jurors who were 'not afraid of Sir Arthur Heveningham nor living under any of the Cornwallises'. A client seeking his patron's help in a suit, sent him advice: 'get a panel returned including men of knowledge in sheriff's matters; if possible, some who have been under-sheriffs or clerks, of which sort there be store about Shipdham where the venue is laid . . . Have this panel filed in court lest the other side, misliking it, defer or dally for better opportunities.' Edward Lord Cromwell thanked

[30] *HMC Gawdy*, pp. 7, 14. BM MSS. Add. 27447, f. 110; 27457, f. 48.

[31] J. Hurstfield, *The Queen's Wards*, 1958, p. 53.

the sheriff for his 'friendly usage towards . . . [him] in setting down names', but warned that his adversary 'hunteth altogether upon advantage and would fain watch a time to get a panel of mean and ignorant persons to his liking . . .' His suit 'is only that the panel may be persons of good calling and of good understanding'.[32]

In fact it was the under-sheriff who normally empanelled juries since he kept the book of freeholders in his office. This meant that a partisan sheriff needed to supervise and control the activities of his deputy. John Wilkinson, writing in the early seventeenth century, advised a sheriff that the easiest way to achieve this was to appoint one of his servants to the under-shrievalty. In this way he would ensure a measure of subservience to his wishes, and by locating the under-sheriff's office in his own household be able to supervise all business. If, on the other hand, he granted the under-shrievalty to someone outside his household he forfeited a large degree of control —both psychological and physical.[33]

As faction in Norfolk increased during the 1590s, sheriffs certainly took steps to ensure a much closer relationship with their deputies than had existed during the former decades of Elizabeth's reign. Then, they had either sold the office to the highest bidder, as in 1565 when Thomas Jermy advised William Paston to dispose of it for his 'further benyfitt'; or they granted it to the nominee of a powerful patron who in turn intended to sell it for profit. Thus, when the elder Bassingbourne Gawdy became sheriff in 1578, he agreed to appoint the Earl of Leicester's nominee, Thomas Wingfield, on condition that he merely took 'the benefit that might arise by the gift of that office' and found a 'skilfuller man to exercise it'. Gawdy appears to have been uninterested in who did the job so long as it was done without cost and trouble to him. Similarly, when he was in the 'Bill' for sheriff in 1575 he promised the office to John Brett of Scarning, but there is no hint in either Brett's letter seeking appointment or in the voluminous Gawdy correspondence that they were closely acquainted.[34]

[32] *HMC Gawdy*, pp. 9, 15, 36, 46, 79. BM MSS. Add. 36989, f. 9; 36540, f. 1. Bodl. MS. Tanner 241, ff. 6–6v. NNRO MS. NAS Safe II.28, ff. 6–6v.

[33] J. Wilkinson, *Treatise . . . concerning the office . . . of Coroners & Sherifes*, 1618, ff. 8v–9.

[34] BM MS. Add. 27447, f. 110. Bodl. MS. Tanner 241, f. 3. NNRO MS. NAS C3/1/9, John Brett to Bass. Gawdy, 15 Nov. 1576.

This attitude is in marked contrast to that shown in the 1590s when sheriffs usually appointed one of their servants or even a close relative as their deputy. In 1589 Sir Robert Southwell appointed the notorious John Ferrour, an attorney retained in his service if not a household official. Thomas Clere ensured his control and direction by making his young son under-sheriff and employing the experienced William Terould to transact the business. In 1599 Nathaniel Bacon appointed Richard Spratt who lived nearby and was already his under-steward for Duchy of Lancaster lands in Norfolk. Richard Jenkinson brought in his brother in 1600, despite a strong plea from the Lord Keeper on behalf of Miles Basspole; while in 1601 Bassingbourne Gawdy promoted his faithful clerk, Robert Bolton.[35]

Besides ensuring that his staff was deployed to the best advantage of his faction, a sheriff in late-sixteenth-century Norfolk had many opportunities personally to influence events. Although debarred from taking his place on the Bench, he remained a dominating figure in local administration since he was invariably named in that unending stream of conciliar letters which authorized special enquiries and demanded *ad hoc* administrative decisions. Moreover these letters went first to the sheriff's office where he had the power to delay or expedite their lordships' commands. As has already been shown, Bassingbourne Gawdy attempted to influence the decision about a grant to repair Terrington's sea-banks by withholding a council letter which arrived during quarter sessions and subsequently convening a special meeting which few justices could attend. In this respect the sheriff was no more a servant of local magistrates than the present-day clerk to a county council is in reality a servant of his council. By subtle means he could control and direct, if he so minded.

The shrievalty could also be significant by virtue of the special relationship it afforded with the assize judges. Through their biannual visits they established an important link between local and central administration and their recommendations to the Lord Chancellor provided one of the principal means of appointment to the Bench. What information they carried back to the Chancellor and Council will never be known, but it is interesting that despite

[35] BM MSS. Egerton 2713, f. 353; Add. 23007, f. 11. PRO E 123/16, f. 179v; St. Ch. 5, W 21/30, H 6/22 (bill). *PRO, Deputy Keeper's Report*, xxxviii, 1887, p. 424. FSL MSS. Bacon–Townshend L.d. 87, 636. *HMC Gawdy*, *passim.*

complaints in parliament about the great expense incurred by sheriffs in their entertainment of the judges—complaints which the Council met in 1573 by granting judges an allowance for board and forbidding all feasting at assizes—Norfolk sheriffs continued to incur 'extraordinary expenses' through the provision of banquets for judges, justices, and the grand jury. The Council, no doubt with justification, accused them of doing this 'some for ostentacon and some others to make themselves stronge amongst the freeholders to sway causes at there will in the countrey to the overthrowe of justice'.[36]

A sheriff's influence was never greater than at an election of knights of the shire. These elections took place at the county court where the sheriff presided, and where, as Professor Neale has shown, he had infinite scope for influence and, in the event of a contested election, even downright corruption. A partisan sheriff might conceal the writ and so delay the election for a month, hoping that opposition freeholders, who had journeyed to the court in vain, would be less willing to return when he executed the writ on the next 'county' day. Another well-known stratagem was to switch the court's venue without informing the opposing candidates' supporters; while they waited at the traditional meeting-place, the sheriff would hurriedly conduct the election elsewhere. He might even try to influence the election by holding it in a town conveniently situated for those freeholders who supported one pair of candidates but necessitating a tedious journey for the others. No doubt Nathaniel Bacon had this in mind in 1603, when, campaigning against three other candidates for the first county seat, he tried to persuade the sheriff to hold the election at East Dereham instead of Norwich. At these elections the freeholders voted by 'voice' or acclamation; it was the sheriff's duty to adjudge the county's will and declare elected the appropriate candidates. This allowed him wide discretion, but if the 'voices' seemed too well balanced, the defeated candidates could demand a poll, in which case he could resort to further stratagems to secure their defeat.[37]

The sheriff's position in local government had undeniably been weakened by the growing authority of J.P.s and the emergence of the lieutenancy, but it should not be assumed that the shrievalty was

[36] CUL MS. Buxton, Box 96, Common Form Book of Edward Honinge, f. 39v. BM MSS. Add. 32323, ff. 125v–126v; 23007, f. 4; Egerton 3048, ff. 63v–64. PRO SP 12/106/18.

[37] Below, p. 330. Neale, *Commons*, ch. III.

merely burdensome and unwanted. Onerous it may have been, but whether men tried to avoid it or campaigned to be appointed was related closely to the political and social state of the county. Just how closely will become clear after the politics of Norfolk have been described in part III below.

PART III

NORFOLK POLITICS 1572–1603

CHAPTER VIII

Introductory: Dramatis Personae

THE character of Norfolk politics changed dramatically with the death of the Duke of Norfolk in 1572. The relative quiet and orderly existence imposed by his pre-eminence were quickly replaced by acute rivalry amongst the principal gentry for social and political leadership. This alone would not be difficult to depict, but in the light of the foregoing analysis it is pertinent to enquire how far the fluid state of the commission of the peace and the intricacies surrounding the choice and appointment of justices exacerbated this situation by providing rival gentry with opportunities to indulge their quarrelsome propensities. It is even more important to watch the development of divergent views about the purpose and methods of local administration, since such disagreement served not only to exacerbate already strained relationships between rival gentry but also eventually to create a fundamental division which was of far greater political import than the unstable situation caused by the death of the Duke of Norfolk. Clearly the story of Norfolk's politics after the Duke's demise is a complicated one which is best approached by introducing its principal characters. Basically they fall into two loose groupings—one led by Sir Arthur Heveningham, the other by Nathaniel Bacon.

Arthur Heveningham came of an old-established East Anglian family which since the thirteenth century had been seated at Heveningham in Suffolk and for much of the Tudor period was prominent in that county's local affairs. Late in the fifteenth century Thomas Heveningham had inherited the Norfolk manor of Ketteringham which soon became the principal family seat. No Heveningham figured in Norfolk affairs, however, until 1574 when Sir Arthur succeeded his half-brother Henry, and immediately shifted the focus of his political and administrative activities from Suffolk into Norfolk. By 1579 he had been appointed to the Norfolk Bench; in 1581 he was chosen as sheriff and in 1588 he became a deputy lieutenant in the county. He also held similar positions in Suffolk, but the manner in which he tried to dominate Norfolk administration testifies to his determination to fill the vacuum in Norfolk society created by the Duke's death. As his neighbour Edward Flowerdew subsequently explained, he 'hath . . . challenged more superioritie, aucthoritie and jurisdicion over other men and their lyvings than the best nobleman that hath lyved in that countrey hath done'.[1]

He produced a pedigree to match his aspirations. Respectable though his ancestry appears to have been, he claimed descent 'from Arphaxad who was one of the knights that watched Christes Sepulchre'. From Walter Heveningham, Lord of Heveningham who 'lived in *anno* 19 of Canut King of England, 1020', the line ran by direct male descent to Sir Arthur. It included such illustrious forebears as Sir William who 'was with King Richard I at the seige of Acon' and who 'in sight of the King in single combatt' slew 'Sapher, Captain of the castell of Acon'.[2]

By 1597 he headed the Norfolk section in Burghley's list of 'principall gentlemen that dwell usually in their contreis'. He must have earned this position by virtue of his dominant role in administrative affairs since in economic terms he was only in the middle rank of East Anglian landowners. For what it is worth, his subsidy assessment during Elizabeth's reign never rose above £30; his principal estates were confined to the vicinities of Ketteringham and Heveningham, and he had no other residences either in East Anglia or London, as did several of his fellow Norfolk gentry; indeed there are even some hints that he was in economic difficulties by the 1590s.[3]

Heveningham was flamboyant, impetuous, and hot-tempered, preferring to duel with weapons rather than words. On one occasion when he clashed with his neighbour, Edward Flowerdew, in debate at the quarter sessions, he openly boasted that 'he would huntt course or drive him out of his countrey'. His overbearing personality could brook no opposition; characteristically, when the corporation of King's Lynn refused to hand over to his collectors a rate which he was levying under royal warrant, he personally rode over to the town,

[1] W. A. Copinger, *The Manors of Suffolk*, ii, Manchester, 1908, pp. 93–4; *NA* iii, 1852, pp. 281–8. Appendix I. *APC, 1587–8*, p. 385. PRO St. Ch. 5, H 18/2 (Flowerdew's answer).

[2] BM MS. Harl. 4031, f. 239.

[3] PRO SP 12/269/46, f. 2. Bodl. MS. Tanner 241, f. 32v. NNRO MS. NAS C3/1/9, subsidy assessment for 1588. In 1591 he was pawning jewels in London (NNRO MS. Aylsham 10). He also sold outlying estates in Norf. (Blomefield, *infra*). BM MS. Eg. 2804, f. 134.

I. Sir Arthur Heveningham

confronted the assembled aldermen, and returned with the money.[4]

Norfolk society did not readily assimilate such a personality. Although many of Sir Arthur's ancestors, including his father and grandfather, had married into Norfolk families, he married the daughter of a Hertfordshire squire. This, in itself, may not be significant, but the marriage pattern of his twelve children strongly suggests his ostracism from Norfolk gentry society. Only his eldest son John Heveningham married into this society and he not until his second marriage in 1601 when he was espoused to Bridget, daughter of Sir William Paston. All his other children appear to have married into families outside the county with the exception of Abigail, one of his youngest daughters, who in 1608 married Augustine Pettus, member of a Norwich aldermanic family.[5]

Sir Arthur Heveningham's complete indifference to the views and feelings of his neighbours made him a willing agent of Crown and Council. For over thirty years he figured on nearly every Norfolk commission and executive body; indeed councillors so valued his participation that occasionally they insisted on his presence before a meeting of commissioners could be quorate. His ruthlessness is indicated by the way in which he rebuilt the steeple of Ketteringham church after it had been destroyed in a storm in 1608. For his contribution he provided the timber and bricks as well as food and drink for the carpenters and masons; but the money for wages etc. he raised by a compulsory levy among his household servants, the parishioners of Ketteringham, and his friends and relations. This he augmented with substantial sums from the county treasury—contributions which were no doubt voted at quarter sessions in response to his forceful demands. A feature of this fund-raising operation was his particular brand of blackmail. First, he arranged to record the names of all contributors in a special volume of the 'Town Books'—a gesture which many of his fellow magnates might have made, but he then rounded off this roll of honour with a further list of names headed 'all these did give noe monye and the most parte of them did nothinge ells about this good worke as all the rest of the townes men doe well know'.[6] 'Nothing by halves' might have been his motto, as successive chapters will show.

4 PRO St. Ch. 5, F 14/17 (Bill). Below, p. 261.

5 NNRO MS. PD 42/9. *NA* iii. 284.

6 BM MS. Add. 27447, f. 139. NNRO MS. PD 42/11 and 13. I am indebted to Mrs. E. Rutledge for bringing this MS. to my attention.

Heveningham found a kindred spirit in Sir Edward Clere of Ormesby and Blickling who frequently supported him in his unpopular and high-handed administrative activities. Clere, too, came of an old-established family which, according to the heraldic devices on his tomb in Blickling church, traced its ancestry back to one of William I's knights. Be that as it may, the Cleres had long resided at Ormesby and played a prominent part in county government. Sir Edward's father had inherited nearly twenty manors in Norfolk and had purchased the reversion of three more, including Blickling, as well as receiving grants of monastic land for military service to Henry VIII. To this substantial holding the young Edward Clere added the extensive Fulmerston lands through his marriage to Frances, daughter and heiress of Sir Richard Fulmerston who died in 1567. Thereafter, with estates scattered across the county and residences at Blickling, Norwich, Thetford, Ormesby, and London, as a property owner he stood second only to the Duke of Norfolk. This was reflected in the subsidy book where, for a time, he was rated at £120; even his regular rating of £100 substantially exceeded that of any other Norfolk gentleman. Since he was also second cousin to the Queen and to Lord Hunsdon, it is not surprising that in 1588 Burghley included his name in a list of prospective barons describing him as a 'knight of great possessions'; but he was 'not to be called therto without some precedent service to deserve the same'. In the event he was not 'called', and a closer look at his affairs may help to explain why.[7]

Despite his wealth in land he lacked an income sufficient to sustain the dignity of a baron. Such of his letters and papers as have survived show him hopelessly caught up in the minutiae of estate management, frequently in debt and having to borrow money, often involved in litigation and usually seeking the help of his friends to influence its processes. In 1577 he asked Bassingbourne Gawdy to lend him £40; in 1582 his payments for his son's rooms at Cambridge were so badly in arrears that the college tutor asked Gawdy to remonstrate with him since 'this dealing is not meet for a man of his worship'; in 1588 he was anxious to lease out a manor in order to pay off some of his debts; in 1591 he complained that he was 'desti-

[7] R. J. W. Swales, 'Local Politics and the Parliamentary Representation of Sussex 1529–1558' (Bristol PhD thesis 1964), p. 95. PCC 33 Stonarde. BM MS. Add. 27960, ff. 3, 6, 27. PRO SP 12/144/41. BM MSS. Lansd. 32, f. 84; 59, f. 145; 104, f. 52. NNRO MS. NAS C3/1/9, subsidy assessment for 1588.

tute of sheepe cattle to store [his] shepes pastures, and of monye to buye till upon [his] next audit tyme or by some sale [he] may be relievid'. By 1594 he was in the Fleet prison, presumably for debt.[8]

His failure to match income and expenditure was probably caused by profligacy—a trait which can be detected in each generation of Cleres throughout the sixteenth century. His father Sir John Clere had this reputation; so, too, did his eldest son Edward, who in 1585 was 'in peril divers ways of imprisonment & shame'. Sir Edward seems to have had doubts about his eldest son's ability to settle down to the tedium of estate management since he left a great deal of his property to his second son Robert; a gentleman 'of admirable temperance . . ., one given to no kind of sports or play, mostly keeping his chamber, . . . very studious . . . and of a tender conscience', commented the rector of Blickling, no doubt contrasting him with his elder brother.[9]

Sir Edward must have been a grasping and unpleasant neighbour. Betwen 1570 and 1575 he quarrelled so violently and so frequently with his tenants that the Council repeatedly called him to account; apparently to no avail since as late as 1579 their lordships were still asking Sir William Butts, Sir Christopher Heydon, and Francis Wyndham to mediate in these controversies. His relations with the townsmen of Thetford were little better, and he conducted a spiteful vendetta against Roger Wyndham of Felbrigg. There are hints of a long-standing feud between the Clere and Wyndham families; if this be so Sir Edward certainly did his best to keep it going. In 1570 he described Roger Wyndham as 'the heire of Sir Edmond Windham . . . not . . . delightinge the company of eny equal or his better'. In 1587 he contrived to get him indicted for felony, while a year later he gave the Council such a hostile version of Wyndham's proceedings in salvaging the cargo of a Scottish vessel wrecked at Runton that the latter described him as his 'mortal enemy'.[10]

He further antagonized his fellow gentry by his willingness to implement policies which ran counter to their interests. Apparently

[8] NNRO MSS. Willcocks (xerox) 29/12/71, Edw. Clere to Bass. Gawdy, 17 Apr. 1591 and 1604, and to Sir Wm. Paston, 26 June 1588. BM MS. Add. 27960, ff. 16, 36–8.

[9] Swales, op. cit., p. 95. *CSPD, 1603–10*, p. 307. *HMC Salisbury*, xvii. 581; xviii. 386–7. *Visit. of Norf.* ii. 279.

[10] *APC, 1571–5*, pp. 99, 141; *1575–7*, pp. 50, 52, 55; *1587–8*, p. 322. NNRO MS. NRS 8528 (21 B 5). H. A. Wyndham, *A Family History 1410–1688*, Oxford, 1939, p. 91. PRO SP 12/67, f. 142; /222/82; /120/15; St. Ch. 5, W 26/23 (Bill).

he alone among Norfolk sheriffs attempted to levy a voluntary contribution from the county towards the repair of Hastings harbour in accordance with the terms of a patent granted to Viscount Montague and Lords Cobham and Buckhurst in 1578. As collector of the loan in 1569–70 he had no qualms about providing the Council with information on his neighbours' wealth which controverted the evidence they presented to justify their claims to exemption. No doubt the more he collected the greater his commission; but accusations were also made that he took 'sondrye somes of money of divers persons under the pretence of privey seales and converted the same to his own use'. Then in 1595, in his capacity as a deputy lieutenant, he was accused by Edward Coke of receiving bribes from men anxious to avoid impressment for service overseas.[11]

If Clere was prepared to undertake many administrative tasks (usually involving the collection of money) which his fellows would have preferred left undone, he, in turn, left undone many things which in their view ought to have been done. In this way he alienated Puritan justices like Nathaniel Bacon and Francis Wyndham who were particularly concerned about the community's moral and social well-being. By the end of 1583 Stephen Drury, a servant of Francis Wyndham who lived at Aylsham, was complaining bitterly to Bacon about Clere's indifference, if not positive hostility, to their endeavours to reform disorderly alehouses and other social evils. Drury ended a long indictment of Clere by remarking that, if the constables 'find not better assistance ellswhere, they will be more slow to execute the justices comandements'.[12]

Clere's unpopularity among his fellow gentry may help to explain his failure to secure that pre-eminence in county government appropriate to his social and economic status. Although he had been appointed to the Bench in 1559–60 when only twenty-three or twenty-four years old, he was dismissed shortly afterwards and did not regain his place until 1583 when he was nearly fifty. His parliamentary career was equally disappointing. When he stood as knight of the shire for Norfolk in 1572 he was decisively rebuffed; in 1586 he claimed that only ill-health prevented him from standing again,

[11] NNRO MS. Willcocks (xerox) 29/12/71, Edw. Clere to various gents. and chief constables, 22 June 1581. PRO SP 12/67, ff. 112–13; /68, ff. 24, 42; /69, f. 71; /71/12. BM MSS. Lansd. 14, ff. 151–4; Add. 27960, ff. 3–6, 30; 32325, ff. 127v–128. PRO St. Ch. 5, A 13/31, 32/39.

[12] FSL MS. Bacon–Townshend L.d. 275.

but in fact he never achieved the distinction of representing his county in parliament. Indeed, apart from his election at Thetford in 1558 and 1563 at the behest of his father-in-law and the Duke of Norfolk, no Norfolk constituency ever elected him.[13] He gained prestige in 1585 when he was appointed to the influential office of deputy lieutenant, but his nomination was almost certainly at the instigation of Lord Lieutenant Hunsdon, his relative and an outsider to the county. Indeed Hunsdon may have chosen him precisely because of his indifference towards his neighbours and his readiness to implement Council policy.[14]

The Heydons also aligned themselves with Sir Arthur Heveningham, although they were too unstable to remain for long identified with any county group. Three generations of this family—Sir Christopher (senior), Sir William and Sir Christopher (junior)—spanned the Elizabethan period and all figured prominently in the Norfolk political scene.[15] The family fortunes had been founded in the fifteenth century by two lawyers—John (d. 1479) and his son Henry (d. 1504). Between them they amassed sufficient wealth to build the great fortified 'pile' at Baconsthorpe. John, who had been a Lancastrian supporter, secured a clutch of lucrative offices during the Duke of Suffolk's ascendancy. His son Henry established the family in the front rank of county society: he was knighted at the coronation of Henry VII, regularly figured in the Norfolk commission of the peace, and was elected knight of the shire in 1489.

The Heydons continued to grow in wealth and power in the early sixteenth century, reaching their peak of ascendancy during the first decade of Elizabeth's reign, when, in the absence of the Duke of Norfolk in 1560, Sir Christopher Heydon (sen.) was appointed joint lord lieutenant with Sir Edmund Wyndham. Ten years later, when lieutenants of counties were again appointed, Sir Christopher served with Sir William Butts as deputy to Lord Wentworth. He had been appointed a J.P. in Norfolk before he was thirty and kept

[13] Appendix I. Above, p. 37. Below, pp. 316, 321.

[14] BM MS. Harl. 474, f. 69. *NRS* xx, 1949, p. 18.

[15] This sketch of the Heydons draws heavily upon a study of the family by Sister Barbara Batten. A copy of this is available in the Colman and Rye Libraries of Local History, Norwich. The interpretation is mine.

his place on the Bench until he died in 1579, becoming *custos rotulorum* in 1564. He was also elected knight of the shire in 1545 and 1571, and was twice pricked sheriff of Norfolk and Suffolk. His port matched his power: his household numbered eighty servants, he entertained lavishly, and ostentatiously built the great gatehouse and forecourt at Baconsthorpe.[16]

Both port and power depended upon a sound economic base; unfortunately there are signs that throughout Elizabeth's reign the Heydons lived beyond their means. Sir Christopher (sen.) apparently bequeathed a debt of £2,400 to his eldest son William who was already £3,500 overspent; to meet his liabilities William had to sell stock and household effects as well as lands worth over £100 annually. Unheeding, he continued to live extravagantly and, despite the sale of further lands valued at £300 per annum, he died in 1594 in debt to the tune of £11,000. His encumbered estates passed to Christopher Heydon (jun.) who had already incurred liabilities of over £3,000 but who continued to spend lavishly—witness the immense monument he erected in Saxlingham church in memory of his first wife. Since his interests lay in astrology rather than estate management, the tottering economy quickly collapsed: in 1600 he mortgaged the ancestral home at Baconsthorpe and fourteen years later it was sold to meet his debts. Financial ruin inevitably brought declining prestige in its wake; people began 'to shun' Sir Christopher Heydon, who never held the shrievalty and figured in the commission of the peace for only two brief periods totalling no more than eight years.[17]

The problem of matching expenditure to income confronted all established gentry families in the period 1540–1640. Like the Heydons, many failed to find a solution and suffered economic decline, but few can have crashed in such a spectacular manner as this family. It may well be that its plight was aggravated by a streak of instability which is apparent in all three generations.

Sir Christopher Heydon (sen.) appears to have been a trimmer since he evinced no qualms about successively implementing the religious policies of Edward, Mary and Elizabeth. In fact, however, the chronology of his shifts in religion is not that of a mere politique, intent upon retaining office and power; rather it also reveals a weak-

[16] Appendix I. BM MS. Add. 27447, f. 104. PRO SP 12/59/57. S. E. Rigold, *Baconsthorpe Castle*, HMSO, 1966, p. 7. *CPR, 1560–3*, p. 219.

[17] BM MSS. Lansd. 67, f. 5; Harl. 6853, f. 185. *NA* xxxiv, 1969, p. 85.

willed man dominated by his wife. At Mary's accession he supported the claims of Lady Jane Grey and it was not until 1554 that he emerged as an active Marian supporter. Under Elizabeth he not only conformed sufficiently to maintain his position in county government, but rapidly emerged as a Protestant zealot who for a decade or more schemed to get Puritans promoted to the Bench. These activities coincided with his second marriage to Temperance Carey, a lady of radical religious views. Then, when she died in 1577, he quickly shifted tack again and associated himself with Bishop Freake and a Recusant faction which was endeavouring to defeat and suppress Puritanism in the diocese.[18]

His son William seems to have been equally fickle in religion. As a young man he displayed excessive Puritan zeal, but by the early 1580s he had dissociated himself from his fellow Puritans and joined with gentry like Heveningham and Clere in their efforts to exploit county administration for profit and power. He was also irascible. When, for instance, Parkhurst refused to appoint his nominee to a benefice he flew into a rage and then just as suddenly regretted his behaviour: 'whatsoever bitter wordes have passed betwene us', he wrote to the Bishop, 'I for my parte do acknowledg myne own ymbecilitie: and desire your lordship of perdon hearin, if I have offended'. It is perhaps further commentary upon the instability of his generation that his brother had to be provided for as an '*ideotus*'.[19]

Sir William Heydon's[20] relations with his eldest son Christopher provide further evidence of his temperamental nature. Trouble arose between them in 1590 when Sir William attempted to meet his debts by selling more property. Christopher, already in debt himself, claimed that this property had been entailed on him by his grandfather, and took legal action to prevent this complete dissipation of his inheritance. Thwarted in this manner, Sir William Heydon resolved to realize such assets as he could by felling the timber in the great park at Baconsthorpe and pulling down the magnificent fortified house which symbolized Heydon pre-eminence in north Norfolk. Clearly this was intended as a vindictive act rather than as a serious solution to his financial difficulties. Although his son raised £800 'by the meanes of his friendes' to purchase the timber from his

[18] Below, p. 222.

[19] FSL MS. Bacon-Townshend L.d.52. Collinson, pp. 192, 203, 257. CUL MS. Ee. II 34, f. 122v. Below, pp. 236–40.

[20] Knighted 1583.

father, Sir William still threatened to demolish the house. This family quarrel became so bitter that several county magnates became involved and even the Privy Council intervened in order to prevent Sir William entering 'into an action so hurtfull to himself & his posteritie'.[21]

Although Christopher Heydon managed to save his ancestral home from destruction at the hands of his vindictive father, he too lacked that moderation and restraint which might have stabilized the family's economy. Instability in his generation manifested itself in a propensity for duelling and an escapist interest in astrology which increased in step with his economic plight.[22]

Thomas Lovell of East Harling, near Thetford, a squire struggling to maintain his family's pre-eminence in south-west Norfolk, was also drawn into Heveningham's clientage network, if not into close political association with him. The Lovells had been established at Harling in the late fifteenth century by Sir Thomas Lovell, friend and adviser to Henry VII. Speaker of the Commons, Chancellor of the Exchequer, Treasurer of the Household and Constable of the Tower under that monarch, he had purchased the manor of East Harling where he built a mansion commensurate with his status at Court. He died in 1524 and was succeeded by his nephew, Sir Francis Lovell, who consolidated the family's prestige in the county by acquiring extensive monastic property, becoming a regular member of the commission of the peace, being pricked three times as sheriff of Norfolk, and marrying his eldest son Thomas to the daughter of Arthur Viscount Lisle. This Thomas, rich with 'goodly possessions of great proffytt', became one of the foremost Marian justices in Norfolk, being knighted by the Queen at her coronation.[23]

Thereafter, however, his undoubted Catholic sympathies, together with the suspicion that his son held similar views, led to the family's

[21] *APC, 1591–2*, p. 116; *1592–3*, pp. 371–2. FSL MS. Bacon–Townshend L.d.69.

[22] Below, pp. 302–4.

[23] *NA* xviii, 1914, pp. 46–59. *CPR, 1485–94*, p. 494; *1494–1509*, p. 651; *1547–8*, p. 87; *1553–4*, p. 22. *L & P H VIII*, i(2), p. 1541; ii(1), pp. 69, 303; v. 78; xiii(1), p. 567; xvi. 143; xvii. 216. PRO C 192/12. *DNB*, s.v. Lovell, Thomas. G. R. Elton, *The Tudor Revolution in Government*, Cambridge, 1962, pp. 27–9, 34, 63. PRO SP 12/67, f. 142v. Bodl. MS. Tanner 241, f. 32v.

political eclipse. Sir Thomas Lovell was omitted from Elizabeth's first commission of the peace for Norfolk and, although he regained his place in 1561 he was dismissed again in 1564. His son, also named Thomas and the subject of subsequent chapters, had to wait until 1585 before gaining a place on the Bench, and thereafter managed to hold it only intermittently. If office in county government be regarded as an index of local status, the Lovells' position had slumped: their name appeared in the Norfolk commission of the peace for only eleven out of the forty-four years during which Elizabeth ruled, whereas in the first half of the century at least one Lovell, and sometimes two, had figured in almost every commission. A glance at the lists of sheriffs and M.P.s reveals a similar eclipse: indeed under Elizabeth no Lovell appears in either.[24]

Thomas Lovell, as will be shown, strove to restore his family's tarnished prestige. He intrigued with some success at Court; he even tried, less successfully, to conform to the Anglican settlement; he quarrelled with those among his neighbours who were granted the offices denied to him, and in the course of these quarrels he was drawn into close association with Sir Arthur Heveningham.[25]

Opposition to the views and activities of Heveningham, Clere, and the Heydons was organized by Nathaniel Bacon and his brother Nicholas. In contrast to their opponents they were 'new men'; indeed few families can have climbed more rapidly into the front ranks of the nation's political, intellectual, and administrative classes than the Bacons. Their father Nicholas Bacon was the son of Robert Bacon, a yeoman of Hessett, near Bury St. Edmunds; Nicholas had risen rapidly in the law and service to the Crown, finally being appointed Lord Keeper and a privy councillor in 1558 when he also received a knighthood. He married twice; by his first wife Jane, daughter of William Fernley a Suffolk merchant, he had three sons—Nicholas, Nathaniel, and Edward; by his second wife Ann, the cultured daughter of Sir Anthony Cooke, he had two more sons—Anthony

[24] Appendix I. 'A collection of original letters from the Bishops to the Privy Council, 1564', ed. Mary Bateson, p. 58, *Camden Miscellany IX* (Camden Soc. N.S. liii), 1895. *APC, 1577–8*, p. 333; *1586–7*, p. 202. BM MSS. Cotton, Titus B.III, no. 66; Lansd. 52, f. 200v–201. PRO SP 12/117/27i; /142, no. 43; /208, no. 16i. *HMC Salisbury*, ii. 194.

[25] *APC, 1586–7*, p. 202. Below, pp. 184–5, 187, 190.

and Francis. True to his motto 'mediocria firma' Sir Nicholas established his three elder sons as substantial county gentry, providing them with estates in Norfolk and Suffolk. Thereafter, as if by intent, they made these counties the focus of their political and social activities. By contrast, Anthony and Francis, children of a brilliant mother, and both minors when their father died in 1579, became leading figures of courtly and intellectual life, Francis becoming Lord Chancellor under James I and a philosopher of European renown.[26]

Nicholas, the Lord Keeper's eldest son, married Anne daughter of Edmund Butts—a marriage which eventually brought him extensive estates in Norfolk and Suffolk. Meanwhile his father had entailed upon him the manor of Redgrave and installed him in the mansion which he had recently completed there. Here, under his father's critical eye, the young Nicholas received a practical training in estate management and business methods which must have contrasted markedly with his formal legal studies at Cambridge and Gray's Inn. Lloyd in his *State Worthies* attributes to the Lord Keeper the maxim 'Let us stay a little that we may have done the sooner'. He undoubtedly had an incredible capacity for hard work and prompt attention to detail; qualities which he instilled into Nicholas (and later Nathaniel) through a spate of letters, remarkable for their precision and plain speaking. 'As touching the warraunt you writt of for money', he wrote in August 1570, 'I meane to grante no such warraunt untill I be advertised from you howe the same shalbe employed, which may easely be done bycause the bargaynes be made of great [*sic*]'. In June 1578 he acknowledged receipt of £100, but pointed out that it is 'wantinge 40/– by reason the Angells were light & sowdered [?] which you are to remember to send up'.[27]

Nicholas Bacon became one of the principal magistrates in Suffolk where he led a dynamic group of radical Protestant justices in opposition to patentees and licensees in general and to Sir Arthur Heveningham in particular. But since Redgrave abutted on the Norfolk border he also figured in the Norfolk commission of the

[26] A. Simpson, *The Wealth of the Gentry 1540–1660*, Cambridge, 1961, pp. 22–115. *Procs. SIA* xxv, 1952, pp. 158–63; xxix, 1964, pp. 1–31.

[27] *Procs. SIA* xxix, 1964, p. 29. NNRO MS. Bradfer-Lawrence VII (b) 1, bundle marked '50 Bacon letters', letter dated 23 June 1578. The letters of the Lord Keeper to his son Nicholas have been edited by E. R. Sandeen in 'The Correspondence of Nicholas Bacon, Lord Keeper' (Chicago MA thesis 1955). A large number of his letters addressed to Nathaniel Bacon are scattered among the Bacon MSS. in the NNRO.

peace, occasionally attending the sessions at Norwich. Generally, however, his brother Nathaniel Bacon led the opposition there, so that in effect each brother had his sphere of influence, although there is abundant evidence that they worked in close association and shared a common outlook towards the affairs of the two counties.

During the late 1560s the Lord Keeper made several attempts to marry Nathaniel into middling Suffolk gentry families, but the young man went his own way and in 1569 married Anne, the natural daughter of Sir Thomas Gresham, the Elizabethan financier. Sir Thomas settled the north-Norfolk manors of Langham, Morston, and Hemsby upon the young couple, while in the following year Sir Nicholas purchased for them the adjacent manor of Stiffkey where he built the magnificent mansion which for many years provided a focus in Norfolk for the opposition to Heveningham's faction.[28]

Nathaniel inherited his father's meticulousness and capacity for sustained effort. Although he remained a county figure, never aspiring to office in central government or a position at Court, he maintained wide intellectual and cultural interests. Educated with his brother Nicholas at Cambridge and Gray's Inn, he amassed an extensive library of printed and manuscript books which had a strong legal bias; his walls were hung with maps and tapestries; a pair of virginals stood in his parlour.[29] His legal ability quickly brought him to the fore as the principal draftsman of a voluminous series of letters from the Norfolk justices to the Privy Council in which government policy was frequently challenged.[30] He was a well-known figure at Court where one of his daughters became a gentlewoman of the Queen's chamber. Usually, as soon as New Year festivities had ended at Stiffkey and Epiphany sessions had closed, he moved his household to London, returning to Stiffkey only with the onset of spring.[31]

His religious views were radical. There is abundant evidence that

[28] Sandeen, op. cit., pp. 83, 92. Simpson, op. cit., pp. 49–50, 96. *CPR, 1569–72*, p. 136.

[29] *CSPD Add. 1580–1625*, p. 544. *NA* xxiii, 1929, pp. 321–334.

[30] Draft copies of these letters, in the distinctive hand of Bacon's clerk Martin Mann, and frequently emended in Bacon's hand, appear in nearly every collection of late-sixteenth- and early-seventeenth-century Norfolk MSS. They are also scattered throughout the Bacon MSS. in the Norf. & Norwich Record Office and the Folger Shakespear Library.

[31] Jeayes, p. 104. NNRO MS. Bradfer-Lawrence VII b(5), Household Accounts 1592–6.

from his first days in Norfolk he consistently supported the Puritan cause, using his patronage to appoint Puritan ministers to livings in the county and frequently persuading other gentry to do the same. In 1574 he presented John Percival to Stiffkey, with the result that for the next two decades puritan 'prophesyings' flourished in the neighbourhood. Although some of his fellow Puritans like Sir William Heydon wavered in their enthusiasm for the movement, his zeal never flagged. In 1576 he invited John More, the great Norwich puritan preacher, to continue his ministry from Stiffkey after he had been suspended by Bishop Freake, and in 1583 he was one of five Norfolk gentlemen who signed a petition on behalf of their Puritan ministers threatened with suspension for refusing to subscribe to Whitgift's articles.[32]

Nathaniel must have been a strait-laced figure who may well have been more respected than liked. He was austere to the point of meanness: witness his disapproval of his second wife's expenditure on jewels and the diminutive monument which he personally commissioned and which still stands in Stiffkey church. His hospitality was modest in style and limited in scale, generally being confined to a small circle of friends and relations. Home-grown fare provided the bulk of the diet with sweetmeats and imported foodstuffs figuring only occasionally in the kitchen accounts. Feasting was rare, even the Christmas menu being indistinguishable from that provided on ordinary occasions; there were celebrations at the New Year but, to judge from the provisions laid in, they were community occasions for servants and tenants rather than for his social equals.[33]

On the whole Bacon seems to have been more concerned with the well-being of his local community than with self-indulgence. His household was provisioned by small purchases made from a large group of servants and tenants rather than by bulk buying in the local markets. Similarly the Stiffkey wool clip—166 stone in 1625—was sold off in small lots to local clothworkers rather than to middlemen dealers. In his will he was extremely generous to his household staff, but while he lived they were probably less enamoured with his ob-

[32] Collinson, *passim.* Raynham Hall MS. photostats *penes* T. S. Blakeney, vol. 27, no. 19. BM MSS. Add. 41655, ff. 23–4; 41140, ff. 2, 9. Collinson, 'Classical Movement', pp. 201–7, 316–17, 880–1. *Stiffkey Papers*, p. 190. NNRO MS. Millican 8/9/70 (xerox), misc. bundle, paper headed: 'Thexercise at Wyveton for thies monethes following. 1585.' Below, p. 237. *The Seconde Parte of a Register*, ed. A. Peel, 1915, i. 225.

[33] *CSPD Add. 1580–1625*, p. 544. NNRO MSS. 20384 (126 X 6); Bradfer-Lawrence VII b(5), Household Accounts 1592–6.

II Sir Nathaniel Bacon

sessive concern for their moral well-being.[34] His muniment room was piled with meticulously recorded depositions relating to all types of moral offences throughout north Norfolk as well as a great number of records relating to the licensing and putting down of ale-houses.

His strictures fell with equal severity upon his social equals and upon friend and foe alike. He wrote sharply to Lady Heydon, wife of the lapsed Puritan Sir William Heydon, reproving her and her husband for harsh dealings towards their son who 'both doth and will beare a good harte towarde ye churche of God and the welfare of his countrey and therefore [is] so mutch the more to be estemed of by me and others. Thus wishing both you Madame & Sir William plentie of the grace of God for the better guiding you in these many trobles wherewith it hath pleased God to exercise you.'[35] When his brother-in-law Sir Robert Mansell purchased the post of vice-admiral of Norfolk and Suffolk, no doubt hoping to make a handsome profit on his substantial outlay, Bacon tendered some unpalatable advice:

> Good brother suffer me a little to advise you. This place of the Vice Admiralty is a place of good creditt and countenance in the county if it be used right, and of small profit either to your self or your officers unless profitt do arise by extraordinary accidents. . . . Therefore . . . let those corrupt ones who will not be content with a lawful gayne be discharged, yea punished according to their deserts; and make not their faults your owne by defending of them, and you will hardly kepe them from corruption for they be nedie & will have their wants supplyed one way or other.[36]

On another occasion when Sir Arthur Heveningham asked him to sign a false muster certificate he commented scathingly: 'I cannot consider upon what iust ground this muster roll should now be sent up, seeing there was another (as I take it) sent up in the end of last somer, & if this be made more perfect by draught than that was, what have we done since to make it more perfect in action?'[37]

Such forthright speech without regard for person coupled with an immense reputation for integrity—his friends referred to him as 'honest Nathaniel Bacon'—meant that his services as a mediator

[34] Simpson, *The Wealth of the Gentry 1540–1660*, p. 194. *CSPD Add. 1580–1625*, p. 544. PCC 2 Swann.

[35] FSL MS. Bacon–Townshend L.d. 48.

[36] Draft letter from Nath. Bacon to Sir Robt. Mansell, 20 Mar. 1599/60, *penes* Mr. B. Cozens-Hardy.

[37] FSL MS. Bacon–Townshend L.d. 115.

were in great demand both by fellow gentry and the lords of the Council. His neighbours' esteem for his impartiality was demonstrated by John Hunt who, after ten years of inconclusive litigation against William Bulwer, persuaded the latter that they should submit their case to arbitration by two referees. Bulwer at once nominated Nathaniel Bacon, 'a knight in his opinion without exception'; so, too, did Hunt, 'at which Mr. Bulwer was so well pleased that presently off went our hats and on went our hands and hearts to a pacification which was the first time that ever we two shook either hands or hearts together'.[38]

His later years seem to have been clouded by tensions with his second wife and her family. After his first wife's death he had married Dorothy, daughter of Sir Arthur Hopton and widow of William Smith of Burgh Castle. The latter had bequeathed his estates to his two sons, making little provision for his widow. Unfortunately she had extravagant taste and badgered Nathaniel into heavy spending on jewels and finery. Pearls were her weakness. He bought her over 2,000 loose ones, not to mention several chains, the finest of which cost £190, or so Nathaniel's accounts recorded. Dorothy subsequently confided to his daughter that it cost more, 'for I must have lost it had I not geven more money sekretly'. Nathaniel probably knew more of her dealings than she thought, for he specified in his will that 'my wife's great pearl chain, which cost me £200, is to be sold for payment of debts, as also the border of diamonds & rubies; if she will give for the pearl and border what they cost me, she is to have them'. Lady Dorothy even made him an exile from Stiffkey since at her 'instanc and earnest request' he bought the manor of Irmingland and built a mansion there in which he frequently resided. Nathaniel, for his part, financed this building from the income of her sons who were his wards; this caused endless bad feeling and ultimately a great deal of litigation between the widow and his children. It is hardly surprising that Bacon sounded weary and broken in some of his letters written from Irmingland at the end of his life; but it is a weariness which strikes one only in contrast to the dynamic magistrate who, as will be shown, did so much to shape to his own ideal the course of Elizabethan government in Norfolk.[39]

[38] Jeayes, p. 65. FSL MS. Bacon–Townshend L.d. 365.

[39] NNRO MS. 20384 (126 X 6). *CSPD Add. 1580–1625*, p. 543. NNRO MSS. NAS Frere K.3(A), Irmingland bundle; 20522 (132 X 6); 20384 (126 X 6); 26629 (148 X 6).

It is perhaps surprising that nobody bothered to inscribe the date of his death on the monument which he had commissioned before he died. That he was so slightly honoured in his parish church must surely be because he had no male heir, his only son Nicholas having died in infancy. Nathaniel bequeathed his property to his three daughters, leaving Stiffkey and much of the estate to Anne, his eldest daughter. After her husband Sir John Townshend had died in 1603, she and her son Roger had returned to Stiffkey and Nathaniel had come to regard his grandson as the future ruler of the godly community he had fostered there. This hope faded in 1619 when Roger began to build his new mansion at Raynham; thereafter Nathaniel knew that not only would the Stiffkey Bacons founder in one generation, but so too, for lack of a resident magistrate, would his godly commonweal.[40]

On most issues Nathaniel Bacon found himself in alliance with Sir Thomas Knyvett of Ashwellthorpe. Knyvett and his wife frequently stayed at Stiffkey and eventually their eldest son Thomas married Bacon's second daughter Elizabeth—a match which clearly delighted the austere squire of Stiffkey since he celebrated it with a gargantuan feast. Sir Thomas Knyvett was the head of a cadet branch of the Knyvetts of Buckenham Castle, a family with a long and distinguished history. The Ashwellthorpe branch stemmed from Edmund Knyvett, serjeant porter to Henry VIII, who in 1501 married Jane, daughter and heiress of John Bourchier, 2nd Baron Berners, and through her inherited Ashwellthorpe together with many other properties in Norfolk, Suffolk, Lincolnshire, Yorkshire, and Staffordshire. It was this great inheritance which in 1562–3 passed to his grandson Thomas Knyvett.[41]

It placed him among the principal gentry in Norfolk; indeed at the end of the century he appeared third in a list of 'principall gentlemen that dwell usually in their contries'. Ironically, by this time Sir Thomas was in financial trouble. Despite serious efforts to

[40] Cockthorpe parish register no. 1. NNRO MS. Bradfer-Lawrence VII b(1), bundle marked '50 Bacon letters', Sir Nich. Bacon to Sir Thos. Gresham, 3 Apr. 1577. *CSPD Add. 1580–1625*, p. 544.

[41] NNRO MS. Bradfer-Lawrence VII b(5), Household Account book 1592–6. *NRS* xx, 1949, pp. 16–17.

increase rents in step with inflation, he was having to sell lands and mortgage heavily, so that at his death in 1617 his extensive inheritance had been reduced to a few manors in Norfolk and Suffolk and two messuages in Norwich. His economic plight had not been improved by his marriage to Muriel, daughter of Sir Thomas Parry. The settlement made by Parry ultimately gave rise to a great deal of litigation which in the long run probably cost Thomas Knyvett more than he gained.[42]

He seems to have shared Bacon's radical religious opinions, although his views are less well documented. His wife appointed a noted Puritan, Samuel Greenaway, to a living in her presentation and subsequently corresponded with John More, the leading Puritan minister in Norwich, about Greenaway's preaching. Their son Edmund provided a revealing glimpse of the sort of upbringing he had when, in 1604, he wrote from Court to his mother, trying to make his peace after some aberration: 'I would endure much more for the obtaining of my father's good favor, and liking again with your lady, if that would do it, but that must come from God who I beseech grant you bothe with us all long life, health and his holy spirit to keepe us in his feare all the days of our life, and then to bring us to his everlasting kingdome which is prepared for his elect people.' Subsequently Sir Thomas and Lady Knyvett gave their grandson a godly upbringing after Edmund died in 1605. For his early education they placed him under John Rawlyns, the Puritan rector of Attleborough, and then in 1612 sent him to Emmanuel College, Cambridge, where that great Puritan Lawrence Chaderton still held the mastership.[43]

The Knyvetts also shared Bacon's concern for the social if not the moral well-being of their local community. Their hospitality towards the poor became legendary, being celebrated in contemporary verse and ballad. Well it might, for in 1587 Sir Thomas even refused to co-operate with his fellow deputy lieutenants in levying soldiers for service in the Low Countries because of its evil social consequences. 'It was too well knowne', he is reported to have said, 'by common experience of a greate nomber that daylie repayred to everye man's gate that was able to geve almes, what good did come of the sendinge men thether.' The soldiers were beggared and, by implication, the

[42] PRO SP 12/269/46, f. 2. *NA* xxxii, 1961, p. 343–52. *NRS* xx, 1949, pp. 18, 19, 24.

[43] BM MS. Eg. 2713, ff. 210–11. NNRO MS. KNY 633 (372 X 5). *NRS* xx, 1949, p. 19. Collinson, 'Classical Movement', p. 1263.

captains enriched. He had no interest in the Council's drive for an improved militia and was positively alarmed by the social and economic consequences of professionalization. When mustering and training increased in 1584 he persuaded the Council to accept his resignation from the captaincy of the bands in south-west Norfolk and to appoint Bassingbourne Gawdy in his stead. Given his attitude, it is difficult to understand why he accepted appointment as a deputy lieutenant in 1585, and there may well be something in the accusation of Lord Hunsdon that he was 'better content with the credyte to beare the name of deputie leiutenant & to put others to the service'.

His courtier-brother Henry regarded him as a tactless man, inexperienced in the ways of the world, who was best left, indeed encouraged, to pursue his wide scholarly interests.[44] Although there is no evidence that he attended university and only a note of his admission to the Middle Temple, he had clearly been educated in the finest Renaissance tradition. He brought together at Ashwellthorpe 'a large library of printed books and choice manuscripts valued on his death at the considerable sum of £700'. It appears to have been much more comprehensive than Bacon's collection, containing books on 'theology, philosophy, medicine, history, mathematics, Greek and Arabic sciences, Greek & Latin classics, law and literature'. Many of his volumes are now in Cambridge University Library and one of them bears testimony that Knyvett himself, in however modest a manner, wrote poetry and translated from the classics.[45] He was also an avid collector of 'antiquities' and 'medales'—his brother Henry's description of the Roman coins for which he scoured London. Indeed Henry Knyvett, desperately struggling to avert poverty by minor office and by military adventures, became one of the principal agencies through which Sir Thomas built his great library, even collecting papers and manuscripts for him during his military service at Calais.[46]

Justice Francis Wyndham (d. 1592) was a firm adherent of the Bacons in their opposition to Sir Arthur Heveningham. The Wyndhams of Felbrigg were a thrusting and ambitious family whose

[44] Blomefield, v. 155. NNRO MSS. KNY 680, 694 (372 X 5).
[45] *Middle Temple Admissions*, p. 25. *NRS* xx, 1949, p. 17.
[46] NNRO MSS. KNY 679, 696, 700, 727, 737, 743 (372 X 5).

members had successfully manoeuvred for power and riches during the unrest in the fifteenth century and then consolidated their position by royal service under the Tudors. Francis was the second son of Sir Edmund Wyndham (d. 1569), one of the foremost gentry in the county under the fourth Duke of Norfolk. While his 'mean grasping and vindictive' elder brother Roger held sway at Felbrigg 'for 30 disastrous years', Francis pursued a brilliant career in the law. He was called to the bar in 1560, became recorder of Norwich in 1575, serjeant at law in 1577, and judge of the common pleas in 1579. With the profits from his successful legal practice he purchased a residence in Norwich and an estate at Pentney.[47]

Wyndham's association with the Bacons first became evident in 1570 when he married Nathaniel's sister Elizabeth. But one suspects that it was essentially rapport in religious and legal matters which turned these brothers-in-law into the Castor and Pollux of the Norfolk political scene. With Bacon usually in the county and Wyndham in London, frequently at Court, they worked in harness to safeguard the 'preciser sort' from ecclesiastical censure and to protect their county commonweal from what they regarded as exploitation at the hands of patentees and deputy lieutenants. In 1591, in the midst of the High Commission's inquisition into the Puritan ministry, it was Francis Wyndham and Edward Coke who inveighed against the bishops' use of the *ex officio* oath. Wyndham reported to Nathaniel Bacon how, 'by reason of a charge geven by me & Mr. Cooke at Sessions *viz* that the ordynarye cowld not cyte men to appere *per* [*sic*] *salute anime* [*sic*] to awnswer upon oathe', the Archbishop of Canterbury had fulminated in Council that 'ecclesiasticall courtes were lyke cleane to be over throwen'. As a result the judges had been summoned informally before the Council and 'commanded from her Majestie to forbeare to geve yt [the charge] any further till more consultatyon were had thereof'. In a letter remarkable for the light it sheds upon the close relationship between the county and the Court, Wyndham went on to recount how, when all the other judges had withdrawn from the Council Board, Lord Hunsdon proceeded to accuse him of having 'sought to dyscontenans hys lordship in his liefetenancy in that shyre [and having] . . . impugned her Majesties comission and all other her service there for levyeng of money'. The incident to which he refers was part of a conflict over the methods of

[47] R. W. Ketton-Cremer, *Felbrigg*, 1962, pp. 20, 26. *DNB* s.v. Wyndham, Francis. Wyndham, *A Family History*, pp. 128–30.

county administration in which Wyndham and Bacon had invoked the law in an effort to thwart the activities of Sir Arthur Heveningham in his capacity both as a deputy lieutenant and a patentee.[48]

Several members of the Gawdy family also became allied with the Bacons both through marriage and by virtue of opposition to Heveningham. Since the Gawdys were a prolific family it is necessary to identify those who played important roles in the ensuing account.[49] Their ancestors had been small landowners living at Harleston, socially no more than yeomen or minor gentry until Thomas Gawdy (d. 1556) became a sucessful lawyer. In addition he married three times, each wife bearing a son who rose to be an eminent lawyer and one of the greatest territorial magnates in the county. It is the principal members of the branches founded by these three sons who will be introduced below.

Thomas Gawdy's eldest son, Thomas Gawdy of Shottesham, Redenhall, and Norwich (d. 1556), had a successful career at the Inner Temple and was then appointed recorder of King's Lynn in 1545 and Norwich in 1550. The third Duke of Norfolk retained him as high steward of his lands in Norfolk and no doubt helped to secure him a place in the commission of the peace in 1540.[50] In 1552 he was made a serjeant at law and in October 1553 was elected to parliament as a burgess for Norwich. By this time he had purchased an imposing residence in Norwich as well as acquiring extensive lands in Norfolk, Suffolk, Hertfordshire, Devon, and Somerset. He, too, married three times, but only his family by his first wife Anne, daughter of John Bassingbourne of Hatfield, calls for attention here.

Their eldest son, Thomas, wasted his inheritance and is of no consequence to this study, but their second son, Bassingbourne, became a gentleman-waiter to the Queen, established himself by marriage at West Harling near Thetford, and rapidly rose to be an

[48] *Stiffkey Papers*, pp. 186–7. This letter has been incorrectly dated 1575. Below, pp. 253–65, 280–81.

[49] Unless otherwise stated the following paragraphs are based upon P. Millican, *The Gawdys of Norfolk and Suffolk*, Norwich, 1939.

[50] NNRO MS. NRS 27260 (361 X 3).

important figure in county administration. He was appointed sheriff in 1578, had become a J.P. by 1581, and entered parliament in 1584 as burgess for Eye in Suffolk, after failing to gain a seat at Thetford. A neighbour and friend of Sir Nicholas Bacon (jun.), he shared the latter's radical religious views, making his mark in county political affairs at the expense of his recusant neighbour Thomas Lovell.[51]

He was succeeded by his son Bassingbourne Gawdy (jun.) who with assistance from his courtier brother Philip edged the Harling Gawdys into the front rank of county society. Bassingbourne Gawdy (jun.) was appointed to the Bench when his father died in 1590, was twice pricked as sheriff of Norfolk, received a knighthood in 1597, and achieved the supreme county honour of being returned knight of the shire in 1601. He not only maintained the family friendship with Sir Nicholas Bacon (jun.) but strengthened it in 1595 by marrying Bacon's daughter Dorothy as his second wife. He, too, had Puritan sympathies: in 1601, for instance, he asked the Lord Keeper to present William Jenkinson, the Puritan vicar of Croxton, to the living at his neighbouring parish of Bridgham.[52] It is hardly surprising, therefore, that he continued the family feud against Thomas Lovell and, as the century drew to a close, became increasingly involved with the opposition to Heveningham and his associates.

Although the Harling Gawdys gained a place among the foremost magnates in the county and played a leading role in its political affairs, they never developed their estates commensurately. Consequently during the late sixteenth century they were overshadowed by the two other branches which Thomas Gawdy of Harleston established through his second and third marriages.

By his second marriage, to Rose, daughter of Thomas Bennett of Rushall, he had another son, also named Thomas (d. 1588) who had an even more successful legal career than his elder half-brother's and who established the Claxton branch. This Thomas also became recorder of Norwich, was made a serjeant at law, had close associations with the Duke of Norfolk,[53] gained a place on the Norfolk Bench (1555), and represented Norwich in parliament (1558); but he surpassed his half-brother when he was promoted judge of the

[51] BM MS. Add. 36990, f. 5. NNRO MS. NAS Safe II.28, loose letter, Edward Eden to Bass. Gawdy, 21 Oct. 1584. Below, pp. 182–92.

[52] NNRO MS. NAS Safe II.28, f. 72. Collinson, p. 366.

[53] *CPR, 1569–72*, p. 450.

Queen's Bench in 1574 and received a knighthood in 1578. He also outdid him in the accumulation of property which he acquired by judicious marriage and steady purchases. He married twice; his first wife Audrey, co-heiress of William Knightley, a prosperous Norwich attorney, brought him the manors of Rockland, Bramerton, and Surlingham; his second wife Frances, daughter of Henry Richers of Swannington, provided sufficient money for him to buy up much of the property of his debt-ridden nephew Thomas Gawdy, including his mansion in Norwich. Besides this he steadily purchased property in Norfolk and Suffolk from the time that he was called to the bar. His extensive investment in land is at least partially reflected in his subsidy assessment which had risen from £33 in 1576 to £60 when he died in 1588.[54]

His estates and legal acumen were inherited by his eldest son Henry Gawdy who became a prominent member of the anti-Heveningham faction and whose activities bulk large in the ensuing chapters. Educated at Cambridge and the Inner Temple, Henry subsequently confined himself to estate management and county administration; here he had few peers, being listed in 1597 among the seven 'principal gentlemen [of Norfolk] that dwell usually in their county'. He was very much a county man; twice sheriff and twice elected as knight of the shire, he served assiduously on the Bench for upwards of forty years. Norfolk was his 'patria'; he viewed national affairs in terms of their impact upon his county. Although he never practised law, he was, like Nathaniel and Nicholas Bacon, acutely aware of the implications for county government of the lieutenancy's growing power and the Crown's increased reliance on patentees. Together with Sir Thomas Knyvett he became a member of that select company which gathered at Stiffkey Hall, and like Sir Thomas Knyvett he married his son to one of Nathaniel Bacon's daughters.

The legal eminence and propensity to estate-building of Sir Thomas Gawdy of Claxton were matched in the career of Francis Gawdy, the third distinguished son of Thomas Gawdy of Harleston, this time by his third wife Elizabeth. He was made serjeant at law in 1577, became recorder of Lynn in 1586, succeeded his half-brother as judge of the Queen's Bench in 1589, and became chief justice of the Common Pleas in 1605. Henry Knyvett regarded him as a judge of outstanding integrity and tipped him to succeed Sir Christopher

[54] BM MS. Lansd. 32, f. 84. Bodl. MS. Tanner 241, f. 32v.

Hatton as Lord Chancellor.[55] This speculation may have been prompted by the marriage in 1588 of Gawdy's only daughter to Hatton's nephew and heir—a marriage which could account for Gawdy's subsequent promotion to judge of the Queen's Bench. He appears to have been less involved in county affairs than his nephews Bassingbourne and Henry Gawdy, but when he did intervene he supported the Bacons in their opposition to Heveningham and the use of the prerogative.

Through his wife Elizabeth, daughter of Christopher Coningsby, he obtained the manor of Eston Hall in Wallington. Here he built a mansion, depopulating the village to make way for his park, and acquired an extensive estate by purchasing numerous parcels of land in the neighbourhood. His active estate policy brought him into conflict with Sir Nicholas Hare who was pursuing a similar policy from his base at Stow Bardolph.[56] Francis seems to have been an unpopular figure among his neighbours—or at least he has had a bad press since Henry Spelman wrote his obituary:

The judge, shortly after being made chief justice of the Common-Pleas (at a dear rate as was reported) was suddenly stricken with an apoplexy . . . and . . . died without issue—male, e'er he had continued in his place one whole *Michaelmas* term, and having made his appropriate parish church a hay-house or a dog-kennel, his dead corps being brought from *London* unto *Walling*, could for many days find no place of burial, but in the mean time growing very offensive . . . he was at last carry'd to a poor church of a little village there by called *Runcton*, and burried there without any ceremony, lieth yet uncovered (if the visitors have not reformed it) with so small a matter as a few paving stones.[57]

[55] NNRO MS. KNY 749 (372 X 5).

[56] *HMC Gawdy*, pp. 9, 14.

[57] H. Spelman, *History of Fate & Sacrilege*, 1698, p. 252.

CHAPTER IX

Private Quarrels and County Government

It has already been shown that the Duke of Norfolk's execution in 1572 gave rise to competition among the principal gentry for the leadership of county society; this, in turn, encouraged jealousy and conflict among their followers and friends. But it was not simply the Duke's death which set one against another; this merely dictated the point in time at which other more deep-seated divisive circumstances began to affect the local scene. During the 1570s conflict between Protestant and Catholic intensified, while inflation and the fluid market in land worked to the advantage of some and the detriment of others. Historians have tended to write as if the tensions created by these religious and economic changes remained latent until the early seventeenth century. This was not so in Norfolk and the Duke's sudden death removed the one force which might have damped them down. His monolithic patronage was replaced by an intricate clientage network which opened up the possibility of local office-holding to a great number of aspirants. In these circumstances there was little to prevent county administration being subverted to private and factious ends. Early in Elizabeth's reign Cecil had observed that 'with the increase of nomber of justices of peace in every shyre . . . the conservation of peace hath decreased and by multitude of an undiscret nomber of men named for justicees, mayntenance, bracery, ryotts and such lyke have multiplyed'.[1] This may not have been too cynical a diagnosis of affairs in mid and late Elizabethan Norfolk since it is possible to reconstruct at least three incidents in which rival gentry conducted their quarrels through the offices of local government.

I

For much of Elizabeth's reign two gentry families from neighbouring villages in the Breckland of south-west Norfolk, the Gawdys of West Harling and the Lovells of East Harling, engaged in a contest for power and prestige which provides a classic example of

[1] PRO SP 12/17, f. 100.

how personal and family rivalry could affect the conduct of local administration.

Until Elizabeth's accession the Lovells had ruled the roost for several generations, but thereafter Thomas Lovell's supremacy was challenged by the Gawdys who suddenly burst into the front ranks of county society. As has been shown, they had lived unobtrusively at Harleston until the early sixteenth century when Thomas Gawdy and his sons all became distinguished lawyers. His grandson Bassingbourne Gawdy, having established himself through marriage at West Harling in 1558, began the challenge to Thomas Lovell's pre-eminence by gaining minor office at Court, appointment to the Bench and the shrievalty, and a seat in parliament. His son Bassingbourne junior challenged Lovell's position even more strongly by becoming the first member of the Harling Gawdys to rank among the foremost county families; besides retaining his father's place on the Bench and twice becoming sheriff, he also twice secured election to parliament, once as knight of the shire for Norfolk.

Both parties in this conflict received backing from the principal East Anglian faction leaders—the Gawdys from Sir Nicholas Bacon, son of Lord Keeper Bacon, the Lovells from Sir Arthur Heveningham. Sir Nicholas Bacon lived a few miles south of Harling, at Redgrave in Suffolk. His uncompromising personality, Puritan beliefs, and common-law training made him particularly sensitive to religious and constitutional issues; indeed this Hampden-like figure was to refuse to pay ship money as early as 1597.[2] Lovell, for his part, received backing from Sir Arthur Heveningham who was an exponent of centralized prerogative government and who despised common lawyers, especially those like the Gawdys and Bacons who elevated common-law principles as a bulwark against every innovation of which they disapproved.

The first signs of tension between Bassingbourne Gawdy and Thomas Lovell appeared in the day-to-day problems of estate-building during the early 1580s. The Gawdys acquired several manors by judicious marriage. The Lovells, however, were more successful at purchase, Thomas Lovell outbidding Bassingbourne Gawdy on at least two occasions and outwitting him on a third. Ill feeling developed as each family extended its estates and their lands became increasingly intermingled. In Brettenham, for instance, where they both owned a manor, the subterfuges employed by their

[2] Below, p. 283.

respective stewards to control the village's agricultural system eventually led to conflict between their tenants and to a Privy Council enquiry.[3]

By 1581 Thomas Lovell had other reasons for jealousy towards Gawdy. Until his father's death in 1566 his family had been unrivalled in the government of south-west Norfolk. For well over half a century, at least one Lovell had figured in the commission of the peace. But Thomas had not succeeded to his fathers' place on the Bench; indeed in 1581, as if to add insult to injury, his neighbour Bassingbourne Gawdy had been preferred in his stead. Furthermore, when militia captains had been chosen Lovell had again been snubbed by the appointment of Gawdy's son to command the company in south-west Norfolk. These were bitter blows to Lovell's pride. As the Council pointed out, he was 'a gent of an auncient howse, and one that seemeth desyerous to maynteyn and contynue a good name and report in the contrye where he dwelleth'. Prestige apart, he knew that the best way to cope with a troublesome neighbour who wielded magisterial authority was to become a magistrate himself.[4]

By the 1580s Lovell desperately needed a place on the Bench; but his suspect religious views militated against this. In 1578 the Privy Council had committted him, together with other noted Recusants, to confinement in Norwich for conference with the Bishop—apparently with little effect since in 1587 he was still noted for his Recusancy. Lovell, however, was not the first to discover that whom he knew mattered more than what he believed. Unlikely to be recommended for a place on the Bench, he probably resorted, as on subsequent occasions, to intrigue with Crown Office officials. Whatever his tactics, by 1585 Lovell had not only been appointed a J.P. but had also succeeded in getting his name placed higher in the order of precedence than Gawdy's.[5] Issue had now been joined between these rival gentry. They had embarked upon a struggle for pre-eminence in south-west Norfolk in which the decisive factors were to be the offices of local government. Neither would be satisfied until the other was expelled from the Bench. It was Bassingbourne Gawdy and Sir Nicholas Bacon who made the first move.

They planned to discredit Lovell at Court in the hope that privy

[3] Smith, 'Norf. Gentry', pp. 125–7.

[4] Appendix I. NNRO MS. NAS Safe II.28, f. 68. Bodl. MSS. Tanner 241, f. 22; Douce 393, f. 31.

[5] *APC, 1577–8*, p. 312. Appendix I. Above, pp. 64–5. Below, pp. 186, 190.

councillors would order his dismissal from the Bench. An opportunity arose in 1586 when, as a result of the controversy over lands in Brettenham, Sir Nicholas Bacon accused Lovell of suborning and corrupting witnesses. The accusation appears to have been made in Lovell's absence and reported to him subsequently. Proud of his recent appointment as a J.P. and angered by Bacon's disparaging remarks, he challenged him to a duel in a letter which must stand as a masterpiece of invective:

I am advertised of words delyvered in my cosen Gawdye his howse at West Harlinge which doe moch intend eyther to my credet or discredet . . . I tell the thowe lyeest; thowe lyest and lyest in thye throte . . . And I doe by this my letter challeng the as a lyeing knight: but if thowe wyll prove thye selfe contrarye then . . . meete me . . . eyther at Flushinge or Myddleburrowe theare to rune three courses with the sharpe lawns.[6] And yf yt be my chawns to fall in to thye hands then cutte my throte withowte merecye. . . . yf fylthye feare cawseth the to refuse this, then serve with me on horseback or foot in three servises, and who doeth fyrst . . . endamage the enemye, let the other be accownted recreant, a dastarde, and a discredyted person in all honourable and honest compenye . . . But if thowe shalt refuse the performans of the one of theis three, then I will secretlye repute the, and openlye blase the, as a dunghell spyryted man, as one that dyd nothing partycipate in thye generatyon with the sylver mowld of thye honowrable father . . .

Thyne enemy Thomas Lovell.'[7]

Sir Nicholas Bacon forwarded this challenge to the Council whither Lovell was immediately summoned and committed to the Marshalsea prison. At this point, however, someone intervened at Court to counter Bacon's moves by claiming that Lovell had been unduly provoked and pleading for leniency towards a gentleman who, so it was asserted, had recently abandoned his Catholic views and conformed in religion. These pleas appear to have been so successful that within days of his imprisonment Lovell had been released and allowed to return triumphantly to Norfolk, while Bacon had to remain at Court to be reprimanded for vindictiveness. The powerful backing which Lovell had received at the Council Board probably came from Lord Hunsdon, who, having recently been appointed lord lieutenant of Norfolk, was about to select Lovell's

[6] Lance.

[7] PRO SP 12/275/22. This letter, dated 1 July, has been incorrectly ascribed to 1600. It is unmistakably referred to in a Privy Council letter dated 4 Aug. 1586.

supporter Sir Arthur Heveningham as his deputy lieutenant.[8]

Bacon's plan had misfired so badly that Lovell not only kept his place on the Bench, but a few months later also appeared in the subsidy commission.[9] A subsidy commissioner had responsibility for the assessment throughout his 'division' of each landowner's income, so that he could favour a friend and victimize an opponent—a situation which Lovell appreciated well enough. The key figures in this sort of manipulation were the subsidy assessors—substantial men in each Hundred to whom the commissioners delegated the work of assessment. Although the commissioners scrutinized the work of these subordinates, sometimes altering individual assessments, they could exercise their partiality most unobtrusively through the careful choice of assessors. So it was that when the commissioners met at Watton in 1591 Lovell joined with two other Catholic sympathizers—Sir Robert Southwell and Thomas Knyvett of New Buckenham—in refusing to appoint Thomas Jeckler as an assessor because he was 'an utter enymie to papistry and a precysian'. The puritan minister John Trendle wrote a woeful letter to Bassingbourne Gawdy, complaining of Lovell's behaviour and concluding that 'except the Lorde stire upp some fewe our ruine is at hande'.[10]

Doubtless Gawdy agreed, but, rather than wait upon the Lord, he had been doing his utmost to help himself. Events had run his way in that Lovell had been dismissed from the Bench in 1587, probably during the summer purge when he had been classified by the Bishop as 'suspected and reputed to be backwardes in religion'.[11] There is nothing to suggest that Gawdy had played any part in this, but thereafter his family had mounted a veritable campaign at Court to prevent Lovell's reappointment to the commission. In May 1588 Gawdy's half-brother Anthony reported that he had been dining at the Lord Treasurer's house, where Sir Thomas Leighton 'spoke openly how proudly and foolishly Mr. Lovell abused him [Bassingbourne Gawdy] since his [Lovell's] coming to Court'; he went on to say that they spoke what they knew of Lovell, which 'was ill enough'.[12]

[8] *APC, 1586–7*, p. 202. Bodl. MSS. Douce 393, f. 31; Tanner 241, f. 25.

[9] Appendix I. PRO SP 12/197, no. 33.

[10] BM MS. Lansd. 55, f. 163. Thomas Knyvett of Buckenham was son-in-law to Thomas Lovell. His wife was a noted Rescusant (PRO SP 12/208, no. 16i). BM MS. Eg. 2713, f. 279.

[11] Above, p. 84.

[12] *HMC Gawdy*, pp. 29–30.

Then in a letter to his father early in 1589 Philip Gawdy described an unexpected encounter he had had with Lovell which suggests that whispering campaigns and intrigues were continuing:

being at court . . . I was talking with my Lord Wharton & Mr. Dacres of the Northe. Mr. Lovell standing a good prety way from us, cam & whispered in Mr. Dacres eare, and sodenly and very softly he spake in my eare to this effecte without any other salutation, . . . "Your father will nowe leave his slaunderous speaches of me", and presently runn his way without suffering me to reply. I followed him as fast as I might, and told him that my father had neither sayde or done any thing, but that he wold iustefy to be honest, and in his absence I wold iustefy it to be true to his face wher he wold disprove me. Well sayeth he, "he hathe used very spitefull and slaunderous speaches touching my creddit". Then I desired to know what the effecte of the woordes shold be; he answered that he wold keepe them to him self, and yow shold heareafter heare of them; then I replyed that I toke it for a lye and him for a lyar in the reporting of it. . . . "Well cosin", saythe he, "I have nothing to say to yow, this matter concerneth your father my great enemy. And he shall answer it els wher, and yf I be not muche abused by my friends I know it to be very true". I urged him farr to have some knowledge therof, but he passed it over and called me cosin, and by no means I cold make him angry with me. . . . But assure yow Sir I gather this of his vilde condition that malice was his mother, and envy nursed him, and shame brought him into the world and never will forsake him till he leave world and all'.[13]

Gawdy's 'spiteful and slaunderous speaches' apparently did the trick since Lovell failed to regain his place on the Bench despite his activities at Court. In November 1588, Philip Gawdy described to his father how 'Mr. Lovell hathe made great suite to serve my Lord Chaunceler dyvers of his men enformed me so. Mr. Goldsmithe and he ar very conversant together and he is a meane of his preferment. Goldsmith told me very lately that he shold be his man and have his lyvery. He meanes to tryumphe over his enemyes.'[14]

In the short term Lovell had failed. He had not been restored to the commission when Bassingbourne Gawdy senior died in 1590, no doubt content in the knowledge that he had finally established his family among the foremost in the county and that his heir, also named Bassingbourne, could look forward to a period of unchallenged supremacy in south-west Norfolk.

But Lovell was not to be so easily ousted. By 1591 he had been

[13] Jeayes, pp. 46–7.
[14] Ibid., p. 42.

reinstated in the commission of the peace.[15] Indeed for the remainder of Elizabeth's reign he struggled with some success against the growing prestige and authority of the younger Bassingbourne. They continued to quarrel over their estates; their tenants quarrelled too; there were inconclusive lawsuits in the Exchequer court and in Star Chamber which usually culminated in sporadic skirmishes which, in turn, gave rise to fresh lawsuits. Matters were bound to continue in this manner so long as both Gawdy and Lovell held influential office, since each could give as good as he got. If Gawdy was to maintain that pre-eminence in south-west Norfolk which his father had achieved he must do as his father had done and oust Lovell from the Bench. To this end he, too, schemed with Sir Nicholas Bacon.[16]

In the post-Armada years, as Englishmen braced themselves for further offensives by the forces of the Counter-Reformation, the activities of priests and Jesuit missionaries aroused such suspicion that any report of Catholic conventicles evoked a prompt conciliar response. In this atmosphere Lovell provided a sitting target for his opponents. His wife was a well-known Recusant; and if he had ever subscribed to the Anglican settlement he had done so with considerable reluctance—at best he was a 'church papist'. In January 1592 Bacon and Gawdy therefore seized the opportunity to inform the Bishop of Norwich, and through him the Council, 'that there is great recorses meetyngs and conventicles at the house of Thomas Lovell'. Their information may have been true, but they could have levelled similar accusations against many other Recusant families of gentry status; the fact that they did not, taken in conjunction with the timing of their accusation, leaves little doubt that they had other motives besides religious considerations. Even the Council was inclined to believe that 'this hard informacion geven against him [Lovell] did proceed of some displeasure'. None the less their lordships reacted predictably, immediately ordering Lovell's dismissal from the Bench and summoning him to answer the charges. He put up such a spirited defence that by May the Council had ordered his restoration to the Bench. Baffled, however, by conflicting information, it also appointed a special commission of enquiry which, despite the intervention of Sir Arthur Heveningham, upheld the original

[15] NNRO MS. NAS C3/1/9, Privy Council to the Bishop of Norwich and Sir Nich. Bacon, 26 Jan. 1591.

[16] *APC, 1590*, pp. 125–6. PRO E 123/18, f. 16.

information. Once more the Council had to turn in its tracks and order Lovell's dismissal from the commission. But this time it refused to be dissuaded and, try as he might, Lovell remained excluded for the next six years. At last it seemed that Gawdy, with his adversary discredited at Court and in the county, had finally triumphed.[17]

Lovell, however, far from accepting defeat, still schemed to restore his credit and to diminish that of his rival. The Council's efforts to improve militia training in the mid 1590s provided his next opportunity.[18] Down to 1596 the county's militia had been mustered and trained in seven large companies or regiments corresponding to the seven 'divisions' of the county, each comprising six or seven hundred men under the command of the foremost local magnate. From at least 1584 Bassingbourne Gawdy junior had led the company drawn from the Hundreds of south-west Norfolk, thereby excluding Lovell from yet another prestigious and influential office. Initially there appeared to be little Lovell could do about this except to flout Gawdy's authority by refusing to send his men and equipment to the musters; but in 1596 the Council provided him with an opportunity to get on equal terms with his neighbour, at least in military affairs, when it ordered a drastic reduction in the size of these companies in an effort to improve the standard of training. Instead of seven large companies based upon the 'division', there were to be thirty-three small ones each recruited from within a single Hundred. As a result of this reorganization Lovell received the captaincy of Shropham company while Gawdy lost his large command and had to be content with a company drawn from Guiltcross Hundred.[19]

In this way Lovell had lessened Gawdy's lead in the contest for pre-eminence in south-west Norfolk. Yet his success was short-lived since almost immediately afterwards Gawdy was knighted (1597). This must have been a bitter pill for Lovell. His father, grandfather, and great-grandfather had all been prominent magistrates in the county, each being honoured with a knighthood. By contrast, in 1597 Lovell, already well past 50, could boast of neither distinction. Honour demanded prompt action, and once more he played courtier. First he sought a knighthood, for which, so we are told, 'he flewe such a pitche as no man did this twenty yeare'. Then, having failed

[17] *APC, 1591–2*, pp. 204, 454. NNRO MS. NAS C3/1/9, Privy Council to Bishop of Norwich and Sir Nich. Bacon, 26 Jan. 1591/2.

[18] Below, p. 287.

[19] *HMC Salisbury*, vi. 223. Below, p. 287.

in this suit, in 1599 he bought his way back into the commission of the peace at a cost, according to Philip Gawdy, of £240. Bassingbourne Gawdy had reason to fear his neighbour's success. With a militia captaincy and a place on the Bench Lovell again presented a serious challenge. But his courtier brother consoled him with the reflection that things could have been worse: Lovell could be turned out of the commission once more, Philip commented, but could never have been deprived of a knighthood.[20]

In any case Gawdy soon redressed the balance. In the summer of 1599 Lovell lost his militia captaincy when the muster commissioners abandoned the scheme for small companies and reappointed Gawdy to his former command. He further increased his ascendancy when he gained a place in the muster commission. Six commissioners had been appointed in 1596 to take over the lord lieutenant's responsibilities on the death of Lord Hunsdon, and Gawdy's inclusion in this commission in September 1599 once more underlined his dominant position in county society.[21]

More immediately it gave him another opportunity to disgrace his neighbour and get him dismissed from the Bench. Ever since Lovell had been deprived of his captaincy he had refused to send his men and weapons to the musters. Nor, so Gawdy claimed, would he contribute to the *ad hoc* levies imposed by the commissioners in order to meet conciliar demands for companies of horse and foot to serve in Ireland. The evidence suggests that he was being rated unduly heavily by the commissioners. Even so, Gawdy persuaded his fellow commissioners to inform the Council of Lovell's refusal 'to shewe unto the captaine of the Lymitt such armes as he hath beene formalie charged to fynde . . . [and] to pay such money as he is assessed for the settinge forth of 100 men that are presentlie to be sent into Ireland'. They concluded by virtually inviting the Council to dismiss Lovell from the Bench by pointing out that as a J.P. he was 'an evill example to the inferior sort which are backward inough to pay unto such charges'.[22] Their lordships acted predictably. Once more they summoned Lovell to their Board and, after dismissing his plea that Gawdy had acted out of 'spleen and malice', committed

[20] Jeayes, p. 111. He dates this letter 19 Dec. [1600]. Internal evidence leaves no doubt that it was written in 1599. Cf. also Appendix I. Above, pp. 64–5.

[21] BM MSS. Kings 265, f. 276; Add. 48591, f. 2. NNRO MS. NAS Safe II.28, f. 78.

[22] BM MSS. Kings 265, f. 289v; Add. 48591, ff. 57v–59. NNRO MS. NAS C3/1/9, undated petition from Thos. Lovell to Sir Robert Cecil.

him to the Marshalsea. But Lovell again side-stepped the full consequences of Gawdy's attack. Far from being dismissed from the Bench, he was released from prison in a matter of days, 'fawning more like a dog than a man', as one reporter put it. As before, Sir Arthur Heveningham had been his 'great advocate' at Court and there are again hints at bribery. Philip Gawdy reported that 'after his commytting, he [Lovell] hade made very great frendes, whiche I understood hathe coste him very deare, and by yowre leave I perceyved by Mr. Wade [one of the keepers of the Marshalsea] that he hathe tasted very deeply of his purse.'[23]

Once back in the county Lovell continued his efforts to regain that power and prestige which had been usurped by the Gawdys. His next opportunity appeared in June 1601 when, on Council instructions, the muster commissioners again reduced large militia companies to smaller ones. This entailed the division of Gawdy's company into two units, and undoubtedly Lovell expected to receive a captaincy. But on this occasion he was disappointed; to his consternation the commissioners appointed Gawdy to command both companies. Lovell's failure to get on equal terms with his neighbour undoubtedly stemmed from Sir Arthur Heveningham's declining influence on the muster commission.[24]

Had Lovell succeeded in regaining the captaincy of Shropham company in 1601 he would well-nigh have restored his family's tarnished prestige, for in the spring of that year he received the knighthood 'for which he flewe such a pitche' three years earlier. Philip Gawdy reported that the Lord Admiral, Charles Howard of Effingham, was the 'meanes' by which he was 'brought to kisse the Quenes hande. The olde [blank] blusshed most extreamly', continued Philip, 'and not without cause, for it is thought he strayned so harde for the favor, as it brought all the blood up in to his face'. A knighthood meant that he sat higher in the order of precedence on the Bench of justices; how much higher was determined by the positioning of his name in the next commission of the peace. Characteristically he intrigued at the Crown Office to be placed above his rival, but Philip Gawdy took care that in the next commission Lovell's name appeared immediately after Gawdy's.[25]

[23] *APC, 1599–1600*, pp. 537, 554, 718, 733. BM MS. Add. 48591, ff. 58v–61. NNRO MSS. NAS C3/2/3, copy of a warrant dated 17 July 1600 and a letter from Privy Council to justices of Norfolk dated 1 Aug. 1600; WALS XVII/1, ff. 40–2. Jeayes, pp. 104–5.

[24] Below, pp. 288–9. BM MS. Add. 23007, f. 21v.

[25] Jeayes, pp. 123, 168.

Gawdy still led by a short head, but within weeks Lovell drew level by gaining a place in the muster commission. Prestige apart, this meant that he would have a voice in the appointment of company commanders and in the military assessments for the limit. Almost immediately he was scheming to deprive Gawdy of his double captaincy, and so secure for himself command of the Shropham company. 'He doth use all meanes he can possible with the Lords of the Councell', Gawdy complained to Lord Thomas Howard, 'to crosse the proceedings of the comissioners here in Norfolk in seeking to take awaye the chieffe part of my soldiours from me in the cuntry, and in the hundred where I doe dwell, which I have had theise xviii yeres, a matter which he hopeth should prove disgracefull unto me, which indeede yt must needes yf he should prevaile.' In the event he failed; Gawdy appears to have maintained his superiority in the militia organization.

Undeterred, Lovell challenged strongly in every other aspect of local administration. By 1601 he had been reappointed to the subsidy commission, a situation which alarmed Gawdy who was disqualified temporarily from this commission by his appointment as sheriff. He clearly feared that in his absence Lovell would appoint new assessors and alter the subsidy book, since he had instructed his courtier brother to try to ensure that Lovell also was left out of the commission. Philip failed, but justified himself by arguing that Lovell was disqualified on a technicality. Apparently he had been entitled 'esquire' in the commission despite his recent knighthood—a flaw, so Philip contended, which was tantamount to exclusion, 'for I assure you he may not sytt'. He also assured his brother that he would secure his restoration to his rightful position in the subsidy commission at the end of his shrievalty and ensure that Lovell was left out. There is no evidence that Philip fulfilled his promise, but there was no lack of effort on his part and on that of others as well. In May 1602 Edmund Moundford informed Sir Bassingbourne Gawdy that 'the great T.L. hath made complainte at the court of most of the justices to be ioyned in combynacions especially against hym'.[26]

Sir Thomas Lovell died in January 1605 having struggled with some success to extend his estates and maintain his prestige in the face of Gawdy's challenge. Like his ancestors, he died a knight and a

[26] BM MSS. Add. 23007, f. 33; 48591, f. 93v. NNRO MS. NAS Safe II.28, f. 37v–38, 68. Jeayes, pp. 116, 124. BM MS. Eg. 2714, f. 197.

justice of the peace, but he never represented his county in parliament, he was never sheriff, nor did he become a deputy lieutenant, and on the few occasions when he was appointed to the Bench he had to sit lower in the order of precedence than his enemy and rival Bassingbourne Gawdy. Whether or not he be judged successful, his career provides a classic example of the way in which private faction influenced the appointment and dismissal of local officials and the day-to-day conduct of their business.

II

In the early 1580s another feud occurred between two neighbouring gentry—Edward Flowerdew of Stanfield Hall, Wymondham, and Sir Arthur Heveningham of Ketteringham.

The Flowerdews of Hethersett, like the Gawdys of Harling, had risen in society through successful legal careers. By the mid sixteenth century John Flowerdew, a 'lawyer-turned-squire' who is remembered only for his part in the opening stages of Ket's rebellion, had secured his family a place among the lesser gentry. His fourth son Edward had an outstanding career at the Bar which culminated in his appointment as serjeant at law in 1580 and third Baron of the Exchequer in 1584. Edward's services were much in demand locally: during the 1570s both the Dean and Chapter and the corporation of Norwich retained him as counsel and subsequently he was appointed recorder of King's Lynn (1576) and Norwich (1580), and steward of Yarmouth (1580), while Castle Rising elected him a burgess to the 1572 parliament, perhaps at the behest of his patron the Earl of Leicester.

As early as 1564 Flowerdew had amassed sufficient wealth to purchase Stanfield Hall from John Appleyard, and thereafter he proceeded to extend his estates by purchasing or renting numerous parcels of land in Wymondham, Hethersett, and Ketteringham. He appears to have bought extensive property from his brothers and nephews, who generally failed to consolidate and improve their inheritances, although it is fair to add that he subsequently bequeathed it back to them. His considerable investment in land is reflected in the subsidy book where his assessment was raised from £20 in 1576 to £40 in 1581. Legal eminence, extensive property, and a powerful patron at Court ensured him a place among the county magnates and, as early as 1569, among its magistrates.[27]

[27] S. T. Bindoff, *Ket's Rebellion*, 1949, p. 3. NNRO RQG I A, handlist of the 'Gurney' MSS. which were at Thickthorn Hall in 1938. BM MS. Lansd. 32, f. 84.

Flowerdew appears to have been a self-righteous grasping man who throve upon the follies and troubles of his relatives and neighbours. He bought out his brothers when they fell on hard times. When his neighbour John Appleyard reluctantly left the county, in debt and in disgrace with his master the Duke of Norfolk, Flowerdew obligingly moved into his fine residence at Stanfield. As a burgess for Castle Rising in the 1572 parliament he tried to get himself promoted to a seat for Norwich in the third session by nudging out alderman Thomas Beaumont.[28] Like any astute lawyer he avoided litigation, but then defied his neighbours to sully his record: 'I have not sued anie, neither have anie sued me, no not for anie cause though waitie', he complained to Heveningham when the latter threatened him with legal proceedings. His self-righteousness made him quick to discern and decry faults in others. Although hardly any older than Heveningham, he lectured him in superior tones for delivering an intemperate note about some straying cattle:

> . . . good honest and quiett behaviour withowt disdaine is best and best allowed emonge men in this world, and if you can be so contented to lyve you shall reape as others fynde which is good will for good will and one good toorne for another. When I remember the quiett disposicion of your father, the neighbourly mynde of your good mother, and the noble, sadd stayed behaviour of your brother Henry, I cane butt marvaile to see you so much degenerate from them by pryde (which so much offendeth others and so greately hurtteth yourself) when they by theire goodnes woonne the good will of all men. . . . Sir Arthur, the day hath ben that you have made some showe of estimacion of your poore neighbours, but nowe you contempne them as base and vile persons far unfitt for your greatenes, and yett when you were either att the meanest or att the greatest they were redy to pleasure you with purse, pastime, credditt and councell: which things I dare saye, nay, I am suer of hitt, you might yett finde emonge them yf you colde butt yett live with them as a neighboure and not as a prince. . . . For men that lyve and dye in this world leave fame behinde them and carry synne with them and no synne allmost greater than to slander your neighbour.[29]

Heveningham and Flowerdew were both ambitious men, but their contrasting temperaments made it inevitable that they should differ in their goals and the means by which they pursued them. Flowerdew, conservative by nature, sought to advance his fortunes by diligent service to the common law and the administration of his county,

[28] NNRO MS. NAS Frere K 12(A), bundle for Humbleyard Hundred, John Appleyard to Edw. Flowerdew, 3 Oct. 1564. *DNB*, s.v. Flowerdew, Edw.

[29] NNRO MS. Aylsham, bundle 74, Edw. Flowerdew to A. Heveningham, 18 Dec. 1582.

as well as by shrewd and sometimes harsh dealings in land. His was the career of the precise common lawyer—a lesser Edward Coke. Heveningham, in contrast, hated lawyers—he once referred to Flowerdew as a 'knavish sergeant'[30]—and he had scant respect for the niceties of the common law. Nor was he interested in enhancing his status in local society through painstaking estate-building and diligent attention to the interests of his county. For him success meant riding roughshod over his neighbours, with powerful backing from influential men at Court; he preferred to act as an agent of the Crown and Council rather than as a local magistrate working within the framework of statute and quarter sessions.

It is possible that religious differences may also have contributed to the bad relationship between these squires. Heveningham appears to have been content with the Elizabethan settlement whereas Flowerdew almost certainly wanted further reform. In the 1581 parliament he spoke in favour of the Puritan Bill 'for a public fast . . . and for a sermon to be had every morning', while as early as 1573 he had delivered a 'charge' at the quarter sessions suggesting that statute permitted the use of 'common bread' at the communion. His will also shows signs of radical views.[31]

Friction between Flowerdew and Heveningham developed soon after the latter succeeded to his inheritance in 1574. The complicated manorial structure of Ketteringham, Hethersett and Wymondham encouraged conflict since parcels of land which Flowerdew had acquired lay scattered among Heveningham's closes and arable lands. Each protested that the other had damaged his crops by allowing cattle to stray, had hunted his game, overstocked the commons, cut his timber, and permitted unlawful enclosure.[32]

By 1582 bad feeling engendered by day-to-day problems of estate management had been exacerbated by two other issues, one public, the other private. The public issue arose from Heveningham's activities as sheriff during the year 1581–2. Flowerdew accused him of allowing his under-sheriff or bailiffs to commit 'divers shameful abuses' and of personally indulging in extortion. He cited the case of John Bate of Burlingham who, when indicted at quarter sessions

[30] PRO St. Ch. 5, F 14/17 (Bill).

[31] Neale, *Parliaments 1559–1581*, pp. 378–9. CUL MS. Ee. II. 34, f. 145v. PCC 23 Windsor.

[32] NNRO MSS. Aylsham, bundle 74, undated letter from A. Heveningham to Edw. Flowerdew and reply by Flowerdew dated 18 Dec. 1582.

for felony, had 'made great sute and meanes unto the said Sir Arthure to purchaze his favourable frendshipp' by offering him £300 if he would empanel a partial jury. Heveningham had accepted the bribe, but when Bate defaulted over payment of the second instalment Heveningham had used his under-officers to endeavour to get Bates reindicted. Flowerdew also asserted that Heveningham had accepted from King's Lynn a £10 bribe to stay the execution of a writ and that his under-sheriff had received a gelding from a Wymondham man anxious to avoid arrest. The most serious allegations against Heveningham concerned his extortionate and apparently unconstitutional behaviour in executing a special commission for the repair of certain highways in south Norfolk and north Suffolk, but this issue transcended his quarrel with Flowerdew and will be dealt with in a later chapter.[33]

Initially these accusations had been levelled in the quarter sessions, where Heveningham had 'burst owt into a greate and vehement kinde of rayling speeche' against Flowerdew', but there is little doubt that they were intended to discredit him at the Council board and so lead to his dismissal from the Bench. If this was Flowerdew's aim it certainly succeeded; Heveningham's name was not restored to the Norfolk commission at the end of his shrievalty in 1582. While he had been sheriff, however, Heveningham had had abundant opportunity to retaliate. He encouraged Peter Pullen to charge Flowerdew with using his authority as a J.P. to protect two of his servants who had 'burglarously and felonously broken into and robbed [Pullen's] dwelling house . . . to the value of £40'. Heveningham also complained to the Council about Flowerdew's attempts to discredit him in his official capacity. Confronted with these accusations their lordships had ordered Flowerdew's dismissal from the commission of the peace—an especial disgrace to an eminent lawyer who upon occasion had acted as chairman of the Bench.[34]

While each sought to discredit the other in his public capacity, they had also become involved in a family dispute which stemmed from the marriage of Flowerdew's daughter to Thomas Shelton. The Sheltons of Shelton were a family of ancient lineage which had been prominent in the county since at least the fifteenth century. Thomas's

[33] PRO St. Ch. 5, F 14/17. A copy of the Bill is preserved among Heveningham's papers (NNRO MS. Aylsham, bundle 152). Below, pp. 253–65.

[34] Appendix I. NNRO MS. NAS Frere K8(B), Hethersett bundle, 'articles exhibited to the . . . Lords of . . . the Councell by Peter Pullen'.

great-grandfather had been responsible for the magnificent perpendicular church at Shelton, while his father had been among those knighted by the Queen during her Progress through Norfolk and Suffolk in 1578. Nothing could better have set the seal upon Flowerdew's newly acquired gentility than a marriage between his daughter and heiress Elizabeth and the heir to this distinguished family. How long he had schemed and planned for this event is not known, but barely two months after Sir Ralph Shelton's death in October 1580 Elizabeth Flowerdew was licensed to marry his son Thomas. After their marriage a serious disagreement developed between the serjeant and his son-in-law. Its cause is unknown but, since Sir Ralph had died intestate, Flowerdew may have interfered in the settlement of his estate; there is some suggestion that Shelton plate and documents were transferred to Stanfield Hall. This disagreement was never resolved and eventually led to an estrangement between Flowerdew and his daughter. Although Elizabeth was his only child, she merely figures in the last paragraph of his will: 'concerning my daughter Shelton, whom for some respects I had not dealt so liberally withall as hertofore I was minded, the gilt cup which the city of Norwich did bestow upon me'.[35]

However great the tension which had developed between Flowerdew and Thomas Shelton, Heveningham managed to increase it. For several generations his family had intermarried with the Sheltons, and he felt that Thomas had degraded himself by his marriage to Elizabeth Flowerdew, heiress to a parvenu, albeit a wealthy one. Consequently, after Thomas Shelton had broken into Flowerdew's house and removed jewels and documents, Sir Arthur Heveningham, despite being sheriff, gave him sanctuary at Ketteringham. As tension rose during the summer of 1582 strenuous efforts were made to reconcile the serjeant with his son-in-law. But a meeting arranged for this purpose was ruined by Heveningham who insisted upon attending and quickly fell to bandying recriminations with his adversary. At the outset Shelton complained that Flowerdew had tried to disgrace him by reporting his escapade at Stanfield Hall to his 'master' the Earl of Sussex. When Flowerdew denied this, Heveningham railed at him, contrasting the meanness of his birth with that of his son-in-law who was 'a gent born'. Flowerdew retorted with equal venom: 'I will tell thee I never yett readd in any cronicle of any wise or valiant man of thy name.' Not surprisingly the meeting ended in

[35] *Visit. of Norf.* ii. 324, 348. PRO St. Ch. 5, H 18/2.

disarray with skirmishes among the servants. Next, in an effort to avoid an open breach of the peace between Flowerdew and Heveningham, Sir Roger Woodhouse arranged for them to discuss their disagreements at Kimberley. This meeting appeared to be more successful since they eventually embraced in show of friendship and promised to offer no further 'uncourtesy' to one another.[36]

But the goodwill which flowed at Kimberley was quickly staunched by the troublesome realities of life. Within weeks Flowerdew's cattle had strayed again and Heveningham had reacted characteristically. In a vindictive letter he claimed that they had 'done . . . [him] more then twentye powndesworthe of hurte', asserted that the incident 'procedethe rather of malice then anythinge ells' and concluded challengingly: 'if yow will not se me satisfied I must seeke my remedy as I maye'. Flowerdew replied with a heavy-handed lecture which refuted Heveningham's claim, hoped that his 'pounds [would] fall to pence', dwelt at great length upon his trespasses against all his neighbours and informed him that he was 'mallicious', that his actions demonstrated to the world how eager he was to seek a quarrel with his neighbour, and that those who were acquainted with his 'humour' knew that he could never control his temper. 'I have enclosed all my heate in a peece of paper', concluded the virtuous and unimaginative serjeant, 'and that can doe you no further harme . . . and thus making an end of my writinge I wish you to make an ende of your wrath and so of such woes as wrath bringeth'.[37]

Nothing could have been more calculated to anger Heveningham; better that his enemy should have resorted to law than to moral invective. He responded by ambushing Flowerdew as the latter was riding to the 1582/3 Epiphany sessions at Norwich. The incident occurred in Ketteringham where the main highway from Wymondham to Norwich, long ago disused, passed close by the hall. As the serjeant rode past, Heveningham galloped out at the head of an armed band, blocked his path, and challenged him to a duel. Flowerdew, pleading that he was about the Queen's business and unarmed, made to ride on, but, so he subsequently asserted, Heveningham spurred his horse after him, threatened to kill him, and struck him on the head 'gyving hym a most greveous and mortall wound of the

[36] PRO St. Ch. 5, H 18/2 (Flowerdew's answer); H 9/35; F 14/17 (Heveningham's answer); F 8/32.

[37] NNRO MSS. Aylsham, bundle 74, undated letter from A. Heveningham to Edw. Flowerdew, and Flowerdew's reply 18 Dec. 1582.

lenght of 5 ynches and in depthe even unto the lower ryme of the brayne'. 'Astonyed', he slid from his horse and was only saved from 'certain death' by the intervention of one of Heveningham's servants and by his promise to fight a duel when he recovered.

Heveningham proceeded to the quarter sessions where he openly boasted that he had given the 'knave sergeant a knock on the cockscombe'. Here, although his name had been left out of the commission of the peace, probably at Flowerdew's instigation, he received such backing that it was only with great difficulty that Flowerdew's supporters managed to get Heveningham and his men bound to keep the peace. Quite clearly the quarter sessions were being manipulated to factional ends by the friends and followers of these quarrelsome gentry.[38]

Eventually Flowerdew obtained redress, but only after he had invoked the law by lodging a bill in Star Chamber, which culminated in a settlement out of court. Heveningham agreed to pay £600 damages in five annual instalments which were to be delivered 'in the south porch of St. Stephens in Norwich'. The final payments remained outstanding when Flowerdew died in 1586, and as late as 1596 his executors were still trying unsuccessfully to exact them.[39]

III

In 1594 yet another quarrel, this time in north Norfolk, resulted in two justices procuring each other's removal from the Bench, one for two years and the other for life. The two gentry concerned were Martin Barney of Gunton and Heveningham's friend Thomas Farmer of East Barsham. They were not neighbours and the quarrel seems to have had its origin in the marriage of Barney's son Francis to Farmer's daughter Mary.

Thomas Farmer came of a wealthy Norfolk family. His grandfather Sir Henry Farmer was a rich London merchant who married into the county, built a beautiful manor house which still stands at East Barsham, and became one of the greatest early Tudor sheep-

[38] PRO St. Ch. 5, F 8/32; F 14/17; H 18/2. NNRO MS. Aylsham, bundle 152, copy of Flowerdew's Bill. NNRO MS. Quarter Sessions minute book 1583–6, entry for 8 Jan. 25 Eliz. For Heveningham's dismissal, see above, p. 195. See also, below, pp. 233–4 for further details of this incident.

[39] NNRO MSS. Aylsham, bundle 74, doc. endorsed 'Articles of agreement between Sir A. Heveningham & Mr. Sergeant Flowerdew'; NAS C3/1/9, transcr. of letter from A. Heveningham to Thos. Knyvett, 11 June 1596, and draft of Knyvett's reply.

masters. Henry Farmer's son Sir William, who ranked among the foremost county gentry when he died in 1558, had greatly expanded his estates with grants of land from Henry VIII. He was succeeded by his nephew Thomas who proceeded to squander his inheritance, eventually selling fifteen or sixteen manors, 'leaving none but his chief house Ba[r]sham'. Such was Thomas's financial plight that apparently he could not give his daughter a dowry. None the less when her husband Francis Barney died leaving a young son, Farmer immediately sued for the wardship of the youth.[40]

By April 1594 Martin Barney had become so suspicious of Farmer's designs upon his grandson's inheritance that he made his will in order to establish 'my smale inheritance, and the same by God's grace nott to be spent and consumed by Mr. Fermor or any his broode, as he in his life sought and purposed to doe in my life, havinge already as the whole world knoweth consumed his owne'.[41] There matters might have rested had not Barney dismissed his servant—George Carr—for eloping with his niece. Whereupon the disgruntled Carr conspired with Thomas Farmer, now 'blynded with his olde mallice', to retaliate against Barney. Carr supplied evidence which enabled Farmer to accuse Barney, a noted reactionary in religion, of allowing mass to be celebrated in his house. The charge, laid at the spring assizes 1595, was well timed since it coincided with one of the Council's periodic attempts to purge county Benches, and on such occasions assize judges were instructed to report any magistrate whom they suspected of Recusancy. Barney's name inevitably went forward and in due course he was put out of the Norfolk commission.[42] Although he subsequently regained his place for a brief period, his dismissal in 1595 effectively marked the end of his magisterial career.

Barney was, however, in a strong position to retaliate, since the judges had also been instructed to seek out the 'meaner sort' of J.P.s, with a view to their removal as well. If he proclaimed Farmer's indigent state, he undoubtedly contributed to the latter's removal

[40] T. H. Swales, 'The Sequestration of Religious Property in Norfolk at the Reformation . . .' (Sheffield PhD thesis 1965), p. 292. Allison, 'Wool Supply', pp. 231–8. H. Spelman, *The History of Fate & Sacrilege*, 1698, p. 262.

[41] PCC 50 Hayes.

[42] PRO St. Ch. 5, B 45/3 (Bill); B 105/10 (Interrogs. and depositions of John Pinchbeck); C 47/25 (Interrog. to Thos. Wyndham); F 20/28 (Interrogs.); F 21/22. Appendix I.

from the commission—a disgrace from which Farmer never recovered since, although he lived for another twenty-seven years, he never again appeared on the Bench.[43]

The three disputes outlined above possess two common features: they all arose from essentially personal issues, and in each case the participants endeavoured to subvert the offices of local government to their particular ends. Indeed the pricking of sheriffs, the choice of muster commissioners, and the appointment and dismissal of justices can only be fully understood in terms of these private feuds.

But in the dispute between Flowerdew and Heveningham there are signs that issues of principle were coming to the fore in these essentially parochial and petty rivalries. In particular, Flowerdew disapproved of Heveningham's activities in, and attitudes towards, local administration. As succeeding chapters will show, during the last two decades of the century Norfolk justices began to differ fundamentally about the purpose of local administration. This disagreement increasingly dictated their relationships with one another as parochial disputes became subsumed within a wider and deeper conflict. The tendency was for personal disputes to escalate into something closely resembling party political conflict. This, in turn, had an even greater effect upon the personnel of local administration and indeed on the activities of the central administration and even parliament itself.

[43] Above, p. 85. There were other reasons for Farmer's removal from the commission, see below, p. 243–4. Appendices I and III.

CHAPTER X

Religion 1570-1585

IN 1576 Chief Justice Wray reported to Burghley upon the state of religion in the Norfolk circuit: in his opinion the Elizabethan Settlement had been widely accepted everywhere except in Norfolk and Suffolk where there abounded 'a multitude of suits and great disorder for religion'. 'There is no county in England', he concluded, 'so far out of order as these two.' He attributed this situation to the presence of extensive and clamorous groups of Puritans and Catholics, many of whom were presented 'for not coming to church . . . [and] varying in all points from the Book of Common Prayer'; many were 'obstinate Papists, but the most of them wilful and undiscreet precisians'.[1] His report did not exaggerate, for even as he wrote the diocese was on the brink of a conflict between 'undiscreet precisians' and their Bishop which must surely have been one of the bitterest of its kind in Elizabethan history.

Its narration will leave no doubt that there were a number of vociferous Puritans and papists in Norfolk and Suffolk, but whether these zealots represented the views of substantial elements within the Norwich diocese is another matter. Since, as has been demonstrated all too frequently, a few extremists can deceive themselves, and others, about the degree of support for their cause, it is worth attempting an assessment of the strength of Puritanism and Catholicism in the diocese, although there are only shreds of indirect evidence upon which to base it; indeed, given the ferment of belief in Elizabethan England, it is doubtful if even contemporaries could have stated the position with any accuracy.

The Recusant rolls, for all their shortcomings, ought to provide some indication as to the extent of Catholicism. From this source one writer has noted 143 Recusant households in late-sixteenth-century Norfolk. Certainly, if the Recusant returns for 1577 and 1588 in any way reflect the distribution of Catholic sympathizers throughout England, they reveal a high density in the Norwich diocese. Dr. Jessopp's study of Recusancy in Elizabethan Norfolk portrays one district where the squires 'were Catholic almost to a

[1] *HMC Salisbury*, ii. 136.

man . . . The Townshends of Rainham, the Cobbs of Sandringham, the Bastards of Dunham, the Bozouns of Whissonsett, the Kerviles of Wiggenhall and many others of less note and importance . . . all within a ten miles' ride of Grimston; the county swarmed with squires who, though they "kept their church" yet had small love for the new order of things, and would have welcomed a change to the old regime with something more than equanimity'. A similar concentration of Recusant squires can be detected in south-west Norfolk where the Woodhouses of Breccles, the Lovells of Harling, the de Greys of Merton, the Townshends of Bracon Ash, the Rokewoods of Euston, the Southwells of Woodrising, and the Bedingfelds of Oxborough must have provided an effective *cordon sanitaire* against the appearance of reformed doctrine in the Norfolk Breckland.[2]

Elsewhere in the diocese Puritanism flourished, especially in cloth-making districts, in the principal towns, and in rural areas where a concentration of Puritan magistrates ensured the thoroughgoing implementation of Calvin's economic, social, and religious teaching.[3] The movement was strong in the Stour Valley where Suffolk clothiers were actively endowing lectureships and frequently leaving legacies to support preachers. Thomas Gale of Edwardstone bequeathed 'to Mr. Nicholsonne my pastor . . . £5, . . . to Mr. Sandes the preacher of Boxford . . . £5, . . . to Mr. Byrde the minister of Boxforde . . . £10, . . . to Mr. Knewstubb the minister of Cockfield . . . £5, . . . [and] to Mr. Welch the preacher of Little Waldingfielde . . . £5'. These calvinist clothiers invested wisely, since their preachers had great influence over the lower orders of society. In the village of Lawshall, for instance, 'fifty persones younge and old' had been won to the gospel by a lecture regularly delivered in their parish church.

Among the East Anglian towns, Ipswich, Norwich, and Bury St. Edmunds had particularly vigorous Puritan communities. At Ipswich, merchants such as John More and his brother-in-law Robert Barker endowed lectureships and, whenever possible, bestowed livings upon Puritan incumbents. At Norwich, where the influential John More, preacher at St. Andrew's, led a group of radical clergy which included canons and minor canons of the cathedral, exercises

[2] *NA* xxxii, 1961, pp. 32–9. *CRS* xxii, pp. 7, 120–6. A Jessopp, *One Generation of a Norfolk House*, 1879, pp. 138–9.

[3] The succeeding paragraphs are based upon Collinson, 'Classical Movement', chap. ix, and his *Elizabethan Puritan Movement*, 1967, esp. pp. 141, 188, 213, 223.

or 'prophesyings' flourished down to 1576. These weekly sessions of Biblical study and exposition appear to have been well attended by citizens and magistrates. As one preacher subsequently reminded them: 'No matters of weight were usually concluded in your common assemblies for the good of your city before ye had first consulted with your grave and godly preachers.' A similar relationship existed at Bury where leading townsmen supported two preachers and tried to drive out the conformist curates whom the Bishop collated to the churches of St. Mary and St. James. In 1582 no less than 175 Bury citizens petitioned the Council to restore these preachers after they had been silenced and forced to abandon their ministry by the Bishop.

The movement in Bury St. Edmunds drew its leadership from Puritan gentry who were as heavily concentrated in this neighbourhood as were Recusants around Grimston: Sir Robert Jermyn at Rushbrooke, Sir John Higham at Barrow, Sir Robert Ashfield at Stowlangtoft, Edward Lewkenor at Denham, and Thomas Poley at Little Saxham—all dwelt within eight or ten miles of Bury, while slightly further afield, at Redgrave, Sir Nicholas Bacon, son of the Lord Keeper, gave powerful backing to the movement. As owners of advowsons, these gentry appointed Puritan ministers to the benefices in their gift; as men of substance they supported unbeneficed salaried preachers; as magistrates they acted vigorously to protect their protégés against ecclesiastical discipline. 'In few other counties', writes Professor Collinson, 'did the Puritan Movement own such whole-hearted and powerful patrons.' Norfolk, too, seems to have been exceptional in this way. In the north of the county Nathaniel Bacon of Stiffkey (the brother of Sir Nicholas) and, initially at least, William Heydon of Baconsthorpe laboured for the 'lifting up of Christ'. They appointed many of the ministers responsible for 'prophesyings' at Fakenham, Wiveton, and Holt, and in 1575 they joined with two other Puritan magistrates–Thomas Barrow of Shipdham and William Blennerhassett of Little Plumstead—in instituting six-weekly sessions or petty sessions at Acle where, like their counterparts at Bury, they endeavoured to impose a strict moral discipline upon the neighbourhood.[4]

By the 1570s there appear to have been districts in Norfolk and

[4] There is considerable coincidence between these late-sixteenth-century centres of Puritanism and the pre-Reformation distribution of dissent in the diocese. For the latter, see *NA* xxxv. 308–26.

Suffolk where heavy concentrations of Puritans profoundly affected many aspects of government and society, and others where a majority of squires inclined towards the old faith. In these circumstances devotees of both persuasions may well have convinced themselves that the religious atmosphere in their locality reflected the national scene; that, as one Recusant put it, 'the state could not longe stand thus; it wold ether to Papistry or to Puritanisme'.[5] They could certainly cite developments outside their local communities in support of this view. Had not zealous protestants in the 1559 House of Commons successfully forced the Queen and her councillors to accept a more radical religious settlement than had been intended? Why should they not secure further concessions both by gradual innovation and radical reformation? Equally, so far as Catholic sympathizers were concerned, had not the Pope, in his Bull *Regnans in Excelsis* (1570), excommunicated and deposed Elizabeth and called upon the faithful to implement his sentence? All in all it is not surprising that substantial numbers of Puritan and Catholic gentry in the Norwich diocese felt convinced that the Elizabethan Settlement was merely an uneasy compromise. Granted this conviction, it was inevitable that they should endeavour by every means possible to change the practices in their diocese, if not the State, in the direction of their own beliefs.

Neither side lacked resourcefulness. Puritan preachers had instituted 'prophesyings' as a method of training ill-educated clergymen in preaching and Calvinistic theology; Puritan gentry bestowed the livings in their patronage upon good preaching ministers; Puritan merchants financed lectureships; Puritan M.P.s, albeit vainly, initiated in the Commons a series of Bills to reform the Prayer Book and church government. Catholic devotees lived in a less optimistic world. Probably few wanted the old faith to be restored through foreign invasion and the deposition of the Queen, but so long as the succession question remained open so, too, did the possibility of a Marian-type reaction; in the meantime the faith had to be nurtured and those in doubt given hope. To this end young East Anglian gentlemen were being trained in continental seminaries for mission work at home, and Catholic sympathizers employed domestic chaplains to celebrate Mass and hold private devotions.

But whether England would 'to Papistry or to Puritanisme' depended upon a third and crucial factor: the rigour with which the

[5] PRO SP 15/25, f. 280v.

government enforced the Elizabethan Settlement; for in the last resort the Queen and her councillors could deploy ecclesiastical and civil administration to suppress the proselytizing activities of both Puritan ministers and Catholic priests. And gradually and rather unwillingly they did. Down to 1570 they had made little effort to secure the enforcement of even the mild penalties against Recusancy formulated in the 1559 Act of Uniformity. But the situation changed when the Pope's excommunication and deposition of the Queen turned Recusancy into a potential source of insurrection. For political reasons the Council determined to act vigorously against Catholic elements in the counties and, although the Queen vetoed attempts in the 1571 parliament to introduce more stringent laws against Recusancy, councillors demanded the vigorous enforcement of those already in existence.

As for Puritanism, down to 1576 repressive measures were sporadic and *ad hoc*, but all the more disconcerting for that. Generally speaking, the Puritan movement, as the most dynamic Protestant element in English society, was a source of strength to Elizabeth's government; moreover it had powerful backing from a section of the Council led by the Earl of Leicester. But periodically the Queen, influenced by personal or diplomatic considerations or by reports from her archbishops, demanded the suppression of Puritan practices which were often countenanced within the Church. In 1565, at the height of the controversy over vestments, she ordered Archbishop Parker to suppress all innovation; as a result, in 1566 many ministers were suspended and even deprived for refusing to conform to his 'Advertisements'. Then, in October 1573, a proclamation 'censured bishops and magistrates for their negligence in suppressing nonconformity, and insisted on imprisonment for anyone who defamed the Prayer Book'. Once more Puritan ministers suffered suspension and deprivation, especially in London where the repression 'most closely resembled a persecution'. Finally, in 1576 the Queen ordered that all exercises of prophesying in the diocese of Canterbury should be suppressed, and the number of preachers reduced to three or four in each shire.[6]

Puritans and Catholics, confronted with varying degrees of repression, naturally sought by every possible means to safeguard practices which they deemed essential to their worship and the propagation of their beliefs. How better could they do so than by

[6] Collinson, pp. 69–74, 150, 152, 191.

securing the appointment of sympathetic magistrates—both lay and ecclesiastical—who, according to their convictions, would either relax or intensify the enforcement of repressive measures? Had not Bishop Parkhurst of Norwich shown 'kind forbearance' towards Puritan ministers in his diocese when he should have enforced Parker's 'Advertisements' in 1566? Although Puritan and Recusant gentry could hardly hope to influence the appointment of bishops, they had plenty of scope in the appointment of J.P.s and diocesan officials.

Puritans also had more positive reasons for displaying great concern about lay magistracy. They made no fundamental distinction between the government of the State and that of the Church; both ought to be ruled in accord with God's law. In their view society was a theocracy in which godly gentry shared with the minister a duty to implement God's will on earth; they therefore might feel a particular responsibility to participate in local government since godly magistrates could do much to implement Christ's teaching, especially in relation to economic and social matters. 'Day by day,' writes Professor Collinson, '"magistracy and ministrye" were working together in a common task of governing the county with godly justice: the minister by preaching and discipline, the justice by government, winning and coercing the people within their charge to a life of godliness and obedience.' In a real sense Puritans 'had a religious view of the nature of magistracy'; they were called to it.[7] Thus, by the 1570s, both radical Protestants and Catholics in Norfolk had good reason to be much concerned about the personnel of local government. The consequences of this, first for the civil and then for the ecclesiastical government of the county, form the subject of this chapter.

Devotees on either side could only hope to pack the Bench with sympathetic magistrates by controlling or at least influencing the channels through which justices were recruited. Although the Lord Chancellor appointed all J.P.s, he needed advice from county magnates who had an intimate knowledge of local affairs; in Norfolk, until 1570, he invariably consulted the Duke of Norfolk and John Parkhurst, Bishop of Norwich. If Parkhurst had had his way Puritan

[7] Collinson, 'Classical Movement', p. 875.

gentry would undoubtedly have gained ascendancy on the Bench. During Mary's reign he had been in exile at Zurich and, once appointed to Norwich, he was remarkably indulgent towards preachers and ministers who worked for the further reformation of the Elizabethan church. 'He winketh at schismatics and anabaptists', Cecil grumbled to Archbishop Parker in 1561. But however great his disregard for ecclesiastical canons and archiepiscopal instructions, his independence collapsed before the dictates of that 'noble prince' Thomas Howard, Duke of Norfolk; or so appointments to the Bench throughout the first decades of Elizabeth's reign would seem to suggest.[8]

The Duke's execution in June 1572 transformed the situation. Thereafter, in the absence of any other nobleman of distinction, Parkhurst was able to speak his mind in recommending magistrates. Moreover his inclination to nominate gentry who held radical Protestant views now received support from Sir Christopher Heydon and Sir William Butts—two magnates whom the Council increasingly associated with him in the leadership of Norfolk. Although Heydon appears to have been inconstant in religion, there is evidence that he supported the radicals during the early 1570s. Sir William Butts's views are not so well documented, but they were sufficiently radical to result in his dismissal from the Bench early in Mary Tudor's reign; a disgrace he suffered until Elizabeth reinstated him, with other good Protestants, at her accession.[9]

Parkhurst, backed by Heydon and Butts, soon began to procure the appointment of magistrates who held radical religious views. In 1570 they secured a place in the commission for young William Heydon, already one of the most ardent Puritans in Norfolk. His appointment is a measure of their determination to strengthen the radical Protestant element among the justices, for they pushed it through despite the Council's avowed disapproval of a father and son sitting concurrently on the Bench. Shortly after Heydon's appointment, Parkhurst successfully sponsored two more Puritan gentry, William Blennerhassettt of Little Plumstead and Thomas Barrow of Shipdham, the father of the Separatist Henry Barrow.

[8] C. Read, *Mr. Secretary Cecil and Queen Elizabeth*, 1955, p. 261. Above, pp. 34–5.

[9] For Heydon, see Sister Barbara Batten's study of the Heydons; a copy is available in the Colman & Rye Libraries of Local History, Norwich. For Butts, cf. *CPR, 1547–8*, p. 87 and Appendix I s.v. Butts, with *CPR, 1553–4*, p. 22 and PRO SP 11/5, no. 6, s.v. Norf.

Then, in 1573, the youthful Nathaniel Bacon, an indefatigable Puritan and the Lord Keeper's second son, was appointed a justice, although he had barely established himself in Norfolk. Only two other magistrates joined the Bench during the years 1570–5—Thomas Hewar and Robert Walpole, both of unknown religious views—so that it is certain that at least two-thirds of the newcomers held Puritan views.[10]

Simultaneously with the appointment of these new men, the Council ordered the dismissal of several justices suspected of Catholic sympathies. This action may have been prompted by Parkhurst and his associates, but since at least one of those who lost office—Sir Nicholas L'Estrange—had been involved in the plot to marry his master the Duke of Norfolk to Mary Stuart, and a second—John Blennerhassett—had also been in the Duke's service, the Council's action may have been a direct consequence of the enquiries which followed the Ridolphi plot. Whatever part Parkhurst, Heydon, and Butts played in the dismissal of these and other Recusant justices, there is no doubt that under their tutelage Puritan adherents dominated the Bench.

This situation changed dramatically when Parkhurst died in 1575. His backing had been crucial to the Puritan movement and its growing ascendancy in county government; without episcopal support Heydon was not sufficiently reliable nor Butts sufficiently radical to maintain this ascendancy. But the new bishop, Edmund Freake, proved extremely unsympathetic to their cause since he had been appointed with a mandate to suppress Puritanism in the diocese. Freake seems to have been prepared to trim his ecclesiastical views to the prevailing wind at Court. As Bishop of Rochester he had taken an indulgent attitude towards Puritan activities in his diocese; but when the Queen's views hardened against the movement he showed no qualms in accepting the more lucrative see of Norwich with a mandate to discipline its Puritans.[11] Undoubtedly Freake's appointment dealt a blow to the movement there, but its supporters had already become so powerfully entrenched in county administration that ultimately they drove him out of the diocese. Not, however, before a bitter struggle had ensued over diocesan administration and

[10] Collinson, pp. 192, 203, 257. Above, p. 80. CUL MS. Ee II 34, ff. 68v, 102v. For Blennerhassett's Puritanism, see Collinson, 'Classical Movement', pp. 883–4. *NA* vii. 87–92.

[11] Collinson, p. 202.

the appointment of a chancellor which, in turn, had extensive repercussions upon the magistracy of Norfolk and Suffolk.

Both Puritans and papists regarded the diocesan chancellor and Official Principal as a key figure in their efforts to protect and propagate their beliefs.[12] As the Bishop's chief legal officer he usually deputized for him in the consistory—the principal diocesan court used for disciplining clergy and parishioners who flouted the Elizabethan Church Settlement. Down to 1581 this court constituted at least a potential threat to Recusants since it had responsibility for enforcing the statutory penalty against them—a shilling fine for every absence from church on Sundays or holy days. By 1577 moves were afoot to increase this mild penalty, and at least one bishop had done so without statutory authority. The consistory court could also be used as a means of compelling puritan conformity in such matters as vestments, ritual, ornaments, and the use of the Prayer Book. For both Puritans and Catholics alike it proved most threatening during an episcopal visitation which was tantamount to the consistory 'on progress', equipped with inquisitorial powers in the form of visitation articles. These comprised an elaborate questionnaire designed by the bishop and his chancellor to elicit information about breaches of ecclesiastical law and to facilitate the scrutiny of any aspect of parish life deemed necessary. These articles, circulated to incumbents and church wardens in advance of the visitation, required the submission of written answers. From this information offenders were summoned to answer before the bishop, or more commonly his chancellor. In such circumstances the latter could do much to intensify or weaken the impact of ecclesiastical discipline. As a Puritan remarked in 1578, it was 'no small ordinary matter for safety of government who supply that place [chancellorship] in this diocese'. Consequently during the 1570s both Catholics and Puritans in turn endeavoured to procure a well-disposed official who, at worst, would shield them against the rigour of the law or the severity of their bishop and, at best, would actively further their cause.[13]

[12] During the Middle Ages the offices of Chancellor and Official Principal were held separately, the Official Principal being the bishop's chief legal officer. But after the Reformation, in the Norwich diocese, both offices were held by the same person. For the rest of this chapter I have followed normal usage and referred to the bishop's deputy in the consistory as 'chancellor'.

[13] R. A. Marchant, *The Puritans and the Church Courts in the Diocese of York 1560–1642*, 1960, esp. chaps. III, X. PRO SP 15/25, f. 272.

Ironically enough, Parkhurst seems to have appointed a chancellor with Catholic sympathies. According to the Puritans this was the result of a deliberate plot. Sir Thomas Cornwallis, a noted Suffolk Recusant, had taken care, so they asserted, 'to settle such a one chancellor of Norwiche as beinge at his devotion, might followe his direction'. Undoubtedly they exaggerated, but it is clear that when the Bishop appointed Dr. William Masters in 1569 he preferred a man whose background and beliefs differed fundamentally from his own. While Parkhurst had breathed the heady Zwinglian atmosphere of Zurich, Masters had studied at Rome and Orleans. Such an education needed to be lived down in Elizabethan England; instead, he married into a Recusant family whose association with the Duke of Norfolk's cause in 1569 rendered his beliefs yet more suspect. Parkhurst eventually doubted his religious loyalty, commanded him 'to shewe his opinions of masse and purgatory', and in 1575 revoked his patent of chancellorship.[14]

Parkhurst died before he could appoint a new chancellor, so that this task confronted Freake on his arrival in the diocese. On 3 December 1575 he chose John Becon from among the canons of Norwich cathedral. He could scarcely have done worse; circumstances had compelled him to select a new chancellor in a factious diocese before he had had an opportunity to assess the problems and personalities involved, and it looks as if he simply appointed Parkhurst's protégé. Why, otherwise, should a bishop, intent upon disciplining the Puritans, appoint a chancellor who shared their views? As if this were not sufficient cause for friction, John Becon also proved to be a quarrelsome lawyer who thrived on conflict. In 1570, as proctor at Cambridge University, he had incited Puritans and younger members of the University to protest against the new statutes. His opponents depicted him as by 'nature given to contention', and his subsequent career certainly confirms this assessment: as chancellor at Norwich he was soon at loggerheads with Freake; then, when his friend Bishop Overton appointed him chancellor of Coventry, he immediately conspired against him. At Norwich he made little effort to temper his radical Protestantism to suit the Bishop and his conservative advisers. On the contrary, simultaneously with Freake's

[14] PRO SP 15/25, f. 272. NNRO MS. REG/13, book 19, 1559–74, f. 260. *CRS* xxii. 63. C. H. and T. Cooper, *Athenae Cantabrigiensis*, ii, Cambridge, 1861, p. 65. PRO SP 12/117/27i; /71/61; 15/25, f. 269v. Masters married Anne, daughter of Eliz. and Thos. Tibbenham.

attempts to suppress the prophesyings in Norwich he propounded a scheme whereby these could be incorporated into the Elizabethan diocesan system in order to improve its spiritual and administrative standards. A man of such beliefs and temperament was ill-fitted to the task in hand, and very soon Freake tried to dismiss him.[15]

The crisis between bishop and chancellor developed swiftly as Freake proceeded to discipline the Puritans. In his primary visitation of 1576 he undertook a wholesale suspension of Norwich preachers; according to one report '19 or 20 Godlie Exercises of preaching and catechising [were] putt downe in this cittie'. He showed no sympathy for those moderate Puritans, led by John More, the preacher at St. Andrew's, who tried to draw up a formula of limited conformity. 'I hear the bishop stormeth' was the comment of one observer when the Council subsequently ordered him to accept it.[16]

Puritans throughout the diocese reacted strongly; perhaps the more so because their bishop, before coming to Norwich, had been a 'moderate puritan who had turned his coat'. When he suspended Mr. More, one of the 'presidents' of the Norwich exercise, the congregation of St. Andrew's greeted the new incumbent, Mr. Holland, with vituperation and passive resistance. They called him 'turnecote and sayed that he preched false doctryne and had betrayed the worde, and that the Byshop who had commanded hym thither had no more authorytye then a comon mynister'. Meanwhile, 'the paryshe clerke of St. Andrew, beyng commanded over night to rynge in the mornyng to the Exercyse as he had wont to do, neyther wold so do nor yet begyn to synge the psalme . . . as he had wont to do'. The Bishop clapped the ringleaders into prison for disorderly conduct, but the occasion was turned into a triumphal feast. As one observer commented: 'yt ys to be marveled at how many came to them to pryson and how they were banqueted, wyne brought to them and on Fryday at night even feastes made them in pryson both of fleshe and fyshe'.

[15] NNRO MS. REG/14, book 20, 1575–1602, introd. f. 1. The revocation of Masters's patent by Parkhurst, and Freake's appointment of Becon is difficult to understand. For a similar incompatible appointment, see R. A. Marchant, op. cit., p. 44. J. B. Mullinger, *The University of Cambridge from the Royal Injunctions of 1535 to the Accession of Charles I*, Cambridge 1884, pp. 230–8. J. Lamb, *A Collection of Letters . . . from the MS. Library of Corpus Christi College, Cambridge, Illustrative of the History of Cambridge*, 1838, p. 355. Strype, *Annals*, iii(1), pp. 135–6; (2), pp. 207–10. *HMC Salisbury*, ii. 195–8.

[16] *The Seconde Parte of a Register*, ed. A. Peele, Cambridge, 1915, i. 145. Collinson, p. 203.

The Puritans did not stop at these popular demonstrations against Freake's disciplinary measures. Some of the gentry petitioned the Council for the restoration of the preachers and very quickly enmeshed the Bishop in a network of plots and intrigues which even went so far as intercepting his correspondence. In 1578 he complained to the Council, with good reason, that his letters were 'published abroad' before he had received them. Indeed, for a time Lord Keeper Bacon appears to have despatched letters to the Bishop via his son Nathaniel Bacon, thereby acquainting him and his fellow Puritans with the Bishop's business before the unfortunate prelate knew about it himself.[17]

Chancellor Becon rallied to defend the Puritan preachers in a more subtle manner. He submitted to the Privy Council a scheme for the reform of diocesan government in which moderate Puritans like John More were given an important role. Basically he proposed that the Puritan innovation of the 'exercise'—a regular meeting of ministers for Biblical study and exposition—should be integrated with the ancient system of diocesan government so that much of the disciplinary work traditionally undertaken by the bishop's commissaries would be conducted in these monthly meetings. They would be directed by 'superintendents'—'certain choice picked men' from among the preachers resident in each deanery. As Professor Collinson has pointed out, none was better suited to this task than a moderate Puritan like John More. 'For upwards of twenty years, More exercised a kind of unofficial superintendency throughout much of Norfolk, and received a respect which was granted to none of the three bishops who occupied Ludham House in the same period.'[18]

In putting down the preachers, Freake had stirred a hornets' nest: congregations protested; influential Puritan magnates schemed to thwart his policy; even his chancellor undermined it. Even so he might have succeeded in his efforts to discipline the Puritans had he been sufficiently strong-minded to keep his own counsels. In fact he appears to have been a weak and insecure man who needed advice and support. To make matters worse he had a domineering wife: it was '*vox populi*, a principle well-knowne throughout all Norfolk . . .

[17] Collinson, p. 202. *Stiffkey Papers*, pp. 185–6. PRO SP 12/126/23. IHR microfilm XD 37 (Transcrs. and originals from the collection of H. W. Saunders) frame 415, undated letter from Sir Nich. Bacon to Nath. Bacon.

[18] *HMC Salisbury*, ii. 195–8. Collinson, pp. 183–7.

that whatsoever Mrs. Freake will have done the Bishop must and will accomplishe . . . If he did not . . . she wold make hym weary of his liffe'. As if these were not insuperable handicaps, either he or his wife was avaricious. On the pretext that his predecessor had allowed the episcopal residences at Ludham and Norwich to fall into disrepair, he attempted to claim upon Parkhurst's estate for their restoration, thereby jeopardizing legacies to the latter's servants and friends. Then, too, rumours were current that he wanted to leave the diocese because it was not well endowed. An irresolute bishop with an overbearing wife and a hankering for worldly goods was ill-suited to stand alone against the vigorous Puritan elements in his diocese.[19]

He reacted by listening all too readily to the persuasive counsels of an anti-Puritan if not Recusant faction which was scheming to influence his policy. The Puritans subsequently claimed that the leaders of this faction had insinuated into the Bishop's household a Recusant called Dr. Brown who had been a fellow student with Freake's son at Cambridge.[20] Brown, having 'discovered the Bishop's disposition to be covetous and ambitious . . . sett him on to abandon the best and surest subiectes' calling them all 'puritans'. Next, according to the Puritans, he encouraged Freake to claim on the estate of the late Bishop Parkhurst for renovations at Ludham. Finally, 'he put in his Lordship's head . . . [the idea of] a sovereignty of governmente if he were only of the *Quorum* in the Highe Commission'. For their part the Puritans claimed that they had advised 'the Bishop to walke warely . . . for the slaunder of the gospell . . . and [had] misliked . . . [his] entended course to scrape up comodities without conscience'. But he, disregarding their advice, 'on a sodayne . . . altered his course and countenance and thereupon his whole affection' so that he had become the creature of a faction. Soon many Recusants, who 'before trembled at his name for their suspected religion', came to his table. Meanwhile he did all in his power to discredit those who questioned his behaviour; for instance he denounced to the Queen 'dyvers . . . gentlemen of Suffolk and Norfolk . . . as hynderers of her proceedyngs and favorers of precysianes and Purytanes'. Well might Robert Downes, an 'obstinate' papist, confidently boast to a friend: 'tushe, tushe, let the protestants

[19] PRO SP 15/25, ff. 270, 278v, 279v. *APC, 1577–8*, pp. 369, 390. *HMC Salisbury*, xiii. 208. Strype, *Annals*, ii(1), p. 514.

[20] Thomas Brown, LL.D. and John Freake were contemporaries at Christ's College, Cambridge (Venn, *Al. Cant.* i. 238 and ii. 176).

prate and talke what they will, I am sure we have the Bishop sure on our side'.[21]

Undoubtedly the Puritans over-simplified and exaggerated the situation when they represented the Bishop as being dominated by a pro-Catholic clique. The guests at a dinner-party at Ludham-House may provide a more reliable index to the religious opinion of those who enjoyed his confidence. Among those present were Sir Thomas Cornwallis, William Paston, Martin Barney, John Holdich, and Miles Corbett. They were certainly his well-wishers, for when they discussed current rumours that Freake might be translated to Worcester and he confirmed that he would like to move to a more wealthy bishopric 'Sir Thomas [Cornwallis] answered, "nay that shall you not my lord, we will rather contribute somewhat", and so Sir Thomas offringe ten pounds yearly, the residue promised severally tenne pounds in like sorte'.[22] Given this determination to keep Freake in the diocese, their religious views may well repay examination.

Sir Thomas Cornwallis had strong Catholic sympathies. Possessed of a sensitive and subtle mind, he approved of much in the Anglican form of worship and criticized many things in the church of Rome, explicitly repudiating the temporal claims of the Pope. 'I have seldom knowen any of that syde so wyse and so conveniently learned', wrote Dean Goodman to Cecil. In 1570, after a year spent in Bishop Jewel's household at the Council's instigation, he had actually accepted the Elizabethan Settlement. But conformity bred 'unquietness' in his mind so that by the mid 1570s he had lapsed into Recusancy again. Martin Barney had similar doubts; at best he was a church-papist. Described by Freake's successor as 'backward in religion' and an associate of Sir Robert Southwell, whose companions were 'for the most part popish', he was eventually charged with allowing the celebration of Mass in his house. Other guests, however, appear to have been more amenable to the Elizabethan Settlement, albeit none belonged to the forward Protestant party. John Holdich was subsequently described by Bishop Scambler as 'backward in religion' and William Paston as an 'observer of law', which presumably meant that he conformed without enthusiasm. There is no indication as to the doctrinal views of Miles Corbett, the remaining guest. If these squires can be regarded as representative of Freake's friends, then Professor Collinson is probably correct when

[21] PRO SP 15/25, ff. 258, 275, 279.
[22] Ibid., f. 273v.

he asserts that the Bishop had been driven by the Puritans into an alliance with 'those elements in the county, catholic, conformist Anglican and merely irreligious who resented both the preachers and the power of the justices who maintained them'.[23]

None the less Puritan accusations that Recusants dominated Freake's counsels were not without substance. Sir Thomas Cornwallis, the only unequivocal Recusant among the Bishop's confidants, appears to have occupied a particularly influential position. Perhaps it could not have been otherwise in view of his background and experience: head of an old-established Suffolk family which had risen to office at Court via the Howard household, he had been a member of the Privy Council under Mary. But there are suggestions that his special place among the Bishop's friends was deliberately contrived. His lands and influence had been concentrated in Suffolk until 1571 when he purchased in Norwich the ex-Chantry College called the Chapel in the Field (now the Assembly House) and undertook extensive renovations to convert it to a grand Elizabethan mansion. Here he resided for long periods as the crisis mounted between Freake and the Puritans, and it is hard to believe that his residing in Norwich at this time had nothing to do with ecclesiastical politics.[24]

There is also abundant evidence of Freake's over-indulgence towards Recusants. He released them from prison on such flimsy pretexts that sometimes the Council had to order their recommitment. 'I have of late received very sharp reprehension from my Lords of the Council for my lenity extended towards you and the rest in question for religion in these parts' he explained apologetically to one noted Recusant when reincarcerating him in 1582. Despite this 'very sharp reprehension', he had not mended his ways a year later. According to Chief Justice Wray, he had taken into custody Recusants committed at the previous summer assizes, and then 'suffered them ever since for the most part to be at large'. Puritan justices complained that he seldom assisted them to seek out and discipline Catholic suspects. When he did 'it was slender in regard of the number presented and it was unprofit through want of christian

[23] *Procs. SIA* xxviii, 1961, pp. 226–71. BM MS. Lansd. 52, f. 201. Collinson, 'Classical Movement', p. 881.

[24] A. Simpson, *The Wealth of the Gentry, 1540–1660*, Cambridge, 1961, pp. 153, 166. Elveden Hall MS., Personal Accounts of Sir Thos. Cornwallis 1557–97. I am indebted to Mrs. Joy Rowe for kindly allowing me to consult her transcript of this MS.

names, surnames, place of abode and other necessary instructions for indictment'.[25] Similar criticism came from the Bishop of Ely who grumbled that whenever he tried to 'persuade' Recusants into conformity many 'shyfted theyre habitations oute of this shire into the dioces of Norwiche'.[26]

Although the degree of Recusant influence over Freake may be unknown and unknowable, the tenor of Recusant advice is clear enough: Becon must go and the chancellorship be restored to Dr. William Masters—the doctrinal conservative whom Parkhurst had dismissed. Becon had aroused this intense antagonism when he took 'a playne directe course . . . in discoveringe the whole rable of papists', thereby making real that threat of persecution which was always latent while a radical Protestant held the chancellorship. This, coupled with his sympathy and support for the Puritans, inevitably united Recusants and Bishop in their determination to be rid of him.[27]

Matters came to a head in 1577 when Freake announced his intention of making a diocesan visitation. A visitation, with its detailed scrutiny of every incumbent and his congregation, would have provided chancellor Becon with abundant opportunities to indulge his radical sympathies by routing out and disciplining Catholic sympathizers. Moreover the announcement came immediately after the Council had summoned a meeting of bishops in London to examine 'how such as are backward and corrupt in religion maie be reduced to conformity and others stayed from like corruption'. Not surprisingly, therefore, Recusant leaders campaigned vigorously to oust Becon from the chancellorship. First, apparently with the Bishop's approval, Sir Thomas Cornwallis offered him 'any ready downe money very frankly' if he would resign in favour of Dr. Masters. Becon, encouraged by Puritan gentry, refused to be bought out; whereupon Freake tried to discredit him before the Council by complaining of his complicity in extortionate and corrupt dealings. The Bishop's real grievances against Becon emerged in one of his more explosive passages:

25 FSL MS. Bacon–Townshend L.d. 904. This MS. is undated, but was probably drawn up in 1582/3 (see L.d. 272).

26 Pembroke Coll. Camb. MS. vol. of letters presented by the Rev. Charles Parkin, f. 46. BM MS. Lansd. 38, ff. 112–13. PRO SP 12/117/28.

27 PRO SP 15/25, f. 272.

he is an instrument to woorke my continewall troble, which effect will never cease till the cawse be removed. For neither the man nor his parte shall at anie tyme want supportacion owte of theise partes againste me . . . In consideracion of the malice rooted in the man againste me I maie not with safetie lodge as it were within me so professed an enimie.

The Council did not respond to Freake's disclosures. Undoubtedly it had heard other versions of this quarrel; there is evidence that the Earl of Leicester had been kept informed of the situation, and he led a group of councillors who favoured plans like Becon's for infusing the Anglican church with moderate Puritanism.[28]

Since Becon would not surrender his patent of chancellorship, and since the Council had not recommended his transfer to another diocese, Freake resorted to a legal subterfuge which enabled him to displace his chancellor during the visitation. He revived a rather obscure pre-Reformation office: that of *auditor causarum*. The early history of this official is by no means clear. He first appears in the later Middle Ages when bishops entrusted most of their ecclesiastical jurisdiction to an Official Principal sitting in the consistory; most, but not all, for they also maintained their own personal court—the court of audience—to deal either with major cases which were beyond the competence of other diocesan courts, or with such cases as they saw fit to withdraw from the consistory. In some instances they appear to have delegated their 'audience' jurisdiction to an *auditor causarum*. The evidence for the appointment and responsibility of this officer is scanty—only one commission surviving for the Norwich diocese. Undoubtedly the office had long been in abeyance there when, on 12 May 1578, Freake revived it, naming none other than Dr. Masters as its incumbent. In this way he enabled Masters to usurp Becon's consistory jurisdiction and so prevent an anti-Recusant campaign during the forthcoming visitation.[29]

Indeed episcopal scrutiny and censure was now likely to fall most sharply upon the Puritans, who reacted by warning the Council of a 'hurliburly like to ensue' if the Bishop held his visitation while

[28] F. X. Walker, 'The Implementation of the Elizabethan Statutes against Recusants 1581–1603' (London PhD thesis 1961), pp. 43–7. PRO SP 15/25, f. 272; 12/126/6; /127, no. 4. FSL MS. Bacon–Townshend L.d. 919.

[29] NNRO MS. ACT/14, book 16. B. Burnham, 'The Episcopal Administration of the Diocese of Norwich in the Later Middle Ages' (Oxford BLitt thesis 1971), pp. 7–62. I. J. Churchill, *Canterbury Administration*, 1933, i. 470–99, ii. 211–16.

Becon's jurisdiction was usurped in this manner. Their lordships listened with sympathy and commanded Freake, pending their further investigation of the situation, to 'surcease his court of audience' and reinstate his chancellor. He reacted to this order by postponing his visitation rather than risk the consequences of conducting it under Becon's auspices.[30]

In July 1578 the Council attempted to resolve the situation by summoning both bishop and chancellor before its board at Greenwich, where it effected a reconciliation in which Freake promised to cease his campaign against Becon and to dismiss Masters from the office of *auditor causarum*. But as soon as he had returned to Norwich his antipathy towards Becon was rekindled by Dr. Brown, Sir Thomas Cornwallis and Mrs. Freake, who apparently would 'not suffer the Bishop and Chancellor to be frindes'. Consequently, despite his recent promises, he retained the court of audience, withdrew more and more cases from the consistory to be heard by Masters, and even forbade the consistory clerk to pay Becon any fees accruing from cases heard in his court.[31]

During August the Queen and her Court came on progress into Norfolk and Suffolk. The surviving records leave more than a suspicion that councillors used the occasion to discipline Freake's Recusant associates and to countenance the Puritans. For instance popish relics were discovered while the Court stayed at Euston Hall; whereupon the Lord Chamberlain commanded its owner, the young Edward Rokewood, to appear before the Council at Norwich. In the event he was only one out of twenty-three well-known Recusants from the Norwich diocese whom the Council disciplined while the Queen held court for five days in the Bishop's palace. Most of them were committed to close confinement 'to be conferred withal by the Bishop'. While councillors subjected Recusants to this inquisitorial treatment, they encouraged the cause of moderate Puritanism by forcing the Bishop both to accept John More's proposals for limited conformity and to reinstate the Norwich preachers whom he had suspended in 1576. It was at this point that Dr. Becon submitted his proposals for incorporating moderate Puritan practices into the diocesan administration. The Council received it enthusiastically and expressed the hope 'that it might form the basis for peace between the preachers & the authorities in other places'. All this acti-

[30] PRO SP 12/127/4; /126/41 no. iii.

[31] PRO SP 15/25, f. 270; 12/127/4.

vity at the Bishop's palace in August 1578 betokened a severe public reproof for Freake's conduct of diocesan affairs.[32]

Even so his resolve to be rid of Becon remained unshaken. Despite a further conciliar order to close his court of audience and to allow Becon to collect his fees pending a settlement by 'the judgement of men learned in both lawes', when the consistory resumed sitting in mid-September he again withheld these fees and continued to refer many cases to Dr. Masters sitting as his *auditor causarum*. Finally, on 22 September, in defiance of yet another Council letter, he revoked Becon's patent of chancellorship, 'makinge choice', as he put it, 'rather with paine to beare the whole burthen thereof, then with perill to have sutch a supporter as my late chancellor'.[33]

The Puritans reacted swiftly. They protested to the Council that Becon's dismissal was clear proof of the Bishop's determination to prevent any reconciliation with his chancellor; that he was bent upon his dismissal. No doubt they were correct. Freake's only rejoinder to the Council's charge that he had deliberately flouted its instructions, was a feeble plea that he had revoked the patent before opening their lordships' letter. In fact he had received it several days prior to his act of revocation. Becon, meanwhile, had challenged the legality of his dismissal and, whenever the Bishop held the consistory, he forced an entry in order to 'make his protestation for safeguard of his patent'. The situation became even more tense when, on 1 October, Freake announced publicly that he had revoked Becon's patent and 'here do revoke it againe and pronounce hym before you all no officer'. As Becon pushed forward, protesting angrily, the Bishop thrust him back commanding his servants to expel him from the court. On three successive days the Bishop announced Becon's dismissal; each time Becon interrupted, only to be dragged from the court by Freake's servants.[34]

These dramatic scenes coincided with the Michaelmas quarter sessions where Becon seized the opportunity to complain of the Bishop's behaviour and the 'violence offred . . . by himself and his men'. It was a shrewd move, made at a time when ecclesiastical

[32] E. Lodge, *Illustrations of British History*, ii, 1838, pp. 119–22. *APC, 1577–8*, pp. 310–13. *CRS* liii, 1961, p. 113. Collinson, p. 203.

[33] PRO SP 12/127/4. *APC, 1577–8*, pp. 320–1, 336–7. NNRO MSS. ACT/13, book 14B, 1577–8; /14, book 15, 1578–9. PRO SP 12/126/6.

[34] PRO SP 12/126/19 & 41.

courts were generally in disrepute and when, as will be shown, Puritan magistrates in the Norwich diocese were making a determined bid to usurp much of the jurisdiction of these courts. Consequently these magistrates were more than willing to use quarter sessions to defend Becon against improper diocesan administration. He could certainly count upon the support of at least five or six puritan justices[35]—'my greatist adversaries', as Freake subsequently described them—but his case must have impressed other justices as well since the Bench, sixteen or seventeen strong, summoned Freake, a magistrate himself, and declared illegal his dismissal of Becon. It then ordered him to allow his chancellor all consistory court fees, including those he had already withheld, and to permit his attendance at all sessions of the court. Finally, aware of the subterfuges which Freake had used to usurp Becon's jurisdiction, the justices demanded his word that, pending judgement at law, whenever he was unable personally to hold the consistory court, 'the chancellor should and none other'.[36]

Few experiences could have been more humiliating for Freake than this public disciplining by his fellow justices. But the incident only made him more vindictive, and so intensified the conflict even further. Heeding the justices' dictates even less than conciliar instructions, he promptly expelled Becon from the consistory court once more. Desperately Becon complained to the Council which, as before, showed strong sympathy with his case; it appointed a commission of six ardent Puritan gentry, together with the two most radical archdeacons in the diocese, to enquire into the Bishops' 'rare and strange' behaviour and, pending its findings, to restore 'Dr. Becon in quiet and peaceable possession of the chancellor's office'.[37]

This the commissioners did in as public a manner as Freake had dismissed him. First they let it be widely known that the Council had ordered Becon's reinstatement, then, late in October, Sir Robert Jermyn and William Blennerhassett accompanied by 200 of the brethren burst in upon Freake's consistory proceedings and in the

[35] Nath. Bacon, Wm. Blennerhassett, Dru Drury, Thos. Gawdy, and Wm. Heydon.

[36] PRO SP 12/126/14 & 41 iii, f. 2.

[37] PRO SP 12/126/3. The commissioners were: Sir Philip Parker, Sir Robt. Jermyn, Sir Thos. Gawdy, Dru Drury, Nath. Bacon, Wm. Blennerhassett, Dr. Fulke, and Dr. Still. For evidence of their Puritanism, see Collinson, 'Classical Movement', pp. 317, 503, 808, 866, 884.

name of the Council restored 'Dr. Becon in full possession of the office of chauncellorshipp [commanding] the proctors and inferior officers to accept him and obey him'. Seldom can the citizens of Norwich have witnessed such scenes as accompanied this bitter conflict for control of the chancellorship. Once more the Bishop had been publicly humiliated and his orders countermanded by his Puritan detractors, this time on the Council's authority.[38]

Once more, too, the incident fortified Freake's resolve to rescind Becon's patent of chancellorship, and pending this he continued personally to hold the consistory throughout November. Becon, meanwhile, asserted his rights by endeavouring to perform his duties, with the result that diocesan government rapidly disintegrated in a welter of orders and counter-orders. The Bishop implored the Council to rescind its instructions for Becon's reinstatement so that he 'may not forbyd that which I commaunde nor commaunde that which I forbyd to the greate troble of the wholl countrey and intollerable vexation and charge of the subiects'. Throughout December ecclesiastical jurisdiction was paralysed: the Bishop appears to have been unable to hold the consistory himself; he would not allow Becon to do so, but could not appoint another chancellor since Becon's patent had not been legally revoked; finally, the Council had forbidden his court of audience and he had eventually suspended his *auditor causarum*. By January 1579, however, either the Council had intervened or good sense had prevailed; George Gardiner, Dean of Norwich, and a moderate puritan, had been appointed 'acting' chancellor until the dispute could be settled.[39]

While the Council took advice as to whether Becon could be deemed to have infringed his patent and so warranted dismissal, the Bishop complained about the procedures of the commission appointed to enquire into his treatment of Becon. He asserted that after depositions had been taken they 'were by the comissioners delivered to Dr. Beacon to be considered of before theie were ingrossed, who, as it is said, had the custodie of them five or six daies'. Such partiality, he maintained, necessitated a new commission directed to 'impartial' gentry. As commissioners he nominated Sir Christopher Heydon, Sir William Butts, Sir William Paston, Sir Henry Woodhouse, Sir Roger Woodhouse, Francis Wyndham, and

[38] PRO SP 12/127/1.

[39] NNRO MSS. ACT/13, book 14B, 1577–8;/14, book 15, 1578–9, entries for 21 Oct., 11 Nov., 27 Nov. PRO SP 15/25, f. 287.

Henry Doyley—squires who, in the main, supported the Bishop in his anti-Puritan, if not his pro-Catholic policy, but whom he may have considered more acceptable to the Council than Catholic sympathizers like Sir Thomas Cornwallis and Martin Barney. Sir William Paston has already been identified as a supporter of Freake. Henry Doyley was subsequently described as 'backwardes in religion', while Sir Roger Woodhouse had little sympathy with puritanism: he was left out of the commission of the peace in the late 1570s, probably at Parkhurst's suggestion, and Bishop Scambler trying to classify his religious views in 1587, could only describe, him as an 'observer of lawe'. It is surprising, perhaps, to find Freake proposing Butts and Heydon—two of Parkhurst's former radical Protestant associates. By 1578, however, Sir Christopher Heydon had been won over to the Bishop's faction and had become particularly intimate with Dr. Masters, Freake's candidate for the diocesan chancellorship.[40]

Freake's demand for a new commission of inquiry evoked no response from the Council; it merely stung Becon into retaliation by agitating for an investigation into 'the notorious offensive misgovernment' of the Bishop's household. To this the Council readily acceded and the subsequent inquiry, even allowing for hostile exaggeration, produced considerable evidence to suggest that the Bishop was little more than a pliant tool in the hands of his wife and a group of Recusant gentry.

The Council, confronted with this evidence and backed by the judgement of common and civil lawyers, decreed in Becon's favour: not only should he remain chancellor, but also he should receive those fees from the consistory court which Freake had withheld; if the Bishop desired personally to hold the court he was to 'do yt to countenance not to discountenance his chancelor', and if he was absent from his diocese he could appoint no other deputy nor 'erecte any other courts'.[41]

Freake had one card left to play: he could threaten resignation and so force the Queen and her Council to choose between himself and his chancellor. It was dangerous play which might have cost him his see, but he took the risk. 'I desier no longer to beare governement then I shalbe . . . master over anie myne inferior officer', he pro-

40 PRO SP 12/127/1; /126/14; 15/25, ff. 273v, 287. BM MS. Lansd. 52, f. 201. Appendix I.

41 SP 12/127/2 & 3; 15/25, ff. 268–80.

tested, therefore 'I will rather submitte my self to hir Majesty's good pleasure to appointe some other in my place' than yield to a reconciliation with Becon. Faced with this choice the Council backed down and arranged for Becon's appointment as precentor of Chichester cathedral. Thereafter Freake and his advisers swept to victory by appointing Dr. Masters to the chancellorship in April 1580 and promptly commencing the diocesan visitation.[42]

This triumph for the anti-Puritan faction, especially its Catholic wing, by no means silenced the Puritan gentry's opposition to Freake. Simultaneously with their struggle to maintain a sympathetic diocesan chancellor, Puritan magistrates in north Norfolk and north-west Suffolk had been usurping the business of the commissaries' courts by extending 'their jurisdiction to cover many purely moral offences which the ecclesiastical courts might well claim as their peculiar preserve'.[43]

Best documented are the proceedings in Bury St. Edmunds.[44] Here, in 1578, Puritan magistrates drew up and exhibited in each church a code of discipline for the better government of the townsmen. They specified punishments for 'papistry, absence from church, disturbance of prayers and sermons, railing at magistrates and preachers, blasphemy, witchcraft, gaming, usury and moral offences'. By 1580 they had pressed their attack on the local ecclesiastical court to the point where they had refused even to acknowledge the authority of the Bishop's commissary Dr. Day. When he had attempted to punish Puritan townsmen for non-attendance at church three of their justices had bound him over for summoning questmen without 'making the justices first privie unto it'. By 1581 they had driven him to distraction: he implored Freake to write to the Queen about 'all our trobles and the justices . . . continewell abusing' of him; he proposed 'to kneale before her Maiestie and to laie open how they . . . [had] dealt with . . . [him] from time to time and for what cause'. His letter ended on a more practical note: he would 'make frendes to be in commission for the peace', thereby exercising as a magistrate the jurisdiction denied him as commissary.[45] He must have lacked

[42] SP 12/126/6. NNRO MS. REG /14, book 20, 1575–1602, preliminary entries ff. 3v–4.

[43] Collinson, 'Classical Movement', p. 875.

[44] Ibid., pp. 860–930. In these pages Professor Collinson has dealt thoroughly with the situation at Bury. My brief account is based entirely upon his work.

[45] BM MS. Lansd. 33, ff. 41–41v.

powerful patrons, or his overtures were blocked by Puritan intrigue, since he never figured in any commission of the peace.

Simultaneously these same Puritan magistrates tried to reform the ministry in Bury. First they forced out the 'conformist' curates from the parish churches of St. Mary and St. James and then refused to accept any candidates put forward by the Bishop, on the grounds that the appointment of new curates rested with the townspeople of Bury in whose name they claimed to act. The parishioners' nominees, however, needed Freake's approval and he, for his part, refused to induct any minister chosen at the instigation of these Puritan justices. Conflict and tension continued for several years. Freake accused the justices of trespassing on his jurisdiction, appealing in vain to both Council and Queen. Such support as he received came from the assize judges who not only drove Puritan ministers from Bury, but also secured the dismissal of four justices who had led the opposition to Dr. Day.

In Norfolk, Puritan justices were more widely scattered than their counterparts around Bury. Consequently their conflict with the Bishop and his officials may have been less well co-ordinated, although there is little doubt that they acted in concert with their fellows in Suffolk. In at least one north Norfolk town they challenged ecclesiastical jurisdiction in the same manner as their brethren at Bury, while in 1583–4, at the height of the Bury Puritans' campaign against Freake and Day, they strove to discredit the Bishop by fostering suspicion that he harboured Recusants in his household. First they procured his exclusion from the commission against Recusancy where he was of the 'quorum', with the plea that 'he could spy out from the furthest [parts] of his diocese some minister of the gospel for omitting the least duty . . . and yet could not spy out any one Mass of so many in Norfolk and Norwich, some of them being in his own parish'. This done, they then 'detected' his butler and lawyer repairing to secret Masses, indicted them for Recusancy at the quarter sessions, and even refused to allow the Bishop—himself a justice—to plead on their behalf. In a pathetic letter to Burghley he complained that, although his servants had deceived him, 'some justices there . . . sought to pervert the actions of those men to his reproach; and so consequently thereby to confirm the untrue reports given out of his supportation of Papists'.[46]

[46] FSL MSS. Bacon–Townshend L.d. 272, 275, 904. NNRO MS. 20432 (126 × 6). Strype, *Annals*, iii(1), pp. 250–1.

Freake, powerless to resist this relentless campaign against his integrity and his diocesan government, spared no effort to procure a transfer to another diocese. That he possessed neither the stature nor the astuteness to discipline the powerful factious elements in this diocese had long been apparent. As early as 1578 he had confided to a few friendly Norfolk squires his hankering for a less troublesome diocese and in June 1579 there had been discussions about his transfer; but Cooper of Lincoln refused Norwich because of 'the troblesomnes and the dainger of the diocesse'. Protracted negotiations for him to replace the aged Bishop Cox at Ely had broken down because the latter had demanded a pension from the temporalities, which Freake refused to grant. In 1581 Aylmer suggested that he should be moved to Lincoln 'where the diocesse is well setlede', but this too came to nothing. In desperation during 1583 Freake sought permission to retire if he could not move 'unto some place of more quiet'. 'No comfort, God knows, have I here', he cried, 'but continual crossing and over-thwarting, to my great grief and unquietness.'[47] Release came in 1584 when he was translated to Worcester and succeeded at Norwich by Edmund Scambler of Peterborough, who quickly allayed controversy and dissension.

The Puritans' conflict with Freake and (in their view) his Recusant accomplices had centred largely on the diocesan chancellorship. But it also had extensive repercussions upon the personnel in the Norfolk and Suffolk commissions of the peace, and it is now appropriate to resume the investigation of the impact of sectional beliefs upon the Norfolk Bench which was interrupted in order to describe the disorders which accompanied Freake's sojourn at Norwich.

By 1575 Parkhurst, Heydon, and Butts had managed to secure places on the Norfolk Bench for an influential group of Puritan gentry which subsequently proved capable of mounting a devastating campaign against Freake and his advisers. In letters to courtiers and councillors, on commissions of inquiry, in quarter sessions and petty sessional gatherings, these magistrates had defended John Becon and embarrassed the Bishop and his diocesan government to the point at which anarchy threatened. Although Parkhurst's death

[47] BM MS. Lansd. 28, f. 161. Strype, *Annals*, ii(2), pp. 261–2; iii(1), pp. 248–9. Collinson, 'Classical Movement', p. 887.

had undoubtedly deprived the Puritans of a powerful patron, it would be a mistake to assume that they lost influence on the Bench. They still had influential friends at Court who could safeguard those places which they had already gained: they had easy access to the Lord Keeper—Sir Nicholas Bacon—through his sons Nathaniel and Nicholas; the Earl of Leicester, that champion of Puritanism and patron of Dr. Becon, took a lively interest in their activities;[48] then too, from among their own ranks, Dru Drury, a gentleman usher of the privy chamber, kept in close touch with affairs in Norfolk. With such backing the Puritan gentry not only managed to maintain their following on the Bench but even to augment it by securing the appointment of Nicholas Bacon and Thomas Knyvett, of Ashwellthorpe.[49]

Freake, confronted by such opponents, countered by attempting to pack the Bench with his own supporters. Although his advice ultimately carried little weight at the Council board, he received strong backing from the two assize judges who had considerable influence on the composition of the Suffolk Bench and probably that for Norfolk as well. It is certainly significant that out of ten justices whom Bishop Scambler subsequently described as 'backward in religion', no less than six—Henry Doyley, Martin Barney, Clement Paston, William Rugg, John Pagrave and Nicholas Hare—had been appointed between 1575 and 1579 at the height of the conflict between Freake and Becon, while a seventh—John Holdich—had been appointed during the Bury crisis in 1582. Furthermore, Sir Nicholas L'Estrange and William Yelverton, both dismissed under the regime of Parkhurst, Heydon, and Butts were restored to the commission of the peace in 1579. The suggestion that these justices provided the nucleus of a pro-Freake group does not rest entirely on the fact that their religious views were conservative. Holdich and Barney had been among the justices who dined with the Bishop at Ludham and supported Sir Thomas Cornwallis in persuading him to remain at Norwich, while Henry Doyley was one of the justices whom the Bishop had nominated to supersede the pro-Puritan commissioners appointed by the Council to enquire into his dispute with Becon.[50]

Several other squires may also have owed their appearance on the

[48] Collinson, 'Classical Movement', pp. 885, 894, 927. [49] Appendix I.

[50] Collinson, 'Classical Movement', pp. 892–930. Appendix I. BM MS. Lansd. 52, f. 201. Above, pp. 214, 221–2.

Bench to Freake's influence. It is noteworthy that John Walpole, a Marian justice who had been excluded from the early Elizabethan commissions, was reinstated in 1577 only to be dismissed again by 1583. Geoffrey Cobb's short-lived magisterial career is equally significant: a gentleman with Recusant connections, he was appointed J.P. in 1578 and remained in the commission until his death in 1581; none of his forebears had been a justice nor were any of his descendants at least down to the Civil War.[51] Even less is known about other justices and it is only possible to record the coincidence between their appearance on the Bench and the development of this prolonged religious conflict. Charles Calthorpe and Richard Kemp, appointed in 1575 and 1580 respectively, were dismissed in 1578 and 1581. Although Calthorpe lived until *c.* 1609 and Richard Kemp until 1600, neither of them reappeared in the commission of the peace.

The dismissal of these and other justices suggests that each side endeavoured, albeit with rather limited success, to oust the other's supporters from the Bench. All that Freake could achieve, even with backing from the assize judges, was the temporary dismissal from the Suffolk commission of four Puritan justices at the height of the Bury conflict.[52] This is not surprising since the mounting threat of invasion and Catholic insurrection strengthened the Council's resolve to maintain a magistracy which was 'well affected' in religion. Good Protestant justices were at a premium. By the same token, Councillors were much more likely to respond to Puritan complaints of waywardness among the Bishop's friends. John Walpole may have fallen victim to these tactics in 1583. Certainly Thomas Townshend and Martin Barney did in 1576. As soon as the Council received information that they 'cume not to the churche' it instructed the Lord Keeper to remove their names from the commission of the peace. Yet so subtle was the network of patronage and so great the difficulties experienced by the Council in discovering the realities of any situation, that even the Puritans had little success in permanently excluding Freake's supporters from the Bench. No sooner, for instance, had they levelled their complaint against Townshend and Barney than Freake denied it; whereupon the Council immediately countermanded its instructions to the Lord Keeper and both justices were reinstated.[53]

[51] A. Jessopp, *One Generation of a Norfolk House*, 1879, p. 138.

[52] Sir Robert Jermyn, Sir John Higham, Robert Ashfield, and Thomas Badby.

[53] *APC, 1575–7*, p. 238.

Inadequate sources prevent a detailed analysis of the effect of this bitter religious conflict upon the personnel of the Norfolk Bench, but its impact is apparent in the rapid increase in the number of justices as each side sought to pack the Bench with its nominees: in 1574 the commission contained twenty-eight names; by 1578 it had expanded to thirty-six and in the following year, at the height of the dispute, it numbered no less than forty-six justices.

CHAPTER XI

Conflict in Local Administration: Patentees, Licensees, and Deputy Lieutenants 1578-1586

SIMULTANEOUSLY with their campaign to undermine diocesan administration, Freake's principal detractors in Norfolk and Suffolk began to oppose what they regarded as harmful innovations in secular administration. They appear to have been particularly concerned about patents and licences through which the Crown empowered particular gentry to undertake administrative tasks which hitherto had been the responsibility of the justices in quarter sessions. That the Crown granted trading and manufacturing patents to reward courtiers and to augment its meagre revenues is well known. But the use of patents in local administration has received less attention. As was suggested in chapter VI, these patents appear to have been granted as a means of overcoming the tardiness and obstructiveness which many justices displayed towards statutes and Council orders. As the threat of Spanish invasion mounted, this quarter-sessional tardiness increasingly frustrated the Council's efforts to ensure that strategic roads, harbours, and sea defences were adequately repaired and that the militia was well trained and thoroughly armed. If the justices would not sanction sufficient rates to facilitate these tasks, then the Crown must find other means. Consequently it began to issue licences and patents which enabled specified persons to raise the money and undertake the work.

The Norfolk gentry who sued for these patents scarcely shared the Council's concern for national security. They were opportunists who quickly perceived that the Crown's willingness to license private individuals to implement government policy could be utilized to enhance their power and augment their fortunes. Among these, Sir Arthur Heveningham stands out as by far the most resourceful and forceful personality. He had become the principal contender for leadership in Norfolk affairs after the Duke of Norfolk's execution in 1572. His tactics testify to his conviction that success at Court paved the way to power in the county. Energetic, flamboyant, irascible, quarrelsome, he displayed supreme contempt for those cumbersome administrative processes which depended upon agreement among justices meeting in quarter sessions; instead, he endeavoured to make his mark by obtaining letters patent which empowered him to bypass these processes.

In opposition to this view, other justices protested that patentees and licensees like Heveningham used their prerogative power to extort and misappropriate money, thereby, so it was claimed, subordinating the public good to private gain. Undoubtedly there were grounds for such accusations, but the justices who voiced them were by no means dispassionate observers of the scene. Whatever power accrued to Heveningham and his like did so at the expense of their fellow magistrates; and in any case the statutes which patentees were empowered to enforce were often those which most magistrates tacitly ignored because they ran counter to a whole range of local vested interests. For a variety of reasons, therefore, many magistrates opposed the activities of patentees and licensees, and in the process became jealous guardians of their statutory administrative powers and particularly their powers in quarter sessions to grant or withhold local rates.

The leader, and perhaps the most sincere member among these magistrates, was Nathaniel Bacon of Stiffkey. Bacon's voluminous papers, now scattered in private and public collections throughout England and America, bear testimony to his almost obsessive concern for the godly and quiet government of north Norfolk. He was particularly critical of magistrates who sacrificed the good of the commonweal to their private gain, and he seems to have spent as much time investigating corruption among those in authority as he did curbing the excesses of the lower orders of society. In these activities he received support from two distinguished lawyers—Edward Flowerdew and his brother-in-law Francis Wyndham—as well as from religious radicals like Dru Drury, William Blennerhassett, and Thomas Barrow, all of whom had been involved in the campaign against Freake's ecclesiastical jurisdiction.

Their initial clash with the patentees can be dated to 1581 when Heveningham procured his first patent.[1] It empowered him to repair the main highway from Cambridge and Bury St. Edmunds to Southwold where it passed through Metfield, a Suffolk parish situated

[1] The petition to the Queen seeking a patent is dated 4 Mar. 1580/1 (Bodl. MS. Tanner 241, ff. 12v–13). It has not been possible to identify the patent from the MS. Indexes in the PRO.

close to the Norfolk boundary.[2] He was to finance the undertaking by submitting his estimates to the Norfolk and Suffolk justices who were then to authorize the constables to collect an appropriate rate. From the Crown's point of view the arguments in favour of this grant were compelling. The 1554 statute for highway repairs had imposed upon each parish the responsibility for upkeep of its roads, but it had made no provision for cases where difficult terrain created engineering problems of such magnitude that, unaided, parishioners could neither provide the resources nor bear the cost. This seems to have been the situation at Metfield where the main thoroughfare was often waterlogged because of drainage difficulties in an area of active springs. Its condition further deteriorated as a result of the amount of traffic it carried since it was one of the main routes to the coast for dairy-produce destined for London from the rich lands of south Norfolk and north Suffolk; thus a good case could be made for the inhabitants throughout the whole area contributing to the repair of the road at Metfield.[3]

But for a variety of reasons many justices in Norfolk and Suffolk did not take this detached view of Heveningham's patent. The more legalistically minded among them considered that it took away their right to decide in quarter sessions whether a rate was necessary and how large it should be, turning them, instead, into mere agents of the patentees.[4] Those from north Suffolk no doubt also felt aggrieved that a member of the Bench should have sought prerogative authority to carry out a task committed to their charge by statute. It is interesting that opposition in Suffolk came from the same gentry of Puritan persuasion and extensive legal education as had led opposition to Freake's diocesan administration—Sir Nicholas Bacon (jun.), Sir Robert Jermyn, Sir John Higham, Sir William Spring, and Sir Thomas Wingfield. Meanwhile in Norfolk Edward Flowerdew was prepared to take the initiative in opposing what he regarded as the dubious activities of his quarrelsome neighbour. He had much in common with these Suffolk justices: he was a distinguished common lawyer, he shared their radical religious views, and, like Nathaniel and Nicholas Bacon, he objected to patents and licences which afforded opportunities for extortion and which therefore subordinated

[2] BM MS. Eg. 2713, f. 133.

[3] The drainage problems are still apparent from a visit to Metfield. See also *Procs. SIA* xxiii, 1939, pp. 144–5.

[4] Below, pp. 255–6.

a community's well-being to the ambition of a few individuals.

Quarter sessions provided the principal platform from which Flowerdew and the Suffolk justices mounted their campaign against the patentee. Heveningham could not escape the necessity of consulting with the assembled justices about his proposed rate, since he depended upon their subordinates—the high and petty constables—for its collection, and these minor officers would only act on the authority of a quarter sessional warrant. There are tantalizing glimpses of bitter debates at the Norwich sessions throughout 1582: Flowerdew openly charged Heveningham with demanding an excessive rate; he even hinted at the ultimate destination of much of this tax by admonishing him for extortion as sheriff. In his complaints against Heveningham's activities Flowerdew received support from Francis Wyndham and 'the graver sortt of the justices'—a group which no doubt included Nathaniel Bacon, William Blennerhassett, and Thomas Barrow, since they all attended these sessions and were simultaneously opposing similar activities in north Norfolk.[5]

Throughout 1582 both sides appealed to the Council for support. When some of the justices in Suffolk petitioned that body against the burden of Heveningham's rate he 'laboured and obtained many signatures of men of good repute' for a counter-petition. He also complained at the Council board about the obstructiveness of his opponents in Suffolk and no doubt in Norfolk too where Edward Flowerdew certainly protested against Heveningham's 'contynuall boorde talke' throughout his shrievalty.[6]

There is little doubt that Heveningham and Flowerdew deployed all the influence they could command at Court in an effort to 'pack' the Norfolk commission of the peace and so ensure that a majority of the Bench favoured their views, Heveningham hoping to gain approval for his rate, Flowerdew scheming to secure its rejection. In these circumstances Heveningham's appointment to the shrievalty in 1581 was surely no coincidence. It may have been the work of his opponents who knew well enough that this office would bar him from the Bench throughout the critical months when quarter sessions would be debating his rate. On the other hand it afforded

[5] PRO St. Ch. 5, H 18/2 (Flowerdew's answer); F 14/17. NNRO MS. Norfolk Q/S minute book 1583–6. Below, pp. 234–41.

[6] PRO St. Ch. 5, H 18/2 (Flowerdew's answer). NNRO MS. Aylsham, bundle 74, Edw. Flowerdew to Sir A. Heveningham, 18 Dec. 1582.

him close contact with the Council which he exploited to good effect. By the end of 1582 his complaints to their lordships appear to have culminated in Flowerdew's dismissal from the Norfolk commission of the peace and the appointment of at least three new justices who shared Heveningham's attitude towards local government.[7] Indeed he seems to have intrigued at the Crown Office in Chancery with such success that when the new Norfolk commission was finally sent down to Norwich, in time for the Epiphany sessions (1582/3), its entire order of seniority had been altered to the humiliation of his opponents and the aggrandizement of his supporters. His friend William Heydon, for instance, then busy exploiting licences in north Norfolk, had been placed above their mutual opponent Nathaniel Bacon, while the latter's Puritan associate Thomas Barrow fell ten places and Heveningham's friend Thomas Farmer rose thirteen.[8]

With this accession of strength and the prospect of his own return to the Bench when his shrievalty expired in November 1582, Sir Arthur had grounds for optimism that his rate would be approved at the Epiphany sessions. But his opponents had not been idle and Flowerdew's friendship with the Lord Chancellor may explain the shock which awaited Heveningham. When the new commission arrived in January 1583 he discovered that his name had not been restored and that in consequence he would still be barred from the Bench when the crucial debate over his Metfield rate took place.[9] With characteristic hotheadedness he ambushed Flowerdew as he rode to the quarter sessions, injured him, and then galloped off to the sessions where he no doubt hoped to persuade the Bench to grant the rate he required. Such was his arrogance that despite being omitted from the commission of the peace, he sat among the justices 'with his hat on his head' and afterwards dined with them at the mayor's house, where he boasted that 'if any man in England shoulde abuse him . . . he woulde kyll him though he were hangyed on a gybett'. Even when one of Flowerdew's servants appeared in court to display his master's blood-stained hat as evidence of Heveningham's

[7] Edward Clere, John Peyton, and Thomas Sidney. For their subsequent conduct in local admin., see above, pp. 161–3, and below, pp. 235–8, 242, 287, 296–7.

[8] Appendix I, cf. lists 29 and 32. For Heveningham's friendship with Thos. Farmer, see PRO St. Ch. 5, F 14/17 (Bill); F 8/32 (Hev's dep.).

[9] PCC 23 Windsor. Flowerdew named Lord Chancellor Thos. Bromley as his executor. Appendix I and above, p. 73.

outrageous breach of the peace, justices like Francis Wyndham and Nathaniel Bacon had the utmost difficulty in persuading the Bench to take bonds for his appearance at the next sessions. Yet as soon as Heveningham complained that Flowerdew's men were preparing to ambush him when he rode home after the sessions, the Court bound them to keep the peace. Such indications of the strength of Heveningham's following in 1583 would suggest that his rate was finally approved, but unfortunately evidence about the outcome of this controversy is lacking.[10]

While, in south Norfolk, Edward Flowerdew strove to prevent Heveningham from implementing his patent, nearer the coast Nathaniel Bacon conducted a vigorous campaign to prevent the Heydons from exploiting other aspects of local administration. Throughout most of the 1570s both Sir Christopher Heydon and his son William had worked in close association with Bacon to advance the Puritan cause in Norfolk. But by 1578 they had sundered themselves 'from the best . . . affected gentlemen of the shire' and, like Sir Arthur Heveningham, with whom they became closely associated, had begun to manipulate administration in Norfolk in order to augment their dwindling income. While Heveningham exploited patents, the Heydons profited from the abuse of licences and from corruption in the vice-admiral's court.[11]

Their opportunity arose from the government's attempts to regulate corn supplies in order to prevent high food prices and consequent social unrest. Two early Elizabethan statutes effectively permitted the export of corn provided its price in English markets remained at a reasonable level; the second statute, however, acknowledged that the Crown might at any time prohibit export either from one district or from the entire country. This it frequently did, even in years when supplies seemed plentiful, permitting export only under special licence.[12] Consequently, for much of Elizabeth's reign, enterprising East Anglian merchants with corn on their hands could export it only by the hugger-mugger loading of grain in

[10] PRO St. Ch. 5, F 14/17; F 5/13. NNRO MS. Norfolk Q/S minute book 1583–6, entry for 8 Jan. 25E. Above, pp. 197–8.

[11] Above, p. 207. Below, p. 237–8. FSL MS. Bacon–Townshend L.d. 353.

[12] 5 Eliz. c. 5; 13 Eliz. c. 13.

remote creeks or by purchasing an export permit from a Crown licensee. A licence to export 100 quarters of grain fetched at least £7, so that trafficking in licences became a profitable business: profitable to the Crown which granted these licences both as rewards to courtiers and to assist coast towns in raising finances to repair harbours and sea defences; profitable, in turn, to licencees who quickly sold them to eager merchants; profitable to the merchant who proceeded to export many times the quantity of corn permitted by his licence; profitable, finally, to men like Sir Christopher and Sir William Heydon who knew how to manipulate the system to their private gain.

By 1578 Sir Christopher Heydon had joined forces with Thomas Sidney of Walsingham to exploit the licensing system. No doubt they were drawn together by the prospect of mutual benefit since between them they wielded influence at all key points in the system. Heydon ranked among the principal magistrates in Norfolk; Sidney, a busy cornmonger with connections at Court through his brother-in-law Sir Francis Walsingham, was in charge of the customs office at King's Lynn. By 1578 he had little to learn about exploiting this position. Instead of trying to check smuggling and illicit grain exports from Lynn and its member creeks, he had compromised his position by personally engaging in the export of unlicenced grain. In 1572 his slackness and suspected collusion in the extensive smuggling activities of Lynn merchants had been disclosed to the Privy Council. Even so the subsequent enquiry came to nothing; Sidney remained in charge of the Lynn customs office and soon resumed his trafficking with Flanders and Spain.[13]

His joint enterprises with Sir Christopher Heydon started in 1578 when, with Heydon's encouragement, the townsmen of Cromer petitioned the Queen for a licence to export 10,000 quarters of grain in order to help finance their sea-defence works. Their petition needed a sponsor at Court; here Thomas Sidney took up the cause and 'followed the matter' for them 'by the helpe of Sir Francis Walsingham, his brother, then Secretary' and an influential privy councillor. As soon as the townsmen received their licence they 'did put Sir Christopher Heidon in trust with the said license'. No doubt he took his fees, but the real significance of this appointment lay in the patronage it afforded him. Licences were in great demand and

[13] *NA* vi, 1864, p. 262. PCC 17 Brudenell. Williams, 'Maritime Trade', pp. 33–4. *EHR* lxvi, 1951, pp. 387–95. N. Williams, *Contraband Cargoes*, 1961, p. 47.

he could dispose of them at will. His first client arrived in haste from London; he was none other than Thomas Sidney bearing letters from Sir Francis Walsingham supporting his claim to purchase at a reduced rate two-fifths of the entire licence as recompense 'for his travell [travail] and charge in obteyning the same'. Heydon granted this concession and eventually Sidney paid £168 for a licence which should have cost him a minimum of £280. He had been well recompensed for his efforts; but what of Heydon? Besides his fees and patronage the evidence suggests that he kept most of the proceeds from the sale of this licence as well. The accounts kept by his deputy Thomas Armiger, which were eventually submitted to the townsmen of Cromer, showed no record of Sidney's payment, but 'during Sir Christopher's life there was never question made thereof nor during the lives of many then inhabitantes and chief of the towne who knew how the busynes was governed'. Thirty years later, however, when the subordination of public interest to private gain had become a major political issue, Cromer tried to recover this money from Sidney's son.[14]

When Sir Christopher Heydon died in 1579 his son William continued the association with Sidney in these shady licensing transactions. In 1582 Cromer procured a second licence, this time to export 20,000 quarters of grain, and appointed Thomas Baxter to administer it. Baxter was supposed to submit his accounts to Burghley and Leicester, but they nominated William Heydon to act in their stead. Once more Sidney purchased part of the licence and within ten years the townsmen, led by John Blofield, had accused Baxter and all the pier-reeves of embezzlement, despite Heydon's inspection of the accounts.[15]

Meanwhile the Queen had granted Sheringham a licence to export 20,000 quarters of grain in order to provide funds for building new breakwaters. Two merchants from Yarmouth and Creake between them purchased a quarter of the licence paying at the rate of £7 for every 100 quarters. Thomas Sidney bought the remaining three-quarters paying £550 down—barely half its market value—the difference still being unpaid when he died in 1585. This time William Heydon feathered his nest by supplying the pier-reeves with timber from his park. While William Spink, Thomas Whisker,

[14] *Stiffkey Papers*, pp. 124–9, 135–6. 'Supplementary Stiffkey Papers', ed. F. W. Brooks, p. 42, *Camden Miscellany XVI* (Camden Soc. 3rd ser. lii, 1936).

[15] W. Rye, *Cromer Past and Present*, Norwich, 1889, Appendix, pp. lvi–lvii.

and Richard Newman sold 500 oaks at an average price of eight shillings each, Heydon provided 920 at just over eighteen shillings each. Either his trees were twice as large as any others or he was profiteering in no trifling manner. There are even hints that many trees, sold according to the pier-reeves' account, still stood around Baconsthorpe ten years later.[16]

In due course Nathaniel Bacon joined with other justices in Norfolk and Suffolk in a successful campaign against other abuses in connection with Sheringham's sea defences, but down to 1586 his disapproval of these subterfuges and his dislike of the personalities involved can only be glimpsed in occasional remarks among his private papers. For instance, when some of the townsmen subsequently petitioned the Crown for another grain licence Bacon warned that 'thei of the towne who preferre the peticon do rather seeke their private lucre than the publick good'. His advice, he claimed, was based upon former experience when 'the towne had a gifte . . . towardes the building of pers by the transportacon of muche corne for which grate somes of money were due whereof . . . much . . . [was] converted to private uses'. He advised Sir Edward Coke, who was handling the matter, to make sure that if the Crown granted another licence 'yt may so be governed as the former abuse may not agayne be suffered'.[17]

Bacon made no attempt to conceal his hostility towards the ringleaders of this 'former abuse'. In 1582, when Lord North reproved him for his unfriendly behaviour towards Sidney, he retorted that he had 'no cause why . . . [he] should yield him any courtesy'. His relations with William Heydon were even worse. No doubt his dislike of the latter's activities was intensified by the recollection that in the early 1570s they had worked in close association to establish 'godly rule' in north Norfolk. As early as 1578, at the height of the Puritans' conflict with Bishop Freake, Sir Christopher Heydon had deserted their cause and began to associate with Freake and Dr Masters. It is not clear whether William lapsed from the godly at the same time as his father, but Bacon subsequently described him as an 'unconstant man' who had deserted his former gentry associates. Certainly by the mid-1580s their relations had become so strained that even 'Mr. Secretary' Walsingham was trying to 'mediate an accorde' between them. Despite these efforts, bad feeling continued. By the 1590s Bacon appears to have been supporting Heydon's

[16] *NA* x. 1888, pp. 250–1. [17] Below pp. 247–53. *Stiffkey Papers*, p. 126.

son, Christopher, in a family quarrel and, when Lady Heydon remonstrated, Bacon retorted bitterly, 'I marveile that you who have these many yeares shewed me so little kindness will nowe challendg me for unkindness . . . I am persuaded that your sonne both doth and will beare a good hearte towarde the churche of God and the welfare of his countrey and therfore so mutch the more is to be estemed by me and others.'[18]

Bacon's hostility towards William Heydon may have been increased by the latter's abuse of his admiralty jurisdiction in Norfolk. Vice-admirals' courts had been instituted during the early sixteenth century when Henry VIII expanded the civil jurisdiction of the admiralty court so that it dealt with every kind of shipping dispute as well as those connected with fishing rights, salvage, and prize. To cope with the increased business it became necessary to decentralize the court's activities by holding sessions in each maritime county under the supervision of a vice-admiral. The procedure in these courts was modelled on that of the civil or Roman law rather than the common law, the defendant being summoned to the court to answer on oath certain unspecified charges, whose exact nature remained unknown until he appeared in court. Trial was not by jury, the case being decided before a judge on the evidence of sworn witnesses.

William Heydon, who had been appointed vice-admiral of Norfolk and Suffolk in 1578, claimed that he paid £300 for his patent. If this be so, he no doubt regarded the office as an investment which must be made to yield a handsome return. He certainly tried to expand his jurisdiction by claiming that he had a grant which permitted informations 'upon certain penal statutes to be laid in his admiral court'. This appears to have been an encroachment upon the jurisdiction of the common law courts, notably Exchequer and quarter sessions, where informations against breaches of penal statutes were usually laid. The townsmen of Lynn, prompted by Nathaniel Bacon, claimed that Heydon had no warrant for 'makinge his courte her Majesty's exchequer'. But warrant or not, informations were laid by his admiralty officers, notably by two summoners or serjeants—James Allison, servant to William Heydon, and James Bourne of Cley, 'a gent . . . [that] had some good patrymony thoughe the same be nowe altogether consumed'.[19]

[18] Above, pp. 207, 222, 165. FSL MSS. Bacon–Townshend L.d. 69, 83, 353.

[19] *APC, 1577–8*, p. 330. *EHR* xxiii, 1908, p. 747. BM MS. Lansd. 67, f. 5. MS. *penes*

Members of those maritime communities which clustered round north Norfolk's creeks and havens must have been especially vulnerable to the informer's activities, since they gained a livelihood as opportunity presented by fishing, trading, smuggling, or even piracy. For such men the threat of an information being laid in their local admiralty court must have been especially intimidating since this court, with its civil law procedures, gave far less protection to the defendants than did the quarter sessions and Exchequer. Indeed the entire procedure provided unlimited opportunities for blackmail. William Sabb reported 'howe James Borne tolde hym howe he had matter against hym whereupon the said Sabb bestowed a Frenche crowne upon him'. Nicholas Ringall, a yeoman of Sharrington, disclosed that in 1581 Bourne had threatened to arrest him but had offered to 'kepe the wolf from the dore' for a fee, 'whereupon . . . Ringall gave . . . [him] a combe of wheate and so staied his suite'. In 1583 John and Richard Young had been arrested by Sharp, an admiralty under-marshal, to whom they were compelled to pay fees of ten shillings. When John subsequently appeared in court he 'could not understand the cause of his arrest', but was eventually constrained by the judge to pay five marks for his discharge. Only then was he told that he had been arrested for transporting eighty quarters of barley without licence—a charge which he vehemently denied.[20]

Heydon supported his officials in their blackmail, taking his cut in kind if not in cash as well. For instance, when, in August 1583, Richard Walsingham and Mathias de Heire sailed into Cley with twenty chaldrons of coal, James Bourne laid an information against them in the admiralty court for breach of a statute against transporting coal in a foreign ship, although they were not told the substance of the information. Then his fellow-summoner, James Allison, seized their ship and carried off eight chaldrons of coal, delivering seven of them 'to two severall howses of . . . Mr. William Heydon' and the other to James Bourne's house. When they appeared in court the judge (Nathaniel Hall) ordered them to give sureties not to board their ship; upon their refusal he ordered the ship to be unrigged, its tackle being carried 'into the house of the

B. Cozens-Hardy, draft letter in Nath. Bacon's hand endorsed 'the coppie of Walsingham's letter to my Lo. Tres. & Sir Walter Mildmay'. NNRO MS. 2647 (3A2). *East Anglian*, N.S. iii, 1889–90, pp. 206–8.

[20] NNRO MS. 20399 (126X6).

said Mr. Heydon, beinge in Claye'. Heydon also sent his servant Allison to fetch the ship's box from Walsingham's home and again summoned them into court to find sureties to be bound in £100 'or ells . . . [they] should not have . . . [their] shipp nor coles'.

Walsingham and de Heire, however, did not compound their offence as Bourne and his associates presumably expected. Instead they petitioned Lord Burghley and Sir Walter Mildmay for the case to be heard in the Exchequer court. Pending that court's Michaelmas sitting, their lordships significantly ordered Nathaniel Bacon and Thomas Farmer—sworn enemy to William Heydon—to investigate the case and if possible restore the ship to its owners. The appointment of these commissioners did not bode well for Heydon who refused to hand back the ship's tackle. The Exchequer verdict can only be surmized from Nathaniel Bacon's claim that on two earlier occasions that court had threatened Heydon with fines of £100 if he persisted with similar cases.[21]

Nathaniel Bacon discharged his Exchequer commission with such vigour, and collected so much incriminating evidence as to suggest that he may even have been responsible for prompting Walsingham and de Heire to petition Burghley for redress. This would not be surprising since throughout the last two decades of the sixteenth century he continually inveighed against the excesses of admiralty officials in Norfolk. He accused them of interference in franchises and private jurisdictions; he charged them with corrupt practices while engaged in pressing seamen; he even complained that admiralty marshals had been used to summon jurors and deliver warrants, thereby depriving bailiffs and high constables of their normal fees. This obsession with admiralty malpractices was undoubtedly born of bitter experience since he lived at Stiffkey on the north Norfolk coast. No doubt, too, his training in the common law had sharpened his antipathy to the civil procedures used in admiralty courts. This shows clearly in the advice he once gave to his kinsmen Sir Robert Mansell who, on being appointed vice-admiral of Norfolk, consulted him about how best to reduce corruption among admiralty officials. 'You shall do well', Bacon replied, 'not to relye alone upon the judgment of the civil lawier, but to use the advise allso of some learned

[21] *East Anglian*, N.S. iii, 1889–90, pp. 206–8. NNRO MS. 2642 (3A2). MSS. *penes* B. Cozens-Hardy, Nath. Bacon, and Thos. Farmer to Wm. Bast [*et al.*], 23 Sept. 1583, and draft letter in Bacon's hand to the Lord Treasurer and Sir Walter Mildmay. *Stiffkey Papers*, pp. 212–13.

common lawier. I heard you at the assizes relye upon Dr. Burman [judge in the vice-admiral's court] as if he had bene able to have defended that which he had done, and in my opinion the man is not worthy to be relyed upon seinge he is not thought of sufficiency eyther for his learninge or experience to discerne aright what is to be done in thes cases'.[22]

Bacon's determination to expose informing in the vice-admiral's court was only part of his wider campaign against the malpractices of common informers generally. In 1582 he joined with his brother-in-law Francis Wyndham and the Puritan William Blennerhassett to investigate the extortion and oppression of John Ferrour. A little later Francis Wyndham so harried the informer Nicholas Wright that, significantly, Sir Arthur Heveningham took up his case at Court. Then, in 1594, when Henry Parnell, a noted informer, laid process at quarter sessions against a number of bakers who had not served their seven years' apprenticeship, Nathaniel Bacon indicted him for illegal and corrupt practices while informing. According to Bacon he had unlawfully compounded with some parties and indulged in victimization by arresting 'many persons to appere at this sessions whoe lie at great charge and [yet he] hath nothing to declare against them'.[23]

It is clear that by the early 1580s Norfolk gentry were deeply divided in their attitude towards the use of patents and licences in local administration. Some, like Sir Arthur Heveningham, the Heydons, and Thomas Sidney, welcomed them as instruments of power, private gain, and even oppression; others, in the main Puritans and lawyers like Nathaniel Bacon and Francis Wyndham, used every

22 MS. *penes* B. Cozens-Hardy, Nath. Bacon to Sir Robt. Mansell, 20 Mar. 1599/1600. BM MSS. Lansd. 142, f. 129; Add. 41306, ff. 12–14; Stowe 150, f. 161. *Stiffkey Papers*, pp. 201–9. NNRO MS. 2647 (3A2).

23 PRO SP 12/155 no. 65, ff. 1–2. *Stiffkey Papers*, p. 188. The latter part of this letter has been omitted and part of another inadvertently substituted by the editor, thus causing it to be wrongly dated to 1575 instead of 18 Feb. 1591/2. The missing section is on IHR microfilm XD 37 (transcripts and originals from the collection of H. W. Saunders). Photostats of Raynham MSS. *penes* T. S. Blakeney, vol. 27, petition to justices against Henry Parnell; memo. dated 7 Jan. 1594. IHR microfilm XD 37 (transcripts and originals from the collection of W. H. Saunders), frame 74.

means at their disposal to expose what they regarded as the malpractices of these patentees and licensees. But whereas down to about 1585 Bacon and his associates directed their complaints at the maladministration and corruption of the grantees, thereafter, as will be shown below, they increasingly challenged the validity of the grants themselves. The crucial factor in the development of this overt opposition to prerogative instruments of government may well have been the appointment of a permanent lord lieutenant.

In the early years of Elizabeth's reign lords lieutenants and their deputies had been appointed only in times of crisis; but by the 1580s, in an effort to overcome the slackness and legalism of muster commissioners and J.P.s, the Council attempted to create a permanent centralized militia administration which would respond to its dictates rather than to those of the local gentry. This it achieved by appointing councillors as lords lieutenants, each assisted by no more than three or four carefully chosen deputies. As part of these reforms Lord Hunsdon was appointed lieutenant of Norfolk and Suffolk in 1585.[24] Inevitably the system was moulded by the men appointed to run it. It may well be, therefore, that in Norfolk and Suffolk the background and personality of Hunsdon accentuated this shift towards centralized control and away from local autonomy. He had no lands in East Anglia and knew little of its society and political undercurrents. Nor by temperament was he likely to be sympathetic to considerations of local autonomy; he appears to have been a bluff, ill-educated soldier who had little comprehension of, and no sympathy for, the legalism of many Norfolk justices. He required that his deputies should readily and ruthlessly implement the Council's instructions and not prevaricate to suit any county interests.

Initially he appointed Sir William Heydon, Sir Edward Clere, and Sir Thomas Knyvett as his deputies in Norfolk. His choice of Heydon is not surprising and requires no comment. Sir Edward Clere, too, was well suited to the job. Ranking among the principal gentry in the county, he was a grasping man who cared little about the views and interests of his fellow gentry. In parliament, moreover, he had already spoken out in defence of the prerogative, albeit rather incomprehensibly.[25] Hunsdon's choice of Sir Thomas Knyvett

[24] J. C. Sainty, *Lieutenants of Counties 1585–1642* (*BIHR* Special Supplement no. 8, 1970), pp. 28, 32.

[25] Trinity College Dublin MS. E.2.9, f. 34v. I have to thank the Hist. of Parl. Trust for this reference.

appears less appropriate. Indeed the subsequent relationship between them suggests that there may have been substance in Knyvett's claim that he had been chosen by the Council rather than by Hunsdon. Socially Knyvett was extremely well qualified, but he was a scholarly man who gave little attention to county administration. When he did, he inclined towards the views held by his friend Nathaniel Bacon. As deputy lieutenant he was soon at odds with his colleagues Heydon and Clere, refusing to participate in levying soldiers for service in the Low Countries on the grounds that the corrupt administration of this campaign beggared the soldiers and enriched the professional captains. Not surprisingly Hunsdon dismissed him in February 1588, appointing in his stead none other than Sir Arthur Heveningham who, according to Knyvett, had 'gaped so wyde after that place'.[26]

A permanent deputy lieutenancy under Lord Hunsdon conferred upon the holder immense power and influence which Heydon and Heveningham had no scruples about deploying in their conduct of other business besides militia affairs. When in 1586 Thomas Farmer accused Heydon of 'phantasying himself to have an absolute power', he understated the case; there was no fantasy about it.[27] By virtue of his commission of lieutenancy Heydon had become an agent of the Privy Council with immediate access, via Hunsdon, to its Board. If his activities in the county were challenged he could be sure of receiving powerful backing at Court. Moreover the opportunity of sending unco-operative persons before Lord Hunsdon or the Privy Council proved a most efficient instrument of coercion which, besides facilitating the deputy lieutenants' imposition of unpopular military burdens, could also be used to bolster their actions as patentees and licensees. Indeed, deputy lieutenants had a whole range of sanctions which could be deployed as occasion demanded, be it in an election campaign, a private dispute, or the enforcement of a patent.

The power of a deputy lieutenant can be illustrated by the way in which William Heydon conducted a feud with Thomas Farmer. In many ways they had much in common. Both lacked business ability, lived beyond their means and attempted to recoup their fortunes by devious methods. Like the Heydons, Thomas Farmer and his brother Nicholas clutched at office to restore their declining

[26] BM MS. Harl. 4712, f. 356v. *APC, 1587–8*, p. 385.

[27] BM MS. Harl. 6846, f. 227.

fortunes; in 1572 Thomas tried unsuccessfully to wrest the customership of Lynn from Thomas Sidney, while in 1576 his brother endeavoured to secure the under-shrievalty of Norfolk. In 1577 Nicholas Farmer also appears to have been counterfeiting coinage, a fact which Heydon discovered and disclosed to the Council, thereby possibly contributing to Nicholas's subsequent suicide. Thereafter Thomas Farmer bore William Heydon a 'deep and inward malice' and, so Heydon claimed, sought 'how he might deface and hinder him not only in matters private . . . but also in public services'. Farmer's appointment as a J.P. in 1579 widened his scope for 'defacing' and 'hindering' Heydon and undoubtedly enabled him to be joined in commission with Nathaniel Bacon in enquiring into Heydon's malpractices as vice-admiral.[28]

It was in the course of this feud that Heydon invoked his authority as a deputy lieutenant. It happened when Farmer issued a warrant in July 1586 for the arrest of one of Heydon's servants on a charge of drunkenness, dicing, and loose living. Heydon retaliated by summoning the constable who had executed Farmer's warrant to appear before the assize judges; the constable, prompted by Farmer, retorted contemptuously 'that he hoped to find as many good frindes in court as Heydon'. Immediately Heydon clapped him into prison and, using his authority as a deputy lieutenant, sent him to London for examination before Lord Hunsdon. Then, a few weeks later, he arrested one of Farmer's servants who had failed to attend the musters—an all too common occurrence—and held him prisoner for three days before 'horsing' him up to London to appear before the lord lieutenant. Farmer interpreted this as 'mere malice in respect he was your said subject's servant' and shortly afterwards did all in his power to hinder Heydon's collection of 'coat and conduct' money for soldiers being sent into the Low Countries.[29]

Heydon, exploiting his ready access to the Council, proceeded to so discredit Farmer that in August 1586 their lordships ordered that he be dismissed from the commission of the peace since he was 'a man shewing him self froward in her majesties services and one against [w]home many exceptions are made'. Farmer fought back with a case in Star Chamber and eventually got himself restored to the Norfolk Bench, but only for a brief period.[30]

28 Williams, 'Maritime Trade', p. 27. *HMC Gawdy*, p. 6. Above, p. 240.

29 PRO St. Ch. 5, F 3/17 (Bill and Answer).

30 *APC, 1586–7*, p. 196. Appendix I, s.v. Farmer.

Deputy lieutenants who could arbitrarily imprison people and send them before the Council Board were formidable adversaries, as Thomas Farmer had discovered. But when, as in the case of Heveningham, they were also patentees who could make use of their lieutenancy powers in implementing their patents, then what had previously looked like the misuse of the royal prerogative by a handful of patentees might begin to appear as a coherent attempt by some local magnates, if not the government itself, to override the interests of the local gentry and to challenge the autonomy of its justices. It may have been such considerations which stimulated justices who were versed in the common law to extend their criticisms of the patentees to criticisms of the validity of their patents. Whether or not this was so, from the mid-1580s opposition hardened towards these prerogative instruments of government. As succeeding chapters will show, many justices and gentry opposed the Crown's constitutional innovations by asserting as an orthodoxy the principle that all administrative innovations which involved taxation should be approved in parliament or sanctioned by a majority of justices in quarter sessions.

CHAPTER XII

Patents and Their Opponents 1583-1593

Down to 1585 magistrates like Nathaniel Bacon, Edward Flowerdew, and Francis Wyndham had been occupied mainly with exposing the corrupt practices of patentees and licensees and had not overtly opposed the grants which enabled these malpractices. But the person could never be entirely separated from the office and there came a point at which opponents of those who abused patents and licences began to oppose the grants themselves. Clearly, it is not possible to date this shift with precision but, as has been suggested, there are reasons for thinking that it coincided with the development of the lieutenancy into a permanent feature of military administration in 1585. This development resulted in a militia administration which was amenable to conciliar demands because it operated independently of the justices in quarter sessions and reduced them to subordinate executives of the deputy lieutenants. Undoubtedly it lowered the prestige of the majority of justices who were not deputy lieutenants; but, above all, it weakened their ability to control the county's expenditure on militia training and organization. Conscious of the loss of this crucial role, they could not fail to see that the use of patents and licences in local administration was also sapping their prestige and undermining their control of local affairs, particularly their control of local taxation. Opposition to patents and licences grew with this awareness.

Those justices who had attacked the corrupt practices of patentees continued to spearhead this opposition, but others joined them, particularly common lawyers who were anxious to defend quarter-sessional authority and prestige for constitutional reasons. These justices deployed a variety of tactics in parliament, the courts, and county administration in order to thwart the implementation of existing patents and to prevent their proliferation. Occasionally they were able to initiate legislation to good effect, but, since parliament met infrequently, their day-to-day opposition took place mainly in the common law courts, especially in quarter sessions. Here, since attack proved the best method of defence, they contested every move made by patentees. Consequently the sessions of the peace at Norwich became the scene of bitter debates and arguments in which constitutional principles were formulated and history falsified to substantiate them. Inevitably voting was keen, so much so that both sides endeavoured to 'pack' the Bench; partial juries delivered their prearranged verdicts; caucuses met to draft petitions or plan the next move in their ceaseless opposition to the implementation of patents and licences.

This clash, between those who defended the autonomy of the justices in quarter sessions and those who exploited the county by acting as agents of the central government, can be traced in three concurrent administrative disputes which divided Norfolk during the years 1583–93. They arose over the repair of Sheringham's sea defences, the maintenance of the Wymondham–Attleborough highway, and the leasing of the estates belonging to the Dean and Chapter of Norwich cathedral.

SHERINGHAM PIERS 1583–1593

Sheringham, situated on the cliff where the mid-Norfolk uplands meet the sea, possessed no natural harbour, and in the late sixteenth century erosion threatened the cliff-face. In earlier centuries the inhabitants had built wooden breakwaters to prevent 'the further washing away of houses by the rage of the sea' and to provide an anchorage for their fishing craft, but by the late sixteenth century these breakwaters had fallen into such disrepair that the townsmen were soliciting a voluntary aid from the entire county to help finance the work of reconstruction. It is now clear that Sheringham's sea defence problems were aggravated by gradual subsidence along the east coast during the late medieval period, but the inhabitants of Tudor Norfolk knew nothing of this and, when asked to assist the townsmen, took the view that they had prior claims upon their resources.[1]

The Privy Council, however, reacted more sympathetically, since it realized that English sea power depended upon flourishing maritime communities. It had already granted the townsmen two licences to export a total of 30,000 quarters of grain whose profits the Heydons and their associates were busily deflecting from sea defence works into their own pockets. Such conciliar concern provided opportunity for further exploitation. In 1583, therefore, Sir William

[1] *NA* x, 1888, pp. 226–7.

Heydon and Henry Lord Cromwell (the impoverished grandson of Henry VIII's famous minister) supported a scheme put forward by Robert Kirk for building larger and more extensive breakwaters. The projectors even proposed to provide military defences by building a blockhouse 'of lyme and stone . . . meete for our great ordynance'. They suggested that these works could be financed by a grant from the Crown of all fines levied throughout Norfolk and Suffolk under two statutes which required farmers to grow one rood of hemp or flax for every sixty acres of land under tillage. On 28 February 1583 a patent not only authorized these proposals for seven years, but also granted Kirk and his associates the power to dispense with the law on receipt of an annual composition fee. It also provided two safeguards against malpractices: first, the justices of assize were to appoint two commissioners to be responsible for the 'true employinge of such somes of money as shall be collected'; secondly, the patentees were to gather only such sums as 'shalbe allotted unto them . . . from tyme to tyme at any quarter sessions' in Norfolk or Suffolk. The judges duly appointed two commissioners but, since they chose Sir William Heydon and Henry Lord Cromwell, no audit ever took place; consequently there was no means of enforcing the second condition.[2]

Kirk appears to have been a man of little substance; 'verie needie . . . and of small accompt . . . and utterly unfytt to have commytted [to him] the governaunce of so great a some' was Nathaniel Bacon's scornful comment. From the outset, backed by Sir William Heydon, he discharged his commission in a high-handed manner, even laying informations in the Exchequer against farmers who had not infringed the statute, thereby terrorizing many into compounding with him without due cause. His patent did not stipulate the composition fee and it was generally felt that he levied an unreasonable sum which varied from person to person. By 1586 he had aroused such widespread resentment that several justices, possibly prompted by Francis Wyndham, complained to the Council.[3]

[2] *NA* x, 1888, p. 253. 24 H VIII c. 4; 5 Eliz. c. 5. A proclamation demanding better enforcement of this statute had been issued in Jan. 1579; see Hughes & Larkin, ii. 435–8. PRO C 66/1224. *APC, 1586–7*, p. 77.

[3] *Stiffkey Papers*, p. 103. NNRO MSS. Sotheby 28/12/67, 'a partecular note as well of the names & surnames . . . 10 March, 1587'; microfilm of MSS. in possession of P. C. Pearson, memo. entitled 'Eynesford Hundred. A note of such somes of money . . .' *APC, 1586–7*, p. 42. When a commission of enquiry was subsequently set up Francis Wyndham was specially instructed to join it. *NA* x, 1888, p. 245.

Their lordships summoned Kirk to London and ordered Sir Arthur Heveningham, Sir Edward Clere, and other justices to enquire into the accusations against him. These justices could not agree how best to do this. The principal opponents of the patent, led by Francis Wyndham and Nathaniel Bacon, embarked upon a long and painstaking investigation which involved the collection of depositions from the constables and other interested parties. Sir William Heydon and Lord Cromwell, however, cut across these elaborate enquiries and, in their capacity as commissioners for overseeing the patentees, ordered that those who compounded 'should paie but v shillings yearlie during the yeeres of continuance of the letters patents'. The Council immediately accepted this pronouncement as a just settlement and instructed all justices of the peace 'to be by all good meanes aiding and assisting' the patentees.[4]

That Heydon and Cromwell had managed to stifle the investigation is not surprising since they were in collusion with the patentees. Kirk and his accomplices claimed that they had 'a sound and suer frind of my Lord Cromwell and that they had gyven him to be theire faythfull and assured frind a cuppe and one other jewell . . . of twenty pound price'. An unknown complainant remarked that 'all the cuntry well knoweth that Sir William [Heydon] hath bene his [Kirk's] only countenance in all those actions', and the depositions taken by Bacon and Wyndham in 1587 reveal that Heydon had been busy indicting farmers who had ignored the laws for sowing hemp. For such support he took his cut. As had happened before,[5] he received twice as much for his trees as other timber suppliers and delivered even less of them: apparently no more than fifty out of at least 400 for which he received payment.

Undoubtedly Lord Hunsdon's backing had helped to allay conciliar doubts about the patentees' activities. Kirk openly boasted that he had 'a sure frind of my Lord Chamberlayne'—probably an exaggerated claim which had substance only in that his principal supporter, Sir William Heydon, was Hunsdon's deputy lieutenant in Norfolk. But the lord lieutenant demonstrated his general sympathy towards patentees when in 1588, at the height of this controversy, he appointed Sir Arthur Heveningham—the doyen of patentees in Norfolk—as one of his deputies. Wholehearted support from the entire Norfolk lieutenancy probably explains how Kirk averted the attempt to discredit him at Court.[6]

[4] *APC, 1586–7*, p. 77. [5] Above, pp. 236–7. [6] *NA* x, 1888, pp. 240–3.

Indeed, when his patent expired in 1590, he had no difficulty in securing its renewal on the same terms, except that the new patent coupled William Garter with him as one of the principals. Garter practised as a London notary, receiving sufficient news of Court affairs to enable him to inform Kirk about the most recent tactics being adopted by their opponents. There had been other instances of administrative patents being awarded to a syndicate of London and county-based patentees—an arrangement which clearly facilitated the efficient execution of their patent. Consequently there was consternation at the news that Kirk's activities were to continue and might even increase. In particular the gentry of West Suffolk, led by their justices, petitioned the Council that the 'wholl Franchise of Bury' should be discharged from such 'unnecessary impositions'.[7]

This petition was promoted by that group of Puritan justices which had played such havoc with Freake's ecclesiastical jurisdiction in 1582 and which had led the protest against Heveningham's patent to repair the highway through Metfield. These justices acted with characteristic vigour and determination. First, they demanded an enquiry into Kirk's conduct; then, when the Council had agreed to this and had appointed commissioners, they badgered the commission, once more divided over procedure, into beginning its investigation; finally, they took care to publicize its damning report at the quarter sessions in Bury, thereby gaining support for yet another protest to the Council.[8]

Despite such determination, Kirk nearly managed to abort this enquiry as well. Everything hung upon the personalities who conducted it. The Council had nominated as commissioners Sir Arthur Heveningham, Sir William Paston, Sir Henry Woodhouse, Sir John Peyton, Nathaniel Bacon, and Clement Paston, stipulating that any four of them could undertake the enquiry. At least Heydon and Cromwell had been excluded this time, but only to be replaced by Sir Arthur Heveningham. He was already deeply involved in the defence of another patent, and his presence at the enquiry would undoubtedly have biased its findings. That this was Kirk's intention

[7] *CSPD, 1581–90*, p. 702. NNRO MS. Aylsham, bundle 75, Wm. Gillett to A. Heveningham, 11 June 1591. Below, p. 254.

[8] The justices who supported the petition were: Sir Nich. Bacon, Sir Wm. Spring, Sir Wm. Waldegrave, Robt. Ashfield, Sir John Higham, John Gurdon, Sir Robert Jermyn, Robt. Drury, and Henry Gilbert. Cf. with pp. 203, 231 above. *NA* x, 1888, pp. 229–37.

and that his opponents countered it is suggested by a delay of nine months before the commission started work.[9]

Eventually the investigation opened in July 1592 with Nathaniel Bacon and William Paston firmly in control. Kirk refused to give evidence before such partial commissioners, but Bacon produced a book of accounts which he had apparently obtained at his inquiry in 1587. On the basis of this incomplete record and the testimony of the high constables, the commissioners drew up a detailed indictment of Kirk's activities: 'many somes are misentred, and there misentry alwaiese resteth in setting downe lesse than was collected', indeed, 'many somes of good valew, which appeare by the certificat of the chiefe constables to have been gathered, are not entred' at all; from the timber he purchased he resold the 'topwood, billet and barke', but the profits from these sales rarely appeared in the accounts; 'he demandeth allowannce as paid to some men for cariadge, [but they] affirme that thei gave the cariadge to the worke'; he demanded £400 for expenses in obtaining Exchequer processes and yet the persons against whom these processes were obtained 'did paye the charges . . . and herof no entry in his booke'. The commissioners concluded that even this falsified account revealed that £1,488 had been collected out of Norfolk and Suffolk during the years 1583–7—an under-estimate since the high constables' certificates suggest that this sum had been raised out of Norfolk alone.[10]

The commissioners went on to argue that in any case the projected piers were a waste of money: they could not be completed and those which had been built 'had not wrought anie benefytt' to the anchorage. They judged it 'altogether labor lost to have the worke proceeded with by building any further into the sea' and recommended that 'the tymbre which hath ben imployed about the north peere [should be] wholly taken up and a great parte of that plucked downe to the sea warde'. Finally they recommended that the patent be rescinded 'for wee be persuaded that . . . it is farre of from her Majesty's pleasure . . . to have the gayne . . . of private persons covered with the shaddowe of a publick benefytt, and there is nothing ells by them sought herin'.

The patentees, meanwhile, anticipating the outcome of this inquiry, had taken steps to ensure the continuation of their project. Since Sheringham formed part of the Duchy of Lancaster estates in

[9] *APC, 1591–2*, pp. 87–8.

[10] *NA* x, 1888, pp. 238–40, 244–54. *Stiffkey Papers*, pp. 102–4. *TED* ii. 267–9.

Norfolk, Kirk had organized a petition to the Chancellor of the Duchy, Sir Thomas Heneage, complaining that the great benefits to be derived from the new anchorage were being jeopardized by 'malignante persones' who sought to overthrow the patent on which the scheme depended for finance. Heneage promptly instructed the deputy lieutenants and justices of Norfolk to report any man who resisted the collection of fines or composition fees 'to thend that suche corse of proceedinge maye be taken against him as shalbe most convenient'. His letter administered a severe snub to the commissioners, still in the midst of their investigations, since it flatly contradicted a Council order forbidding Kirk and Garter to collect any fines or compositions until the commissioners had completed their inquiry. It also suggested that Court sentiment favoured the maintenance of the patent and that the commissioners laboured in vain; a fact which was subsequently confirmed when the Council took no action on their report.[11]

Despite Kirk's apparent success, his opponents ultimately carried the day. Having failed to get the patent rescinded, they proceeded to secure the repeal of the statute upon which it was based. The evidence suggests that Kirk's patent provided one of the issues in the 1593 election in Norfolk. From among the patentees Sir Arthur Heveninghan canvassed vigorously for his own return, only to be opposed by Nathaniel Bacon and Edward Coke who were both elected. It is difficult to reconstruct what took place in parliament, but if Bacon led a campaign against the statute for sowing hemp and flax he was hardly raising new issues, since informers had been granted patents to enforce this Act in other counties and their activities, or those of their deputies, had evoked widespread complaints. A proclamation issued in 1589 had blamed any malpractices upon 'certain lewd & evil disposed persons, pretending . . . to have power & authority to execute the penalty of the statute made for the sowing of hemp & flax seed'. Although it forbade their activities, it left the patents intact, which suggests that the patentees, when faced with censure, had disowned the activities of their deputies. Be that as it may, the proclamation is evidence of the widespread depradations of men like Kirk and Garter. This was the atmosphere in which the Commons considered renewal of the 1563 Act for sowing hemp and flax. On 19 March Francis Bacon reported on a 'conference had with the lords for continuing of former statutes' and

[11] *NA* x, 1888, p. 236. Heneage's letter dated 25 Aug. 1592.

when he came to this statute he proposed that it 'be restrayned to some contryes only that are fittest'. In the event the statute was allowed to lapse rather than be modified in this fashion. There is no record of the debate leading to this decision, so that the part played by Nathaniel Bacon can only be surmised. The situation in Norfolk and Suffolk was probably well to the fore in any debate since Kirk and Garter had petitioned Secretary Sir John Wolley, M.P. for Surrey, presenting him with a cogent case against the 'proposed repeal of the Act'.[12]

In this controversy a group of justices led by Sir Francis Wyndham, Sir William Paston, Nathaniel Bacon, and his brother Sir Nicholas were in fundamental disagreement with Sir William Heydon, Henry Lord Cromwell, and Sir Arthur Heveningham over both the purpose of the patent and the abuse of its provisions. The latter group supported it and condoned Kirk's extortionate behaviour to the point of taking their cut of the profits. The former demanded that it be revoked on the grounds that its purpose was futile and that it provided a pretext for the misappropriation of public funds.

Generally, the initiative in opposing Kirk's patent seems to have come from that remarkably dynamic group of justices around Bury; at times they appear to have been pressing their Norfolk counterparts into action. If this be so, it may have been because the latter were simultaneously engrossed in conflict with Sir Arthur Heveningham over his implementation of another patent for the repair of roads in south Norfolk.

WYMONDHAM-ATTLEBOROUGH HIGHWAY, 1588–1593

In 1588 Sir Arthur Heveningham and Edward Honing of Darsham[13] led a group of gentry in petitioning for a patent to repair Christmas Lane in Metfield, Suffolk, uninhibited by the fact that, according to the terms of the 1582 patent, this piece of road had already been repaired. This time they also proposed to repair a particularly 'noisome way' in south Norfolk where the London to Norwich road crossed Attleborough fen. Maintenance of this highway had long proved beyond the resources of the townsmen of

[12] Hughes & Larkin, iii. 43–4. BM MS. Cotton Titus F ii, f. 64v. *CSPD, 1591–4*, p. 339. W. Rye, *Cromer Past and Present*, Norwich, 1889, appendix pp. lxi–lxiv.

[13] Son of Wm. Honing, clerk to the Privy Council. He was receiver of Crown rents in Suffolk.

Wymondham and Attleborough and its eventual repair was only satisfactorily undertaken in the late seventeenth century when Sir Edwin Rich gave generously towards this task.[14]

At Court Lord Hunsdon backed the petition, and no doubt arranged that his son John Carey should be named a commissioner together with Heveningham and Honing when the patent was granted in April 1588. The recipients constituted a powerful team; Heveningham was already a deputy lieutenant and one of the foremost magistrates in Norfolk, while John Carey provided the essential link with the Court. Their commission empowered them to estimate the cost of repairs and to raise the required sum by an annual levy for five years upon the inhabitants of Norfolk and Suffolk.[15]

For a variety of reasons this patent met with immediate opposition. In the first place Heveningham's fellow gentry had every reason to resent any further extension of his authority. His arrogant behaviour both during his quarrel with Edward Flowerdew in 1582 and while implementing the earlier highway patent no doubt still rankled. Even if old wounds had begun to heal they had recently been reopened when Sir Thomas Knyvett had been peremptorily dismissed from his deputy lieutenancy and Heveningham appointed in his stead.[16] Personal animosities apart, the patent was bound to arouse opposition since it imposed further taxation on the county at a time when the incidence of subsidies, forced loans, and military rates had reached an unprecedented level. In 1586 parliament had voted a subsidy, although the collectors had barely brought in the final yield from that granted in 1584. Almost monthly, as the Council struggled to prepare defences against invasion, constables received warrants to levy rates for militia training and equipment; then in June 1588 Norfolk had been called upon to provide £1,200 for the erection of fortifications at Yarmouth, and immediately afterwards privy seals had been despatched for the special Armada loan. Simultaneously with these demands, Kirk was extorting considerable sums

[14] NNRO MS. Aylsham, bundle 17, MS. endorsed 'A informacon to the grand jury concerning Attleborough Waye'. BM MS. Lansd. 55, f. 114. The memorial commemorating Rich's generosity still stands beside the A11 midway between Wymondham and Attleborough.

[15] PRO C 66/1308, mm. 1, 2. BM MS. Lansd. 55, f. 114.

[16] Heveningham had been appointed a deputy lieutenant only two months before the patent was granted. Above, p. 243.

of money for the ostensible purpose of improving the anchorage at Sheringham.[17]

Heveningham's patent, moreover, specifically empowered him to surcharge that section of the community most capable of coherent opposition. Indeed, by authorizing the commissioners 'to collect receyve and gather of welthy grasiers, cornemongers, cheesemongers . . . and other welthie traffiquers . . . as much contribution towardes their work in the discrecon of our commissioners . . . as of those which are to be charged by reason of a ploughland', his patent established a new criterion for rating assessments and enunciated the principle that the cost of road repairs should be borne by those who stood to gain most and who, through the vagaries of the rating system, normally contributed relatively little.

Suspicion that much of this rate was destined for Heveningham's coffers or the pockets of his deputies also caused resentment. Flowerdew had hinted at embezzlement in 1582; this time the principal opponents of the patent made no effort to disguise their fears. In Star Chamber they directed many of their interrogatories towards this issue. For instance, one of Heveningham's servants deposed that £1,500 had been rated on towns and Hundreds in Norfolk and that only £500 had been spent on the highway. Another deponent, speaking for the townsmen of Aylsham, declared that 'the some of twoo hundred powndes woulde repayre the saide waye and, if all were taxed after the rate of Aylesham, they thoughte it woulde amounte unto three or four thowsand poundes'. Shortly after the patent had been granted, Francis Wyndham implored Burghley to 'cause a present view to be had by the justices of peace . . . of the imployment of such somes of money as have been lately . . . collected . . . whereby there will be wrought a marvaylous great satisfaction and contentment to all hir majesty's subjects . . . when they shall thereby understand how these excessive and great colleccons have been bestowed and imployed'.[18]

Perhaps most importantly, justices could not escape the conclusion that their control over the incidence of county rates had been weakened by a patent which empowered the grantee to decide whether a rate should be levied and how much that rate should be.

[17] Below, p. 278. BM MS. Kings 265, ff. 266–8. For the incidence of taxation during the years 1586–9, see esp. F. C. Dietz, *English Public Finance 1558–1641*, New York, 1932, pp. 53–63.

[18] PRO St. Ch. 5, P 31/11 (John Brown's dep.); H 3/7 (Henry Norgate's answer).

As in the case of lieutenancy administration, it robbed justices of their local autonomy and reduced them to mere subordinates of Crown agents. Moreover, it embodied a dangerous precedent about how highway maintenance should be financed. Whereas the 1555 statute placed responsibility for this on each parish, the patent authorized a county-wide rate to assist a particular parish with its highway repairs. This principle of county responsibility had been implicit in the 1555 statute in so far as it permitted a county-wide rate for the repair of bridges, but Heveningham's opponents would have been quick to point out that the justices in quarter sessions authorized these special rates, not the Crown, Council, and patentee—a fact which made all the difference, as the inhabitants of Aylsham stressed when 'with one voice' they refused to pay Heveningham's rate, 'some of them affirminge . . . that they shoulde receave litle or noe profitt by the makinge of the saide highe waye and that there were manie highe waies in Norfolk that were verye fowle and moore profitable for them to be repayred'.[19]

Widespread dislike of this rate was transformed into positive opposition by the same justices as had protested against Kirk's patent—Sir Nicholas Bacon, Sir Robert Jermyn, Sir John Higham, and Sir William Spring from Suffolk, and Nathaniel Bacon, Francis Wyndham, and Sir William Paston from Norfolk. On this occasion they were joined by Henry Gawdy, William Blennerhassett, a well-known Norfolk Puritan, and Francis Gawdy who had recently been promoted a judge of the Queen's Bench. Such keen legal minds had no difficulty about reformulating in legal and constitutional terms their neighbours' subjective reasons for opposition, thereby drawing 'the cuntrye . . . unto a wonderfull contempte of her Majesty's prerogatyve and the Counsells aucthorytye'. Francis Wyndham reported how he had told Lord Hunsdon and other members of the Council that Heveningham's patent 'was no lawfull warrant to levye money', at which 'the Lordes marvelled that I shuld so farre impech the Great Seale. I sayd that yt was a very frequent thynge in all the Quenes courtes to decyde of the vallydytye of her patentes as yt was of the subjectes evydens.' Apparently he had challenged Heveningham 'that if he would shewe his pattent to the Judges at London at anie tyme when they were assembled that he should have their opinion in lawe whether the said letters pattent wer warrantable by Lawe'. Sir Robert Jermyn referred to this grant as 'a greater and

[19] PRO St. Ch. 5, H 3/7 (Henry Norgate's answer).

more weightie cause than I thinke is considered of . . . the *president*[20] is it that is so offensive'. Nathaniel Bacon bluntly declared that 'hir maiestie coulde not make or graunt suche a commission to leavie money out of . . . [his] lands'. Such views sound like a rehearsal of some of Edward Coke's arguments in the early seventeenth century. Indeed, they may well have been, for men who were involved as judges, M.P.s, and J.P.s in the development of local administration based upon common law and parliamentary statute, regarded the special powers granted under the Great Seal to Kirk and Heveningham as unwelcome innovations which could be countered only by extending the claims of common law to meet this challenge from the prerogative.[21]

The quarter sessions at Norwich inevitably provided the forum in which such claims were initially propounded since Heveningham's grant stipulated that the justices in sessions must sanction any rate which the patentees proposed to levy. In any case he needed their approval since high and petty constables could collect rates only on the authority of a warrant signed by the justices. Heveningham first asked the Bench to approve his rate in January 1589, only to discover that he had sparked off a lively debate which culminated in many justices petitioning the Council against his patent rather than granting the warrants he sought. The Council must have had considerable sympathy with their case: it had already advised Heveningham to moderate his demands in view of 'divers chardges for the publique defence of the coast and countrie' which had been imposed upon Norfolk, and in February Lady Digby informed him that unless the advocacy of his commission 'be better followed [it] ys very like to be utterly dashed and overthrowne'. In the end the Council proposed a compromise quite outside the terms of the patent: instead of the patentees recouping their outlay through a county rate, they should do so by compounding with persons who had failed to perform their statutory highway duties at the rate of two shillings for every day's default.[22]

[20] Meaning 'precedent'. The italicizing is mine.

[21] NNRO MSS. Aylsham, bundle 16, Robt. Jermyn to A. Heveningham, 6 July 1589; bundle 17, A. Heveningham to Justice Gawdy, 23 July 1590. *Stiffkey Papers*, p. 188; this letter should be dated 18 Feb. 1591/2 (see above, p. 241, n.o). PRO St. Ch. 5 H 3/7 (Francis Wyndham's answer); H 43/39 (dep. 5).

[22] *APC, 1588*, pp. 45–6. NNRO MSS. Aylsham, bundle 16, Lady Abigail Digby to A. Heveningham, 7 Feb. 1588/9; bundle 17, A. Heveningham to Justice Francis Gawdy, 23 July 1590; inhabitants of Aylsham to A. Heveningham, 9 June 1592.

The justices of Norfolk and Suffolk considered this proposal at quarter sessions and assizes in April. It appears to have been sufficiently attractive to weaken the well-nigh unanimous opposition mounted at the January sessions. At Norwich ten or eleven justices accepted it, but about twenty refused 'to medle . . . towchinge anie suche imposicon' because it was not according to the commission and 'in manie respects unfitte and inconveniente'. The Suffolk justices debated the proposal at the Bury Assizes where Sir Nicholas Bacon and that influential group of Puritan justices persuaded them to reject it unanimously and to present instead a 'supplication' against the patent which appears to have been received in an indulgent manner by Justice Peryam.[23]

Despite this intransigence at Bury, the willingness shown by a substantial number of Norfolk justices to implement the Council's compromise may have encouraged Heveningham to force the issue. As soon as the Easter sessions had closed he lobbied a few justices to sign a warrant for the rate which he then blandly dispatched to the high constables as if it had received quarter-sessional approval. The county stood aghast at such high-handed behaviour, most constables reporting widespread refusal to pay the rate. The high constables of Laundich most eloquently expressed this dissent when they informed Heveningham that they had sent out his warrants to all petty constables 'and have receyved ther severall aunswers indorsed upon the backsyde of everie of ye said warrants, all in effect tending to this purposse, viz. that ther ys no money to be gotten for that they can not se nor learne howe they shalbe dyscharged of anie ther sex daies work appoynted to be done by statute by reason of the extreme fowlnes of our owne wood countrie lanes and waies which are contynuallie punyshed and will not be amended with dubling of those working daies'.[24]

Again both sides appealed to the Council. This time their lordships ordered the justices and constables to implement Heveningham's warrants and threatened that 'refusers [shall] answer their

[23] PRO St. Ch. 5, H 3/7 (Sir Wm. Paston's answer). NNRO MS. Aylsham, bundle 17, undated letter from Edw. Honing to A. Heveningham, clearly written in the spring of 1589.

[24] NNRO MSS. Aylsham, bundle 16, Robt. Jermyn to A. Heveningham, 23 Apr. 1589; bundle 17, Constables of Laundich to A. Heveningham, 26 Apr. 1589; 'certificate from Wm. Basspole . . . touchinge the collection for Attleborough More'; Constables of Long Stratton to A. Heveningham, 28 May [1589]; Constables of N. Greenhoe to A. Heveningham, 18 July 1589.

obstinacies before us'. Such forthright conciliar backing may have been premature since Heveningham had not yet exhausted his own stratagems. At the Michaelmas quarter sessions he indicted the chief constables of Loddon and Taverham Hundreds for failure to execute his warrant and, without waiting for a verdict, demanded their dismissal. Inevitably, 'a great variance and controversie' ensued as the justices responsible for these Hundreds—especially Henry Gawdy, Sir William Paston, and William Blennerhassett—protested against Heveningham's interference in their divisional affairs and received widespread support from other opponents of the patent. 'The cause of dyslike was long debated and heard by the rest of the justices of peace assembled at Norwich, yet the same could not be determined to the contentacon of both parties.' Once more the Council intervened and referred the dispute to the mediation of the justices of assize. They, with more than a hint of sympathy for the views of Heveningham's opponents, ordered that the two chief constables 'be sufferid . . . to remaine still in . . . [their] rome till the nexte Assizes at which tyme we will heare the causes . . . obiected against [them]'. In due course they affirmed the illegality of Heveningham's warrants and endeavoured to persuade him to collect a rate only from the areas adjacent to the highway.[25]

Such mediation was belated and irrelevant, for already Heveningham, acting in his capacity as deputy lieutenant, had dismissed the chief constables. Since, however, they were normally appointed by the justices, their dismissal on the authority of a deputy lieutenant required some justification.[26] This Heveningham provided by blandly rewriting history:

I have made diligent inquirie of the begininge of cheiffe constables and it is affirmed by men of greate experience that they were ordeyned first for martiall affayers and appointed by them that had aucthorite in such causes, and are so still at this hower, but were continewed to execute some matters belonginge to justices of peace for levyeng of money and assistinge purveyeurs . . . and this is all that chief constables are to do under you [justices], but petie constables are the officers that are to serve the justices turnes in returninge their warrants in

[25] Bodl. MSS. Tanner 241, ff. 37–37v; Douce 393, f. 107. BM MS. Add. 33597, f. 18. PRO SP 12/227/18; St. Ch. 5, P 45/4 (Heveningham's dep.); H 3/7 (Nath. Bacon's answer).

[26] NNRO MS. Aylsham, bundle 17, A. Heveningham to Henry Gawdy, 3 Dec. 1589.

matters of justice . . . therfore the choice of chief constables remayne in the lord liefe tenaunte (or his deputie leife tenaunts).[27]

Henry Gawdy refuted this justification for the lieutenancy's interference by reading his history differently. He asserted that high constables had been 'ordeyned even before justyces of peace' but that their authority had been taken from them and given to commissioners of the peace, the constables being left merely as 'ministers' to execute the justices' commands and as such could only be appointed and dismissed by them. He went on to argue that Heveningham's justification for his 'displacing of such as handle martial matters' (i.e. constables) would also enable him 'to remove justices whoe many tymes take musters, viewes of horses etc'—a tendentious conclusion which was not implicit in Heveningham's claims but which reveals the nagging fear among J.P.s that their authority and influence was being subordinated to that of the lieutenancy.[28]

Throughout the rest of this controversy Heveningham continued to counter opposition to his patent by invoking Lord Hunsdon's authority. He was well placed to do this by virtue of his deputy lieutenancy in Norfolk and Suffolk and because his co-patentee was Hunsdon's son John Carey. Like William Garter in the previous incident, Carey remained at Court using his influence to procure a stream of warrants and letters in support of Heveningham's action in the county. Clearly their partnership prospered: 'whatsoever Sir Arthur informeth, my Lord [Hunsdon] will nedes have it true', Francis Wyndham remarked bitterly to Nathaniel Bacon. Nor is there any doubt that Heveningham's deployment of these lieutenancy powers incensed his opponents and increased their determination to oppose his activities through every administrative device and legal argument which they could bring to bear.[29]

In the spring of 1590 Heveningham dispatched further warrants for the collection of his rate, but these, too, had only been signed by a minority of justices after quarter sessions had closed. No doubt he hoped that the constables, mindful of the fate of their fellows in Loddon and Taverham, would implement his warrants this time.

[27] Ibid., bundle 17, draft letter from A. Heveningham to Henry Gawdy, 10 Dec. 1589.

[28] Ibid., bundle 17, Henry Gawdy to A. Heveningham, 11 Dec. 1589.

[29] IHR microfilm XD 37 (transcrs. and originals from the collection of H. W. Saunders), Francis Wyndham to Nath. Bacon, 18 Feb. 1591/2. NNRO MS. Aylsham, bundle 17, John Carey to A. Heveningham, 16 May 1590.

Even so he took the precaution of procuring authority from the lord lieutenant to commit any 'obstinate' persons to the custody of a pursuivant 'to be brought upp to answere ther refusall therein before my Lords of her majesty's Privie Cowncell'. Many constables, faced with these formidable sanctions, would undoubtedly have levied the rate had not Francis Gawdy, Nathaniel Bacon, and others 'conspired together how to abridge' Lord Hunsdon's authority and frustrate Heveningham's actions by publicly declaring that if the Council committed anyone for refusing to contribute, 'they would have a *habeas corpus* to remove them'. Such a pronouncement encouraged constables to stand their ground; those from North Greenhoe, for instance, curtly informed Heveningham that 'our hundred holy are determyned to paye nonne'.[30]

Sometimes Heveningham intervened personally to expedite the collection of his rate. On one occasion, after King's Lynn had repeatedly refused to pay its contribution, he rode over and terrified the aldermen into convening an extraordinary council meeting by brandishing the lord lieutenant's warrant to summon 'obstinate persons' before the Council Board. Without more ado the corporation 'condiscended and agreed that there shall be bestowed upon him 20 Angels of good value £10, in consideration of Sir Arthur Heveningham's good will and favour towards this town, being one of the deputy lieutenants for this county—not in respect of his demands . . . by virtue of her Majesty's commission to him'; a clever, albeit cowardly, response in which the townsmen seized upon Heveningham's deliberate confusion of his powers as a patentee and deputy lieutenant in order to maintain their legal objections to his warrant and at the same time avoid the unpleasant consequences which would follow further refusal to pay.[31]

Heveningham's opponents countered his high-handed tactics by threatening to indict for extortion any constable who implemented his warrants. In June 1590 Stephen Drury, an Aylsham lawyer in the service of Francis Wyndham, began proceedings against the chief constables of South Erpingham for rating Aylsham at £10. His tactics failed, for the jury 'being synisterlie solycited and moch

[30] PRO St. Ch. 5, H 3/7 (Nath. Bacon's answer). NNRO MSS. Aylsham, bundle 17, Lord Hunsdon to deputy lieuts. of Norfolk, 16 May 1590; draft letter from A. Heveningham to Lord Hunsdon, 28 July 1590; Chief Constables of N. Greenhoe to A. Heveningham, 25 July 1590.

[31] KL Muniments, Congregation book 5, f. 408v.

laboured to the contrarie and also put in terror and feare by the said Sir Arthur, did not find or present the same'. Yet this move had not been in vain; as Heveningham complained to Hunsdon, the incident had 'brought the contrie unto such troble as they are more afrayed of him [Drury] and of thes justices' thretninges then they be of your Lordships' and your authoritie'.[32]

Characteristically 'Sir Arthur did growe unto exceeding hatred and malice toward the said Drury'; by July he had issued a warrant in Lord Hunsdon's name for the arrest of the 'pryckeared knave' and for his appearance before his lordship in London. In fact Drury had little to fear since the constables of Aylsham not only refused to arrest him, but also ignored Heveningham's rating demands. Perhaps they withstood this lieutenancy warrant against Drury with such confidence because they knew that it was technically invalid. Apparently Hunsdon had stipulated that such warrants must be signed by two deputy lieutenants, but for some reason both Heydon and Clere had withheld their signatures and Heveningham had therefore dispatched them on his sole authority. Late in July he had complained bitterly to Lord Hunsdon about Sir William Heydon's tardiness: despite 'faier wordes and many promises made unto my cosin John Carie . . . [he] will neither meete me nor joyne with me in any warrant for the sendinge up of any obstynate person as your Lordship's letter doth require him'. However, by the autumn Heveningham had managed to overcome Heydon's scruples and had procured a spate of valid warrants directing the pursuivant Ralph Mason to arrest recalcitrant constables, including those at Aylsham. They were imprisoned at Norwich pending their journey to London to appear before the Council, but the imminence of this dreaded experience weakened their resolve and they hastily paid over the £10 due from the township.[33] Although Aylsham's constables had capitulated when confronted with the might of the lieutenancy, other townsmen under the tutelage of Stephen Drury took issue with Heveningham—not least the incoming constables who refused to collect the rate needed to reimburse their predecessors. Heveningham immediately dispatched pursuivants to arrest these

[32] PRO St. Ch. 5, P 62/28 (Bill). NNRO MS. Aylsham, bundle 17, draft letter from A. Heveningham to Lord Hunsdon, 28 July 1590.

[33] PRO St. Ch. 5, P 62/28 (Bill); P 45/4 (Interrogs. 17, 18, 51, 56, and Drury's dep.). NNRO MS. Aylsham, bundle 17, draft letter from A. Heveningham to Lord Hunsdon, 28 July 1590.

constables but his men only succeeded in becoming involved in a brawl with Stephen Drury.[34]

Amid this mounting tension quarter sessions opened at Norwich in January 1591 and proceeded in a predictable manner. First, Heveningham attempted to legalize his position by obtaining retrospective approval for the rate he was in process of levying, but although for 'two several dayes togeather [he] moved the justices of peace then and ther assembled to have them condicend and agree to a rate', Wyndham's followers so dominated the proceedings that it 'was at both tymes denied and utterly reiected'. Then, when he had failed in this, he 'solicited and labored divers of the said justices of peace privately, and so by this means drew some of them to subscribe to a rate . . . by him self preferred'. He also presented several constables for refusing to levy his rate, but the Bench promptly discharged them; whereupon 'in open court' he committed them to prison, on the pretext that the lord lieutenant had summoned them to London. In the midst of this uproar Aylsham's new constables arrived to complain about 'certaine speeches and threttninges' used by Heveningham during his abortive attempt to arrest them. Small wonder that the Bench responded by rebuking Heveningham in the most public manner possible: it bound him over in open sessions to keep the peace—the greatest humiliation that could have been devised for one of the foremost gentry who held office as a justice and deputy lieutenant in both Norfolk and Suffolk.[35]

Responsibility for allowing the sessions to proceed in this unseemly manner must have rested with the chairman of the Bench—on this occasion, and hardly by coincidence, none other than Francis Wyndham. He certainly had no scruples about the impartiality of the chair; rather he took the opportunity to inform the assembled constables and bailiffs that 'whosoever gathered anye monye by vertue of anie commission or letters from the Lords of [her] Maiesties heighe councell, it was extortion'. This pronouncement by such a distinguished chairman—for many years a justice of the Common Pleas—reassured Heveningham's opponents and served as a clarion call to action: Sir William Paston, Nathaniel Bacon, and William

[34] PRO St. Ch. 5, H 60/11 (Heveningham's interrogs. to Henry Norgate); H 3/7 (Answers of Drury and Norgate).

[35] *Stiffkey Papers*, p. 188. PRO St. Ch. 5, H 3/7 (Bacon's answer, Henry Norgate's answer and Stephen Drury's dep.); P 62/28 (Bill); H 60/11 (Interrogs.); H 43/39 (Interrog. 13 and Nath. Bacon's answer).

Blennerhassett, together with Wyndham's servant Stephen Drury, immediately ordered chief and petty constables to pay back any money they had levied on Sir Arthur's warrants.[36]

Nor surprisingly, at this point the Privy Council intervened and, in an effort to achieve a compromise between the two factions, arranged a meeting between Francis Wyndham and Lord Hunsdon at the Lord Chancellor's house. In fact the occasion merely provided opportunity for further intemperate exchanges. Wyndham reported that Lord Hunsdon accused him of attempting 'to dyscontenans hys Lordship in his liefetenancy in that shyre' and of impugning 'her Majesty's comission and all other her service there for levying of money' and then 'fell to partycularities towching . . . Drurye . . . [and said] he had 20 other matters I should answer hereafter'. Wyndham apparently stood his ground and retorted that Heveningham's grant 'was no lawfull warrant to levye money'. He closed a long letter to Nathaniel Bacon on a bitter note which bore no hint of a reconciliation: 'this is the some of this tragedie with many evill wordes of you and Sir Nicholas Bacon . . . thus for ought I see our commonwelth will still receyve oppression. God send it better when it pleaseth him.'[37]

Despite this inauspicious meeting, in June the Council proposed a compromise which they hoped would be acceptable to Heveningham's opponents although it yielded little to their case. The patent was to stand; the rate was to be levied; but where some 'towneshipps perchance have found them selves surcharged in the taxations assessed uppon them . . . [these] maie be moderated with the goodwill of them which shalbe assessed'. With these proposals went an exhortation that all bitterness between the parties should cease; so, too, should all suits at law.

This compromise in no way met the objections of the Bacon–Wyndham group who continued both to oppose the rate and to obstruct its collection. Even as the Council devised its compromise formula, Robert Gibson of Beckham was organizing a petition to the Lord Treasurer in protest against Heveningham's activities. Barely four months later Hunsdon accused Wyndham of 'prosecuting' Sir Arthur 'as if there hadd ben no end made before the Lords.' There is certainly plenty of evidence that widespread resistance to the

[36] PRO St. Ch. 5, H 3/7 (Bill).

[37] *Stiffkey Papers*, p. 187; for the dating and missing portion of this letter, see above, p. 241, n.o.

rate continued. The response of the constables of Smithdon Hundred to a further warrant from Heveningham typifies reaction throughout the county: 'dyvers of the townes abovesaid make answer that they will paye yf the Quenes Majesty hir pleasure and the Counsailes so be; . . . others that they wille paye none; others that charges growe daylie upon them more than their abilitie wille beare; dyvers others that they have payed all or the most parte.' Similar certificates from other constables indicate that it was, on the whole, gentry and substantial yeoman who continued to refuse to pay.

Even as late as 1593 the Council was still summoning to its Board leading opponents like Stephen Drury, presumably in the hope of persuading them to comply; but with little apparent success since at the end of May Heveningham complained that he had 'bestowed greate somes of money in finisheing of those ways . . . [but] can by no meanes gett the money' he had disbursed. Much of the rate remained outstanding in 1594 when Heveningham may have admitted defeat; clearly the parties did not reach accord and, as will be seen, there was to be no peace and friendship between them.[38]

MARTHAM PARSONAGE 1583–1598

The final dispute which contributed to the cleavage among Norfolk gentry in the period 1583–93 arose from attempts by a group of patentees to deprive the Dean and Chapter of Norwich of their property. The activities of these patentees had county-wide ramifications, not least because by Elizabeth's reign many of the principal gentry had become capitular lessees.[39] The pretext for this appropriation of capitular property was that it had been 'concealed' from the Crown since the Reformation. The difficulty of preventing landholders from 'concealing' estates which should have either escheated to, or been confiscated by, the Crown had long vexed royal administrators, and there is no doubt that at the Dissolution a good deal of monastic property, which should have passed to the Crown, had been appropriated by private individuals.

[38] NNRO MSS. Aylsham, bundle 75, Wm. Gillett to A. Heveningham, 11 June 1591; bundle 182, copy of letter from Lord Hunsdon to Francis Wyndham, 25 Oct. 1591; bundle 17, Certificate of Wm. & Robt. Read, chief constables of Smithdon, 9 Sept. 1591; inhabitants of Aylsham to A. Heveningham, 9 June 1592; A. Heveningham to Lord Treasurer, 25 May 1593. *APC, 1591–2*, pp. 397, 442.

[39] Bodl. MS. Gough Norf. 33, ff. 44–44v. Norwich Cathedral, Dean and Chapter MS. Account Roll for 1591.

Early in her reign Elizabeth tried to recoup this loss. She either sold 'concealed' lands at cut rates to those who discovered them, or, if these busy-bodies were royal officials who merited reward, she granted them the lands as payment for their services. This was good economy since it enabled the Crown to augment its resources by utilizing what, *de facto*, it did not possess. A less healthy situation developed in the 1570s when the Queen began to license courtiers to seek out 'concealed' lands. In 1570 she granted to Thomas Lord Wentworth 'his heirs and assigns . . . so much concealed lands as he, his heirs, executors or assigns shall discover to the yearly value of £200 [and] . . . if any of the lands shall afterwards be lawfully recovered from him . . . he shall receive other concealed lands in compensation'. By granting away 'concealed' land before it had been discovered, the Crown encouraged Wentworth, or his assigns, to fabricate charges of concealment.[40]

They had little difficulty in doing so against the Dean and Chapter of Norwich since the latters' succession to the title of the former cathedral priory property had been ineptly established. After the Prior and monks had surrendered their property to Henry VIII in 1538, he had regranted it to them, naming the Prior as Dean and some of the monks as prebendaries and canons. This surrender, however, had been invalid at law because the Bishop of Norwich, as successor to the founder of the priory, had not consented to it; therefore Henry's grant had also been invalid. In order to secure proper title the Chapter resurrendered the lands to Edward VI who reconstituted it and regranted most of the lands which had belonged to the former priory. But in the process of removing one legal flaw the Dean and Chapter had created another: they had made this second surrender in their own name, but since Henry VIII's grant had not been legally valid there could have been no Dean and Chapter to surrender the lands. Edward VI could not, therefore, have regranted them and they must have remained 'concealed' in the possession of the Prior and monks until the last monk died (in 1586). Or so the assignees of Wentworth's patent for 'concealed' lands successfully argued in the Exchequer court where judgement was given in their favour in 1583.[41] Shortly afterwards they leased much of this property to Sir

[40] *CPR, 1563–6*, pp. 52–3, 62–7, 237–8, 476–7; *1566–9*, pp. 46–9, 51–2, 162–3, 225–7, 353–4; *1569–72*, pp. 5, 38–42, 43–4, 156–9, 167, 227–30, 239, 334, 369–71. Stone, *Crisis*, p. 415.

[41] Theophilus and Robert Adams.

Thomas Shirley, William Downing, 'and other needy and indigent persons who endeavour[ed] to repair their poor declining estates by the dissolution of the Cathedral Church'. The Dean and Chapter, however, refused to accept this Exchequer judgement and sought to safeguard their title by an Act of parliament. Pending legislation, they continued to grant leases in their name.[42]

Unfortunately the Bill foundered in the 1584–5 parliament, leaving the tenants of each party with little prospect of peaceful occupation. In an attempt to avert years of litigation and local conflict, Burghley asked the Attorney and Solicitor Generals to negotiate an equitable settlement. They proposed that both parties should surrender their titles to the Queen, that she should then reconstitute the Dean and Chapter and regrant the property to them, but with certain stringent conditions. These stipulated that the lands should revert to the Chapter only after they had been leased for 99 years to Thomas Fanshawe, Remembrancer of the Exchequer, and Peter Osborne 'for the behoofe of the patentees and their assignees'. Fanshawe and Osborne were instructed to sub-lease the lands to former capitular tenants, provided the latter gave 'reasonable composition' to the patentees and their assignees. Only if these tenants refused to compound were the lands to be sub-leased outright to the tenants of the patentees. In the event the cathedral Chapter refused to proceed with this settlement on the grounds that the patentees had not surrendered *all* the capitular lands which had been granted to them. Instead it again tried, unsuccessfully, to establish its title by Act of parliament (1588).[43]

This deadlock encouraged the respective parties to attempt to substantiate their claims through the courts and the machinery of county administration, with the result that by 1588 the fate of capitular property had become a county issue. Sir Arthur Heveningham supported the patentees and their tenants, while many of his opponents in the previous controversy backed the Dean and Chapter. Several capitular supporters held capitular lands but many, including leaders like Francis Wyndham and Henry Gawdy, did not. Such justices appear to have supported the Dean and Chapter in order to safeguard their 'commonwealth'—to use Wyndham's term for the county—against further exploitation by patentees.

[42] PRO C 66/679, m. 28; /801, m. 29. Strype, *Annals*, iii(1), pp. 488–92; iii(2), pp. 376–9. D'Ewes, p. 323.

[43] BM MSS. Lansd. 55, f. 184v; 58, ff. 14v–16. Strype, *Annals*, iii(2), 56–62, 577–9.

The entire controversy centred upon the possession of Martham parsonage, and its glebe and tithes.[44] By 1585 Sir Thomas Shirley had leased it to his fellow assignee William Downing, a Yarmouth attorney and M.P. for Orford. Three years later, in May 1588, the Dean and Chapter leased the same property to Thomas Eden, a yeoman who already held land in Martham. The Chapter clearly regarded the ensuing dispute between Eden and Downing as a test case since it levied a special rate on all its tenants in order to sustain Eden's litigation.[45]

Trouble began immediately Eden took possession of the property. Finding one of Downing's men at work in the fields, he impounded his horses on the pretext that they had strayed on to his land. A day or two later Downing arrived with an array of servants and dispossessed Eden who, however, returned in August to reap where he had not sown, apparently harvesting much of the corn despite resistance from Downing's servants. During the autumn of 1588 Sir Arthur Heveningham widened the dispute by riding over to Martham, restoring Downing to the parsonage house, and using his position as a deputy lieutenant to ensure that the Council summoned Eden to answer for his riotous behaviour. Further skirmishing took place at seed-time and harvest in 1589, but by December Eden again had possession of the property. Then five days before Christmas Downing dispossessed him with the support of Sir Arthur Heveningham, Philip Woodhouse, and an array of servants, who 'did not onlye picke and loosen the walles but with a pece of tymber forciblye rune and beate the same downe'. Once more, at Heveningham's instigation, the Council summoned Eden to answer for his behaviour.[46]

As this conflict developed, the justices who supported the Dean and Chapter took action in quarter sessions and other common law courts to safeguard Eden's possession. For instance, at the sessions in January 1590 Francis Wyndham, Sir William Paston, Henry Gawdy, and William Blennerhassett successfully indicted Downing

[44] This controversy has been largely reconstructed from the following Star Chamber cases: PRO St. Ch. 5, D 15/32, 33, 34; D 16/12; D 27/6; D 29/39; D 31/21, 25; E 11/38; 13/29; 14/9; H 3/7. Hereafter I have cited them only when quoting extensively.

[45] FSL MS. Bacon–Townshend L.d.265. PRO St. Ch. 5, E 11/38. Norwich Cathedral, Dean and Chapter MS. Ledger Book 3, f. 158.

[46] PRO St. Ch. 5, E 11/38 (Eden's Bill and Downing's dep.); E 14/9 (Interrog. 3 and Downing's dep.).

for forcibly entry to the parsonage, the court ordering Eden's immediate restoration to the house and lands. Simultaneously with these proceedings in quarter sessions, Eden, prompted by Francis Wyndham, brought an action of trepasss in Queen's Bench against Downing's servant Edward Brown. The case was heard at Thetford assizes where the sheriff, Henry Doyley, himself a capitular tenant, had empanelled a sufficiently partial jury to ensure that the court found Brown guilty despite the judge's direction to the contrary.

Downing countered by appealing to the equity jurisdiction of the Exchequer court which had previously ruled that the lands of the Dean and Chapter were 'concealed' and therefore forfeited to the Crown. On 20 June 1590 this court issued 'An injunction against Thomas Eadon and William Franklyn . . . comanding them . . . not to prosecute the same accon any further in the said court of Kinges Bench . . . nor to intermedle with the possession of the premisses [at Martham]'. As a result Downing took possession of the parsonage and its lands, only to be once more indicted for forcible entry by Francis Wyndham and other supporters of the Dean and Chapter at the Michaelmas quarter sessions. Once more, too, the indictment was found and Eden restored, despite strong opposition from Heveningham and his supporters.[47]

His occupation of the property ended abruptly when Heveningham arrived and reinstated Downing; but both, in turn, found themselves indicted for forcible entry at the next quarter sessions. These were the memorable sessions in January 1591 at which Sir Arthur suffered the indignity of being bound over to keep the peace. No doubt his activities in support of the patentees of 'concealed' lands had angered the justices who were already incensed by his endeavours to levy a rate for the Wymondham–Attleborough highway repairs. Certainly Francis Wyndham, as chairman of the court, made no attempt to conduct the case impartially. When Downing and Heveningham asked to be tried by travers, as if they had committed a misdemeanour rather than a felony, Wyndham 'sittinge there as the cheif addresser and director in matters of justice . . . [and] bearing affeccon towards [Eden and his friends] . . . against lawe and justice did utterlie refuse and deny the parties greved to travers the said indictments'.[48]

[47] PRO E 123/17, ff. 79–79v.

[48] PRO St. Ch. 5, H 3/7 (Bill).

Since these quarter-sessional verdicts successfully countered the Exchequer decrees, Downing tried to enlist support at Court in an effort to overcome local opposition. He 'obteyned and procured to be openly published in open sessions at Norwich Castle certain letters, some from divers right honourable personages of her Majesties most honorable Pryvie Counsell, and one from her Majesties then Attorney General now Lord Chief Justice . . . in lawful favour of . . . [his] possession of Martham'. One of these 'honourable personages' may well have been the Earl of Essex, who subsequently supported Downing's claim and with whose entourage Downing became closely associated. Probably Lord Hunsdon also intervened at the instigation of Sir Arthur Heveningham. Such backing undoubtedly swayed the waverers when the case was discussed at the next quarter sessions. Robert Buxton, 'spake openlie againste [Eden's] restitution', and there is evidence that John Pagrave, Philip Woodhouse, Thomas Farmer, and Richard Kemp supported the patentees at this time. In consequence 'it was . . . generally agreed for staie of restitution [to Eden] and it was then staied'.[49]

Eden retaliated by lodging a Bill in Star Chamber, while his supporters secured another quarter-sessional warrant for his restitution. Downing claimed that the decision to grant a warrant had been reached by 'privitie and subtill meanes . . . Henry Gawdie Myles Corbett and William Blennerhassett [sitting] longer than any of the rest of the justices at the benche at that tyme, and when the residue were gone, they there onely alone awarded restitucon'.[50]

At this point the Council again tried to implement the proposal for a settlement which had been rejected by the Dean and Chapter in 1588. In June 1591 their lordships directed Thomas Fanshawe and Peter Osborne to open negotiations on the basis of these proposals. Eden, however, rejected them and refused to appear at the Exchequer in order to prove his right to tenancy and to compound with William Downing. The case therefore went by default and on 23 June 1591 process was awarded out of the Exchequer for Downing to be 'quietlie settled' in possession of Martham since he had 'nowe

[49] PRO St. Ch. 5, D 27/6 (Bill); D 29/39 (dep. of Downing's servant); PRO E 178/1600; 123/17, f. 368v. *HMC Gawdy*, pp. 40, 42. NNRO MS. WALS. XVII/I, ff. 15v, 16. Bodl. MS. Douce 393, f. 40. Lambeth Palace MS. 660, ff. 100, 238, 364.

[50] PRO St. Ch. 5, D 27/6 (Interrogs. to Wm. Blennerhassett); D 29/39 (Layton's dep.).

obteyned a good lease of the saide parsonadge from Thomas Fanshawe Esq.'[51]

Process was one thing: its implementation another. This rested with the sheriff, Henry Doyley, who, as a tenant of the Dean and Chapter, ignored the writ. In despair Downing turned for assistance to the neighbouring justices, but they too refused to reinstate him; finally he took the law into his own hands and laid siege to the parsonage. Eden, confident of at least tacit support from the sheriff and nearby justices, taunted Downing and his followers 'that thoughe . . . [they] colde gett no justices to come thither, yett . . . [he] wolde have Justices there shortely that shold drive [Downing] and all his from off the grownde'. His servants were even more arrogant and shouted from the rooftop that 'come justices, come Lordes, come the Quene her selfe they wold not yelde'. Eventually he broke the siege with a sortie in which several of Downing's men were injured, one fatally. Downing pleaded with the local justices to arrest Eden for forcibly resisting the execution of an Exchequer warrant, but in turn the Bishop of Norwich, Henry Gawdy, William Blennerhassett, and Thomas Barney refused to act. Eventually John Pagrave drafted a warrant for Eden's arrest, but it was nullified by William Blennerhassett who signed it but struck out Eden's name.[52]

In January 1592 Heveningham again intervened in an effort to overcome this conspiracy of county administrators against Downing and the patentees of 'concealed' lands. He rode over to Martham, reinstated Downing and arrested Eden and his servants. On 24 January they appeared in the Exchequer court and were committed to the Fleet prison for three weeks 'for dyverse contempts by them committed concerninge the possession of the parsonadge of Martham,' eventually being released on payment of bail of 200 marks. Meanwhile the Exchequer commissioned Sir Arthur Heveningham, Nathaniel Bacon, John Pagrave, and Robert Buxton—all of them, Bacon apart, supporters of Downing and the patentees—to 'enquire of the iuste and trewe valewe of the corne soe carried awaie' by Eden during his 'unlawfull' possession of the parsonage. Finally Heveningham and Downing endeavoured to complete Eden's defeat by indicting him for the murder of Downing's servant who had died in February 1592 from wounds received in the fracas at the parsonage during the previous summer.

[51] PRO E 178/1600, 123/17, f. 338v.

[52] PRO E 123/17, f. 368v; St. Ch. 5, D 29/39 (Layton's deps); D 15/32.

At this point it seemed as if the combined authority of the Council, Exchequer court, and Norfolk lieutenancy was about to compel the Dean and Chapter and their tenants to accept the fact that the profits of their lands would have to be shared with the patentees and their lessees.[53] But when Eden was indicted at the Lent assizes, Miles Corbett, another capitular tenant who had recently been appointed sheriff, saved the day by empanelling a jury which dismissed the case with total disregard for all the evidence. Joshua Downing, William's brother, recollected the event six years later:

the inquest wold not fynde the said indytement, and then the nowe Lord Chief Justice of England sent the said Inquest out agayne commandinge them specially to fynde it, and said the matter was verie apparant. Whereupon they went forthe agayne, and then some of the inquest toke evidence on the parte of the defendents not sent from the courte, and one other of them said, that he wolde be hanged hymself, before that he wold fynde it, and they came into the courte agayne, and wolde not fynde it. . . . Then the Chief Justice beinge informed of the aforesaid speeches dyd swere divers of the great inquest, and examyned them towchinge those words and for takinge of evidence without dyrection of the court for the defendents, and at last one Mr. Holditche confessed the taking of such evidence and it was then confessed that some of the jurye would have fownde those inditements, and others of the inquest wold not agree therunto and then the said Lord Chief Justyce sent them out for the thirde tyme, and yet they retorned agayne and wold not fynde the inditement.[54]

Despite this incredible display of partiality, Downing and Heveningham again indicted Eden at the next assizes before accepting the fact that no court depending upon a local jury would give a verdict against him.

With such backing in the county Eden once more aspired to take the profits of the parsonage from which he had been excluded for several months. On the 3 August, he procured an injunction for his restoration 'unlawfully made out by some of the Attorney's clerks or Court of Exchequer officials'. Miles Corbett, the sheriff, speedily executed the injunction, despite Heveningham's protests that it 'was made upon an iniuste warrante' and despite his repeated commands 'to forbeare the execution thereof'. As before, the injunction was annulled but by then Eden had harvested the corn.[55]

[53] PRO E 123/18, f. 1, /19, f. 17; St. Ch. 5, D 29/39.

[54] PRO St. Ch. 5, D 29/39 (Joshua Downing's dep.). Sir John Popham was the judge.

[55] PRO St. Ch. 5, D 27/6 (Bill); D 29/39 (Interrogs.).

This protracted dispute took a decisive turn when, on 4 January 1593, writs were issued summoning a new parliament. Undoubtedly this controversy, coupled with the dispute over Kirk and Garter's patent, contributed to the bitter electoral contest which ensued.[56] As has been indicated, Sir Arthur Heveningham canvassed vigorously for his own return, but the gentry and freeholders elected Edward Coke, who was chosen as Speaker of the House, and Nathaniel Bacon. It is probable that Coke had all along counselled the Dean and Chapter to stand out for an Act of parliament to safeguard their title.[57] It may not therefore be fortuitous that this parliament attempted to settle the dispute by an 'Acte explaining the statute of 34 Henry VIII touching graunts' which removed the grounds on which the patentees of 'concealed' lands had rested their case. 'Towchinge and concerning the validitie of the ereccons of Deanes and Chapters by the late Kinge Henrie the Eight . . .', it declared, 'all and everie Honors mannors landes tenements and hereditaments which at any tyme heretofore were the possessions of any abbey monastery priorie [and] . . . came to the handes or possession of the saide late Kinge Henrie theight . . . shalbe . . . adjudged to have bene lawfullie and perfectlie in the actual and reall possession of the saide late Kinge and his heires and successors, at such tyme as the same did so come to his majesties handes and possession . . . notwithstanding any defecte wante or insufficiencie'.[58]

The Bill had been introduced in the Lords but the Commons passed it 'with a very frank & free I[ay]', rejecting with 'great scorne' several provisos brought in by 'concealers', including one by Sir Thomas Shirley that 'a certaine lease of landes belonging to the Deane & Chapter of Norwich . . . should not be impeached by this act'. Significantly the Act was one of two singled out for special praise by Speaker Edward Coke in his closing oration, while one diarist recorded that 'It was counted the most beneficiall bill that came this Parliament into this House and a bill of that prise as it alone was worth our three subsidies'. It is not necessary to posit that this diarist 'must surely have held monastic land perhaps by insecure title' in order to explain his satisfaction at the passage of the Bill. It was satisfaction enough that this Act, like that repealing the statute for growing hemp and flax, struck at one of the

[56] Below, pp. 323–5.

[57] Coke, *Reports*, 1602, pt. iii, ff. 73–6. Coke, *Institutes*, iv, 1644, p. 257.

[58] 35 Eliz. c. 3.

devices by which patentees were exploiting county communities.[59]

In Norfolk it only remained for Eden to re-open the case against Downing so that a verdict could be given in the light of the new statute. This he did at the next assizes, taking possession of the property at Martham in July or early August, but certainly in time for the harvest. His restoration appears to have been the occasion for a celebration which was attended by the sheriff, his under-sheriff, the Dean, several prebendaries, and an appropriate array of servants.

But, alas, this did not settle the matter. Downing very quickly claimed to have found a flaw in the Dean and Chapter's title which had not been rectified by the Act of parliament passed in the previous February. He agreed that this Act had made valid Henry VIII's grant to the Dean and Chapter and that therefore the subsequent capitular surrender of lands to Edward VI was valid at law, but he argued that a verbal flaw had invalidated Edward's regrant of the property. Whereas Edward had incorporated the Chapter '*per nomen Decani et Capituli Ecclesiae Cathedralis Sanctae et individuae Trinitatae Norwicensis ex fundatione Regis E. 6*', the patent by which he had regranted its lands omitted the words '*ex fundatione Regis E. 6*'. This omission had not been rectified by the recent Act and therefore the Dean and Chapter's estates were in fact still 'concealed' Crown property.[60]

The case was reopened in the equity court of the Exchequer where Downing's counsel was sufficiently persuasive for the Chancellor and barons to instruct Mr. Fanshawe to issue a *supersedeas* with a clause ordering Downing's restitution to the parsonage. Henry Gawdy, however, who had succeeded Miles Corbett as sheriff, delayed execution of the writ while Eden obtained a letter from the Chancellor annulling the warrant for Downing's restitution and ordering that 'the profitts of the sayd parsonage sholde in the meane tyme be sequestered from the partyes on both sides'. Gawdy's under-sheriff, William Torrold, immediately sequestered the profits 'into the hands of one Henry Elwyn, (who is a brother by maryage to Thomas Eden) collorably letting the said Eden to occupye and enioye the said parsonage & the proffits thereof'.[61]

[59] BM MS. Cotton Titus F ii, ff. 95–95v. D'Ewes, pp. 463, 465–6, 518, 520–1. Neale, *Parliaments 1584–1601*, p. 319.

[60] Coke, *Reports*, 1602, pt. iii, f. 73.

[61] PRO St. Ch. 5, D 27/6 (Bill); D 15/34 (Interrogs. and Torrold's dep.); D 15/32 (Interrogs. and Eden's dep. 43).

The familiar pattern of events quickly re-emerged: Heveningham again intervened; the case was reopened at assizes and in the Exchequer court; both parties laid claim to the crops; the new sheriff, Bassingbourne Gawdy, acted with partiality towards Eden and the Dean and Chapter; Downing, meanwhile, obtained further letters of support from courtiers, notably the Earl of Essex who even tried to nominate the under-sheriff. The wearisome round of possession and dispossession continued in this manner down to 1598 when the dispute was finally settled in favour of the Dean and Chapter and their tenants in a judgement given in the Michaelmas term after conference between the Lord Keeper, the two chief justices, and the chief baron of the Exchequer.[62]

The three incidents narrated above reveal that during the years 1583–93 the county was more clearly divided over issues of government than had previously been the case. In this decade justices like Francis Wyndham, Nathaniel Bacon, and Henry Gawdy openly thwarted the implementation of patents and even began to express serious doubts about their validity. It is unfortunate that no clear statement of their criticisms has survived, but these obviously had to do with the extent to which, and the circumstances under which, courtiers could exploit the local community, or the Crown impose taxation upon it without consent either in parliament or at quarter sessions. There is, too, the clear implication that the Crown had been badly advised in making some of these grants since they were not directed to the realistic solution of significant problems, but merely provided devices through which patentees could extort money from the county's landowners. Opponents stressed that the haven at Sheringham would not be improved by the large piers which Kirk proposed to build; nor would communications in south Norfolk be any better as a result of Heveningham's proposed highway repairs.

Finally the study of these incidents has revealed the mechanism of opposition to patents in local administration. In particular it has demonstrated the importance of quarter sessions as a focus for this opposition. Many justices, besides their judicial and administrative responsibilities, were developing a political role as the guardians of

[62] Bodl. MS. Douce 393, f. 40. NNRO MS. WALS XVII/I, ff. 15v–16. *HMC Gawdy*, p. 42. Coke, *Reports*, 1602, pt. iii, ff. 73v–76.

the county community against the rising incidence of taxation and central interference, and against exploitation by courtiers who masqueraded as agents of dynamic central government. Furthermore, when opportunity presented, justices and gentry showed their awareness of the potential of parliament as a bulwark against the 'oppression' of their 'commonweal'.

CHAPTER XIII

Military Affairs and Purveyance 1590-1603

IN the controversies described above, quarter sessions provided the principal venue for resistance to 'prerogative' government. Clearly there was a divergence of opinion between the Crown, with its desire for more dynamic and efficient administration, and many local gentry, entrenched at quarter sessions, who resisted administrative innovations in order to minimize the financial exactions which fell upon the local community. The legalistic conservatism of this county opposition in turn drove the Crown into greater reliance upon such gentry as were prepared to implement new policies through their powers as patentees or deputy lieutenants and who, so it was claimed, exploited these powers for private gain. This conflict between 'court' gentry and 'county' gentry intensified during the 1590s as a result of two concurrent controversies: one concerned with military affairs and the other with purveyance.

By the early 1580s, as has already been suggested, the Council realized that its efforts to persuade commissioners for musters to modernize and make more efficient their local militia forces had been relatively unsuccessful; that it had failed to provide sufficient well-trained militiamen to safeguard the realm against invasion. Consequently it became more resolute about introducing reforms and less willing to compromise with the county view. But the Council's determination to impose more stringent standards and new methods of training was matched by mounting stubbornness in the counties. Only the threat of Spanish invasion produced sufficient unity of purpose to conceal this divergence until after 1588. This increasing intransigence on both sides was due to two developments. First, the appointment of permanent deputy lieutenants from 1585 onwards provided the Council with its own military agents in the counties so that it no longer needed to depend upon the justices' co-operation. It could issue instructions and expect them to be implemented. Secondly, and partly as a result of this, the incidence of conciliar demands for militia improvements, increasing as the threat of invasion mounted, imposed a heavy financial burden, particularly upon the maritime and south-eastern counties.

There is no doubt that in pre-Armada years these counties bore the brunt of military preparation against invasion and of the indirect taxation which went with it. Whereas, for instance, they kept beacon-watch night and day from March until the end of October, 'remote Lancashire only watched its beacons from 10 July to 30 September'. Similarly, Norfolk, in great haste and at great expense, had to prepare coastal defences against an enemy landing; it spent £1,186 on the fortifications of Yarmouth and Weybourne alone, excluding the cost of manning them and providing stores of arms. It has been estimated that all in all in 1588 Norfolk contributed £4,240 towards resisting Spanish invasion in contrast, for instance, with £1,300 raised in Northamptonshire.[1]

As well as these extraordinary expenses, the county had to meet many recurrent costs in the ceaseless endeavour to produce a battle-worthy militia. In 1572 the government had introduced its scheme for 'trained bands'; this required commissioners for musters in every county to select 2,000–3,000 of the most suitable militiamen, organize them into companies, and provide them with regular training which lasted several days at a time. For every day spent at the musters a militiaman received compensation for loss of earnings ranging from 8*d.* for a soldier to 5 shillings for a lieutenant. In Norfolk this entailed an outlay well in excess of £100 for each day's training which had to be raised by yet another *ad hoc* rate. But this was only a start; more money was needed to purchase powder, shot, uniforms, and artillery. There is no doubt that training, as opposed to mustering, proved expensive, the more so for counties in south-eastern England where intensive preparation against invasion began in 1583—two or three years before its extension to Midland and northern England. The government further inflated costs during the early 1580s when it sent professional captains into the counties to train the militiamen to a higher standard. These 'muster-masters', inevitably appointed earlier in the maritime counties than elsewhere, usually had no local roots and cared little about the escalating costs of their training programmes.[2]

Norfolk's militia rates remained heavy in the post-Armada period since frequent mustering and training continued under the vigorous supervision of deputy lieutenants who, like the muster-masters, showed more concern for military efficiency than for the problem of finding the money to achieve it. In 1592 Sir Arthur Heveningham

[1] Boynton, pp. 132–3, 157–8. [2] Boynton, *passim.*

even hinted that the lord lieutenant should order more thorough mustering, training, and inspection of weapons: 'I thinke it my dutie to advertise your lordship of the weake state of our contreye,' he wrote, 'how unprovided every captaine ys of his bande, and what great defects there is both of men armer and horses. . . . For we which are your honors deputies are carefull in the time of peace to provide for warre and to call upon [the county] to have all things necessary.'[3]

As well as financing this regular militia training and the purchase of new weapons the county had to meet additional demands during the 1590s. The professional muster-masters who had been attached to county militias during the crisis of the 1580s were not withdrawn after 1588: instead, as if to add insult to injury, their salaries, which had initially been a charge against the Exchequer, were made a county responsibility. Then in 1596 the Council called upon the eleven maritime counties from Yorkshire to Cornwall to assist their port-towns in providing ships for the Cadiz expedition—an innovation which, as will be shown, met with widespread opposition in Norfolk. Furthermore, between 1596 and 1599 the government, fearing Spanish landings, annually demanded special defensive preparations in Norfolk and other south-eastern counties. Finally, throughout the 1590s the county received three or four warrants annually to impress soldiers for service in Ireland, each warrant necessitating an *ad hoc* levy for coat and conduct money which, at best, was only repaid in part. During 1601, for instance, Norfolk was successively called upon to provide 3 light horse for Ireland, 300 men for the Low Countries, and 200 men for Ireland, necessitating county rates of £151, £1,110, and £984 respectively.[4]

It is important to remember that while the deputy lieutenants were trying to impose the necessary rates to implement these conciliar requirements they were also involved in exacting money as patentees and licensees. Not without reason, therefore, many justices and gentry felt that the lieutenancy too readily collaborated in policies which ran counter to their interests. But how to oppose these policies was another matter. Outright resistance was not a possibility

[3] NNRO MS. Aylsham, bundle 17, draft letter from A. Heveningham to Lord Hunsdon, 31 May 1592.

[4] Boynton, pp. 180, 191–206. A. H. Lewis, *A Study of Elizabethan Ship Money 1588–1603*, Philadelphia, 1928, pp. 27–42. NNRO MSS. NAS Safe II.28, f. 11–11v; WALS XVII/I, pt. ii. ff. 72, 87, 98v.

since few if any gentry would have disputed the Queen's prerogative right to take such precautions as she deemed necessary for the defence of the realm. Somehow, without refusing to fulfil the Crown's demands, they had to oppose and expose the activities of deputy lieutenants, patentees, and professional captains who all too frequently seemed to be subverting government policy to their private ends. And so they scrutinized the validity of every warrant, constantly quoted precedent, and even sought redress in parliament.

Quarter sessions provided the greatest opportunity for such scrutiny and procrastination since all rates, whether for military or other purposes, had to be approved by the Bench before any constable could collect them. During the 1590s a number of influential justices became increasingly reluctant to sanction militia rates, especially those imposed to finance innovations which had been introduced by the deputy lieutenants without prior consultation with the Bench. In particular they contested the deputy lieutenants' demands for the muster-masters' salary. Muster-masters epitomized professional extravagance; they caused 'the collonells and captaines to gather their whole companies together, and so keeping them three or foure daies, make them walke upp and downe and labor in unnecessarie actions to litle purpose, saving for the spending of a great deale of powder wastfullie and twelve pence a daie for everie soldier with other exactions for officers'. From the outset many Norfolk justices refused to grant a rate to pay these unwanted officials so that there 'had been great difficulty in raising the amount'. Most likely, as in Wiltshire and Somerset, the deputy lieutenants had been forced to make up the muster-master's salary by a 'voluntary subscription'.[5]

But opposition to the muster-master and his salary was only part of a general reluctance to approve any military rates, and, knowing this, constables showed equal tardiness over their collection. By 1591 Francis Wyndham and Nathaniel Bacon had so successfully organized resistance that Heveningham complained to the lord lieutenant that 'yf your honour seke not by some meane to abate his [Wyndham's] pryde, I knowe his aspiringe mynde is suche that he wolde have all the contrie of Norfolk at his commaundement . . . [and] he wolde have your honours aucthoritie lyttle regarded'. Wyndham appears to have employed the same tactics as he had used to thwart

[5] Henry Knyvett, *The Defence of the Realme*, 1596, ed. C. Hughes, 1906, p. 34. NNRO MS. WALS XVII/I, f. 10. 'Supplementary Stiffkey Papers', ed. F. W. Brooks, p. 27, *Camden Miscellany XVI* (Camden Soc. 3rd ser. lii, 1936). BM MS. Add. 48591, f. 161.

the implementation of Heveningham's patent: he persuaded the justices in quarter sessions to countermand and challenge the deputy lieutenants' orders. 'When we comitt anye for not findinge armor or any such thinges belonginge to the good of the contrie', bemoaned Heveningham, 'they are bayled by some of the justices or discharged from us by a *habeas corpus*, and we thretned to be sued upon false imprysonment, and some chiefe constables nowe sued for leveying of moneye by our warrantes for beacon watche.'

A year later, when the deputy lieutenants endeavoured to levy thirty men for service in Ireland under Captain Warlock they again met with spirited opposition. Once more they informed Lord Hunsdon that 'the lawyers carrey such a swaye amongest us that we canot nor dare do any thinge but by good aucthoritie least we here of our doings to our greate troble. Beside that they have taught the comon people to be so obstynate that they will aske councell before they obeye any aucthoritie, which . . . [we] thinke is not used in no place in Englonde but here in Norfolk.' If Captain Warlock was to get his soldiers, they concluded, 'your honour must directe some other course'. He did; when the next incident arose two months later the Council instructed the deputy lieutenants to bring the more obstinate constables before its Board. Even so these deputies continued to be 'laughed to skorne for [their] labour, and little regarded'. By May 1596 opposition had been so successful that the Council summoned Nathaniel Bacon, Henry Gawdy, and 'sondrie other justices of peace' to explain why 'her Majestys service in [Norfolk] . . . hath failed of the proporcions of former tymes and [why] many there are backward in the performance of their dutie'. Details of the charges are lacking, but the situation was sufficiently tense for Bacon and Gawdy, both already in London when summoned by the Council, 'of purpose [to] departe the cittie'.[6]

Their summons may have been occasioned by their reluctance to sanction a county contribution to help King's Lynn and Yarmouth defray the expenses of providing two ships for Essex's expedition to Cadiz. Early in 1596 both towns had complained to the Council about the burden of laying out £3,000 to furnish and provision these ships, and had requested assistance from the county. On 4 April their lordships responded by instructing the deputy lieutenants 'to deale with the inhabytauntes and the rest of the shire' to contribute

[6] NNRO MSS. Aylsham, bundle 182, A. Heveningham to Lord Hunson, 15 Feb. 1590/91, 31 May 1591, 26 Mar. 1592. *APC, 1595–6*, pp. 404–5, 413.

£700 towards the expenses of the two port towns. The deputy lieutenants appear to have acceded readily to this demand but they still had to obtain quarter-sessional authority for a rate to be levied. This was no easy matter; at its next sessions the Bench deferred consideration of the Council's letter until the assizes in July. There, justices again temporized until after harvest, when, rather condescendingly, they informed the Council that they would make some contribution, but could not 'performe the whole sum': surely a realistic statement of the political rather than the economic state of the county. Indeed, almost a year later, Lynn and Yarmouth had not received even this modest contribution. Two delegates whom they sent to the Easter quarter sessions at Norwich to receive such sums as had been gathered, were informed by 'sundry of the constables' that they had been unable to collect the money 'sett down' for their Hundreds, and that they desired 'to have new warrants from the Justices in that behalf'. In an effort to expedite the collection of this ship-money several justices, including the Bishop and Lord Cromwell, signed a warrant, but 'some of the chief of the said justices beynge made sute unto in that behalf refused to sett their hands to the said warrantes'. Inevitably many constables refused to execute warrants which had been sanctioned by only a minority of justices, and the burgesses of Lynn, thwarted yet again, hastily despatched a messenger round the county to solicit further signatures. Eventually some constables did collect the rate, but even these refused to hand it over until all Hundreds had sent in their contributions. Lynn and Yarmouth probably never received even the reduced contribution which the county had promised, since four years later some Hundreds still held out. An entry in the Lynn Congregation book as late as June 1601 records that 'this day John Atkyn is appoynted to traveyll to the justices . . . for the lymytts of the Hundreds of Launditch, Gallow, Brothercross, North Greenhoe, and Holt about suche monyes as are yet unpaid in the said hundreds for the shippes set forth . . . upon the Cadis voiadge'. It need hardly be said that the Hundreds lay within Nathaniel Bacon's 'division' and he was named as one of the recalcitrant justices whom John Atkyn was to visit. Clearly his appearance before the Council at the beginning of this dispute—assuming that he obeyed the summons—had been to no effect.[7]

Although initially Norfolk justices had reluctantly promised a

[7] *APC, 1595–6*, p. 328; *1596–7*, pp. 6–7, 64–5, 461; *1597*, pp. 285–6. *HMC Salisbury*, vi. 272. KL Muniments, Congregation book 1591–1611, ff. 126v–127v, 228.

reduced contribution towards the port towns' outlay on ship-money, their reluctance had quickly hardened into refusal. Two events may have helped to stiffen their resolve. First, in July 1596 Lord Hunsdon died and the lieutenancy in Norfolk lapsed; with it lapsed the extraordinary powers of his deputies and their opportunities for easy access to the Council. The abeyance of the lieutenancy no doubt encouraged many justices to take a bolder stand against the policies for which it had stood. Secondly, when the Council's request for ship-money was first received in 1596 many Norfolk justices may have awaited the reaction of their fellows in Suffolk before joining in a forthright refusal. If this be so they were not long left in doubt. Suffolk justices led once more by Sir Robert Jermyn, Sir William Spring, Sir Nicholas Bacon, and Sir John Higham refused outright to contribute towards Ipswich's ship-money costs. They spurned Council exhortations, ignored summonses to its Board, and even sent out warrants which forbad the collection of any ship-money rate, 'aggravatinge the matter and dyswadinge the same by perillous arguments, meeter to move the people to dyscontentment than to concurr in her Majesty's service'.[8]

From her study of Elizabethan ship-money Mrs. A. H. Lewis gained the impression that 'the constitutional aspects of the extension inland of the ship levy' were not 'in any way clearly apprehended, . . . rather was it an ominous grumbling on the part of a few of the more isolated localities'.[9] Yet, as has been shown, the gentry who refused to levy ship-money in Norfolk and Suffolk were also the outspoken opponents of patents, licences, and rates levied by the lieutenancy. The consistency of this opposition over these varied issues amounted to far more than 'ominous grumbling', and one cannot escape the conclusion that these men—lawyers in the main—fully realized the constitutional implications of these innovations in local administration.

Ironically enough these constitutional conservatives frequently held radical Protestant views which were usually associated with a demand for an aggressive foreign policy and strong defences against the forces of the Counter-Reformation. They would appear to have come near to willing the ends while denying the Crown the basic military and naval strength to achieve them. But this ambivalence may well have been more apparent than real. They were not

[8] Above, p. 231. *APC, 1596–7*, pp. 553–4.

[9] Lewis, op. cit., p. 70.

opposed to improvements in military training; they merely held a particular view about what constituted improvement and felt, not without justification, that all innovation was not necessarily progress —especially when advocated by those with vested interests. The ship-money they had refused to contribute would not have provided more ships for the Queen's fleet, but only enabled King's Lynn and Yarmouth to pay less. By the same token, the appointment of muster-masters provided jobs at the county's expense for superannuated professional soldiers who might introduce the corrupt practices associated with military campaigning—consequences which might more than offset the advantages of any experience they brought.

These justices produced plenty of evidence of corruption in the Norfolk militia administration. During 1594 Edward Coke brought a case in Star Chamber against both the muster-masters, several servants of the deputy lieutenants, and William Gresham, one of the few justices who co-operated with the lieutenancy, accusing them of corrupt practices both at musters and in levying soldiers for overseas service. Others complained that 'sondry somes of money' had been levied 'wherof dyvers somes . . . do yet remayne in the hands of such as had authoritie to collect the same'. The upshot was a commission directed to Edward Coke, Sir Thomas Knyvett, Nathaniel Bacon, William Blennerhassett, Bassingbourne Gawdy, Sir William Paston, Henry Doyley, Nicholas Hare, and William Rugg—it reads like a roll-call of Heveningham's opponents—empowering them to examine the appropriate accounts.[10]

Preparations for the expedition to Cadiz in 1596 also evoked allegations against the lieutenancy in Norfolk and Suffolk of 'dysorders & abuses as namely in exacting or taking somes of money or other composicons of dyvers persons to kepe them from being ympressed, and in changing & dismissing others for brybes, that were levyed, as also in defrauding the countrye of armes & other furnitures that after ymployments should have bene restored'. Once more the Council empowered the same justices to make enquiries and report their findings. This they did with maximum effect: 'we have selected some of the principall abuses & cer[t]ified the same . . . If we should have particularly noted every farther abuse we should have bene over tedious . . .'[11]

[10] PRO St. Ch. 5, A 13/31, 32/39. BM MS. Lansd. 78, f. 48. NNRO MS. WALS XVII/I, f. 21.

[11] NNRO MSS. WALS XVII/I, ff. 10v, 24v; NAS Safe II.28, ff. 11–11v.

Justices who opposed the lieutenancy's activities also resisted government attempts to introduce professionalism into county militia training and administration. During the 1590s a lively debate developed as to how best to prepare county militias and more particularly their trained bands for modern warfare. Professional soldiers, no doubt with an eye to their future, argued forcefully that training should be in the hands of officers with experience in recent continental warfare, and that the trained bands, usually 500–600 men strong, should be divided into smaller companies numbering no more than 150–200 men, in order that militiamen could be trained to execute the manoeuvres which had been developed by commanders like Maurice of Nassau. This view was presented in a spate of books, pamphlets, and memoranda typified by George Wyatt's 'Treatise on the Militia' and Matthew Sutcliffe's *The Practice, proceedings and lawes of armes*. Arguing in Renaissance style from classical experience, they pointed out that the Romans and other ancient peoples who had been successful in battle had admitted none to 'any office either of armes or meere civil, that had not first served 10 years in the wars' and were 'of chiefe account for their understandinge and experience of millitarie science'. These states had invariably adopted small companies as their basic military unit which resulted in 'better understandinge & obaiinge of commands'; the greater number of 'leaders' necessitated by small companies meant that the army was 'stronger against th enimie as an hedge that hath more stakes'. Moreover, captains of small companies were 'les dreadful to the state by les eminencie of authoritie each over other, and the chargise recompensed with more effectual performance of service, as the cost of wel stockinge land is repaired in the goodnes of the crop'.[12]

The principal gentry in each county, who for almost a generation had each commanded a large company, stood to lose prestige and power if the Council accepted the proposals of these professional captains and ordered that each company be divided into two or three smaller ones. It would be difficult to exaggerate the importance which a county magnate attached to the captaincy of a large company in the trained bands. In such a status-ridden society, the size of his command reflected accurately his position within a rigid social hierarchy. Thus Edward Lord Cromwell, the sole resident nobleman

[12] *The Papers of George Wyatt Esquire*, ed. D. M. Loades (Camden Soc. 4th ser. v, 1968) pp. 77, 86.

in late-sixteenth-century Norfolk, considered the captaincy of even a large company to be beneath his dignity; only the lieutenancy itself would fittingly mirror his eminence. As he explained to Burghley in 1596 when seeking to succeed Hunsdon as lieutenant in Norfolk, 'there liveth not within the county any other of my rang, and for me to live there as a private justice of the peace, subject to the commandment and directions of others, I doubt not but you will conceive how unpleasing a taste it may have'. The foremost gentry likewise demanded a military command commensurate with their status. They considered it quite inappropriate that they should lead small companies which differed in no way from those commanded by their inferior neighbours, let alone by 'Low Country captains'. Bassingbourne Gawdy protested that it would be 'disgraceful' for half his soldiers to be taken from him and placed under the captaincy of his neighbour and bitter rival, Thomas Lovell.[13]

The case for large companies commanded by resident magnates was presented by Sir John Smythe in his *Discourses* and *Instructions, Observations and Orders Military* and by Sir Henry Knyvett in *The Defence of the Realme*. They maintained that captains should be chosen from 'the noblemen, knightes, esquires and gentlemen of the country inhabiting within the circuit where the said soldiers are levyed'. 'Low Country captains', as Smythe disparagingly called them, were 'more hungry after charge, spoil and gain than skilful to do any great service or to win reputation in the love of their soldiers'; such men should be 'distributed and placed throughout . . . great bands as sergeants or ensign-bearers under such discreet and worshipful gentlemen to the intent that they might first learn to obey'. Both Smythe and Knyvett also inveighed against the professional muster-masters who had been sent into the counties to train the militia. They considered 'that the muster-maister of horsemen and foot-men of every shire should bee a knight or an esquire of great worship of the same shire'. The present 'ignorant and base muster-masters' should be discharged 'with a strict injunction to command them either abroad into som forrayn warres or else at home to their old occupation and trades'.[14]

Privy councillors seem to have preferred the professionals' view-

[13] *HMC Salisbury*, vi. 294. Above, p. 191.

[14] Henry Knyvett, *The Defence of the Realm*, 1596, ed. C. Hughes, 1906, pp. 31, 33. J. Smythe, *Certain Discourses Military*, ed. J. R. Hale, New York, 1964, pp. 47, 51. J. Smythe, *Instructions Observations & Orders Military*, 1595, p. 205.

point, and the Norfolk lieutenancy readily fell into line by employing two 'low country' muster-masters—captains Jackson and Lewis—throughout the early 1590s. Indeed Hunsdon may even have set the pace, for as early as 1588 he had appointed a professional soldier—Sir John Peyton—as one of his deputies in Norfolk. As well as being a professional, Peyton was also a 'stranger' who had married into the county in 1578 and, when not on military service, resided at Outwell. In 1596 he had submitted to the Council a memorandum on the militia which advocated that trained bands should be divided into small companies–a proposal Lord Hunsdon immediately implemented in Norfolk, where Sir Arthur Heveningham, to the consternation of the established commanders, hastened to divide the seven large companies into thirty-three smaller ones.[15]

Heveningham clearly seized this opportunity to satisfy the aspirations of a group of lesser gentry and professional captains at the expense of his fellow magnates. As one of them subsequently suggested: 'Sir Arthur's greatness or insolencye can appoint what captaynes he pleas in . . . our limitts.' He incensed Bassingbourne Gawdy by halving his company and placing the remainder under the captaincy of Thomas Lovell.[16] He treated Henry Gawdy even more harshly, creating four companies out of the latter's former command, appointing professional captains to command two of them,[17] and bestowing leadership of the third upon his friend and relative Edward Everard—an insignificant gentleman who had recently appeared in the commission of the peace. In north Norfolk he appointed Wimond Carey, a cousin of Lord Hunsdon and a newcomer to the county, to the captaincy of Freebridge Lynn company, ignoring Sir Robert Mansell, brother-in-law of Nathaniel and Nicholas Bacon, and the most distinguished magnate in the area, although also a newcomer. In east Norfolk he halved Sir Henry Woodhouse's command, creating two new companies and appointing his client Thomas Clere, a minor gentleman, to command them both.[18]

As long as Lord Hunsdon and his deputy Sir Arthur remained in

[15] *HMC Salisbury*, v. 523; vi. 223. *APC, 1587–8*, p. 385. *DNB*, s.v. Peyton, John. He had married Dorothy, widow of Sir Robt. Bell. BM MS. Lansd. 81, ff. 37–38v. Bodl. MS. Tanner 241, f. 22.

[16] BM MS. Eg. 2714, f. 122. Above, p. 188.

[17] Gilbert Havers and Humphrey Coppledick. Havers had been a muster-master in Suffolk.

[18] NNRO MS. CCN, 1600, no. 99. PCC 28 Fenner. Smith, 'Norf. Gentry', p. 302.

office the displaced commanders were powerless to redress this indignity. But the balance of power shifted dramatically when, a few months later, Hunsdon died and the Council put the lieutenancy of Norfolk into commission. This meant that gentry who disliked the creation of small companies could seek a place in the muster commission through the usual patronage channels; and once in the commission they could influence militia policy either by direct representation to the Council or by so executing its instructions that these had a minimal impact upon the county.

Their awareness of this situation was reflected in the composition of the first commission. Although it included the four ex-deputy lieutenants, Nathaniel Bacon was also a member. Further support for the anti-professional view came from a succession of sheriffs each of whom was appointed to the commission during his period of office. Then in 1598 the Council nominated three more magnates—Sir Christopher Heydon, Sir John Townshend, and Sir Philip Woodhouse. Of these only Sir John Townshend, son-in-law of Nathaniel Bacon, evinced strong sympathy for the 'county' view, but thereafter Bacon's associates steadily gained ground with Bassingbourne Gawdy, Sir Robert Mansell, and Henry Gawdy joining the commission during the years 1599–1601. Demand for a place in this commission had caused its membership to double from six in 1596 to twelve in 1602.[19]

The consequences soon became apparent in Norfolk's military organization. By 1599 the balance of opinion within the muster commission had shifted sufficiently for the opponents of professionalization to abolish the small companies.[20] Their opportunity came during the summer when Sir Arthur Heveningham was either ill or out of the county.[21] Immediately Bacon, Townshend, and Clement Spelman (the sheriff) voted to restore the seven large companies, reappointing three of the old commanders—Henry Woodhouse, Bassingbourne Gawdy, and Henry Gawdy—and choosing four new ones from

[19] *APC, 1596–7*, p. 53; *1597–8*, p. 484; *1598–9*, pp. 344–5. *HMC Gawdy*, pp. 70, 72, 79. Below, p. 302. BM MSS. Add. 23007, f. 17v; 29313, f. 3; 48591, ff. 70v, 129v–130. NNRO MS. NAS Safe II.28, f. 78. For Mansell's relations with the Bacon–Gawdy group, see below, p. 304.

[20] In 1598 Sir Robt. Southwell died and Sir John Peyton became Lieutenant of the Tower.

[21] He did not sign any orders made by the muster commissioners between early May and late August 1599. See, Philip Woodhouse Letter Book, *penes* Earl of Kimberley. Holkham MS. General Estate Deeds, Misc. bundle A, no. 7. BM MS. Add. 48591.

among the muster commissioners—Sir John Townshend, Clement Spelman, Christopher Heydon, and Philip Woodhouse.[22]

They kept within the letter of the 1596 reform by retaining small companies as subordinate units within these larger commands, but broke its spirit by authorizing each commander to appoint his own captains, thereby maintaining their pre-eminence and preventing the intrusion of professional captains, to say nothing of Sir Arthur Heveningham's client gentry. The Council, no doubt deploring this entire reorganization, scotched a proposal that the new commanders should be called colonels and insisted upon the hum-drum title of 'superintendent'.

Several 'superintendents' demonstrated their concern for status rather than improved military training by failing to appoint any captains—negligence which enabled Heveningham and the Council to insist that this reorganization be abandoned. In May 1601 their lordships ordered that the trained bands should again be organized in small companies and the captains appointed by the commissioners for musters. Bassingbourne Gawdy and Philip Woodhouse thought that this order would result in the abolition of their 'superintendencies' and tried to get it rescinded. Sir Robert Mansell was less pessimistic. He did not think that it was intended 'to deprive the 7 commanders of theyr comande of superintendencye but [that it was] for reducinge every privatt companye to or under the number of 200'. He also pointed out that there was now no reason why the appointment of captains should not be entrusted to the muster commissioners since the anti-professional, anti-Heveningham group had recently managed to dominate this commission.[23]

He was right. The new captains whom the muster commissioners appointed in June to command small companies were certainly not Heveningham nominees. Bassingbourne Gawdy retained the captaincy of two companies drawn from the Hundreds in which his estates lay, whereas in 1596 his rival Thomas Lovell had been appointed to command one of these. He also secured the appointment of his friend William Barwick to the captaincy of another company in his limit. In north Norfolk Sir Robert Mansell became captain of the company drawn from his own Hundred of Freebridge Lynn and also that from Clackclose Hundred, whereas in 1596 he had received no command at all. On the other hand Wimond Carey,

[22] BM MS. King's 265, ff. 276–9.

[23] Ibid. BM MSS. Add. 23007, f. 18; 48591, f. 59v; Eg. 2714, f. 122.

who had been given a company in this limit in 1596, failed to regain it in 1601. In the Hundreds of Gallow and Brothercross, Nathaniel Bacon was able to secure a captaincy for his son-in-law Sir John Townshend. In the east of the county James Scambler, an opponent of Downing and the patentees of concealed lands, and Richard Jenkinson, son-in-law of Henry Gawdy, replaced Heveningham's client Thomas Clere in West Flegg and Walsham Hundreds respectively. Heveningham may have influenced the choice of captains in Henry Gawdy's 'limit', but even here Edmund Doyley, an established squire and friend of Henry Gawdy, replaced the upstart Gilbert Havers as the captain in Henstead Hundred.[24]

Opponents of the Council's attempts to reform and professionalize the militia not only conducted a rearguard action in the county, they also counter-attacked in parliament. Two late Marian (1558) Acts provided the statutory basis for the Elizabethan militia. The first laid down that everyone who had property with a yearly value of over £5 should provide weapons, each person contributing according to his means on a ten-point scale. The weapons it specified, however, were largely traditional to late-medieval warfare and took no account of current developments in military science. The second statute made it obligatory for everyone to attend musters with his weapons, but omitted to specify the frequency of mustering or to make provision for instruction in the use of weapons and for payment of those who attended.[25] Early in Elizabeth's reign it had become clear that these Acts had made inadequate provision for an up-to-date well-trained citizen army. Even worse, by the 1580s, they provided unwilling gentry with an excuse for resisting conciliar and lieutenancy efforts to produce a battle-worthy militia. From the government's standpoint these statutes needed revision. Instead, they were repealed in an Act of 1604 which marked the culmination of a parliamentary conflict in the course of which county interests successfully withstood government efforts to provide statutory backing for an improved militia under lieutenancy administration. This conflict can be traced through a series of unsuccessful militia Bills.[26]

The first, 'for furniture of armour & weapons', was introduced in the Commons in 1581 where it received short shrift on its first reading. The text has not survived, but it may well have been an attempt

[24] BM MSS. Add. 23007, f. 21v; King's 265, ff. 298v–299.

[25] 4 & 5 Philip and Mary, cc. 2, 3.

[26] 1 James I, c. 25.

to compel counties to provide the most up-to-date weapons together with appropriate training in their use. In 1589 two more Bills were introduced, this time in the Lords, one for 'having horse armour & weapons', the other 'concerning captains & soldiers'. Once more no texts have survived, but the speed with which both passed the Upper House and the urgency with which that House commended them to the Commons suggest concern among lords lieutenants and lords of the Council to secure statutory backing for regular musters and for the provision of more sophisticated weapons. In the event the Commons never read the first Bill. The second was clearly disliked: twice committed, it remained a subject of conference with the Lords when parliament was dissolved.[27]

In 1597–8 parliament considered two more militia Bills. The first originated in complaints voiced in the Commons by opponents of the lieutenancy. Early in the session George More, knight of the shire for Surrey, drew attention to the 'great & burthensome charge of the subjects . . . being compelled upon great penalties with the keeping & having of sundry sorts of armour & weapons'. The House appointed a committee which framed a Bill 'concerning armour & weapons', but nothing further is heard of it. Shortly afterwards the Commons received a Bill from the Lords 'for the reforminge of sundrie abuses comitted by soldiers & others used in her Majesties services concerning the warres'. This Bill was concerned with military efficiency rather than the protection of county interests. Coming at a time when deputy lieutenants were heavily engaged in levying soldiers for service overseas and when their efforts were impaired by extensive desertions between impressment and embarkation, it provided swingeing punishments for this offence: 'everie person soe offending shall . . . be . . . adiudged a felon & suffer & be executed as in case of felony'. Not surprisingly this Bill also foundered in a Commons' committee.[28]

The conflict between those who advocated militia reforms and their opponents is most apparent in the business of the 1601 parliament. Early in the session the Lords read a Bill entitled 'An acte concerninge musters soldiers & other thinges apperteyninge thereunto'. It was a composite measure compiled from two or more unofficial draft Bills which clearly reflect a militia-efficiency 'lobby'.

[27] D'Ewes, pp. 290, 423–5, 447, 450. BM MS. Lansd. 58, f. 164.

[28] D'Ewes, pp. 537, 541–4, 552–3, 556, 566, 589–92. HLRO Main Papers (Supplementary) 1597–1601, ff. 169–172v.

The Bill gave lieutenants and their deputies, or commissioners appointed in their stead, far-reaching powers to discipline anyone who attempted to avoid impressment:

everie person . . . soe offendinge upon sufficient proofe thereof or confession of the partie so offendinge (to be examined upon his oathe) before suche persons as are or shall be lievetenantes or lievetenante of the same countie or otherwise before the [deputy?] lievetenantes or commissioners for musters . . . or any twoe or more of them shalbe committed to the gaole . . . theri to remaine without baile or mainprise by the space of three monethes.

Even more significantly this Bill gave deputy lieutenants and commissioners for musters unlimited authority to enforce payment of any military rates they saw fit to impose:

wheare greate trouble and contention often groweth in sondrie partes of this her Majesties realme . . . touchinge the ratinge & leavyinge of such somes of money and payments as are thought fitt to be rated sett or raised . . . not onlie to the greate hinderaunce of her majesties services, but verie often to the greate burthen and chardge of such as intermedle with the collectinge of the same. Be yt therfore enacted . . . that all such questions and controversies shalbe ordered and determined by the lievetenantes . . . or otherwise by the deputy liuetenantes or comissioners for the musters . . . or any two of them, whoe shall have powre and aucthoritie by vertue of this acte to rate & taxe what [sic] everie person or persons . . ., and shall give warrant to leavy the same by waie of distres and sale therof, or otherwise by comittinge the parties not obeyinge their order to prison, theare to remaine untill such tyme as they shall obey and performe the same.[29]

The Lords committed this remarkable Bill to Archbishop Whitgift, Lord Buckhurst, and other peers, afforced by six law officers including the two chief justices and Attorney General Edward Coke. Their protracted deliberations suggest difficulties if not disagreements. Eventually they reported 'so many imperfections in the . . . [Bill] as it could not conveniently be amended'. Instead they presented a new Bill entitled 'An act concerning captains soldiers mariners & other the Queenes services in the wars'. This Bill retained the substance of its predecessor in that it gave statutory powers to the lieutenancy, but it also associated the J.P.s with them in all enforcement clauses, thereby weakening the *de facto* authority of the lieutenancy since, given the situation in Norfolk, the odds were strong that cases would be heard before justices who opposed the lieutenancy. The Lords hurriedly passed this more moderate

[29] HLRO Main Papers (Supplementary) 1597–1601, ff. 73–5v.

Bill, but even in this form it had little to commend it to the county interests represented in the Commons where it was 'dashed' at the second reading.

The parliamentary deadlock over militia affairs throughout the 1590s prevented the government from procuring a realistic statute of arms. Consequently prerogative powers had to be invoked to implement regular musters and training as well as to impose extraordinary demands in times of crisis. The counties baulked at these demands by constantly appealing to the Marian statutes so that by 1604 the government may well have felt that no statutes were better than inadequate ones—hence the repeal of these Marian statutes in the first parliament of James I.[30]

Simultaneously with the development of opposition to the lieutenancy and the plans for an improved militia, Norfolk justices disputed over whether the county should compound its obligation to supply provisions to the royal Household in order to avoid the depredations of purveyors. For a time the county was so badly split on this issue that some southern Hundreds, led by Sir Arthur Heveningham, had compounded for meat, while central and northern Hundreds, led by Nathaniel Bacon, refused to make any agreement for the supply of grain.

Although the Crown's right to purchase provisions for the Household at a rate below market price was a well-established part of the prerogative, the harsh dealings of purveyors gave rise to constant complaint in parliament.[31] By the end of Mary's reign several statutes had been enacted to curb the oppressive activities of these officials, but the resourcefulness of purveyors apparently outstripped that of parliamentary draftsmen since the counties seemed no less aggrieved under Elizabeth.[32] She, however, refused to allow any further statutory restrictions upon the activities of her Household officials. Instead she endeavoured to allay complaints by encouraging

[30] D'Ewes, pp. 602–4, 609–13, 684–8. H. Townshend, *Historical Collections*, 1680, pp. 327–9. HLRO Main Papers (Supplementary) 1576–1593, ff. 99–102v; this Bill has been incorrectly ascribed to 1588/9.

[31] In the following paragraphs I have drawn heavily upon Allegra Woodworth's *Purveyance for the Royal Household in the Reign of Elizabeth*, Philadelphia, 1945.

[32] Neale, *Parliaments 1559–81*, pp. 122–3; *1584–1601*, pp. 187–8, 207–15.

the Board of Green Cloth—the officials of the Lord Steward's department—to negotiate composition agreements in which counties contracted to supply the royal Household annually with a fixed quantity of foodstuffs at an agreed price; in return the Crown undertook, with certain provisos, to withdraw purveyors from these counties. In agreeing the rate at which the Crown could purchase provisions the Lord Steward's officers drove hard bargains, sometimes offering a county only half or one-third of the goods' market value. If the justices agreed to compound they then had to recover the difference between their receipts from the Crown and their outlay on provisions by levying a county rate. County Benches were free to make their own decisions as to whether or not to negotiate an agreement with the Board of Green Cloth; frequently they compromised by compounding for the supply of certain foodstuffs, particularly meat and poultry, leaving purveyors to purchase the rest—notably supplies of grain. They could repudiate their agreement after a year had elapsed, on giving six months' notice. To judge from the number of counties which broke agreements, compounding does not seem to have provided a panacea for all the evils of purveyance.

This flexible procedure ended in 1591 when the Queen, in response to clamour in the 1589 parliament for yet more legislation against purveyors, appointed a commission of privy councillors led by Burghley—'the commission for household causes'—to consider reforms in Household administration. The commissioners proposed that each county should make a comprehensive composition agreement for all provisions normally supplied to the Household. They ordered twenty-six counties, including Norfolk, to send delegates to Court by the 24 October 1592 empowered to negotiate 'for some composition to be made for her majesty's household without offence by purveyors'. It was the activities of this commission which precipitated further conflict among the Norfolk magnates.

Nathaniel Bacon led the opposition to compounding. Despite his desire to prevent the harsh dealings of the purveyors, he considered that compounding made the situation worse. His objections appear to have been essentially legal and constitutional. For instance, after the county had eventually compounded, he informed the Lord Chief Justice:

. . . it is better for the contry to performe whatsoever it shall please her Maiestie by her prerogative touching the purvey of her provision to laie upon it, than to have it goe on as it doth without some better provicon wherein it were to be wished that a new lawe were established by parliament if ther maie apper cause to repeale the old.[33]

He was even more explicit in a letter to Sir Charles Cornwallis: '. . . it was better to have the former corse when the purveyors were prescribed to take by a corse of lawe though it had been harder for the subject, than to endure this corse of composicon which is without the compasse of the lawe.'[34] True to form, he wanted the administration of purveyance brought more fully within the purview of the common law and the justices in quarter sessions. In his view, composition, for all its superficial attractions, did just the reverse; it nullified such statutory limitations as had already been imposed upon purveyors by supplanting them with officials —namely compounders and their undertakers (frequently purveyors in another guise)—whose activities had not been circumscribed by statute. Consequently any person in dispute with these compounders or their deputies had no redress at common law; he had to appear before the Board of Green Cloth whose officers had good reason for backing compounders. Bacon saw clearly that such a situation was the abnegation of much that the opponents of purveyance had sought to achieve in their 1589 parliamentary campaign. Then, one of the principal aims had been to 'prevent any purveyor, regardless of the service in which he was employed, from summoning persons before the Board of Green Cloth, except upon certificate obtained from two J.P.s'.[35] In other words their Bill was a serious attempt to withhold purveyance disputes from the prerogative Court of Green Cloth and to settle them in the county, without actually challenging the final authority of this court. Compounding contributed nothing towards such aims.

Undoubtedly many justices and gentry joined with Bacon in opposing composition because they feared that the consequent rate would fall most heavily upon substantial property owners instead of the 'poorer sort' who had hitherto born the brunt of purveyance. There is plenty of evidence that the Council, as in its attitude towards military taxation, was anxious that these new rates should be levied upon justices, gentry, and the wealthier members of the community.

[33] NNRO MS. 2645b (Box 3A2).

[34] IHR microfilm XD 37 (Transcrs. and originals from the collection of H. W. Saunders), Nath. Bacon to Chas. Cornwallis, 26 July 1602.

[35] Woodworth, p. 23.

Warrants from the compounders repeatedly instructed constables 'to rate indifferently upon the townships . . . according to the habilitie of the several inhabitants there, wherein you are to have care for the sparing of the pore and unable sort'.

Although it is not possible to be more precise about objections to composition, they would appear to have been legal and political rather than practical since vehement opposition to any form of agreement arose as soon as it was mooted. A majority of the Bench refused to co-operate with Burghley and the commissioners when they tried to present their new composition proposals in the most favourable light by instituting an enquiry into the iniquities and deceits of purveyors. They had briefed the justices in elaborate detail:

> . . . calle before you all the highe and pettie constables and suche other of everie parishe as you shall think to be most fytt and by oathe and oathes and otherwise by your discrecon . . . examyne and fynd owt all the [abuses] . . . and certifie the same to us in wrighting . . . sealed in some boxe or bagge not to be opened untill it shall come to our handes or to some of us.

But eight months later Norfolk justices had submitted no sealed box or bag—a situation at which the commissioners expressed surprise 'consideringe the usuall complaints made in parlyament'. When Heveningham, Heydon, and Clere—deputy lieutenants to a man—ordered the constables to submit their returns at Attleborough in April 1592 the justices in north Norfolk, led by Francis Gawdy, sabotaged the meeting by summoning all their Hundred constables to appear at Lynn sessions 'there to performe such service as to them shall be enioyned'. 'Wherefore I doubt not', wrote Edmund Moundford in apparent innocence to Heveningham, 'but you will have our cheyfe constables excused in not proceading in the further executing of your warrants. Thus . . . I leave you to the tuycon of the Almighty.' Even by the end of the year many constables still had not submitted their returns, although there is evidence that they had completed the inquisition.[36]

By this time, in any case, the occasion for such disclosures had

[36] NNRO MSS. Aylsham, bundle 17, Privy Council to justices of Norfolk, 29 July 1591; Privy Council to justices of Norfolk, 25 Feb. [1591/2]; Edw. Clere and Wm. Heydon to chief constables of Earsham and Depwade, 12 Mar. 1591/2; Edm. Moundford to A. Heveningham, 7 Apr. 1592; draft letter from A. Heveningham to justices of Norfolk, 16 Oct. 1592. *History Teacher's Miscellany*, ii. 143–4. *Stiffkey Papers*, p. 66. IHR microfilm XD 37 (Transcrs. and originals from the collection of H. W. Saunders), frames 52, 64–6.

passed, since in August 1592 the 'commission for household causes' had propounded its scheme for compounding, supposedly as a means of freeing the county from the oppressive activities of purveyors as revealed in this non-existent indictment. It implemented these proposals in January 1593 by instructing the Norfolk justices to appoint some of their number 'sufficientlye furnished with authoritie to accorde and conclude' a composition which would be acceptable to both the county and the royal Household. The sheriff convened a meeting accordingly on 22 January 1593, but many justices boycotted this and all subsequent attempts to comply with the commission's requirements. This was undoubtedly a tactical error since, inevitably, initiative passed into the hands of a clique, headed by deputy lieutenants Heveningham and Peyton, which constantly associated itself with the interests of the Court rather than the county. 'I need not care whose fryndship I loose in this accon', Heveningham informed Henry Gawdy, 'beinge well assured of her Majesty's favior.'[37]

Those who attended the meeting authorized Heveningham and Peyton, together with Miles Corbett and Robert Buxton, to negotiate a composition agreement; or rather a part-agreement since the intransigence of justices from central and northern Norfolk meant that the county's delegates had been empowered to compound only for provisions from the wood–pasture area where Heveningham held sway. Indeed it seems doubtful whether there was even unanimity among the four delegates, since only Heveningham and Peyton appeared before the commissioners in London, while Miles Corbett subsequently joined the opposition to compounding. The commission for household causes, with good reason, 'toke some exceptions in regarde that . . . [the delegates] were not sufficientlye aucthorised' and ordered them back to Norfolk for further briefing. A second meeting of justices, called by the sheriff on 6 March, resulted in 'manye speaches . . . but no agrement or order taken'. Heveningham endeavoured to convene the justices for further discussions on 23 April but the majority from central and northern Norfolk still refused to attend.[38]

[37] NNRO MSS. Aylsham, bundle 17, Privy Council to sheriff and justices of Norfolk, 7 Jan. 1592/3; 2645d (Box 3A2).

[38] NNRO MSS. 2645g (Box 3A2); Aylsham, bundle 17, draft letter from A. Heveningham and John Peyton to justices of Norfolk, 13 Feb. 1592/3; A. Heveningham to justices of Norfolk, 18 Apr. 1593.

Late in May the commissioners reluctantly bowed to the inevitable by compounding with the southern Hundreds for supplies of oxen, mutton, lambs and stirk, but corn, the principal commodity from west and north Norfolk, and poultry continued to be taken up by purveyors—a disconcerting compromise which the commissioners endeavoured to end as quickly as possible. They informed the recalcitrant Hundreds that purveyors would be commissioned to take 'a farre greater proportion then now is demanded . . . for the ease of other shires that have compounded', and that these officials would be ordered to 'ease the poorer sortes of yomen and farmers . . . and to charge the best able within the said hundreds'. They also ordered the sheriff to convene the justices once more for negotiations about composition and to report any who refused to attend. These threats seem to have swayed a sufficient number to enable Heveningham and Peyton to negotiate a county-wide composition agreement during the summer of 1593. It was to be financed by a rate of 4*d.* in the pound levied upon the wealthier inhabitants according to the assessments in the subsidy book.[39]

Despite this agreement, opposition to compounding was such that Heveningham and Peyton could not even levy the money to meet their first purchases. In mid-September they complained that 'certeyne hundreds have not as yett answered any parte of the saide rates and moste partes of the other hundredes behynde halfe the some they were to satysfie unto us'. In December Heveningham threatened to send recalcitrants before the Council commissioners, a threat which he was soon forced to implement. During 1594 and 1595 at least two Council pursuivants were active in Norfolk summoning those who refused to pay. But far from overriding the opposition, these pursuivants exacerbated the situation since the fees they exacted amounted to many times the sums they had been sent to collect. Robert Hall, for instance, levied fees totalling 77*s.* 10*d.* while trying to collect 19*s.* from sixteen defaulters.[40]

[39] NNRO MSS. Aylsham, bundle 17, Privy Council to sheriff and justices of Norfolk, 23 May 1593; undated draft letter from justices to constables.

[40] NNRO MSS. Aylsham, bundle 17, A. Heveningham and J. Peyton to the justices of peace for Diss, Earsham, Depwade, and Henstead, 17 Sept. 1593; warrant from A. Heveningham [to constables?], 15 Dec. 1593; Privy Council to messenger of the Counting House, 20 June 1594; warrant from compounders to messenger of Counting House, July 1594; Henry Walker to A. Heveningham, 8 July 1594; bundle 173, A note of such money which the Knight Marshall's deputy hath received . . ., 8 Aug. 1600.

Many who refused to pay the rate did so, no doubt, because they considered it extortionate. They frequently insinuated, and sometimes asserted outright, that both commissioners for compounding and pursuivants were making considerable profits. As early as 1594 the constable of Hardingham observed that in barely twelve months his parish rates had been raised from under 20*s.* to 26*s.* Then, in 1596, Edward Coke complained that William Southis, a messenger from the officers of the Green Cloth, had 'by colour . . . of certain directions from one deputie lieutenante above . . . [i.e. Sir Arthur Heveningham] comitted many notable misdemeanors and extorcions'. Coke also claimed that during 'the three yeres before the composicon', Launditch Hundred 'was charged towards her majesties provision but at £19, and thes last three yeres sithence the composicon have bene charged towards her majesties provision for the same things at £70.9.0.' Forty years on it was claimed that compounders had been averaging a steady annual profit of £200–£250 in each county.[41]

Council pursuivants, Household pursuivants, summonses to the Council Board, the arbitrary procedures of the officers of the Green Cloth: these aspects of government had become all too familiar to local administrators during the past decade. Compounding for purveyance merely increased their incidence; hence its immediate rejection by many justices. But outright rejection or tacit opposition merely inflamed the situation by forcing the compounders to rely more heavily upon intervention by the Board of Green Cloth. Very quickly, therefore, those justices who had initially refused to compound saw the realization of their worst forebodings, and decided to repudiate the agreement.

Led by Nathaniel Bacon, his brother Nicholas, and Henry Gawdy, in February 1600 twenty-two justices gave notice of their intention to end the composition agreement. The officers of the Green Cloth rejected it on two counts. First they argued that the letter had not been signed by Sir Arthur Heveningham or Sir John Peyton, the two principal commissioners for compounding. To this Nathaniel Bacon retorted that of the four original commissioners Sir John Peyton no longer lived in the county, Robert Buxton was in prison, Sir Miles Corbett had signed the letter, 'and if Sir Arthur should refuse to allowe of that which hath ben certefied, yet we trust no

[41] NNRO MS. Aylsham, bundle 17, Francis Tilney to Mr. Brown, 7 July 1594. BM MS. Lansd. 82, f. 216v. *Econ.HR* 2nd ser. x, 1957, p. 88.

such construccion will be made of that which hath ben done, as that the countryes breaking, or not breaking should alltogither rest upon anie one man's determinacon'. The officers of the Green Cloth hastily shifted their ground and next argued that, although the letter giving notice to break the agreement had been signed by many justices, their views did not reflect a consensus of opinion throughout the county. Those 'names we thinke have bene severally procured rather than by any generall consente . . . . We ar gyven to understand that their ar sondry gents of good sorte in this county . . . which very willingly and dutifully do and will embrace this composition . . .'. Their letter closed with the threat that if the agreement were to be broken 'we mind to . . . [impose] a larger proportion of provisions out of your countrye'.[42]

The justices, however, refused to withdraw their notice. Faced with this recalcitrance, the Council intervened and in December 1600 instructed them to sound out more thoroughly opinion in the county before breaking their agreement. Constables were to consult '. . . carefully the mindes and desires of all the yeomen farmers' and then to report their findings at a special meeting with the justices during the next quarter sessions. In order to ensure that the anti-compounders did not sabotage these proceedings by arranging special meetings, as had Francis Gawdy in 1592, their lordships insisted that Heveningham must be present at all discussions. Their letter ended with the ominous statement that they would not permit the composition agreement to be broken simply by a majority vote of justices: 'wee must needes give better allowance of two or three carefull for their countrye . . . then of twenty to the contrarye'.[43]

But even Council directives left the opposition unmoved. It refused to meet Heveningham or to summon the chief constables, informing the Council that neither procedure served any purpose since the decision to break the composition agreement had been taken only after 'we had ben satisfied by sondrie gentlemen being no justices of peace, by the chief constables, and by some yeomen also of the better sort that the contry was unwilling to be anie longer tied to the composicon'. Bacon and his fellow magistrates were adamant that their notice had now stood for six months and that the agreement had therefore been terminated. Accordingly at the January

[42] NNRO MSS. NAS Safe II.28, ff. 31v–35v; 2645g (Box 3A2).
[43] NNRO MS. NAS Safe II.28, ff. 44–5.

quarter sessions they refused to sanction the annual composition rate.[44]

Heveningham, recalling how councillors had previously coerced his opponents into compounding, continued to act as if the agreement still stood. Having failed to get a composition rate approved at the quarter sessions, he tried to arrange an *ad hoc* meeting of justices late in January 1601. 'There must be no delay in this service', he informed Henry Gawdy, 'because the poultry must be served presently and the wheate before the 10th day of March, which yf yt be delayed will growe to a higher price.' Would Gawdy therefore 'cause the justices about Norwich to meete uppon Monday at the signe of the Crown to consider what is fitest to be done herein'; he had already discussed the situation with Sir Philip Woodhouse, Sir Bassingbourne Gawdy, Mr. Houghton, and several other lawyers and justices who had promised to attend the meeting and grant a rate. His postscript went to the heart of the matter: 'I pray Sir move Mr. Bacon herein: for I am very lothe to loose any man's love.' It is doubtful whether Henry Gawdy even tried; certainly the meeting proved a fiasco since only Henry Woodhouse attended. Heveningham claimed that Thomas Barney and Robert Houghton had given written consent to a rate, but Barney appears to have denied this. A laconic note in the sheriff's letter book records that 'the whole chardge of the composition for the Queenes provision for Norfolk . . . [was] agreed uppon by some five or sixe of the justices and no more'.[45]

Thwarted in this way, Heveningham proceeded to collect the rate without quarter-sessional approval. Early in February 1601 he called '. . . before himselfe privately manie Chief Constables . . . and made shewe . . . that he called them before him to be informed what powder and shott did remaine in their hands for the defence of the countrye, and sone after dealt with them about the composicon, with whome by perswasion and otherwise he prevailed so farre forth as he got manie of them to subscribe and yeelde their consentes for the continuance of the composicon'. He apparently 'prevailed' upon the constables from twenty-three out of the thirty-three Hundreds. Taking this as a mandate from the county, he issued warrants authorizing a rate to be levied. At this Nathaniel Bacon 'storme[d] greatlye', declared the warrants to be unlawful, and instructed

[44] NNRO MS. 2645c (Box 3A2).

[45] NNRO MSS. 2645d (Box 3A2); NAS Safe II.28, f. 58.

constables throughout the county to desist from collecting any money. Heveningham retaliated by threatening to send before the Council any constable who failed to deliver his Hundred's purveyance money on time. The Lord Chief Justice endeavoured to break the deadlock at the Lent assizes and after some persuasion he left the justices 'willing to take present order therein'. None the less six months later the money had still not been collected. This unsatisfactory situation continued throughout 1602 with many justices refusing to levy the composition rate, while Sir Arthur Heveningham and the officers of the Queen's household blandly ignored the notice to end composition and held splinter meetings of justices in order to obtain a token sanction for collecting the rate.[46]

As a result of these disputes over purveyance and militia administration, tension at quarter sessions reached such a pitch that in January 1601 the Lord Chief Justice instructed magistrates to ensure that 'no weapons be worne' during the sessions in view of the 'hartburning which at this instant is thought to remayne unquallyfied betwixt divers of the chief men of our cuntry'. This was a timely precaution since during the summer sessions Sir Christopher Heydon had challenged Sir John Townshend to a duel which had been averted only by conciliar intervention. The exact nature of their dispute is unknown, but almost certainly it related to the issues in county administration which have just been outlined. Heydon 'taxed' Townshend in his 'public service', and it is significant that each adhered to one of the contending groups in county government. Sir Christopher Heydon had aligned himself with the Heveningham faction after his father had died in 1594, whereas Sir John Townshend, son-in-law of Nathaniel Bacon, had opposed the professionalization of the militia. That Edward Coke, who had recently been involved in exposing corruption in militia and purveyance administration, offered to stand bail for him is further proof of Townshend's association with Heveningham's opponents.[47]

[46] NNRO MSS. 2645a & e (Box 3A2); NAS Safe II.28, ff. 72v, 73, 112; WALS XVII/I, pt. ii, f. 158v. Philip Woodhouse Letter Book, *penes* Earl of Kimberley, Privy Council to A. Heveningham, 18 Oct. 1601.

[47] Philip Woodhouse Letter Book, *penes* Earl of Kimberley, Chief Justice Popham to justices of Norfolk, 8 Jan. 1600. BM MSS. Add. 23007, f. 7; 27961, f. 7. *HMC Salisbury*, X. 367, 458. Jeayes, p. 107.

The Council had scarcely averted this duel when a second quarrel broke out, this time between Sir John Heydon, younger brother of Sir Christopher, and Sir Robert Mansell. This dispute, which began at the Michaelmas quarter sessions, culminated in a duel near Norwich on 2 October 1600. First reports gave both knights as dead. 'It shold seem by the number and the manner of theyre hurts (the one having sixe and the other fowre) that they ran at tilt with theyre rapiers,' wrote John Chamberlain. Subsequently he had better news: both had survived 'though they had double the number of woundes' that he had previously reported.[48]

This duel took place during the quarter sessions at which the justices disputed over whether they should break their composition agreement; indeed it may even have arisen out of attempts to solicit signatures for a petition against compounding. Mansell subsequently recounted how, at the end of the duel, when Heydon sought mercy, 'I drew out my articles from my brest where I carried them and brought them with ink & penn to him [Sir John Heydon] to signe'. If the timing suggests that the duel reflected county politics, so too do the personalities: both duellists were closely associated with one of the county political groupings. Sir John Heydon received backing from Sir Arthur Heveningham who lost no time in supplying the Council with a version of the incident which reflected creditably upon Heydon's part in the affair. Mansell, by contrast, had the support of the anti-lieutenancy group. To second him he nominated Thomas Knyvett, son-in-law of Nathaniel Bacon and heir of Sir Thomas Knyvett, the former deputy lieutenant who had been dismissed by Hunsdon in order to make way for Sir Arthur Heveningham. Moreover, as soon as the duel had ended Mansell and Knyvett returned to Norwich where Sir John Townshend awaited them 'with many gentlemen of worth'. Sir Bassingbourne Gawdy was undoubtedly among this company since he subsequently witnessed depositions about the duel which were taken at Mansell's instigation.[49]

It would be misleading, however, to suggest that this serious rift among the gentry had arisen entirely from their disagreement over aims and methods of county government. Division within the county had been heightened by the Essex–Cecil conflict at Court. Both Christopher and John Heydon were Essex clients, having been

[48] *Visit. of Norf.* ii. 214–16. PRO SP 12/275/89, /94.

[49] NNRO MS. NAS Safe II.28, ff. 46v–48. BM MS. Add. 27961, ff. 3, 7. Above, p. 243.

knighted by the Earl at Cadiz and in Ireland respectively, and both subsequently staked what remained of their family fortune and prestige in support of his abortive rebellion. Sir John Heydon's second in his duel with Mansell—Sir Edwin Rich—also had Essex connections, his brother being married to Essex's sister Penelope. Townshend and Mansell, by contrast, had close associations with the anti-Essex courtiers—notably with the Lord Admiral, Lord Howard of Effingham, and Lord Thomas Howard, marshal of the forces which besieged Essex in his house in London. Townshend also received support from Edward Coke, another of Essex's principal detractors since the Earl had supported Francis Bacon in his contest with Coke for the attorney generalship and his suit for the hand of Lady Elizabeth Hatton.[50]

The impact upon the county of faction at Court in the closing years of the Queen's reign may explain why Sir Robert Mansell appears in temporary alliance with the county-orientated justices although he was basically a courtier, as was to be shown by his subsequent career as a monopolist.[51] The crucial factor was Essex's support for the policies and personnel associated with Heveningham: he intervened on behalf of William Downing and the patentees of concealment in the dispute over the possession of Martham parsonage; he supported the moves to improve militia training and he tried to obtain the muster-masterships for his clients. Inevitably, therefore, Cecil and Howard clients like Mansell were driven into an uneasy alliance with Heveningham's opponents, an alliance made easier in Mansell's case since he had married Nathaniel Bacon's sister Elizabeth after the death of her first husband, Francis Wyndham, in 1592.[52]

[50] Neale, *Commons*, pp. 57–8. BM MSS. Add. 23007, ff. 8–9; 27961, f. 3. NNRO MS. NAS, Safe II.28, ff. 48v–49. *HMC Salisbury*, xi. 88. *Burke's Extinct Peerages*, iii. 452. J. E. Neale, *Queen Elizabeth*, 1934, pp. 334–5. C. W. James, *Chief Justice Coke*, 1929, pp. 9, 27. Birch, *Memoirs*, ii. 347. *DNB*, s.v. Howard, Charles and Thomas. *HMC Gawdy*, p. 79. Above, p. 302.

[51] For a sketch of Mansell's later career, see R. W. Kenney, *Elizabeth's Admiral*, 1970, pp. 295–6.

[52] Above, p. 270. Lambeth Palace MS. 660, ff. 100, 121, 238, 280, 364. NNRO MS. WALS XVII/I, pt. ii. f. 22v. *Visit. of Norf.* ii. 213.

PART IV

CONCLUDING

CHAPTER XIV

Politics and Office Holding

In order to depict the divisive issues within Norfolk administration it has been necessary to look separately at several controversies which, in fact, especially after 1585, were developing concurrently. This has inevitably obscured the full impact of faction and politics upon the appointment and dismissal of justices, the selection of sheriffs, and the conduct of parliamentary business. This chapter will therefore attempt to assess the combined effect of these controversies upon office holding in the county.

A. JUSTICES OF THE PEACE

As has been suggested, gentlemen did not automatically become justices by virtue of their wealth and status, nor did a son necessarily succeed to his father's place on the Bench. The situation appears to have been much more open and flexible, with a large group of gentry competing for relatively few places in the commission. It also appears that justices had little security of tenure; they were frequently dismissed, a few several times over. Of course there were families in which son succeeded father on the Bench for several generations, each holding office without interruption for life as if possessed of a piece of inalienable property. But cases to the contrary, even if not the norm, are too frequent to be treated as exceptions. The numerous short-term appointments, frequent dismissals, and general lack of continuity merit an explanation.

Undoubtedly the Council's efforts to reduce the number of justices introduced a measure of instability; undoubtedly, too, access to a powerful patron explains why some gentry gained office while others failed. As Burghley told his son, a gentleman without a patron is 'like a hop without a pole'.[1] But besides such general explanations, in each county particular factors may have been making for frequent changes among the personnel of the Bench; certainly it is worth considering how far the political divisions among Norfolk gentry affected the Norfolk Bench.

The foregoing narrative has shown the crucial role of quarter

[1] J. Hurstfield, *The Queen's Wards*, 1958, p. 257.

sessions in the conduct of both private quarrels and public disputes over methods of county administration. The importance attached to debates, voting, petitions to the Council, and signatures upon warrants to constables must have encouraged contentious gentry to intrigue for the dismissal from the Bench of their opponents and the appointment of their friends. There is considerable evidence about dismissals: Flowerdew and Heveningham in turn both lost their places on the Bench during their bitter controversy in 1582 and 1583; Thomas Lovell's chequered career as a magistrate is explained by his struggle with the Gawdys for supremacy in south-west Norfolk; Thomas Farmer twice lost his place, once when he challenged the authority of Sir William Heydon, and again in the course of a family row with Martin Barney; Thomas Knyvett was dismissed from both magistracy and lieutenancy for refusing to implement militia policy; Martin Barney and Thomas Townshend were dismissed at the instigation of a Puritan faction during its conflict with Bishop Freake, while four Puritan magistrates in Suffolk received similar treatment at the hands of Freake's allies; Martin Barney was put out of the commission a second time ostensibly on religious grounds but in fact on the initiative of his enemy Thomas Farmer; both Christopher Heydon and Sir Robert Mansell were dismissed after their bitter quarrel in 1600, as had been Sir John Townshend at a slightly earlier point in this conflict; finally, Sir Nicholas L'Estrange and John Blennerhassett lost their places in 1572 through being too closely involved with the Duke of Norfolk.[2]

It is less easy to assess the impact of faction and dispute upon appointments to the Bench, but here again the evidence is at least suggestive. It is significant that Thomas Sidney, customer of Lynn and an accomplice of the Heydons in their shady corn-licensing transactions, appeared in the commission of the peace during the period (1581–2) when Nathaniel Bacon was making determined efforts to expose his sharp practices. Similarly, Thomas Farmer's appointment in 1579 undoubtedly related to his feud with the Heydons, as did his subsequent dismissal. Both Sidney and Farmer came into the commission to meet the exigencies of the moment; neither of them 'inherited' a family place on the Bench nor did a relative succeed them; their names suddenly appear in the commissions for a few years and then vanish for at least a generation.

[2] Above, pp. 181–92, 195, 199–200, 208, 227, 243–4. Appendix I.

Christopher Heydon's case was different. The Heydons had served on the Bench for several generations, but instead of Christopher succeeding his father in 1594 he was appointed to sit concurrently with him in 1586. This premature appointment probably arose from the need to boost his electoral appeal during his campaign against Farmer, and also from his father's desire for strong quarter-sessional backing during his conflict with Nathaniel Bacon over the conduct of local administration. Christopher was subsequently dismissed and not reappointed until four years after his father's death, a delay which undoubtedly also relates to the Heydon–Bacon conflict.[3]

The appointment of only a small number of justices can be explained in these direct and personal terms. However, in the struggle between Freake and the Puritans it has already been shown how each side attempted to pack the Bench with gentry of a sympathetic religious outlook; it may therefore be worth enquiring how far this pattern holds good for other disputes, especially those manifesting an ideological element. Between 1583 and 1593 Norfolk gentry were involved in three concurrent disputes: one about the status of the Dean and Chapter's lands, the others about the validity of patents to repair the highway between Wymondham and Attleborough, and to finance the rebuilding of Sheringham's piers. What relationship can be traced between the parties in these disputes and the newcomers to the Bench?

The protracted litigation between Eden and Downing over tenure of Martham parsonage and its lands appears to have been a test case which, had it been won by Downing, would have jeopardized the episcopal estates as well as those of the Dean and Chapter and their tenants. Each party received support from the foremost justices: Sir Arthur Heveningham backed Downing and the patentees, while Henry Gawdy led a powerful group in defence of Eden and the Dean and Chapter. The ramifications of this were soon apparent in the recruitment to the Bench. In 1591 Dr. Thomas Dove, Dean of Norwich, and Dr. Robert Redmayne, Chancellor of the diocese, appeared in commission although hitherto no dean or chancellor had been a member of the Bench. Equally significant was the timely appointment of four other justices—Miles Corbett (1590–1), Thomas Barney (1592–3), Gregory Pratt (1592–3), and James Scambler (1593)—all of whom were either episcopal or capitular

[3] Above, pp. 235–41, 243–5. Below, pp. 319–21. Appendices I and III.

tenants, three of them residing in the 'division' of Norfolk in which Martham parsonage was situated.[4]

These justices, all of whom acted with partiality over matters connected with Martham parsonage, were no doubt also available at quarter sessions to join with Nathaniel Bacon and Henry Gawdy in preventing Heveningham from collecting a county rate under his highway patent. As well as this accession of strength the Bacon–Gawdy following at quarter sessions was further reinforced in 1591 by the appointment to the Bench of Edmund Moundford and Clement Spelman.

If Heveningham was to make any headway against such a powerful opposition he needed sufficient supporters at quarter sessions to outvote it. This presented few problems since he had ready access to the Council and Court through Lord Hunsdon. Hence, presumably, Wimond Carey's appointment to the Bench in 1590–1. Carey, a stranger to Norfolk who had recently settled at Snettisham, had no particular claim to magistracy except that he was Lord Hunsdon's cousin and that Heveningham needed support on the Bench. Hence, too, the appointment of Robert Buxton and Richard Kemp in 1591. Buxton, a former household official to the Duke of Norfolk, assisted Heveningham in both the Martham parsonage and the Wymondham–Attleborough highway disputes; Kemp may have been less closely involved, but certainly acted with him in the Martham affair. Furthermore at least five other justices who were appointed in 1593 had associations with Heveningham: Edward Everard was a relative and godfather to his eldest son; Edward Barthlett assisted him in both implementing and exploiting the Council's militia policy; so too, did Thomas Clere who was one of the new company commanders whom he appointed in 1596. Richard Frestone and John Hunt, both justices in Suffolk throughout the 1580s, may also have owed their places on the Bench to Heveningham since he remained an influential magnate in Suffolk, holding a deputy lieutenancy there as well as in Norfolk. It is difficult to explain in any other way how two Suffolk squires suddenly appeared in the Norfolk commission, only to be dismissed two years later.

Numerically stated this means that during the period 1588–93, sixteen out of twenty-five newly appointed justices can be linked with these local controversies. That the majority of newcomers were associated with one or other of the contending parties suggests that

[4] For the date of appointment of justices, see Appendix I.

the three issues which so bitterly divided the gentry had a considerable influence upon the choice of personnel for the Bench. It is also significant that, as in the conflict between Freake and the Puritans, the number of justices in commission increased from forty to fifty-eight during the period of most intense controversy (1588–93).

By the turn of the century two other issues divided Norfolk justices and gentry. These arose from Council schemes to reorganize militia administration and the system of purveyance—schemes which Heveningham tried to implement and which Bacon and Gawdy opposed as being detrimental to the interests of the commonweal. Composition for purveyance, like Heveningham's highway patent, became a major quarter-sessional issue and one on which its opponents outnumbered its supporters. Once more, therefore, Heveningham could implement the scheme only if he could gain a majority on the Bench.

Once more, too, the justices appointed between 1598 and 1602 closely reflect this situation. No less than six out of the nine justices who met privately with Heveningham to sanction a composition rate were appointed during this period.[5] Indirect evidence suggests that he also brought in several other supporters: Thomas Talbot (1600), judge of the vice-admiral's court, had long been in conflict with Nathaniel Bacon, while Thomas Bennett (1602) and Clement Higham (1601) were Suffolk men who, like their counterparts in 1592, appeared in commission briefly and then vanished for ever. Indeed at least six of these new pro-Heveningham justices remained on the Bench for only a short period before being dismissed, never to appear again.

Although Nathaniel Bacon and Henry Gawdy had less need to augment their following they may well have had a hand in the appointment of several justices, notably Bacon's son-in-law Sir John Townshend (1598), and his friends Richard Gwynne (1601) and Henry Windham (1599); the latter became a leading opponent of composition as did Henry Spelman and Anthony Browne, appointed in 1598 and 1600 respectively.[6]

Only seven other justices, none of whom had any apparent connection with this issue, were appointed during the period 1598–

[5] Edmund Doyley, Barth. Cotton, John Kemp, Chas. Cornwallis, Thos. Guybon, Clippesby Gawdy.

[6] PCC 2 Swann. BM MS. Stowe 150, f. 186. NNRO MSS. Bradfer-Lawrence VIIb (unfoliated household account book); Aylsham, bundle 173, MS. dated 8 Aug. 1600.

1602, so that once more the selection of personnel for the Bench would appear to have been extensively influenced by the current local controversies. Once more, too, the size of the commission increased, although less dramatically, from fifty-one in 1598 to sixty-one in 1602.

B. SHERIFFS

Two points emerged from a study of the shrievalty in chapter VII: first, there was considerable competition for this office among the principal gentry in late Elizabethan Norfolk; secondly, it provided the holder with abundant opportunities to subvert the processes of the courts in the interest of a friend or faction. It now remains to consider whether the former was a direct result of the latter; whether, in fact, the factions and 'parties' in late-sixteenth-century Norfolk deliberately attempted to dominate the shrievalty in order to further their own cause and hinder that of their opponents.

This would appear to have been so during the controversy over the tenancy of Martham parsonage, since all candidates for office—Henry Doyley, Miles Corbett, Henry Gawdy, Sir Arthur Heveningham, and Thomas Clere—were involved. It is even more significant that two of the successful candidates—Doyley and Corbett—held property from the Dean and Chapter, and, once appointed, each took great care to ensure that the case went in Eden's favour.

It is worth enquiring whether a similar situation arose during the controversies over militia affairs and composition for purveyance. Undoubtedly the sheriff had an important role in militia administration since he was an *ex officio* member of the small muster commission which replaced the lieutenancy in 1596. *De jure* he was its executive officer, but *de facto* he could become the key figure in a commission which rarely numbered above six or eight members and in which the parties were so evenly balanced that he might well have the controlling voice. To what extent, then, did the protagonists in the controversies of the period 1597–1602 compete for the shrievalty?

Heveningham and those who shared his view of county administration certainly did. In 1600, at the height of the conflict over purveyance and militia organization, he made great efforts to gain the office. Philip Gawdy reported from the court that he 'wold fayne have been sheriff', but he missed the 'cashion': he failed to get into the provisional list from which the sheriff was pricked, as he had failed in 1593 and probably on other occasions as well. There is evidence that Sir William Paston sought the position with greater assiduity but a similar lack of success. His name appeared in the sheriffs' roll every year from 1597 until 1601 but, surprisingly in view of his eminence in the county, he was never pricked. Paston's association with Heveningham was recent. The two magnates had originally been opponents, but during the 1590s they had drawn together, becoming friends in the early seventeenth century, when Paston's grand-daughter married Heveningham's son. The change which gradually came over Paston did not pass unnoticed; 'Sir William Paston, who might have been called Passion for his former pity, but now is Paston because he is become as hard as stone', was the epithet of one contemporary observer.[7]

The failure of Heveningham and Paston to gain the shrievalty contrasted markedly with the success of their opponents. Sir Nicholas Bacon was pricked in 1597. In the following year Clement Spelman, an advocate of large militia companies, held the office, only to be succeeded in 1599 by Nathaniel Bacon—the principal opponent of composition for purveyance. In 1600 the Queen pricked Richard Jenkinson in preference to Sir William Paston, Sir Arthur Heveningham, and Edmund Doyley. Since he had not hitherto figured in county government, his appointment had been 'contrarie unto the expectacon of some who . . . labored both to disappoynt & disgrace' him. But his success is no doubt explained by his adherence to the anti-Heveningham group: he was a son-in-law of Henry Gawdy and had been strongly backed at Court by Edward Coke. In 1601 Sir Bassingbourne Gawdy was chosen after his name had been added to the sheriffs' roll at the last minute. Finally, and rather belatedly, Heveningham gained the office in 1602. His eventual success is perhaps convincing proof that in the event of serious county dispute, the protagonists regarded the choice of sheriff as a significant factor in its outcome.[8]

C. DEPUTY LIEUTENANTS AND COMMISSIONERS FOR MUSTERS

Effectively the lieutenancy operated in Norfolk only during the years 1585–96, when Lord Hunsdon held the office without interruption. Apparently the Council appointed his deputies, but undoubtedly on his nomination. Initially he chose three, their

[7] PRO C 227/15A, 16, 17, 18, 19. NNRO MS. PD 42/9, 3 Nov. 1601. *CSPD Add. 1580–1625*, p. 543. *HMC Salisbury*, xiii. 169.

[8] PRO C 227/18 & 19. BM MSS. Eg. 2804, f. 140; Add. 23007, f. 9v.

commission running for an unspecified period, a fourth being appointed after 1590. Such a small number of virtually permanent deputies offered little scope for place-seekers. Moreover, since Hunsdon controlled their appointment they tended to reflect his attitude towards militia administration, the one exception being Sir ThomasKnyvett, and he was quickly dismissed. Thus, unlike magistracy and the shrievalty, the lieutenancy did not provide a series of neutral offices which could be 'utilized' by factions and political groups: rather it represented a type of government which was unacceptable to many justices and gentry, and which became a central issue of political conflict.

The muster commission, on the other hand, did reflect faction and county politics. Its members, appointed by the lord chancellor on the nomination of the Council, had responsibility for militia administration when the lieutenancy was in abeyance. Since the militia reforms of the 1590s became a divisive issue, both advocates and critics endeavoured to pack this commission. There is considerable evidence that patrons managed to obtain their clients' appointment, but, in contrast to the commission of the peace, no evidence that they succeeded in getting opponents dismissed. The personnel of this commission also seems to have been influenced by private quarrels, this being particularly apparent in the struggle between the Gawdys and Thomas Lovell.

D. KNIGHTS OF THE SHIRE

Three points emerge from a study of county elections in late-sixteenth-century Norfolk: first, the electorate was large; secondly, almost every election was contested; thirdly, intending candidates felt it necessary to take extensive soundings before presenting themselves for election. It is impossible to be precise about the size of the electorate, but there are contemporary estimates as to the number of voters present at two elections. In 1586 the sheriff deposed that at least 3,000 freeholders assembled on Castle Hill, while in 1593 Edward Coke, having been chosen as first knight of the shire, recorded for posterity that he had been elected by 7,000 and more.[9] Although both estimates were made by interested parties, they indicate the availability of a very substantial body of freeholders. It would be surprising if this fact did not relate to the type of electioneering and to the number and pattern of contested elections.

[9] Neale, *Commons*, p. 83. *Collectanea Topographica et Genealogica*, ed. Nichols, vi. 115.

Would-be knights of the shire began to sound the county at the slightest hint of a parliament, proceeding with a thoroughness which has not hitherto been sufficiently emphasized. They were rarely content simply to elicit promises of support from the principal gentry, but as well as this they enlisted agents to campaign among the freeholders, usually casting the high constables in this role. Sir Edmund Moundford reacted typically when, after receiving 'cert-tayne intelligence of a parlament to be very shortly houlden at West-minster . . .', he wrote to the chief constables of Wayland 'to commend to the severall townes and parrishes of your hundred re-questinge the men of worshipp, gentalmen and freehoulders whoe only have voice in this popular and free election, to be redy uppon reasonable warninge to shew ther good loves unto Mr. Cooke by ther paines in chusing him'. Despite such preparation, often undertaken long before any election writ had been issued, candidates remained uncertain about the outcome: even Nathaniel Bacon, on the eve of being elected knight of the shire for the third time, had to admit that he could 'arrive at no nomber of voices' and might be 'stodde againste and loose the place'.[10]

Elaborate campaigning, contested elections, and considerable uncertainty as to their outcome suggest that many Norfolk free-holders refused to be martialled as pawns on the electoral board; that when occasion demanded they voted according to their own preference. But to vote in such a positive manner implies an ability to think politically. This the freeholders may well have acquired through their involvement in the issues described above. As partici-pants at assizes, quarter sessions, and petty sessions, as constables collecting—or refusing to collect—rates, and as wealthy freeholders upon whom parliamentary and unparliamentary taxation fell with increasing frequency, they could hardly avoid taking sides in any discussions or dispute over the aims and methods of county govern-ment. It is not inconceivable that freeholders, like many gentry, had begun to regard a knight of the shire as 'a speciall phisytion that will put his best indevour to purge and cure those maladies' inflicted upon the county by patentees, licensees, compounders, and deputy lieutenants.[11]

Whether or not there is substance in these speculations depends

[10] NNRO MS. Aylsham, bundle 16, Edm. Moundford to the constables of Wayland, 13 Jan. 1592/3. FSL MS. Bacon–Townshend L.d. 103.

[11] NNRO MS. Raynham Hall temp. deposit, 252.

upon the extent to which county political issues influenced the course and conduct of elections. Prior to 1572 the Duke of Norfolk so completely dominated county society that no matters, whether political, personal, or factious, were allowed to ruffle its outward calm. But the atmosphere changed immediately the Duke's controlling hand had been removed; even the 1572 election was contested. Although it is difficult to pinpoint the issues in this election, most likely they arose from a combination of religious and family factors. The Council had entrusted supervision of the Norfolk election to Lord Keeper Sir Nicholas Bacon whose estates at Redgrave abutted upon the boundary of Norfolk. He probably encouraged Francis Wyndham and Henry Woodhouse to stand for the county seats, since he had close family ties with them and shared their radical religious views.[12] In opposition Sir Edward Clere also stood for election. One of the greatest landowners in Norfolk and son-in-law to the Duke of Norfolk's former treasurer,[13] Clere was a contentious man who had lost his place on the Norfolk Bench, probably at the instigation of Bishop Parkhurst and his radical Protestant associates who dominated local affairs during the early 1570s. Clere's bitter feud with Sir Roger Wyndham, elder brother to Francis, may have prompted him to contest the latter's election. In the event, he failed to gain a seat and, true to form, took his defeat with bad grace, directing a series of bitter letters to Sir Richard Southwell for failing to support his candidature. In fact Clere was never a serious contender; as one observer put it: 'a great number of the shire' were 'evil affected towards him'. Inevitably therefore victory went to Wyndham and Woodhouse.[14]

When a new parliament met in 1584, Norfolk gentry had already clashed over administrative matters. Nathaniel Bacon, Francis Wyndham, and Edward Flowerdew had openly accused Heveningham and the Heydons of corruption in implementing patents and licences. Undoubtedly, as has been shown, this early opposition to unpopular developments in local administration had been stimulated by family feuds, religious conflict, and personal antipathies—

[12] Collinson, pp. 53, 62, 182. For Wyndham's Puritan sympathies, see above, p. 176. Both Wyndham and Woodhouse married daughters of Lord Keeper Bacon.

[13] Sir Richard Fulmerston.

[14] Above, pp. 161–2. BM MS. Add. 27960, ff. 9–10v. NNRO MS. Aylsham, bundle 16, Edw. Clere to Thos. Billingford, 18 Apr. 1572. Part of this paragraph is based upon information from the History of Parliament Trust.

the perfect formula for a contested election, although there is no positive evidence for one. Moreover, the two candidates who were elected—Sir Dru Drury and Nathaniel Bacon—can scarcely have been unopposed. Both were Puritans who had divided the diocese by their attack upon Freake's episcopal government—an incident which had only just ended by 1584—and neither was sufficiently pre-eminent in the county to command widespread support. Drury was a younger son of a Buckinghamshire squire who had married into the county in 1565; although he had become a prominent magistrate, succeeding Sir Christopher Heydon as *custos* in Norfolk in 1583, he was also a member of the Queen's Household and spent a great deal of time out of the county.[15] By contrast Nathaniel Bacon was a thoroughgoing county figure; yet even he had no strong claim to a county seat; as a younger son of Sir Nicholas Bacon, in 1584 he stood relatively low in order of precedence within the county and many Norfolk squires—not least Sir Arthur Heveningham himself—might reasonably have expected to represent their county in parliament in preference to the young Nathaniel. In any case Heveningham's friend Sir Roger Woodhouse who had been returned for Norfolk in a by-election in 1581, but with scarcely time to take his seat before parliament ended, might well have expected re-election in 1584. It is possible that Bacon and Drury owed their election, in part at least, to a Puritan campaign to dominate this parliament; moreover, since there appears to have been a marked coincidence in Norfolk between religious radicalism and the opposition to patentees and licensees, administrative and religious considerations may have combined to ensure their return. Both the personalities involved and the pattern of county politics suggest that the election may have been contested despite the absence of any direct evidence to this effect.[16]

In 1586 there is clear evidence of a bitterly contested election which related directly to the political situation in the county. By this time division among the gentry had sharpened considerably as Bacon and his associates increasingly opposed the activities of Heveningham, Heydon, and Clere. This division is clearly discernible in the candidates seeking election as knights of the shire. The Bacon–Wyndham group backed Thomas Farmer, Heydon's 'deadly enemy',

[15] Blomefield, i. 278. Appendix I. *DNB* s.v. Drury, Dru.

[16] NNRO MS. Aylsham, bundle 175, Roger Woodhouse to Mr. Doyley, 19 Feb. 1580/81. BM MS. Add. 36989, f. 5. Ascribed to Nov. 1580 on internal evidence. Collinson, pp. 277–88.

who had become closely associated with them in discrediting Heydon and who had recently been put out of the commission of the peace at the latter's instigation. Heydon and Clere, both deputy lieutenants, supported William Gresham—one of the few justices who was prepared to co-operate wholeheartedly in implementing the Council's military instructions.[17]

In its early stages, however, this election campaign seemed exceptionally muted for a county which manifested such bitter divisions. Each party, for instance, put forward only one candidate, which suggests that both sides wished to avoid a contested election. Strange though such collusion may appear in the circumstances, the choice of candidates is even more perplexing since neither Farmer nor Gresham possessed that status and precedence within the county which had become a virtual prerequisite for standing as knight of the shire.

The Farmers, by this time desperately attempting to stave off complete economic collapse, no longer ranked among the foremost gentry. Thomas had never been chosen sheriff, nor elected to parliament, even for a borough; his career as a justice had been chequered, and on the rare occasions when he appeared in the commission he stood low in the order of precedence. William Gresham had even less claim to be a knight of the shire. His family had relinquished its long-established interests in Norfolk early in the sixteenth century when its principal members became successful London merchants. Since the family rarely used its ancestral home at Holt, William's grandfather Sir John Gresham had founded and endowed a school there. As a result William had no connection with the county until 1579 when he inherited from his cousin Sir Thomas Gresham the remaining family property at Intwood, and for a time resided there, trying to reassert his family's former influence.[18] That such inappropriate candidates gained any support is even more surprising in view of the Council's request that whenever possible former knights of the shire should be re-elected. Both Sir Dru Drury and Nathaniel Bacon appear to have been available for re-election, yet neither stood,

[17] PRO C 219/30, f. 60. The first four signatures on this return were those of Francis Wyndham, Sir Thos. Knyvett, Sir Nich. Bacon, and Sir Henry Woodhouse. Above, pp. 240–4, 284. Gleason, p. 149.

[18] Above, pp. 199, 243–4. Appendix I. C. L. S. Linnell & A. B. Douglas, *Gresham's School. History and Register 1555–1954*, Ipswich 1955, pp. 11–12. Wm. Gresham left the county again in 1593 when he inherited his father's estates at Titsey in Surrey.

despite the renewed efforts by Puritan leaders to gain more seats in parliament.[19]

A snap election, which caught county leaders totally unprepared at a time of acute controversy, undoubtedly created this strange situation. That few people expected a new parliament in the autumn of 1586 is suggested by a nationwide absence of electioneering letters prior to the despatch of writs for an election. Indeed there were positive reasons for considering an election unlikely. Although the problem of Mary Queen of Scots had required parliamentary attention throughout the summer of 1586 and there had been pressure in the Council for an immediate election, the Queen had made clear her preference to wait until 14 November when she would recall the parliament prorogued in 1584. Opinion in the country backed the Queen against her Council. Then suddenly on 9 September she allowed a new parliament to be called in great haste. If the issuing of the writ on 15 September really provided the first intimation of an election, then leaders on both sides in Norfolk must have been in a quandary. Only eleven days remained before the next county-day on 26 September when the election had to be held. Such a short period was manifestly inadequate for prospective candidates to sound the county—an essential preliminary without which the foremost gentry rarely hazarded their credit in a contested election, least of all in a county as divided as Norfolk. In such circumstances both sides may have preferred to put up mediocre candidates and if possible to avoid a contested election.[20]

The election might have passed off quietly had not the young Christopher Heydon upset a delicate situation by announcing at the last minute his intention to stand in opposition to Thomas Farmer. He claimed that he had not intended to do so until incited by Farmer's 'immoderate bragge', but it looks as if his father Sir William Heydon, no doubt in consultation with Heveningham and Clere, had decided to change tactics and to run candidates for both seats—a decision bound to precipitate a bitter contest. Although there are no details about the conduct of the election, subsequent recriminations leave little doubt that it was an unruly affair. Sir William Heydon and his fellow deputy lieutenant Edward Clere complained that the sheriff had 'proceaded to that election unorderly,

[19] *APC, 1586–7*, p. 227.

[20] Neale, *Parliaments 1584–1601*, p. 104. PRO SP 12/193, nos. 37, 38. D'Ewes, p. 396.

not regarding also suche letters as were sent from theyr Lordships by her Majesties specyall appointement in that behalf'. Christopher Heydon's accusations were more precise: 'due sommons was not given to the freeholders of the shire . . . [and] proclamation was not duly made'. In defence the under-sheriff asserted that the sheriff had received the election writ only two days before county-day. Whatever actually happened, the freeholders had foreknowledge that 'there would be variance about the election' and an estimated 3,000 mustered on Castle Hill to support their respective candidates.[21]

The sheriff, Henry Hogan, unhesitatingly declared Farmer and Gresham elected knights of the shire, and Francis Wyndham, Sir Thomas Knyvett, Sir Nicholas Bacon, and Sir Henry Woodhouse signed the return. Although Hogan appears to have been a friend of Bacon and Wyndham, there is no reason to assume that he acted partially; evidence from subsequent Norfolk elections suggests that a majority of freeholders were vehemently opposed to the administrative activities of Heydon, Clere, and Heveningham. None the less the two deputy lieutenants refused to accept the sheriff's verdict and complained to the Council that Hogan had mishandled the election. Lord Hunsdon probably persuaded councillors to give credence to that complaint. Consequently on 8 October their lordships instructed the Lord Chancellor to issue a writ for a new election and also reprimanded the sheriff for allowing himself and other gentlemen of note 'to be labored to choose one for knight of the sheere whom they had for his misdemeanors thought unfyt to be of the commission of the peace'—a pointed reference to Farmer's recent dismissal from the Bench.[22]

Sixteen days remained before the next county-day, time enough for both parties to try to strengthen their position. It is possible that Sir Thomas Knyvett agreed to pair with Thomas Farmer in opposition to any candidates put forward by the two deputy lieutenants. If this is so, his appearance in harness with Farmer is further evidence that the conflict over aims and methods of county government dominated this election, since Knyvett was in substantial agreement on these issues with his friend Nathaniel Bacon and opposed to the practices of Heydon and Clere. His willingness to stand against the lieu-

[21] BM MS. Eg. 2713, f. 190. *APC, 1586–7*, p. 241. D'Ewes, p. 396.

[22] G. A. Carthew, *The Hundred of Launditch*, ii, Norwich, 1877, p. 693. *APC, 1586–7*, pp. 241–2.

tenancy candidates would have been a particularly defiant gesture since he, too, was a deputy lieutenant; but a recalcitrant one who had already refused to cooperate with his fellow deputies in implementing the Council's military demands, and who proved so unacceptable to Lord Hunsdon that barely a year later he dismissed him, appointing in his stead none other than Sir Arthur Heveningham.[23]

Lord Hunsdon was undoubtedly incensed by Knyvett's behaviour in this election. His two other deputies, Heydon and Clere, tried to counter Knyvett's influence by seeking more experienced and influential candidates than Christopher Heydon and William Gresham. Clere claimed that he would have stood himself had he not been unwell; instead, rather surprisingly, he invited Bassingbourne Gawdy to become a candidate. Gawdy must have declined the invitation since at the second election Christopher Heydon and William Gresham opposed Thomas Farmer, possibly now paired with Sir Thomas Knyvett. There are no details as to the tactics adopted by Heydon and Clere beyond a reference to 'the indiscrete and rashe dealynges of Sir William Heydon who hathe done enoughe to sett the whole countrye uppon an uprore,' and some evidence that the deputy lieutenants gained support from the Council. Whatever their methods they succeeded in securing victory for their candidates, for it was Heydon and Gresham whom the sheriff duly declared elected and it was Sir Arthur Heveningham and Sir William Heydon who were the first to sign the election return. Well might Henry Knyvett write to his brother in amazement 'that the affection of so manye frends colde be prevayled uppon sutche a sodayne to shrinke from hym whome with one voice theye before had chosen'.[24]

Nonetheless the tone of much of this letter suggests that Knyvett's involvement in this second election may have been a gesture against his fellow deputy lieutenants rather than a serious attempt to defeat their nominees. Indeed there is more than a hint that Nathaniel Bacon and his associates had deliberately shifted the weight of their campaign from the county to parliament and the courts, where the radicals immediately challenged the Council's right to quash the first election and authorize another. From the outset they seemed confident about the success of these tactics. 'The oppinyon of the judges & the beste lerned in the lawe is that the first election is good

[23] NNRO MSS. KNY 691, 692 (372X5).

[24] BM MS. Add. 27960, f. 27. NNRO MSS. NAS C3/2/9, copy of election return, 24 Oct. 1586; KNY 691 (372X5).

& cannot be altered,' wrote Henry Knyvett to his brother. 'When the matter shall be discussed in the parliament house', he reported several days before it was first raised,[25] 'my younge master [Christopher Heydon] shall be discharged, to the shame of hym selfe & his descrete father that wolde nedes have hym selfe and his sonne recorded for fooles by Act of parliament.' Obviously the issue had been discussed and a campaign concerted before parliament had been opened, possibly even before the second election had taken place. As Knyvett predicted, a group in the Commons challenged the Council's right to authorize the second writ, claiming that it was a privilege of the House to adjudicate in a disputed election. No sooner had members assembled and elected their Speaker than they vented their views 'touching the choosing and returning of the knights for the county of Norfolk'. The Queen immediately rebuked them through the Speaker and commanded the Lord Chancellor and judges to decide upon the validity of the election as 'justice and right' demanded. In due course the latter pronounced in favour of Farmer and Gresham. But the House was not to be silenced; 'motions and speeches' about its liberties continued, culminating in the appointment of a committee of fifteen upon whose advice the House declared the first election valid and decreed that Farmer and Gresham should be received into their assembly as 'allowed and admitted only by the censure of this House, and not as allowed of by the said Lord Chancellor or judges'.

So ended an election which had been contested in Norfolk on issues in local administration, and which had been finally settled in parliament with some novel assertions about the relationship between Crown and Commons. The issue at stake both locally and in parliament was essentially the same: how far could Crown and Council, whether through the Chancellor or through patentees, licensees or deputy lieutenants, dictate the course of elections or the implementation of policies which ran counter to the wishes of a substantial element of county society.[26]

The 1589 election seems to have been uncontested. Probably the Spanish threat produced an atmosphere of compromise; the outcome certainly suggests that, as in the preliminary stages of the 1586 election, the leaders on both sides agreed to put up one candidate each. As a result Christopher Heydon finally gained a seat, but he

[25] His letter is dated 28 Oct.; the matter was first raised in parliament on 31 Oct.

[26] Neale, *Parliaments 1584–1601*, pp. 184–7. D'Ewes, pp. 395–9.

had to share the honour with Sir Henry Woodhouse, brother-in-law to his opponents Nathaniel and Nicholas Bacon, and a magnate who sympathized with their view of county government.

Once the threat of imminent invasion had passed, however, controversy among the Norfolk gentry exacerbated the electoral scene once more. Indeed by the time parliament met in 1593 Francis Wyndham, Nathaniel and Nicholas Bacon, and Henry Gawdy had ranged themselves in opposition to the activities of Sir Arthur Heveningham and Sir William Heydon in several spheres of local administration. They had opposed militia reorganization and the increased taxation which went with it; they had refused to authorize Heveningham to arrange composition for purveyance; they had thwarted his attempts to implement his patent for repairing Christmas Lane and the highway across Attleborough Fen; they had exposed the extortionate activities of Kirk and Garter which Heydon and Heveningham certainly condoned and may even have encouraged; they had endeavoured to protect the Dean and Chapter's lands against the subterfuges of patentees of concealment who likewise seem to have had Heveningham's approval. In quarter sessions and the central law courts they had stubbornly resisted all these innovations, but increasingly they resorted to legislation in order to defend their county interests. The repeal of one statute was to end the activities of Kirk and Garter, while the enactment of another would safeguard Martham parsonage for the Dean and Chapter, and with it all the other capitular property. It is, therefore, hardly surprising that these controversies influenced the 1593 election.

In January 1593 Edmund Moundford informed his neighbours that 'the greattest part of the justices doe thinke hir majesties soliciter Mr. Cooke . . . for his knowledg, wisdome and power to doe us good, to be one of the metest gentilmen' to represent them in parliament. 'Though he only shall have occasion to advance all his wittes to the requitinge of so many good friendes', continued Moundford, '. . . yet all our cuntry shall reap the benefit therof.'[27] This is one of the clearest statements of the positive role demanded of their M.P.s by gentry who resented the power and practices of men like Heveningham. They had no cause to regret the choice of Edward Coke as candidate for the first county seat, particularly when Nathaniel Bacon stood with him for the second.

27 NNRO MS. Aylsham, bundle 16, Edm. Moundford to the constables of Wayland, 13 Jan. 1592/3.

Heveningham also respected Edward Coke's ability, but for reasons which made him as anxious to prevent Coke's election as was Moundford to secure it. He therefore decided to stand for the first county seat himself. So, too, did Sir Robert Southwell, a squire who had successfully restored his family's tarnished prestige under the patronage of Lord Admiral Charles Howard of Effingham. In 1585 Southwell had ousted Sir William Heydon from his post as vice-admiral of Norfolk, then, when the latter died in 1594, he succeeded to his deputy lieutenancy. Heveningham may have detected a kindred spirit in this thrusting young courtier; this would explain his proposition that their respective ambitions would best be served if they joined forces, since alone neither could expect to prevail against the extensive backing which Bacon and Coke commanded among the freeholders. Southwell, however, prevaricated in the hope of running with a less controversial figure. In any case he, too, wanted to be chosen first knight of the shire. When he expressed doubts that their pairing might lose him votes, Heveningham retorted, with characteristic self-confidence, that 'those whom peradventure you wold make choyce of [for their votes] relie so muche upon yow, as yow cannot loose there frendshipps for if theye sholde there credicts were nothinge'. Heveningham appears to have made little headway in his overtures to Southwell since a week before county-day he proposed that they should meet to discuss their strategy. Prejudging the outcome of these discussions, he drafted an electioneering letter which asked his supporters to give their first 'voice' to him and their second to Sir Robert Southwell. Unfortunately he had misjudged this young knight who refused to be pushed into second place and compelled him instead to redraft his letter so that it merely asked the gentry and freeholders to vote for himself and Southwell without specifying who was to have the first seat. These inconclusive negotiations with Southwell proved useless, since in the event the assembled county—7,000 strong so Coke claimed—rejected them both in favour of Bacon and Coke.[28]

Lord Hunsdon reacted violently to this defeat of his principal deputy lieutenant in Norfolk. He accused Sir Nicholas Bacon of encouraging Southwell to stand for the first seat in order to draw

[28] NNRO MSS. NAS C3/1/9, A. Heveningham to Sir. Thos. Knyvett, 18 Jan. 1592/3; Aylsham, bundle 16, Sir Robt. Southwell to A. Heveningham, 19 Jan. 1592/3; Heveningham's draft reply, 28 Jan. 1592/3; Heveningham's undated draft electioneering letter (with amendments).

away votes from Sir Arthur Heveningham. 'We have hard a greate deale of unkyndenes aboute the chosinge of the Knights of the Shire,' wrote Henry Knyvett from the Court, and in a subsequent letter, now badly mutilated, he seems to indicate that blows were actually threatened between Hunsdon and Sir Nicholas Bacon.[29]

When the Queen again summoned parliament in 1597 the gentry and freeholders of Norfolk remained divided in their attitude to purveyance and military affairs; indeed, their disagreement deepened in 1596 when the lieutenancy attempted to levy ship-money throughout the county. In this charged atmosphere Sir Arthur Heveningham's determination to avenge his defeat in the 1593 election was such that he began to sound the county at least six months before any formal intimation of an election had been received.[30] His haste availed him nothing; at the county-court the gentry and freeholders once more rejected him, electing instead two of his opponents—Henry Gawdy and Sir John Townshend. Details of this election have not survived, but indirect evidence suggests that a lively contest ensued between Heveningham and his opponents. At the subsequent election the sheriff referred to 'the unrulynes of the common people which I saw . . . at the last election of knightes of the shire, whose fury (if by the great diligence & discretion of the Queen's Attorney it had not been stayed) was lykely to have growen to great inconvenience'. The Queen's Attorney was, of course, Edward Coke, by this time the most distinguished of Heveningham's opponents. He had travelled to Norfolk just prior to this election and conferred with Sir Nicholas Bacon at Godwick. That they had organized the freeholders and gentry is suggested by the signatures of those who witnessed the sheriff's return. These read like a roll of Heveningham's principal opponents: Edward Coke and Sir Nicholas Bacon headed the list, followed by Nathaniel Bacon, Bassingbourne Gawdy, Isaac Astley, and Thomas Barney, the return being convincingly rounded off with several signatures of their principal supporters among the lesser gentry and freeholders.[31]

29 NNRO MSS. KNY 646, 705 (372X5).

30 NNRO MS. NAS C3/1/9, transcr. of a letter from A. Heveningham to Sir Thos. Knyvett, 27 Dec. 1596. The election writ was issued on 23 Aug. 1597.

31 BM MS. Add. 23007, f. 10v. C. W. James, *Chief Justice Coke*, 1929, p. 23. Holkham MS. 724, entry for 5 Sept. 1597. PRO C 219/33/131.

The rancour which underlay this contest had in no way abated by the 1601 election. Disputes continued over purveyance and militia organization, tension being increased by personal animosity, particularly that between Bassingbourne Gawdy and Thomas Lovell. These circumstances undoubtedly account for the interminable electioneering which preceded the summoning of Elizabeth's last parliament in September 1601.

Prospective candidates might reasonably have been expected to begin electioneering six months before this parliament met since its summons had been expected early in 1601, only to be delayed by the Essex revolt. But in Norfolk candidates had started to make their preparations during the summer of 1600—at least six months before the first hint of a parliament. From the outset Bassingbourne Gawdy made the running. His feud with Heveningham's client Thomas Lovell strengthened his alliance with Nathaniel and Nicholas Bacon and Henry Gawdy, so that once he had resolved to stand for election as first knight of the shire, he lost no time in negotiating for their support. Having secured this he proceeded to pair himself with Sir Robert Mansell, who was optimistic enough to stand for the second seat although still smarting from his duel with Sir John Heydon—another Heveningham man.[32]

In mid-October Ralph Rabbards, a court gossip, informed his friends in Norfolk that 'there is some muttering generally and bruit of a parliament'. Tension was running so high in the county that this rumour was sufficient to trigger off electioneering on a scale normally reserved for that brief hectic period which followed well-founded news of a parliament. Bassingbourne Gawdy immediately stepped up his campaign; in London his brother Philip solicited support from courtiers who commanded the loyalty of any freeholders in Norfolk; at home Bassingbourne dispatched electioneering letters to numerous gentlemen and all the chief constables. Meanwhile advice flowed in about how best to make his final dispositions: he should write to Mr. Godbould (servant to his uncle Justice Francis Gawdy) to procure support from the chief constables of Clackclose, Freebridge Lynn, and Freebridge Marshland Hundreds; he should procure the Bishop's support as well as that of Sir John Townshend; a letter to Richard Bunting, bailiff of the Duchy lands in Norfolk, should bring in good dividends; all these, together with support

[32] Neale, *Parliaments 1584–1601*, p. 370. NNRO MS. NAS Safe II.28, ff. 49v–50. BM MS. Eg. 2804, f. 140. *HMC Gawdy*, p. 74.

from Henry Gawdy, which in turn would guarantee many votes from the tenants of Edward Coke, should 'furnish him well'.[33]

Clearly Bassingbourne Gawdy was preparing for a bitter contest which must surely imply opposition or at least the expectation of opposition. Unfortunately the activities of his opponents are not well documented—for reasons which will become apparent as the story unfolds—so that the first intimation of any rival electioneering appears only in January 1601 when Sir Christopher Heydon sent letters to constables and gentry throughout the county begging them to withhold their 'voices' from Sir Robert Mansell, his brother's duelling opponent. Significantly, though, he recommended no alternative candidate. 'I doubt not', Heydon concluded rather flatly, 'but that we shall fynd of our owne country men [a candidate] more suffycient than any stranger . . . [who] wilbe propounded unto you by deliberate advise and generall aprobacon at the election.'[34] Why was Heydon either reluctant or unable there and then to name an opponent to Mansell, and, for that matter, to Gawdy as well? Why indeed did Heydon, as he put it, 'mean not to stand' himself? Even more to the point, why did Heveningham not stand for the first seat as he had in 1593 and 1597?

It is conceivable that Heveningham was holding back until the writ had been dispatched, but this is unlikely since such punctiliousness was out of keeping with his character; moreover all the electioneering letters—Heydon's as well as Gawdy's—are insistent upon the imminence of an election. Sir Robert Mansell may have been nearer the truth when he wrote from London that the wisest observers considered that Heydon and Heveningham were driven to this 'indirect' course because of their weak following in the county. This, in turn, reflected their lack of powerful backing at Court since Hunsdon was dead, Essex in disgrace, and the lieutenancy in abeyance. In such circumstances, and after his resounding defeat in the two previous elections, Heveningham may well have been chary of running against the Bacon–Gawdy group with all the support they clearly commanded among the electorate. Instead he may have set his sights upon the negative achievement of preventing his opponents' election. This would explain why he sought the shrievalty of Norfolk in November 1600, just as Gawdy was mounting his intensive election campaign, and why his failure even in this

33 NNRO MS. Rye 72, p. 41. Jeayes, pp. 105, 107. *HMC Gawdy*, pp. 71, 72.
34 BM MS. Add. 23007, f. 10.

limited aim 'put him in a great chafe'. Well it might, since, with the help of Sir Edward Coke, this key electoral position had gone to Richard Jenkinson, son-in-law of Heveningham's opponent Henry Gawdy.[35]

The realization that Heveningham could not significantly influence the outcome of the election may have weakened the cohesiveness of his opponents. By December 1600, Nathaniel Bacon and Henry Gawdy were threatening to withhold their electoral support from Bassingbourne Gawdy if he remained paired with Sir Robert Mansell. Although Mansell was Bacon's brother-in-law they had little in common. Mansell, as Heydon had indicated, had no roots in Norfolk; he hailed from Glamorgan and had settled at Pentney, near Lynn, only after his marriage to Elizabeth, widow of Sir Francis Wyndham and sister to Nathaniel and Nicholas Bacon. Nor did his views on administration square with those of his strait-laced, county-orientated relatives. Nathaniel Bacon had already proffered him some unpalatable advice about the conduct of admiralty affairs in the county, so that it was probably no surprise when in January 1600 both Bacon and Henry Gawdy refused to support him for the second seat, and advised Bassingbourne Gawdy that to remain paired with him was the best 'waie to cause you to be reiected yourself'. They cited Mansell's duel with Sir John Heydon as their reason for withholding their support: 'he that is appointed by authoritye a keeper of the peace', argued Bacon, 'should not be a breaker of the peace, and therefore his remove [from the commission of the peace] verie iust, and this notwithstanding, for him to seeke to have himselfe countenanced here belowe, when he is discountenaunced above is not as yt should be.'[36]

At this point Clippesby Gawdy of Little Wenham in Suffolk, half-brother to Henry Gawdy, came forward as candidate for the second county seat, but it is not clear if Bacon and Henry Gawdy supported him as a counter to Robert Mansell. If they did, they failed to persuade Bassingbourne Gawdy to join with him since, although Essex's rebellion delayed an election until the following October, Bassingbourne still stood with Mansell. On the day, however, the 'popular' party once more asserted itself by electing Bassingbourne Gawdy as first knight, choosing Henry Gawdy, apparently against his will, for

[35] Above, p. 148. BM MS. Add. 23007, f. 9v.

[36] *HMC Gawdy*, p. 71. NNRO MS. NAS Safe II.28, ff. 49v–50.

the second seat, and leaving the discomfited Mansell to console himself with a seat for King's Lynn.[37]

Controversy over purveyance and militia organization remained unresolved as Elizabeth lay dying in the early spring of 1603. Moreover, despite her promises to rescind obnoxious patents, the oppressive activities of patentees and their deputies continued. They certainly remained an issue in Norfolk: 'I hope he will gett a patente of it', Sir Arthur Heveningham remarked bitterly upon hearing that his opponent Henry Gawdy proposed to stand for the county seat again, despite his success in the 1597 and 1601 elections. These issues continued to polarize the gentry into two distinct groups so that the slightest hint of a parliament sparked off vigorous electioneering. The Queen's death proved no exception: within a matter of days both parties had started to campaign for King James's first parliament.

By 1 April 1603 Nathaniel Bacon and Henry Gawdy had announced that they intended to stand in harness for the county seats. Neither, however, was willing to accept the second seat; Bacon made his position quite clear: 'I am not like to serve often hereafter in anie parliament', he wrote, 'and having served twice already in the second place, I hope that no man shall have iust cause to iudge amisse of me though now I seke the first . . . and if some more creditt be gott by having the first than the second I see not whie I should debarr my self of it yf I can obteyne it.' By midsummer Henry Gawdy, who had already twice sat for the county, had stood down, thereby enabling Bacon to pair with Sir Charles Cornwallis who appeared to be willing to accept the second place.[38]

Heveningham and his associates, too, had problems over their choice of candidates. Office barred Sir Arthur Heveningham since he was currently serving his second term as sheriff, while Sir Christopher Heydon had been discredited for his part in the Essex revolt. In these circumstances Heveningham proposed to Sir Thomas Knyvett that their sons, John and Thomas respectively, should stand for the county seats; with this in mind he sounded the county without actually naming his candidates. Although he optimistically

[37] BM MS. Add. 36989, ff. 11, 12. NNRO MS. NAS C3/2/9, sheet of undated draft letters, endorsed in later hand 'Parlt. men for Norf.' *HMC Gawdy*, p. 74. BM MS. Eg. 2715, f. 15.

[38] NNRO MS. NAS C3/1/9, transcr. of a letter from A. Heveningham to Sir Thos. Knyvett, 1 Apr. 1603. FSL MSS. Bacon–Townshend L.d.102, 105.

assured Knyvett that the Hundreds in south Norfolk would 'wholye goe with us', he knew from his own bitter experience that these candidates could not compete against someone of Bacon's stature among the freeholders. His only hope of securing their return rested upon his ability to show his opponents 'a tryck of [his] office', as he confided to Knyvett. The entire proposal seems bizarre. Neither candidate had held any office in the county, although Thomas Knyvett junior had sat in parliament for Aldeburgh in 1593 and Thetford in 1601. It would be interesting to know how Sir Thomas Knyvett reacted to Heveningham's overtures in view of their earlier relations and his close associations with Nathaniel Bacon.[39]

In the event James did not summon an autumn parliament, and when writs for an election were finally dispatched in the New Year, the situation in Norfolk had changed. Heveningham, having completed his term as sheriff, had decided to stand for the first seat, probably paired with Sir Miles Corbett. His opponents were ill prepared to meet this challenge, since the partnership between Bacon and Cornwallis had virtually foundered when Cornwallis developed aspirations for the first seat. Their alliance seemed so tenuous that at the last moment Bacon tried to persuade the sheriff to hold the election at Dereham, a good venue for his supporters from north-west Norfolk, but inconvenient for Heveningham's freeholders from the south. His stratagem failed, but the freeholders proved it unnecessary by decisively electing him as their first knight, still paired with Charles Cornwallis who, at the last moment, must have agreed to accept the second seat.[40]

The most significant aspect of these elections is the electorate's constant rejection of Heveningham and his associates, despite his powerful position at Court at least down to 1596. This suggests that the majority of gentry and freeholders supported the stand which gentry like Bacon, Wyndham, and Gawdy had taken against patentees, deputy lieutenants, purveyors, and licensees; that they realized the potential of parliament as a means of thwarting these agents of

[39] NNRO MSS. NAS C3/1/9, transcr. of two letters from A. Heveningham to Sir Thos. Knyvett, 1 and 3 Apr. 1603.

[40] NNRO MS. NAS Safe II.28 (loose MS.), George [?] Brown to Mr. Bowlton, 25 Jan. 1603/4. FSL MS. Bacon–Townshend L.d.107.

Crown and Council and of furthering the good of their commonweal.

This positive attitude towards parliament is revealed in a sheaf of Nathaniel Bacon's papers relating to James's first parliament. Some of his own views are explicit in a memorandum he prepared for his guidance in the House:

To consider of provisions, whereby the subiect may be secured for the enioying of that which the King departeth with. For if the Act of Parliament for thes thinges be once past, and the King in quiet possession of this support, then no countie alone, much lesse anie private person shalbe able to withstand the King's authority, though the gifte given be not enioyed. And this may appeare in the example of the purveiance, wherin the King now claymeth that as his right and due from the subiect, which by Acts of parliament may be proved to have been gott rather by incrochment, and what the remedy shalbe to prevent this.

To have it debated if it be not fitt to mak it praemunire or treason for anie person to maintayne or hold opynion that the parliament may not bind both King and subiect even in matter of prerogative. . . .'

Even more significant is the number of people who asked Bacon to seek parliamentary redress for their grievances, some of them even preparing draft Bills: twenty-five master bakers petitioned for redress against abuses under the statute of apprentices; the inhabitants of Wells complained about the 'decay' of their fishing, entreating the knights of the shire 'that nowe at the next Parlament some such course may be taken for the releife of the saide towne . . . as in your good discretions shall seeme fitt and convenient'; one unknown writer sent a list of 'reasons to inforce the bill for the ministers of Norwich rather then any other bill whatsoever'; another proposed measures to reform the abuses practised by under-sheriffs and councillors; Richard Stubbs submitted detailed proposals for three Bills designed respectively to prevent secret outlawries, to reform the procedures employed by escheators, and to avoid exceptions to general pardons; Thomas Baker, one of the greatest corn merchants in King's Lynn, proposed emendations to two statutes regulating the export of corn in order to ensure as great a freedom of transportation as possible; the inhabitants of Marshland petitioned for parliamentary 'reliefe' against the losses they had sustained 'by the overflowing of the sea'.[41]

[41] NNRO MSS. 1620i(1C9); Sotheby 28/12/67, MSS. endorsed 'the Bakers Peticon', 'Concerning Norwich ministers', and 'Touching abuses in Sheriffs & Councellors;'

These letters, together with the interaction between the controversies among the gentry and the conduct of county elections, suggest that there may have been a much closer relationship between parliamentary business and the conduct of local affairs than has previously been realized.

Bradfer-Lawrence VIb (v), Wells petition 1603; VIIb(1), bundle marked 'Statute notes & worsted weavers ordinances', MS. entitled 'certen causes & Reasons whie the Statute made in the XXIIIrd yere . . . for the encrease of marryners and mayntenance of navigacon should be repealed', and MSS. endorsed 'touching utlarye & ye Escheator', and 'concerning ye Navy'; Raynham Hall temp. deposit, 252–4.

CHAPTER XV

General Conclusions

ADMINISTRATION in late sixteenth-century Norfolk had engendered political controversy. To suggest that the gentry had divided into parties over administrative issues would be to over-simplify a very complicated situation. None the less, during the period 1585–1603 two conflicting views of county government tended to polarize the gentry into coherent and reasonably stable groups. Justices like Arthur Heveningham, Edward Clere, William Heydon, John Peyton, and Robert Buxton consistently took a 'Court' view; they were willing, indeed eager, to become patentees and to support the activities of licensed informers; they worked efficiently, if not ruthlessly, as deputy lieutenants and commissioners for purveyance, no matter what additional financial burdens they imposed upon the county in the process. It is a nice point whether they should be regarded as forward-looking men, who considered that local administrators should implement policies formulated in 'national' terms by the central government, or as selfish men who aimed at enhancing their prestige and increasing their income through acting as agents of the Crown.

Gentry like Nathaniel and Nicholas Bacon, Henry Gawdy, Francis Wyndham, and William Blennerhassett were equally consistent in their opposition to the activities of these 'Court' justices. They took the view that, while magistrates were responsible for the enforcement of statutes and the implementation of all Crown and Council instructions, they had an overriding duty to reconcile county interests—by which they really meant landowners' interests—with national requirements as seen by the Crown and Council. It is difficult to assess how far they were conservatives, intent upon protecting men of property against the Crown's demands for increased contributions towards the cost of defence and other aspects of national administration, and how far they were precocious political observers who had begun to divorce public office from private gain and were genuinely bent upon establishing new standards of public morality by exposing corruption among the courtiers. Not for the first time, perhaps, the self-justification of one generation has provided the political maxims of the next.

There is no doubt that behind most disputes between 'Court' and 'county' justices lurked the issue of who paid for what. Most gentry, contentedly under-assessed in the subsidy books, were reluctant to contribute towards the cost of administration through indirect taxation. This reluctance may have been provoked as much by the frequency of these taxes as by their total burden. Rates for militia training, rates for equipping overseas levies, rates for coat and conduct money, rates for ship-money, rates to repair highways and bridges, rates for provisioning the royal Household, rates for the muster-master's salary, rates for building bridewells and for poor prisoners in the King's Bench and Marshalsea, rates for sea bank and harbour repairs: the sheer number and high incidence of these rates may have produced resistance on psychological as well as economic grounds. Certainly at least one M.P. argued that the declining subsidy assessments were a direct result of the gentry's desire to mitigate the burden of indirect taxation:

> according to a mans valuacon in subsedye are they att all other charges as to warres and in tyme of muster with horse and armour and this charge maketh men unwillinge to be raised in the subsidye. But if theis subseydes brought no other charge with them but subsedye they would be yealded willinglie, but the taile and appendage of yt being great & higher than the subsedye yt selfe is the reason that men are soe unwillinge to yealde it.[1]

The evidence from Norfolk suggests that there was some truth in this view.

An intensely political situation developed when those who tried to mitigate the incidence of county rates began to argue their case on constitutional grounds. This led to frequent debates about who did what and on whose authority. 'Courtier' justices like Heveningham and Clere justified their rating activities by reference to the Queen's prerogative. County-orientated justices like Wyndham and the Bacons declined to authorize these rates by appealing to precedent and statute, challenging the need for them, insinuating extravagance, and even hinting at downright corruption in their collection and application. By the 1590s deputy lieutenants and patentees had become so frustrated by these tactics that they themselves began to authorize constables to collect their rates. This, in turn, sparked off debates as to the authority under which constables acted.

These constitutional wrangles were not confined to members of

[1] BM MS. Cotton, Titus F ii, f. 52.

the Bench. They impinged upon a large number of freeholders and substantial yeomen who, as high and petty constables, were confronted with conflicting warrants and conflicting advice as to which warrants they should and should not implement. Whatever action they took, they risked indictment by those justices whose warrants they had ignored—a situation bound to lead to complaints and discussion among constables and would-be constables. Then, too, in the course of these disputes each side tended to appeal for support as widely as possible. For instance, in the controversy over composition for purveyance both the officers of the Green Cloth and those in the county who opposed their scheme sought the freeholders' approval for their proposed activities.

Administrative disputes which frequently gave rise to constitutional debates among the gentry and freeholders of the county were likely to have an impact upon the parliamentary scene. Their significance for elections has already been demonstrated, but several of these disputes also culminated in parliamentary legislation or contributed towards its initiation. Such links between county affairs and parliamentary business may help to explain that heightened political awareness noted by Professors Plumb and Zagorin. 'Men of the meaner sort', writes Professor Plumb, 'did not in Tudor or Stuart England take themselves forty miles across a county in order to vote for a man they did not know or for men of whose principles they were ignorant . . . If these Tudor freeholders were becoming active, it was because they were becoming recognized as useful by men who wished to get into Parliament.'[2] Professor Zagorin has commented upon the increased interest in parliamentary business, upon the 'extraordinary increase in the dissemination of parliamentary news and speeches, so that the import of the conflict at Westminster between the Court and the Country was communicated to every quarter'.[3] Both historians note this awakened political conscience; neither fully explains it. Evidence from Norfolk can help. It suggests that widespread interest in parliamentary business arose because much of that business was concerned with settling issues which had already been debated in the county and which had, in a sense, been submitted to parliament for final resolution. It suggests that the political issues of the early seventeenth century did not originate in parliament by some process of self-generation and then filter down to the county; rather

[2] *P & P* xlv, 1969, p. 94.

[3] P. Zagorin, *The Court and the Country*, 1969, p. 108.

they had their origins in county communities which regarded statute as the ultimate solution of their constitutional, social, and economic problems. There is no doubt that gentry in late sixteenth-century Norfolk regarded local politics and parliamentary business as two aspects of a continuing process. Those of them who sat in parliament can have had little in common with their counterparts in Somerset who, even three decades later, 'sat in the Commons . . . passively listening to the tumult raised by those who had joined an issue as yet but faintly perceived in the county', and who after each parliament 'had returned to Somerset apparently unaffected by what they had heard, to take up once more the normal round of magisterial duties'.[4]

These observations about the interrelationship between local and national politics would be of more significance were the Norfolk scene typical of that in other counties. This certainly cannot be assumed. Indeed it is possible that particular circumstances in late Tudor Norfolk gave rise to a constitutional conflict which was as exceptional as it was premature. After 1572 the county's lack of a resident nobleman of any standing resulted in the appointment of a lord lieutenant (Lord Hunsdon) who had no roots in Norfolk and who was therefore untrammelled in his implementation of Council orders and his support for the activities of patentees. Then, too, his background and personality had similar consequences. A bluff, ill-educated soldier who owed his position entirely to his kinship with the Queen, he not unnaturally gave wholehearted support to the Crown's attempts to improve militia training and military preparation. Nobody could have been less suited to direct the activities of cultured, legally trained and county-orientated justices like Thomas Knyvett, Nathaniel Bacon, and Francis Wyndham.

The political developments in Norfolk may, therefore, have been exceptional, but they are unlikely to have been unique. Unfortunately at present it is not possible to set them in a wider context because there are few studies of Elizabethan county administration with which to make comparison. However, a similar constitutional conflict in Somerset and Wiltshire during the period 1602–6 is revealed in the Earl of Hertford's lieutenancy papers.[5] On this

[4] Barnes, *Somerset*, p. 308.

[5] *The Earl of Hertford's Lieutenancy Papers 1603–1612*, ed. W. P. D. Murphy (WRS xxiii, 1969). *The Parliamentary Diary of Robert Bowyer 1606–1607*, ed. D. H. Willson, Minneapolis, 1931, pp. 130, 154–6.

occasion the dispute arose over payment of the muster-master's salary and it proceeded in an almost identical manner to the militia dispute in Norfolk. First the lieutenancy's attempt to levy a rate was blocked at quarter sessions; next the Lord Lieutenant sent warrants direct to constables authorizing its collection; many constables ignored these warrants, whereupon the lieutenancy resorted to imprisonment and summonses to the Council Board; finally, in 1606, complaints were voiced in the Commons against the Lord Lieutenant's administration—complaints which drew sufficient support from other members of the House for them to be embodied in the Grievances presented to the King in May 1606. By contrast Dr. Lloyd's study of the gentry in Pembroke, Carmarthen, and Cardigan (1540–1640) depicts an a-political society whose reaction to demands for money for royal service, 'far from . . . [being] founded upon principle, was largely one of excuse backed by dishonesty and prevarication'. 'Political activity in this region', writes Dr. Lloyd, 'suggests a minimal grasp of significant political principles and a dogged introspectiveness unshaken . . . by the constitutional conflict at the centre. The duties of local administration, increasing in complexity in this period, were understood and performed by the local gentry in a manner showing awareness neither of the nature of their role in the overall structure of government nor of a recent emancipation.'[6]

The absence in Wales of political disputes similar to those depicted in Norfolk and detected in Somerset and Wiltshire prompts a generalization which can perhaps be tested by further county studies. If, as has been suggested, the constitutional arguments among the Norfolk gentry arose, in part at least, as a result of the weight and incidence of county taxation, it may be that an important factor in a county's political precociousness was the amount of *ad hoc* taxation which it was called upon to bear. Dr. Boynton's study of the Elizabethan and Stuart militia suggests that the greatest burden of military taxation fell upon the southern and south-eastern counties and the least upon the north-western counties. From what is known of the administration of purveyance and ship-money under Elizabeth this also seems to have been the case. Admittedly the south-eastern counties, constituting the wealthiest and most heavily populated area of England, could afford to contribute most, but the incidence of *ad hoc* rates was not governed by such equitable considerations—

[6] H. A. Lloyd, *The Gentry of South-West Wales, 1540–1640*, Cardiff, 1968, pp. 120, 211.

even supposing the distribution of wealth and population was recognized by Tudor administrators. Rather was it dictated by practical considerations like the preparation of defences against Spanish invasion and the convenience of purveyors.

Whatever the relationship between county constitutional opposition and the incidence of county taxation, it was only one among a variety of factors which contributed to the development of a county's political attitudes and which included the religious and educational background of its principal gentry. The role of Puritanism in the emergence of Tudor and Stuart constitutional opposition is an immensely complicated subject, but one to which the foregoing account of Norfolk affairs may have some relevance. Professor Neale has shown that Puritans, in their desire for further reform within the Anglican Settlement, became radical innovators so far as parliamentary procedure was concerned. He and Professor Collinson have demonstrated the potential of Puritanism for organizing pressure groups which might even influence elections. Others, writing about the seventeenth-century political developments, have depicted Puritanism as an ideology of opposition; but its role in the development of constitutional attitudes at the county level has been less well explored. It is possible that the Puritan ethic encouraged gentry of that persuasion to participate in lay magistracy;[7] in which case it may also be pertinent to enquire whether it in any way influenced a justice's attitude towards particular constitutional innovations in local administration.

The evidence from Norfolk and Suffolk suggests that it did. The principal East Anglian Puritans—Nathaniel and Nicholas Bacon, Robert Jermyn, John Higham, and William Blennerhassett—together with a group of radical Protestants—Thomas Knyvett, Francis Wyndham, and Edward Flowerdew—were consistent in their opposition to all attempts by patentees and deputy lieutenants to levy rates which had no authorization either in parliament or at quarter sessions. That much is fact; to explain why is another matter. It has been suggested that the teaching of Puritan preachers encouraged these magistrates to be critical of the assumption that office was a piece of property which could be exploited for private gain.[8] There is no denying their constant complaints that patentees subordinated public good to private interests, indulged in extortion,

[7] M. Walzer, *The Revolution of the Saints*, 1966, p. 265.

[8] Ibid. pp. 232–6.

and failed to apply the rates they levied to the avowed purposes of their patents. In their view licences to export corn had led, not to the repair of harbours at Sheringham and Cromer, but to the enrichment of Thomas Sidney and the Heydons; the dispensing patent of Kirk and Garter had enabled them to mulct the county with but little benefit to Sheringham's piers. Similar criticisms were both explicit and implicit in their opposition to Heveningham's highway patents and to the growing number of rates which the lieutenancy demanded for militia reforms. Their attitude appears to have been consistent in so far as none of them became patentees and only three were appointed deputy lieutenants. Of these one was dismissed and the other two opposed the lieutenant's policy.

Opposition to administrative innovations in late Elizabethan England may also have been roused by the legal implications of these developments. The procedures used in the vice-admiral's court and by the provost-marshals, the proposed procedures by which deputy lieutenants and muster commissioners were to enforce payment of their rates, not to mention the *de facto* procedures frequently used such as arbitrary imprisonment pending the recalcitrant's summons before the Council Board: all smacked of the Roman civil law, of the practices of the church courts, even of the *ex officio* oath. It is perhaps not without significance that the antagonism of East Anglian Puritans towards administrators who resorted to these procedures coincided with the Puritan attack upon the proceedings in the Court of High Commission. When, in the parliament of 1593, James Morice spoke to his Bills against unlawful oaths, inquisitions, and subscriptions in ecclesiastical courts, and against unlawful imprisonment and restraint of liberty, the arguments he developed had implications for the procedures of other courts or quasi-courts as well: 'We . . . the subjects of this kingdom, are born & brought up in due obedience, but far from servitude & bondage; subject to lawful authority & commandment, but freed from licentious will & tyranny; enjoying by limits of law & justice our lives, lands goods & liberties in great peace & security.'[9] Only months previously William Lambarde had warned the jurors at Maidstone quarter sessions that, unless presenting juries presented, the common law procedures, already being eroded by civil law practices, would be 'quite overthrown'. In certain English counties by the 1590s some gentry detected the development of a 'droit administratif' and in Norfolk it

[9] Neale, *Parliaments, 1584–1601*, p. 269.

was primarily the Puritan magistrates who had set themselves firmly against such tendencies.

On the other hand, it is quite possible that the criticism of these magistrates were prompted less by their Puritan consciences than by their devotion to the principles of the common law in which the majority were well schooled. Both Nathaniel and Nicholas Bacon were 'ancients' of Gray's Inn; Francis Wyndham and Edward Flowerdew were sufficiently eminent in the law to be appointed judges; Henry Gawdy had studied at the Inner Temple; Thomas Knyvett at the Middle Temple.

The emergence of county politics probably intensified gentry demand for Court patronage. Indeed all that has been said about the large group of potential office holders in relation to the relatively small number of county offices and about the consequent competition for office, the significance of office in factional and political controversy, and the methods of appointment to the commission of the peace, underlines the need among the gentry for Court patronage; conversely, the county scene provided a much greater clientage for the patronage brokers at Court than has hitherto been allowed by historians. A gentleman who aspired to be a deputy lieutenant, sheriff, or magistrate, an attorney who wanted an undershrievalty, or a professional soldier wishing to retire into a mustermastership, all needed, and apparently readily received, support from the principal courtiers.

As a result it is possible to detect faction leaders at Court building a following in the county. The Earl of Essex, of course, made the running, although his activities in Norfolk were not on the same scale as in south-west Wales and the Marches, where, as he was reminded by one hostile observer, 'most of them that wears your honour's cloth in this country is to have your honour's countenance, and to be made sheriffs, lieutenants, stewards, subsidy-men, searchers, sergeants on the sea, mustermen—everything is fish that comes to their net.'[10] Even so the range of his patronage in Norfolk was surprisingly wide. Inevitably the new militia organization was his particular preserve. He regularly nominated the two muster-masters, reacting swiftly in 1596 when the county tried to cut costs by dispensing with one of them. While he wrote personally to the muster commissioners to persuade them to appoint his nominee 'because the countie ys large', his secretary Anthony Bacon wrote to

[10] Lloyd, op. cit., p. 115.

his half-brother Nathaniel—a rare occurrence indeed—asking him 'to give my Lord that contentment and to doe my selfe that brotherly favour and to countenance & assist Captain Bozome'.[11] The Earl also wrote regularly to the Norfolk sheriffs supporting clients for the under-shrievalty, although with less success than in the military sphere.[12] In 1596 he may even have backed his companion in arms Edward Lord Cromwell to succeed Lord Hunsdon as lord lieutenant of Norfolk. In the event the lieutenancy was put into commission and a rather disgruntled Lord Cromwell had to content himself with the rank of 'a mere justice'—a position which, in any case, Essex may have procured for him.[13] Then, too, he intervened in the dispute over the Dean and Chapter's property, making particular efforts to mitigate the hostility of justices and sheriffs towards Downing and the patentees for 'concealed' lands.

Although Essex and his agents appear to have 'cultivated the county'—to borrow a phrase from later politics—with greater assiduity than other courtiers, the Howards ran him a close second in this client-mongering. As soon as Charles Howard of Effingham had been appointed Lord Admiral in 1585 he dismissed Sir William Heydon from the lucrative post of vice-admiral of Norfolk and Suffolk in order to make room for his son-in-law Robert Southwell. When Southwell died in 1598 Howard brought in Sir Robert Mansell, a distant relative who was to have a noted career as a naval commander and admiralty official, but a man with no roots in East Anglia. His patronage was not entirely nepotistic; indeed, as the century closed he can be detected supporting an anti-Essex group in Norfolk. It was his client Robert Mansell who fought a duel with Essex's supporter, John Heydon. Then, too, his patronage was extended to the Gawdys in their contest for power with Thomas Lovell. In 1603 Bassingbourne Gawdy, upon being informed (incorrectly as it turned out) of the imminent appointment of a lord lieutenant for Norfolk, was optimistic that the Lord Admiral would secure him a deputy lieutenancy.[14]

Finally, if only by way of drawing attention to problems

[11] BM MS. Eg. 2714, f. 3. NNRO MS. WALS XVII/I, pt. ii, f. 22v. Lambeth Palace Library MS. 660, ff. 115, 121, 280.

[12] NNRO MS. WALS XVII/I, f. 14. BM MS. Harl. 4712, f. 279.

[13] *DNB*, s.v. Cromwell, Edward. He was appointed a J.P. in 1593 when Essex became a privy councillor.

[14] *HMC Gawdy*, p. 79.

requiring further investigation, it is worth noting one particularly intractable situation. In view of the backing which Heveningham received from Lord Hunsdon and the support which he gave in the county to conciliar policy, there are certain strange lacunae in his career: he never gained a seat in parliament; he was not pricked as sheriff throughout the period of acute controversy in the 1590s, although his name frequently figured in the 'bill'; nor was he able to bring sufficient supporters into the commission of the peace to give him a commanding position at quarter sessions; indeed he could not even trim the muster commission in order to maintain a majority which was sympathetic to a professional approach in military affairs. That the freeholders refused to elect him to parliament is not surprising, but his failure to secure, either for himself or his supporters, those county offices which were granted by Crown and Council suggests the need for a more thorough understanding of conciliar parties and policies and of Chancery procedures, both formal and informal, by which sheriffs' 'bills' and the whole gamut of commissions relating to local government were compiled.

Appendix I

CHART SHOWING JUSTICES' PLACING IN COMMISSION AND ATTENDANCE AT QUARTER SESSIONS

Key

The career line of each justice is plotted annually thus: [34 / 6] The upper number indicates his placing in the commission; the smaller and lower number indicates the number of days he attended quarter sessions during each year.

[✓] indicates positive evidence that a justice was in commission, but the source gives no information about the order of precedence.

▮ indicates year of death. Where the date of death falls outside the scope of this chart it has been indicated in the final column.

[C] indicates *custos rotulorum.*

[S] indicates year in which a justice was sheriff.

Explanatory Note

i. The career line of any justice provides information on:
(a) when he was in the commission and when not;
(b) whether he rose or fell in the order of seniority and where he sat on the Bench in relation to his fellows;
(c) the regularity and frequency of his attendance at quarter sessions.

ii. Inadequate sources (*BIHR* xxxii. 221–42) present problems about interpreting this table.
(a) For 17 years of Elizabeth's reign there are no complete lists of justices. This means that a gap in the table may indicate the lack of a list and not the ommission of a justice from the commission.
(b) Occasionally a justice appears to attend quarter sessions (lower number) when his name does not figure in the commission for that year (see, e.g. the first entry for Nathaniel Bacon). This anomaly arises from the lack of precision in the sources. It is not possible to tell, for instance, whether a wage claim for 4 days' attendance at the sessions represented a day at each quarter sessions or 4 days at the last sessions for the year. Then, too, commissions of the peace, appointing or dismissing a justice, were issued with great frequency (5 or 6 a

year were common), but it is rare to have a copy of more than one of these. Consequently it is possible for a justice who does not figure in the extant list for a particular year to have been appointed subsequently and attended at least some quarter sessions for that year.

iii. Because several commissions might be issued in one year, all extant commissions have been presented in this chart; thus it includes 58 lists covering the 44 regnal years. It is therefore important to differentiate clearly between the number of the column (top line of table) and the regnal year (second line of table).

iv. Noblemen have been listed under their titles.

Sources

Attendances at quarter sessions

PRO E 372/404–447.

This source records annually each justice's sessional attendances as submitted by the sheriff when making his claim for justices' allowances. For a critical appraisal of these enrolments, see above, p. 90 n.o.

Lists of J.P.s

Lists of justices appear in a wide variety of sources. Many of these lists are undated; the following critical notes about dating and other problems are intended to explain how each list has been used in this table.

Column	Regnal Year	Date	
1	1	Dec. 1558 or Jan. 1559	BM MS. Lansd. 1218. An undated *liber pacis*. Dated on internal evidence. The Norfolk list is torn after the first six names. Comparison with lists for other counties in this MS. suggests that two names have been lost. Allowance for this has been made in arriving at the total number in commission.
2	1	Early 1559	PRO SP 12/2/17. Not a *liber pacis*. Undated; internal evidence suggests early 1559. The first nine names in commission, all *ex officio*, have been omitted from this list. Apart from this, it is identical with Lansdowne 1218, except that the Norfolk section has been emended to record changes in the commission during approximately the first half of 1559. Column 2 is based upon these emendations.

Column	Regnal Year	Date	
3	2		
4	3	*Post* July 1561 [?]	PRO SP 12/2/17. This list, compiled in 1558–9 and emended during 1559, was subsequently annotated by placing the letters 'g', 'm' and 'n' after many of the names. These letters probably indicate each person's worth in commission (see Gleason, pp. 60–2) and were almost certainly added after July 1561 when Cecil proposed to reduce the number of justices in commission. It has been assumed therefore that names to which a code letter is not appended had been omitted from the commission by the time this annotating was undertaken, and column 4 has been compiled on this basis.
5	3/4	Nov./Dec. 1561	BM MS. Lansd. 1218. A *liber pacis*, extensively annotated in Cecil's hand. Internal evidence suggests that it had been compiled by Dec. 1561 and that it probably represents the state of the commission at the end of 3 Eliz. after the Council had purged it (see, above pp. 81–2).
6	4	11 Feb. 1561/2	PRO C 66/985. An enrolled commission.
7	5		
8	6	1 June 1564	PRO C 66/998. An enrolled commission.
9	7		
10	8		
11	9		
12	10		
13	11	Oct. 1569	PRO SP 12/59, f. 52. Not a *liber pacis*. This list is headed *Nomina Justics et aliis*. It is doubtful if it is a full record of justices in commission.

Column	Regnal Year	Date	
14	12	Dec. 1569	PRO SP 12/60, f. 2. Not a *liber pacis*. This list has been compiled from the signatures of justices appended to a letter endorsed 'touchinge the estatute of dyvyne service & dewe ministracon of sacramentes . . . [for] all suche as heretofore hath bene within the commission of peace'.
15	13		
16	14		
17	15		
18	16	*c.* Nov. 1573	PRO SP 12/93 pt. ii. A *liber pacis*, entitled in a different hand *Liber Pacis de anno Regni Regine Elizabeth Sexto Decimo 1573*. Internal evidence suggests that it is late 1573.
19	16	late 1573 or early 1574	BM MS. Egerton 2345. A *liber pacis*.The lists have been emended slightly and those for some counties have been annotated in Burghley's hand. The unemended Norfolk list, dated 16 Eliz., has been shown in this column.
20	17	24 June 1575	PRO SP 12/104. Not a *liber pacis*. It is a copy of returns made by the *custodes rotulorum* showing the Hundreds, 'divisions', and names of J.P.s within them. Names of *ex officio* justices are omitted. Compiled in response to conciliar instructions (*APC 1571–5*, p. 398). BM MS. Stowe 570 is an identical copy.
21	18		
22	19	1 July 1577	NNRO MS. NAS C3/2/12. A copy of a commission of the peace.
23	19	late 1577	PRO SP 12/121. A *liber pacis*, dated 19 Eliz. Internal evidence suggests that it is slightly later than the July commission above.

Column	Regnal Year	Date	
24	20	late 1577 or early 1578	Hatfield MS. 223.7. A *liber pacis*, dated 20 Eliz. The MS. has been extensively emended but this column shows it in its unemended state.
25	20	late 1578 [?]	NNRO MS. NAS C3/2/12. A copy of a commission of the peace. The date has been torn away. Internal evidence suggests that the commission was issued late in 1578.
26	21	8 July 1579	NNRO MS. NAS C3/2/9. A list of names appended to a letter sent 'to all justices in Norf'. *Ex officio* members of the Bench were not included.
27	21	late 1579	PRO SP 12/145. A *liber pacis*, dated 1580 in the calendar. Internal evidence suggests a date towards the end of 1579. The MS. has been slightly emended and annotated. Column 27 represents the MS. in its unemended state.
28	22	*c.* 1580	Hatfield MS. 223.7. See list 24 above. This list is the emended version of the MS. Internal evidence suggests that it was kept up to date down to 1580.
29	22	late 1580	NNRO MS. NAS C3/2/12. Undated list of justices. Not a commission. Internal evidence suggests a date late in 1580.
30	23		
31	24	mid 1582	BM MS. Lansd. 35, f. 130. Not a complete list; shows only the last eleven names in the Norfolk commission.
32	25	early 1583	BM MS. Royal 18 D III. Not a *liber pacis*. MS. undated, but internal evidence suggests a date early in 1583. The lists of justices have been entered on the *verso* of county maps; some have been emended in Burghley's hand, but not that for Norfolk. Non-resident, *ex officio* members of the commission were not included.

Column	Regnal Year	Date	
33	25/26	late 1583	BM MS. Harl. 474. An undated miniature *liber pacis.* It is bound with a list of sheriffs for 1584–5, but internal evidence suggests that it is a list for late 1583. It is clearly a copy of a *liber pacis* as there are obvious errors of transcription.
34	26	early 1584	BM MS. Lansd. 737. A miniature *liber pacis*, dated 1584 in a later hand. It has been extensively emended. In its unemended form, recorded in this column, the Norfolk list appears to have been compiled shortly after Harl. 474.
35	27	late 1585	Bodl MS. Barlow 13. Not a *liber pacis.* Undated. Almost certainly a list of justices for late 1585, but it omits *ex officio* and non-resident members of the commission.
36	28	1586	BM MS. Lansd. 737. This undated list, probably compiled in 1584, has been extensively emended until late in 1586. The justices recorded in column 36 are those indicated by this MS. in its emended state.
37	29	20 Jan. 1586/7	PRO SP 12/197/33. MS. headed 'The division of the shire agreed upon by the justices at Norwich 20 Jan. 1586'. Endorsed, 'touching the said orders for graine'. Omits *ex officio* names and justices who were essentially non-resident.
38	30	1588	PRO E163/14/8. A *liber pacis* which has been extensively emended. In its unemended state it is identical with Lansdowne 737 (column 34). It has been emended until well into 30 Eliz. and it is the emended version which is recorded here.
39	31		
40	32		

Column	Regnal Year	Date	
41	33	mid 1591	Hatfield MS. 278. Not a *liber pacis*. MS. undated, but ascribed to mid 1591 from internal evidence.
42	34		
43	35	mid 1593	Kent R.O. MS. U.350.03. A miniature *liber pacis*, endorsed 'justices of peace in England & Wales 1598'. Internal evidence suggests that the Norfolk list was compiled in mid 1593.
44	35 36	late 1593 or early 1594	Hatfield MS. 278. Not a *liber pacis*. MS. undated. Subsidy assessments have been inserted and annotations made probably in connection with the dismissal of justices in 1595 (above, p. 85). The Norfolk list appears to have been compiled late in 1593 or early in 1594.
45	36	March 1593/4	Pro C 66/1421. An enrolled commission.
46	37	Feb. 1595	Northants. R.O. MS. Wingfield (Tickencote) Collection, box X 511. Not a *liber pacis*. Dated within.
47	37	July 1595	PRO C 66/1435. An enrolled commission.
48	38	Early 1596	PRO SP 13, case F, no. 11. Entitled '*liber pacis* 1596'. The Norfolk list has been emended slightly and in its emended state is identical with list 49. Since it was compiled after list 47 it must be dated late in 1595 or early in 1596.
49	38	July 1596	PRO C 66/1468. An enrolled commission. Dated July 1596, although enrolled on dorse of Pat. Roll for 39 Eliz.
50	39	July 1597	PRO C 66 1468. An enrolled commission.
51	40	16 March 1597/8	NNRO MS. NAS C3/1/9. MS. entitled 'a division of the shire agreed upon by the Justices assembled at Norwich 16 March 1597'.

Column	Regnal Year	Date	
52	40	July 1598	PRO C 66/1482. An enrolled commission.
53	41	July 1599	PRO C 66/1493. An enrolled commission.
54	42	May 1600	PRO C 66/1523. An enrolled commission.
55	43	March 1600/1601	NNRO MS. NAS Safe II.28, ff. 53–4. Copy of a commission.
56	43	June 1601	PRO C 66/1549. An enrolled commission.
57	44	June 1602	PRO C 66/1594. An enrolled commission.
58	1 James	12 April 1603	NNRO MS. NAS C3/3/3. A commission of the peace.

LIST No.	1	2	3	4	5	6	7	8	9	10	11	12	13	14	15	16	17	18	19	20
REGNAL YEAR	1	1	2	3	3/4	4	5	6	7	8	9	10	11	12	13	14	15	16	16	17
DATE	Dec 1558–Jan 1559	Mid 1559		*Post* July 1561	Nov/Dec 1561	11 Feb 1562		1 June 1564					Oct 1569	Dec 1569				c. Nov 1573	late 1573/early 1574	June 1575
EDMUND ANDERSON																				
JOHN APPLEYARD	24$_{3}$	23	S													▨→				
HENRY FITZALAN EARL OF ARUNDEL	3	?			4	4		4												
PHILIP HOWARD EARL OF ARUNDEL																				
ISAAC ASTLEY																				
NATHANIEL BACON																		$_{2}$	$_{2}$	✓$_{4}$
NICHOLAS BACON (Sen.)	1	?			1	1		1										1	1	
NICHOLAS BACON (Jun.)																				
ROBERT BALAM													✓$_{4}$	$_{5}$		▨				
JOHN BARNEY	33		▨																	
MARTIN BARNEY																				
ROBERT BARNEY	27	▨																		
THOMAS BARNEY																				
THOMAS BARROW				$_{2}$													$_{2}$	19$_{13}$	18$_{13}$	✓$_{3}$
EDWARD BARTLETT																				
EDMUND BEAUPRE	29$_{4}$	27	$_{7}$	20$_{8}$	22	21$_{5}$	$_{1}$	23$_{3}$				▨								
EDMUND BELL																				
ROBERT BELL								26				$_{2}$	✓$_{7}$	✓$_{21}$	$_{2}$	$_{3}$	$_{5}$	10$_{8}$	10$_{8}$	✓$_{1}$
THOMAS BENNETT																				
JOHN BLENNERHASSETT					17	16$_{1}$	$_{2}$	18$_{8}$	$_{5}$	$_{3}$		$_{2}$	$_{6}$				▨			
WILLIAM BLENNERHASSETT																		26	25	✓
JAMES BOLEYN	10$_{C\ 25}$	10	$_{26}$	$_{20}$ ▨																
THOMAS BRAMPTON				$_{2}$																
WILLIAM BRAMPTON	36$_{2}$	33		26			▨													
THOMAS BROMLEY																				
ANTHONY BROWNE	6	?			7	7		8			▨									
ANTHONY BROWNE																				
THOMAS SACKVILLE LORD BUCKHURST																				
WILLIAM CECIL LORD BURGHLEY																		2	2	
WILLIAM BUTTS	19$_{4}$	19	$_{6}$	15$_{9}$	14	11$_{11}$	S	12$_{9}$	$_{12}$	$_{11}$	$_{7}$	$_{13}$	✓$_{17}$	✓$_{19}$	$_{10}$	$_{18}$	$_{16}$	8$_{19}$	8$_{19}$	✓$_{15}$
ROBERT BUXTON																				
CHARLES CALTHORPE																				✓
WIMOND CAREY																				
ROBERT CATLIN		?			6	6		7										5	5 ▨	

LIST No.	21	22	23	24	25	26	27	28	29	30	31	32	33	34	35	36	37	38	39	40
REGNAL YEAR	18	19	19	20	20	21	21	22	22	23	24	25	25/26	26	27	28	29	30	31	32
DATE		1 July 1577	late 1577	late 1577/early 1578	late 1578	8 July 1579	late 1579	c. 1580	late 1580			early 1583	late 1583	early 1584	late 1585	1586	Jan 1586/7	1588		
EDMUND ANDERSON													9	9		8		7		
JOHN APPLEYARD																				
HENRY FITZALAN EARL OF ARUNDEL								▨												
PHILIP HOWARD EARL OF ARUNDEL												4	3	3	?					
ISAAC ASTLEY																				
NATHANIEL BACON	$_{1}$	20$_{7}$	19$_{7}$	19$_{8}$	21$_{8}$	✓$_{9}$	27$_{9}$	23$_{12}$	24$_{12}$	$_{15}$	$_{13}$	25$_{14}$	25$_{14}$	26$_{14}$	25$_{5}$	28$_{14}$	S	24$_{6}$	$_{12}$	$_{15}$
NICHOLAS BACON (Sen.)		1	1	1	1	▨														
NICHOLAS BACON (Jun.)					14	✓	17	15$_{3}$	15$_{3}$	$_{9}$	$_{4}$	16$_{3}$	16	16	8$_{3}$	17$_{9}$		14		
ROBERT BALAM																				
JOHN BARNEY																				
MARTIN BARNEY	$_{3}$	33$_{9}$	32$_{9}$	32$_{5}$	34$_{5}$	✓$_{1}$	43$_{1}$	41$_{1}$	39$_{1}$	$_{2}$	✓	36$_{5}$	38$_{6}$	40$_{6}$	31$_{3}$	42$_{6}$	✓$_{5}$	33$_{3}$	$_{2}$	$_{5}$
ROBERT BARNEY																				
THOMAS BARNEY																				
THOMAS BARROW	$_{3}$	22$_{7}$	21$_{7}$	22$_{1}$	24$_{1}$	✓$_{3}$	29$_{3}$	27	26	$_{4}$	✓$_{4}$	35$_{7}$	36$_{10}$	38$_{10}$	30$_{9}$	40$_{8}$	✓$_{4}$			▨
EDWARD BARTLETT																				
EDMUND BEAUPRE																				
EDMUND BELL																				
ROBERT BELL		6$_{2}$	▨$_{2}$																	
THOMAS BENNETT																				
JOHN BLENNERHASSETT																				
WILLIAM BLENNERHASSETT		31	30	30$_{4}$	32$_{4}$	✓$_{3}$	41$_{3}$	38	38	$_{3}$	✓$_{3}$	37$_{4}$	39$_{3}$	42$_{3}$	45	46$_{9}$	✓	34$_{6}$	$_{5}$	$_{15}$
JAMES BOLEYN																				
THOMAS BRAMPTON	▨																			
WILLIAM BRAMPTON																				
THOMAS BROMLEY							1	1	1			1?	1	1	?	1	▨			
ANTHONY BROWNE																				
ANTHONY BROWNE																				
THOMAS SACKVILLE LORD BUCKHURST																				
WILLIAM CECIL LORD BURGHLEY		2	2	2	2		2	2	2			2?	2	2	?	2		2		
WILLIAM BUTTS	$_{7}$	10$_{16}$	9$_{16}$	9$_{20}$	10$_{20}$	✓$_{15}$	11$_{15}$	10$_{15}$	10$_{15}$	$_{2}$	$_{5}$	12 ▨								
ROBERT BUXTON																				
CHARLES CALTHORPE		35$_{7}$	34$_{7}$	36$_{1}$																
WIMOND CAREY																				$_{2}$
ROBERT CATLIN																				

LIST No.	41	42	43	44	45	46	47	48	49	50	51	52	53	54	55	56	57	58	
REGNAL YEAR	33	34	35	35/36	36	37	37	38	38	39	40	40	41	42	43	43	44	1J	
DATE	June 1591		mid 1593	late 1593/early 1594	March 1594	Feb 1595	July 1595	early 1596	July 1596	July 1597	March 1598	10 July 1598	10 July 1599	23 May 1600	March 1601	June 1601	June 1602	April 1603	
EDMUND ANDERSON	7																		
JOHN APPLEYARD																			
HENRY FITZALAN EARL OF ARUNDEL																			
PHILIP HOWARD EARL OF ARUNDEL							▨												
ISAAC ASTLEY								47$_{4}$	48$_{4}$	51$_{8}$	$_{7}$	▨$_{7}$							
NATHANIEL BACON	23$_{16}$	$_{21}$	23$_{18}$	23$_{19}$	21$_{19}$	20$_{22}$	23$_{22}$	21$_{21}$	23$_{21}$	24$_{21}$	✓$_{25}$	25$_{25}$	27$_{18}$	27S	28$_{11}$	28	27$_{15}$	26	d. 1622
NICHOLAS BACON (Sen.)																			
NICHOLAS BACON (Jun.)	15$_{3}$	$_{5}$	13	13	11	11	13	13	13	13	✓	\$13	14	14	13$_{5}$	13	12	12	d. 1624
ROBERT BALAM																			
JOHN BARNEY																			
MARTIN BARNEY	34	$_{3}$	33$_{13}$	37$_{6}$	34$_{6}$	34				32$_{2}$	✓$_{4}$	31$_{4}$							d. 1605
ROBERT BARNEY																			
THOMAS BARNEY		$_{4}$	47	51	47	47		41	42	44	✓$_{10}$	42$_{10}$	44$_{11}$	43$_{6}$	44$_{5}$	43	42		d. 1618
THOMAS BARROW																			
EDWARD BARTLETT			49$_{9}$	53$_{8}$	49$_{8}$	49$_{4}$	46$_{4}$	43$_{13}$	44$_{13}$	46$_{2}$	✓$_{14}$	44$_{14}$	46	45$_{4}$	47	45	44	42	d. 1605
EDMUND BEAUPRE																			
EDMUND BELL													31$_{12}$	31$_{13}$	32$_{19}$	33	32$_{8}$	31	d. 1607
ROBERT BELL																			
THOMAS BENNETT																	25		
JOHN BLENNERHASSETT																			
WILLIAM BLENNERHASSETT	35$_{14}$	$_{18}$	34$_{15}$	38$_{13}$	35$_{13}$	35$_{15}$	32$_{15}$	30$_{13}$	30$_{13}$	33$_{18}$	✓$_{21}$	32$_{21}$ ▨							
JAMES BOLEYN																			
THOMAS BRAMPTON																			
WILLIAM BRAMPTON																			
THOMAS BROMLEY																			
ANTHONY BROWNE																			
ANTHONY BROWNE														25$_{4}$	26$_{2}$	27	26$_{8}$	25	d. 1628
THOMAS SACKVILLE LORD BUCKHURST													2	2	2	2	2	2	d. 1608
WILLIAM CECIL LORD BURGHLEY	2		2	2	2	2	2	2	2	2	▨								
WILLIAM BUTTS																			
ROBERT BUXTON	39	$_{18}$	37$_{15}$	41$_{9}$	37$_{9}$	37	34	32$_{8}$	32$_{8}$	34$_{3}$									d. 1607
CHARLES CALTHORPE																			d. 1616
WIMOND CAREY	44$_{10}$	$_{10}$	45$_{10}$	49$_{6}$	45$_{6}$	45$_{2}$	43$_{2}$	40$_{8}$	41$_{8}$	43$_{11}$	✓$_{8}$	41$_{8}$	43$_{8}$	42$_{6}$	43$_{8}$	42	41$_{8}$	40	d. 1612
ROBERT CATLIN																			

LIST No.	1	2	3	4	5	6	7	8	9	10	11	12	13	14	15	16	17	18	19	20	21	22	23	24	25	26	27	28	29
REGNAL YEAR	1	1	2	3	3/4	4	5	6	7	8	9	10	11	12	13	14	15	16	16	17	18	19	19	20	20	21	21	22	22
DATE	Dec 1558–Jan 1559	mid. 1559		*Post* July 1561	Nov/Dec 1561	11 Feb 1562		1 June 1564					Oct 1569	Dec 1569				*c.* Nov 1573	late 1573/ early 1574	June 1575		1 July 1577	late 1577	late 1577/ early 1578	late 1578	8 July 1579	late 1579	*c.* 1580	late 1580
ROBERT CLARKE																													
EDWARD CLERE			$_{5}$	$_{3}$								S																	
HENRY CLERE																													
THOMAS CLERE																													
GEOFFRY COBB																								35_{1}	38_{1}	✓$_{6}$	42_{6}	43_{5}	41_{5}
WILLIAM COCKETT	35	32		25																									
EDWARD COKE																													
ROBERT COKE	30_{20}	28	$_{24}$	21_{17}	23																								
RICHARD COOTE														✓$_{3}$	$_{4}$	$_{10}$	$_{2}$	27_{5}	26_{5}	✓		32_{6}	31_{6}	31_{2}	33_{2}				
MILES CORBETT																													
CHARLES CORNWALLIS																													
BARTHOLOMEW COTTON																													
EDWARD CROMWELL, LORD CROMWELL																													
HENRY CROMWELL, LORD CROMWELL																											6	6	6
ANTHONY DEATH																													
THOMAS DOVE																													
EDMUND DOYLEY																													
HENRY DOYLEY																			S	✓$_{3}$	$_{4}$	24_{3}	23_{3}	24_{4}	26_{4}	✓$_{3}$	31_{3}	29_{9}	28_{9}
DRU DRURY											$_{5}$	$_{3}$	✓$_{3}$	✓$_{13}$		$_{3}$	$_{10}$	15	15	✓	$_{6}$	16 $	15	15_{15}	17_{15}		25	19_{22}	18_{22}
THOMAS EGERTON																													
EDWARD EVERARD																													
JOHN EYRE	28_{2}	26	$_{3}$	19																									
THOMAS FARMER																										✓$_{3}$	39_{3}	37_{8}	36_{8}
EDWARD FENNER																													
EDWARD FLOWERDEW														$_{2}$	$_{9}$	$_{15}$	$_{12}$	21_{11}	20_{11}	✓$_{9}$	$_{3}$	25_{5}	24_{5}	25_{11}	27_{11}	✓$_{9}$	32_{9}	30_{12}	29_{12}
RICHARD FRESTONE																													
RICHARD FULMERSTON	23_{3}	22			16	15_{2}	$_{5}$	17_{11}	$_{10}$	$_{5}$																			
BASSINGBOURNE GAWDY (Sen.)																										S	S		
BASSINGBOURNE GAWDY (Jun.)																													
CLIPPESBY GAWDY																													
FRANCIS GAWDY								28		$_{6}$	$_{5}$	$_{10}$	$_{6}$	✓$_{7}$	$_{2}$	$_{6}$	$_{8}$	14_{7}	14_{7}	✓$_{6}$		15_{7}	14_{7}	11_{5}	13_{5}	✓$_{6}$	22_{6}	13	20
HENRY GAWDY																													
THOMAS GAWDY (Sen.)	31_{5}	29	$_{11}$	22_{17}	24	23_{6}	$_{7}$	25_{3}	$_{8}$	$_{10}$	$_{7}$	$_{11}$	$_{6}$	✓$_{12}$	$_{2}$	$_{6}$	$_{2}$	9_{12}	9_{12}	✓$_{10}$	$_{3}$	8_{6}	7_{6}	7	8	✓	9	9_{2}	9_{2}
THOMAS GAWDY (Jun.)	32	30		23																		28	27	27	29	✓	36	33	33
GILBERT GERRARD	7	?																6	6			7	6	6	7		8	8	8
WILLIAM GRESHAM																													

LIST No.	30	31	32	33	34	35	36	37	38	39	40	41	42	43	44	45	46	47	48	49	50	51	52	53	54	55	56	57	58	
REGNAL YEAR	23	24	25	25/26	26	27	28	29	30	31	32	33	34	35	35/36	36	37	37	38	38	39	40	40	41	42	43	43	44	1J	
DATE			early 1583	late 1583	early 1584	late 1585	1586	Jan 1586/7	1588			June 1591		mid 1593	late 1593/ early 1594	March 1594	Feb 1595	July 1595	early 1596	July 1596	July 1597	March 1598	10 July 1598	10 July 1599	23 May 1600	March 1601	June 1601	June 1602	April 1603	
ROBERT CLARKE																		7	7	7	7		7	8	8	7	7	6	6	d. 1607
EDWARD CLERE	S		13_{8}	13_{12}	13_{12}	13_{3}	14_{12}	✓$_{6}$	12_{12}	$_{9}$	$_{?}$	12_{4}	$_{5}$	10_{4}	10_{9}	8_{9}	8_{3}	10_{3}	10_{4}	10_{4}	10_{10}	✓$_{13}$	9_{13}	11_{13}	11	10_{5}	10	9_{2}	9	d. 1606
HENRY CLERE																		36			36	✓	34	35	34	35	36	35	34	
THOMAS CLERE															56	52	52_{4}	$_{4}$	S	S										d. 1619
GEOFFRY COBB	$_{3}$																													
WILLIAM COCKETT																														
EDWARD COKE							47	$_{3}$	35		$_{14}$	36	$_{5}$	20	20	17	17_{4}	19_{4}	18	20	21	✓	23	24	21	22	24	23	23	d. 1634
ROBERT COKE																														
RICHARD COOTE																														
MILES CORBETT											$_{11}$	40_{14}	S	35_{8}	39_{13}	36_{13}	36_{15}	33_{15}	31_{5}	31_{5}	20_{18}	✓$_{21}$	17_{21}	19_{15}	18_{15}	18_{13}	19	18_{14}	18	d. 1607
CHARLES CORNWALLIS																										45	30	29	28	d. 1629
BARTHOLOMEW COTTON																												61	58	d. 1613
EDWARD CROMWELL, LORD CROMWELL														5	5	3	3	5	5	5	5	✓	5	6	6					d. 1607
HENRY CROMWELL, LORD CROMWELL			7	7	7	6	6	✓	5			5																		
ANTHONY DEATH														48_{7}	52_{2}	48_{2}	48_{9}	44_{9}	42_{13}	43_{13}	45_{8}	✓$_{7}$	43_{7}	45_{7}	44_{11}	46_{4}	44	43_{8}	41	d. 1612
THOMAS DOVE												21_{3}		21	21	18	18	20	19	21	22	✓	24	25	22	23				d. 1630
EDMUND DOYLEY																							40_{5}	42_{15}	41_{8}	42_{5}	41	40	39	d. 1612
HENRY DOYLEY	$_{6}$	$_{8}$	26_{9}	26_{9}	27_{9}	19	29_{9}	✓$_{12}$	26_{12}	$_{12}$	$_{18}$	24S	$_{9}$	24_{11}	24_{17}	22_{17}	22_{11}	24_{11}	22	24	25									
DRU DRURY	$_{20}$	$_{24}$	19_{18}	$18_{C\,25}$	$19_{C\,25}$	16_{21}	$20_{C\,21}$	✓$_{23}$	17_{21}	$_{22}$	$_{31}$	$17_{C\,?}$	$_{29}$	$15_{C\,29}$	$15_{C\,27}$	13_{27}	13_{29}	$15_{C\,29}$	$15_{C\,30}$	$15_{C\,30}$	$15_{C\,31}$	✓$_{35}$	$15_{C\,35}$	$16_{C\,30}$	$16_{C\,29}$	15_{27}	15_{C}	$14_{C\,30}$	14	d. 1617
THOMAS EGERTON																			1	1	1		1	1	1	1	1	1	1	d. 1617
EDWARD EVERARD														39	43_{8}	39_{8}	39_{4}	37_{4}	35_{8}	35_{8}	37	✓$_{14}$	35_{14}	36_{15}	35	36				
JOHN EYRE																														
THOMAS FARMER	$_{9}$	$_{13}$	24_{12}	24_{9}	25_{9}	24_{6}	27_{6}		25					$_{6}$	26_{4}	25_{4}	25_{3}													d. 1621
EDWARD FENNER														7	8	6	6													d. 1612
EDWARD FLOWERDEW	$_{3}$	$_{9}$	$_{3}$	21_{10}	22_{10}	22	12																							
RICHARD FRESTONE														52	57	53	53													d. 1616
RICHARD FULMERSTON																														
BASSINGBOURNE GAWDY (Sen.)	$_{3}$	$_{2}$	29_{6}	31	32	28	34	✓	30_{3}	$_{5}$																				
BASSINGBOURNE GAWDY (Jun.)												37_{7}	$_{9}$	31_{8}	34	32S	32	28	26	27	28_{5}	✓$_{4}$	22_{4}	23_{16}	20_{13}	21_{10}	22	21	21	d. 1606
CLIPPESBY GAWDY																										53	52	53	50	d. 1619
FRANCIS GAWDY	$_{1}$	$_{2}$	20_{6}	20_{4}	21_{4}	21_{2}	23_{4}	✓$_{4}$	21_{6}	$_{2}$	$_{2}$	10_{2}		8	7_{4}	5_{4}	5	8	8	8	8	✓	8	9_{6}	9_{2}	8	8	7	7	d. 1605
HENRY GAWDY					36	43_{3}	38_{9}	✓$_{3}$	31_{3}	$_{3}$	$_{14}$	$27_{?}$	$_{18}$	S	28_{12}	23_{12}	23_{15}	25_{15}	23_{17}	25_{17}	26_{18}	✓$_{21}$	26_{21}	28_{15}	28_{17}	29_{5}	29	28_{7}	27	d. 1621
THOMAS GAWDY (Sen.)	$_{3}$		10	10_{5}	10_{5}	9	10_{2}	✓	9																					
THOMAS GAWDY (Jun.)			28	30	31	36	33	✓																						
GILBERT GERRARD			9?																											
WILLIAM GRESHAM				29_{3}	30_{3}	35_{6}	32_{9}	✓	29		$_{4}$	28_{7}	$_{18}$	27	29_{9}	27_{9}	27													d. 1624

LIST No.	1	2	3	4	5	6	7	8	9	10	11	12	13	14	15	16	17	18	19	20	21	22	23	24	25	26	27	28	29
REGNAL YEAR	1	1	2	3	3/4	4	5	6	7	8	9	10	11	12	13	14	15	16	16	17	18	19	19	20	20	21	21	22	22
DATE	Dec 1558–Jan 1559	Mid 1559		*Post* July 1561	Nov/Dec 1561	11 Feb 1562		1 June 1564					Oct 1569	Dec 1569				*c.* Nov 1573	late 1573/ early 1574	June 1575		1 July 1577	late 1577	late 1577/ early 1578	late 1578	8 July 1579	late 1579	*c.* 1580	late 1580
HUMFREY GUYBON																													
THOMAS GUYBON (Sen.)			(2)	(8)	20	19 (12)	(6)	21 (16)	(4)		(3)	(12)	(16)	✓															
THOMAS GUYBON (Jun.)																													
RICHARD GWYNN																													
NICHOLAS HARE																										(2)	34 (2)	32 (6)	31 (6)
MARTIN HASTINGS				28 (2)																									
CHRISTOPHER HATTON																													
WILLIAM HATTON																													
ARTHUR HEVENINGHAM																											14	17 (6)	12 (6)
THOMAS HEWAR (Sen.)																	(4)	24 (8)	23 (8)	✓ (5)		29 (7)	28 (7)	28 (5)	30 (5)	✓ (7)	37 (7)	35 (4)	34 (4)
THOMAS HEWAR (Jun.)																													
CHRISTOPHER HEYDON (Sen.)	13 (13)	13	(16)	10 (17)	10	10 (13)	(14)	11 (12)	(7)	(12)	(12)	(16)	✓ (12)	S	(15)	(24)	(23)	7 C 27	7 C 27	✓ (23)	(10)	9 (26)	8 C 26	8 C 25	9 (25)	✓ (22)	10 C 22		
CHRISTOPHER HEYDON (Jun.)																													
WILLIAM HEYDON															(5)	(12)	(5)	23 (17)	22 (17)	✓ (11)	(2)	27 (11)	26 (11)	21 (11)	23 (11)	✓ (14)	28 (14)	26 (9)	25 (9)
CLEMENT HIGHAM																													
HENRY HOBART (Sen.)	21 (3)	20	(3)	16																									
HENRY HOBART (Jun.)																													
MILES HOBART																													
THOMAS HOGAN														(8)	(1)	(10)	(10)	25 (16)	24 (16)	✓ (6)		30 (7)	29 (7)	29 (9)	31 (9)	✓ (8)	38 (8)	36 (9)	35 (9)
GEORGE HOGARD				27							→																		
HENRY HOLDICH																													
JOHN HOLDICH																													
ROBERT HOLDICH	20																												
ROBERT HOUGHTON																													
THOMAS HOWARD																													
WILLIAM HUNGATE																													
WILLIAM HUNSTON														(5)	(3)	(6)		22	21			26	25	26	28	✓			
JOHN HUNT																													
JOHN JAY																													
RICHARD JENKINSON																													
JOHN KEMP																													
RICHARD KEMP																												40	
ROBERT KEMP (Sen.)																													40
ROBERT KEMP (Jun.)																													
WILLIAM KEMP																													
THOMAS KNYVETT (Sen.)	17 (3)	17								(4)	(9)	(3)																	

LIST No.	30	31	32	33	34	35	36	37	38	39	40	41	42	43	44	45	46	47	48	49	50	51	52	53	54	55	56	57	58	
REGNAL YEAR	23	24	25	25/26	26	27	28	29	30	31	32	33	34	35	35/36	36	37	37	38	38	39	40	40	41	42	43	43	44	1J	
DATE			early 1583	late 1583	early 1584	late 1583	1586	Jan 1586/7	1588			June 1591		mid 1593	late 1593/ early 1594	March 1594	Feb 1595	July 1595	early 1596	July 1596	July 1597	March 1598	10 July 1598	10 July 1599	23 May 1600	March 1601	June 1601	June 1602	April 1603	
HUMFREY GUYBON						34 (2)	48 (8)	✓ (5)	37 (6)	(8)	(8)	41 (8)	(8)	40 (11)	44 (6)	40 (6)	40 (6)	38 (6)	36 (8)	36 (8)	38S	✓ (10)	(10)	37 (2)	36 (6)	37 (6)	37			
THOMAS GUYBON (Sen.)																														
THOMAS GUYBON (Jun.)																					(6)							48 (4)	46	d. 1605
RICHARD GWYNN																											49	49 (8)	47	d. 1630
NICHOLAS HARE	(3)	✓ (6)	33 (8)	34 (6)	35 (6)	(6)	37 (8)	✓ (3)											34	34										
MARTIN HASTINGS																														
CHRISTOPHER HATTON									1			1																		
WILLIAM HATTON														18	18	15	15	17												
ARTHUR HEVENINGHAM	(3)	S		12 (3)	12 (3)	10 (9)	13 (9)	✓ (11)	11 (6)	(12)	(18)	11 (14)	(18)	9 (15)	9 (17)	7 (17)	7 (15)	9 (15)	9 (17)	9 (17)	9 (18)	✓ (21)	9 (21)	10	10 (15)	9 (18)	9	8 (4)	8	d. 1630
THOMAS HEWAR (Sen.)	(5)	✓ (8)	(4)	37 (8)	39 (8)	42 (4)	41 (2)																							
THOMAS HEWAR (Jun.)										(2)	(8)	46 (8)	(8)	51 (8)	55 (6)	51 (6)	51 (6)	47 (6)	45 (8)	46 (8)	48 (6)	✓ (8)	46 (8)	49 (8)	49 (8)	52 (6)	51	51 (4)	49	d. 1630
CHRISTOPHER HEYDON (Sen.)																														
CHRISTOPHER HEYDON (Jun.)							43 (6)	✓ (6)	(6)	(2)	(10)												18 (10)	20 (20)	(12)					d. 1623
WILLIAM HEYDON	(9)	(17)	21 (13)	19	20S	12 (5)	21 (18)	✓ (18)	18 (6)	(2)	(19)	18 (13)	(26)	16 (10)	16 (5)	(5)														
CLEMENT HIGHAM																											17	16 (14)	16	d. 1634
HENRY HOBART (Sen.)																														
HENRY HOBART (Jun.)														42 (7)	46 (12)	42 (12)	42 (12)	40 (12)	38 (9)	38 (9)	40 (5)	✓ (16)	37 (16)	39 (13)	38 (11)	39	39	37	36	d. 1625
MILES HOBART					41	40	45 (3)	✓																						
THOMAS HOGAN	(6)	(10)	31 (5)	33 (13)	34 (13)	29 (7)	36S																							
GEORGE HOGARD																														
HENRY HOLDICH																								53	53 (8)	57	56	57	54	d. 1618
JOHN HOLDICH	(3)	✓	40 (4)	43	46	37	52 (6)	✓ (2)	39																					
ROBERT HOLDICH																														
ROBERT HOUGHTON														41	45 (8)	41 (8)	41 (8)	39 (8)	37 (9)	37 (9)	39 (5)	✓ (16)	36 (16)	38 (11)	37	38	38	36 (3)	35	d. 1624
THOMAS HOWARD																							3	4	4	4	4	4	4	d. 1626
WILLIAM HUNGATE																									56 (2)	49 (2)	47	46	44	d. 1606
WILLIAM HUNSTON																														
JOHN HUNT														29	32	20	21 (3)	22 (3)	(1)	(1)										d. 1630
JOHN JAY																												52		d. 1619
RICHARD JENKINSON																					50	✓	49 (5)	52 (7)	52	56S	55	56	53	d. 1623
JOHN KEMP																										60	59	59	56	d. 1610
RICHARD KEMP												43 (10)	(18)	44 (11)	48 (8)	44 (8)	44 (3)	42 (3)	39	40	42 (5)	✓ (7)	39 (7)	41	40	41				
ROBERT KEMP (Sen.)	(3)	✓ (4)	39 (1)	41	44	32	49 (5)	✓																						
ROBERT KEMP (Jun.)																												60	57	d. 1612
WILLIAM KEMP																											60			
THOMAS KNYVETT (Sen.)																														

LIST No.	1	2	3	4	5	6	7	8	9	10	11	12	13	14	15	16	17	18	19	20	21	22	23	24	25	26	27	28	29	30	31	32	33	34	35	36	37	38	39	40	41	42	43	44	45	46	47	48	49	50	51	52	53	54	55	56	57	58	
REGNAL YEAR	1	1	2	3	3/4	4	5	6	7	8	9	10	11	12	13	14	15	16	16	17	18	19	19	20	20	21	21	22	22	23	24	25	25/26	26	27	28	29	30	31	32	33	34	35	35/36	36	37	37	38	38	39	40	40	41	42	43	43	44	1J	
DATE	Dec 1558–Jan 1559	Mid 1559		*Post* July 1561	Nov/Dec 1561	11 Feb 1562		1 June 1564					Oct 1569	Dec 1569				*c.* Nov. 1573	late 1573/early 1574	June 1575		1 July 1577	late 1577	late 1577/early 1578	late 1578	8 July 1579	late 1579	*c.* 1580	late 1580			early 1583	late 1583	early 1584	late 1585	1586	Jan 1586/7	1588			June 1591		mid 1593	late 1593/early 1594	March 1594	Feb 1595	July 1595	early 1596	July 1596	July 1597	March 1598	10 July 1598	10 July 1599	23 May 1600	March 1601	June 1601	June 1602	April 1603	
THOMAS KNYVETT OF ASHWELLTHORPE																									37	✓	18	S	S			15	15	15	15	16	✓			$_{6}$	14		12	12	10$_{4}$	10	12	12	12	12	✓	12	13	13	12	12	11	11	d. 1617
THOMAS KNYVETT (Jun.) OF BUCKENHAM																																									29$_{8}$			30	28	28 ▨													
WILLIAM LEWES																																								$_{11}$	38$_{6}$	$_{6}$	36$_{3}$	40 ▨															
THOMAS LOVELL (Sen.)	$_{4}$			$_{5}$	15	14$_{4}$	$_{2}$	16$_{3}$			▨																																																
THOMAS LOVELL (Jun.)																																			27	24$_{6}$	✓	22															26	26	27	23	22$_{7}$	22	d. 1604
ROBERT MANSELL																																												35	29	29$_{9}$	29$_{9}$	27	19	19$_{5}$	✓$_{13}$	21$_{13}$	22	$_{25}$	20	21	20	20	d. 1656
LE STRANGE MORDAUNT																																																									39	38	d. 1627
EDWARD PARKER LORD MORLEY																									5		5	5	5			6	6	6	?	5																							d. 1618
EDMUND MOUNDFORD																																									$_{2}$	$_{8}$	38$_{11}$	42$_{8}$	38$_{8}$	38$_{4}$	35$_{4}$	33$_{8}$	33$_{8}$	35$_{6}$	✓$_{8}$	33$_{8}$	34$_{10}$	33$_{8}$	34$_{8}$	35	34$_{8}$	33	d. 1617
FANCIS MOUNDFORD																																					$_{2}$	36$_{6}$	$_{8}$	$_{8}$	$_{2}$ ▨																		
OSBERT MOUNDFORD	22$_{11}$	21	$_{3}$	17$_{10}$	18	17$_{2}$	$_{7}$	19$_{6}$	$_{8}$	$_{3}$		$_{8}$	✓	✓				11	11	✓		12						▨																															
RICHARD NICHOLS												$_{8}$	$_{10}$	✓$_{7}$	$_{3}$	$_{9}$	$_{1}$	▨																																									
THOMAS HOWARD DUKE OF NORFOLK	4	?			3	3		3					✓			▨																																											
EDMUND FREAKE BISHOP OF NORWICH																						4	4	4	4		4	4	4			5	5								▨																		
EDMUND SCAMBLER BISHOP OF NORWICH																																		5	?	4		4			4		4	4	▨														
JOHN PARKHURST BISHOP OF NORWICH								6					✓					4	4	▨																																							
WILLIAM REDMAN BISHOP OF NORWICH																																															4	4	4	4	✓	4	5	5	5	5 ▨			
THOMAS OXBOROUGH																																																44	45	47	✓$_{8}$	45$_{8}$	47$_{8}$	47$_{8}$	50$_{8}$	48	47$_{8}$	45	d. 1623
JOHN PAGRAVE																											33	31$_{10}$	30$_{10}$	$_{14}$	✓$_{15}$	32$_{9}$	27$_{8}$	28$_{8}$	39$_{15}$	30$_{20}$	✓$_{17}$	27$_{10}$	$_{10}$	$_{23}$	25$_{15}$	$_{21}$	26$_{21}$	27$_{15}$	26$_{15}$	26$_{22}$	27$_{22}$	25$_{22}$	26$_{22}$	27$_{25}$	✓$_{25}$	27$_{25}$	29$_{16}$	29$_{11}$	30$_{6}$	31	30$_{8}$	29	d. 1611
PHILIP PARKER																																			18																								
CLEMENT PASTON																							18	18	20	✓	26	22	23	$_{3}$	$_{2}$	22$_{5}$	22$_{3}$	23$_{3}$	33$_{4}$	25$_{5}$	✓$_{12}$	23S		$_{4}$	22$_{4}$		22	22	19	19	21	20	22	23 ▨									
WILLIAM PASTON	26	25	$_{5}$	18$_{8}$	21	20$_{8}$	$_{9}$	22$_{12}$	$_{9}$	S	$_{5}$	$_{10}$	$_{9}$	✓$_{15}$	$_{11}$	$_{14}$	$_{13}$	13$_{12}$	13$_{12}$	✓$_{9}$	$_{9}$	14$_{12}$	13$_{12}$	14$_{11}$	16$_{11}$	✓	16	18$_{6}$	14$_{6}$	$_{3}$	$_{4}$	14S	14$_{3}$	14$_{3}$	11$_{4}$	15$_{9}$	✓$_{12}$	13$_{9}$	$_{9}$	$_{8}$	13	$_{9}$	11$_{15}$	11$_{13}$	9$_{13}$	9$_{4}$	11$_{4}$	11$_{9}$	11$_{9}$	11$_{18}$	✓$_{9}$	11$_{9}$	12$_{8}$	12$_{4}$	11$_{18}$	11	10$_{7}$	10	d. 1610
WILLIAM PERIAM																																				9		8			8																		d. 1604
JOHN PEYTON																										$_{2}$	$_{2}$	$_{6}$	$_{6}$	$_{5}$	$_{8}$	30$_{8}$	32$_{8}$	33$_{8}$	41$_{9}$	35	✓$_{3}$	20$_{9}$	S	$_{6}$	20$_{12}$	$_{8}$	19$_{14}$	19$_{13}$	16$_{13}$	16$_{8}$	18$_{8}$	17$_{11}$	17$_{11}$	17$_{6}$	✓	16	17	17	16	16	15	15	d. 1630
ROBERT PEYTON																											35	34	32											▨																			
JOHN POPHAM																																											6	6	4	4	6	6	6	6		6	7	7	6	6	5	5	d. 1607
GREGORY PRATT																																										$_{2}$	50$_{8}$	54$_{6}$	50$_{6}$	50$_{3}$	45$_{3}$	46$_{8}$	47$_{8}$	49$_{2}$	✓$_{8}$	47$_{8}$	50$_{8}$	50$_{8}$	54	53	54$_{2}$	51	d. 1609
JOHN PUCKERING																																											1	1	1	1	1	▨											
ROBERT REDMAYNE																																									32	$_{5}$	30	33	31	31$_{2}$	31$_{2}$	29$_{4}$	29$_{4}$	31$_{24}$	✓$_{13}$	30$_{13}$	33$_{9}$	23$_{8}$	24$_{8}$	25	24$_{3}$	24	d. 1625
HENRY REPPES				29		22	$_{3}$	24$_{2}$	$_{5}$	▨ $_{3}$																																																	
JOHN REPPES																																						38$_{6}$	$_{8}$	$_{8}$	45$_{8}$	$_{8}$	46$_{4}$	50$_{6}$	46$_{6}$	46$_{2}$	$_{2}$							46	48	46	45$_{4}$	43	d. 1612
JOHN REYNOLDS																											40	39	37		?		▨																										
WILLIAM RUGG																								33$_{2}$	35$_{2}$	✓$_{15}$	44$_{15}$	44$_{4}$	42$_{4}$	$_{4}$	✓$_{10}$	34$_{9}$	35$_{8}$	37$_{8}$	38$_{12}$	39$_{8}$	✓$_{8}$	32$_{7}$	$_{10}$	$_{20}$	31$_{6}$	$_{21}$	28$_{18}$	31$_{13}$	30$_{13}$	30$_{14}$	30$_{14}$	28$_{13}$	28$_{13}$	30$_{16}$	✓$_{12}$	29$_{12}$	32$_{5}$	32$_{6}$	33$_{4}$	34	33$_{2}$	32	d. 1616
JAMES SCAMBLER																																												58	54	54$_{8}$	48$_{8}$				✓$_{5}$	48$_{5}$	51$_{10}$	51$_{4}$	55$_{8}$	54	55$_{3}$	52	d. 1633
RALPH SHELTON										$_{7}$	$_{9}$	$_{7}$	$_{9}$	✓$_{17}$	$_{11}$	S	$_{13}$	16$_{5}$	16$_{5}$	✓$_{13}$	$_{5}$	17$_{10}$	16$_{10}$	16$_{20}$	18$_{20}$	✓$_{4}$	15$_{4}$	20$_{14}$	13 ▨ $_{14}$																														
THOMAS SIDNEY																														$_{4}$	✓$_{7}$	38$_{7}$	40$_{5}$	43$_{5}$	▨																							

LIST No.	1	2	3	4	5	6	7	8	9	10	11	12	13	14	15	16	17	18	19	20	21	22	23	24	25	26	27	28	29
REGNAL YEAR	1	1	2	3	3/4	4	5	6	7	8	9	10	11	12	13	14	15	16	16	17	18	19	19	20	20	21	21	22	22
DATE	Dec 1558–Jan 1559	Mid 1559		*Post* July 1561	Nov/Dec 1561	11 Feb 1562		1 June 1564					Oct 1569	Dec 1569				*c.* Nov 1573	late 1573/ early 1574	June 1575		1 July 1577	late 1577	late 1577/ early 1578	late 1578	5 July 1579	late 1579	*c.* 1580	late 1580
ROBERT SOUTHWELL																													
THOMAS SOUTHWELL												▨$_{3}$																	
CLEMENT SPELMAN																													
HENRY SPELMAN																													
JOHN SPELMAN																										✓$_{5}$	46_{5}	45_{5}	44_{5}
THOMAS STEYNINGS	37_{6}	34	$_{7}$	$_{11}$	19	18_{14}	$_{7}$	20_{15}	$_{13}$		$_{2}$							12	12			13	12	13	15		24	16	22
JOHN STEWARD																													
NICHOLAS LE STRANGE	18_{4}	18		14_{3}	13	13_{8}	$_{4}$	15_{14}	$_{11}$	$_{5}$	$_{2}$	$_{12}$	✓$_{16}$														13	12	▨
HENRY RADCLIFFE, EARL OF SUSSEX																													
ROBERT RADCLIFFE, EARL OF SUSSEX																													
THOMAS RADCLIFFE, EARL OF SUSSEX	5	?			5	5		5										3	3			3	3	3	3		3	3	3
THOMAS TALBOTT																													
FRANCIS THORESBY	25_{6}	24											▨→																
THOMAS THROWER				$_{2}$																									
ROBERT TILNEY																													
JOHN TOWNSHEND																													
THOMAS TOWNSHEND															$_{5}$	$_{15}$	$_{6}$	20_{3}	19_{3}	✓$_{13}$	S$_{3}$	23_{6}	22_{6}	23_{4}	25_{4}	✓$_{9}$	30_{9}	28_{3}	27_{3}
THOMAS TYNDALL	15_{9}	15	$_{9}$	12_{6}	12	S		14_{3}																					
JOHN WALPOLE																						34	33	34	36	✓	45	42	43
ROBERT WALPOLE																		28	27										
EDWARD WARNER								13_{6}	▨																				
HENRY WESTON																						11_{6}	10_{6}	10 $	11	✓$_{6}$	12_{6}	11_{2}	11_{2}
WILLIAM PAULET MARQUIS OF WINCHESTER	2	?			2	2		2								▨													
HENRY WINDHAM																													
ROBERT WOOD																													
HENRY WOODHOUSE													✓	$_{17}$	$_{13}$	$_{6}$	$_{11}$	17_{7}	$_{7}$	✓$_{7}$		18_{13}	17_{13}	17_{6}	19_{6}	✓	19	21	16
PHILIP WOODHOUSE																													
ROGER WOODHOUSE (Sen.)	16	16	$_{2}$	13▨																									
ROGER WOODHOUSE (Jun.)										$_{8}$	$_{14}$	$_{9}$	$_{3}$					29_{4}	28_{4}	✓$_{6}$	$_{6}$	21_{13}	20_{13}	20_{16}	22_{16}	✓$_{9}$	20_{9}	24_{16}	17_{16}
THOMAS WOODHOUSE	14	14	$_{11}$	11_{11}	11	12_{4}	$_{9}$	S	$_{5}$	$_{10}$	$_{5}$	$_{6}$	✓$_{3}$			▨													
WILLIAM WOODHOUSE (Sen.)	11_{9}	11	$_{3}$	8_{3}	$_{C}8$	$_{C}8_{18}$		$_{C}9_{25}$	▨																				
WILLIAM WOODHOUSE (Jun.)																													
EDMUND WYNDHAM	12_{17}	12	$_{11}$	9_{11}	9	9_{9}	$_{9}$	10_{14}	$_{10}$	$_{17}$	$_{15}$	$_{24}$	✓$_{18}$▨																
FRANCIS WYNDHAM													$_{9}$	$_{19}$	$_{11}$	$_{8}$	$_{18}$	18_{17}	17_{17}	✓$_{14}$	$_{6}$	19_{15}	11_{15}	12_{3}	12_{3}	✓$_{6}$	21_{6}	14	19
CHRISTOPHER WRAY																						5	5	5	6		7	7	7
HENRY YELVERTON																													

LIST No.	30	31	32	33	34	35	36	37	38	39	40	41	42	43	44	45	46	47	48	49	50	51	52	53	54	55	56	57	58	
REGNAL YEAR	23	24	25	25/26	26	27	28	29	30	31	32	33	34	35	35/36	36	37	37	38	38	39	40	40	41	42	43	43	44	1J	
DATE			early 1583	late 1583	early 1584	late 1585	1586	Jan 1586/7	1588			June 1591		mid 1593	late 1593/ early 1594	March 1594	Feb 1595	July 1595	early 1596	July 1596	July 1597	March 1598	10 July 1598	10 July 1599	23 May 1600	March 1601	June 1601	June 1602	April 1603	
ROBERT SOUTHWELL						7	22_{3}	✓$_{8}$	19	$_{6}$	S	19		17_{4}	17_{8}	14_{8}	14_{9}	16_{9}	16_{11}	16_{11}	16_{8}	✓	▨$_{3}$							
THOMAS SOUTHWELL																														
CLEMENT SPELMAN												42_{8}	$_{16}$	43_{8}	47_{8}	43_{8}	43_{4}	41_{4}	$_{4}$	39_{4}	41_{6}	✓$_{12}$	38_{12}	40S	39_{6}	40_{10}	40	38_{8}	37	d. 1609
HENRY SPELMAN																							50	54_{12}	54_{6}	58_{2}	57	58_{2}	55	d. 1641
JOHN SPELMAN	▨																													
THOMAS STEYNINGS																														
JOHN STEWARD	$_{2}$	✓$_{8}$	41_{8}	44_{8}	47_{8}	44_{9}	53_{8}	✓$_{3}$	40																					d. 1605
NICHOLAS LE STRANGE																														
HENRY RADCLIFFE, EARL OF SUSSEX			3	4	4	?	3		3			3		3	3▨															
ROBERT RADCLIFFE, EARL OF SUSSEX																		3	3	3	3		2	3	3	3	3	3	3	d. 1629
THOMAS RADCLIFFE, EARL OF SUSSEX			▨																											
THOMAS TALBOTT																									24	25	26			d. 1628
FRANCIS THORESBY																														.
THOMAS THROWER																														
ROBERT TILNEY																							51	55_{8}	55_{6}	59_{2}	58▨			
JOHN TOWNSHEND																							19_{2}	18_{26}	$_{16}$	17_{11}	18	17_{6}	17	d. 1603
THOMAS TOWNSHEND	$_{6}$	$_{6}$	27_{9}	28_{9}	29_{9}	23	31_{6}	✓$_{12}$	28_{6}	$_{12}$	$_{18}$	26▨																		
THOMAS TYNDALL					▨																									
JOHN WALPOLE				42	45	47	51		▨																					
ROBERT WALPOLE																														
EDWARD WARNER																														
HENRY WESTON	$_{9}$	$_{2}$											▨																	
WILLIAM PAULET MARQUIS OF WINCHESTER																														
HENRY WINDHAM																								48	48_{7}	51_{2}	50	50_{6}	48	d. 1627
ROBERT WOOD						17					▨																			
HENRY WOODHOUSE	$_{6}$	$_{6}$	17_{6}	17_{9}	17_{9}	S	18_{6}	✓$_{3}$	15_{12}	$_{6}$		$16_{?}$	$_{5}$	14	14_{8}	12_{8}	12	14	14	14	14	✓	14	15	15_{4}	14	14	13	13	d. 1624
PHILIP WOODHOUSE								✓$_{2}$		$_{5}$	$_{4}$	30_{10}	$_{14}$	25_{4}	25_{8}	24_{8}	24 $	26	24_{5}	18_{5}	18_{16}	✓$_{19}$	20_{19}	21_{18}	19_{17}	19_{13}	20	19_{14}	19	d. 1623
ROGER WOODHOUSE (Sen.)																														
ROGER WOODHOUSE (Jun.)	$_{6}$	$_{8}$	18_{8}	$_{9}$	18_{9}	14_{12}	19_{17}	✓$_{13}$	16_{3}▨																					
THOMAS WOODHOUSE																														
WILLIAM WOODHOUSE (Sen.)																														
WILLIAM WOODHOUSE (Jun.)							44																							d. 1639
EDMUND WYNDHAM																														
FRANCIS WYNDHAM	$_{3}$		11	11	11	20_{5}	11	✓$_{11}$	10_{12}	$_{9}$	$_{4}$	9_{4}	▨																	
CHRISTOPHER WRAY			8?	8	8		7		6			6	▨																	
HENRY YELVERTON						46_{2}	50_{10}	✓$_{7}$	$_{3}$	$_{4}$	$_{10}$	33_{8}	$_{9}$	32_{8}	36_{4}	33_{4}	33_{2}	$_{2}$			29_{10}	✓$_{15}$	28_{15}	30_{8}	30	31	▨			

LIST No.	1	2	3	4	5	6	7	8	9	10	11	12	13	14	15
REGNAL YEAR	1	1	2	3	3/4	4	5	6	7	8	9	10	11	12	13
DATE	Dec 1558–Jan 1559	Mid 1559		*Post* July 1561	Nov/Dec 1561	11 Feb 1562		1 June 1564					Oct 1569	Dec 1569	
WILLIAM YELVERTON (Sen.)	34_{17}	31	$_{15}$	24_{19}	25	24_{12}	$_{13}$	27_{20}	$_{16}$	$_{10}$	$_{10}$	$_{22}$	$_{?}$		
WILLIAM YELVERTON (Jun.)															
TOTAL IN COMMISSION	37	34		29	25	24		28							

LIST No.	16	17	18	19	20	21	22	23	24	25	26	27	28	29	30
REGNAL YEAR	14	15	16	16	17	18	19	19	20	20	21	21	22	22	23
DATE			*c.* Nov 1573	late 1573/early 1574	June 1575		1 July 1577	late 1577	late 1577/early 1578	late 1578	8 July 1579	late 1579	*c.* 1580	late 1580	
WILLIAM YELVERTON (Sen.)												23	25_{7}	21_{7}	$_{9}$
WILLIAM YELVERTON (Jun.)															
TOTAL IN COMMISSION			29	28			35	34	36	38		46	45	44	

LIST No.	31	32	33	34	35	36	37	38	39	40	41	42	43	44	45
REGNAL YEAR	24	25	25/26	26	27	28	29	30	31	32	33	34	35	35/36	36
DATE		early 1583	late 1583	early 1584	late 1585	1586	Jan 1586/7	1588			June 1591		mid 1593	late 1593/early 1594	March 1594
WILLIAM YELVERTON (Sen.)	$_{8}$	23_{6}	23_{3}	24_{3}	26_{2}	26_{2}									
WILLIAM YELVERTON (Jun.)															
TOTAL IN COMMISSION		41	44	47	47	53		40			46		52	58	54

LIST No.	46	47	48	49	50	51	52	53	54	55	56	57	58	
REGNAL YEAR	37	37	38	38	39	40	40	41	42	43	43	44	1J	
DATE	Feb 1595	July 1595	early 1596	July 1596	July 1597	March 1598	10 July 1598	10 July 1599	23 May 1600	March 1601	June 1601	June 1602	April 1603	
WILLIAM YELVERTON (Sen.)														
WILLIAM YELVERTON (Jun.)											32	31_{6}	30	d. 1631
TOTAL IN COMMISSION	54	48	47	48	51		51	55	56	60	60	61	58	

Appendix II

CHART SHOWING THE INTERRUPTED TENURE OF JUSTICES

Key

—— indicates periods of tenure.

▧ left-hand edge indicates approximate date of death.

▧→? indicates that date of death is unknown, but that it was subsequent to date shown by bar.

Note

Ex officio members of the commission (judges, bishops, noblemen, and principal officers of state) have been excluded.

The omission of a justice from the commission during his shrievalty has not been indicated.

Sources

For the Elizabethan period, unless otherwise indicated, this chart is based upon information presented in Appendix I.

Sources used for the pre- and post-Elizabethan period are set out in Appendix III.

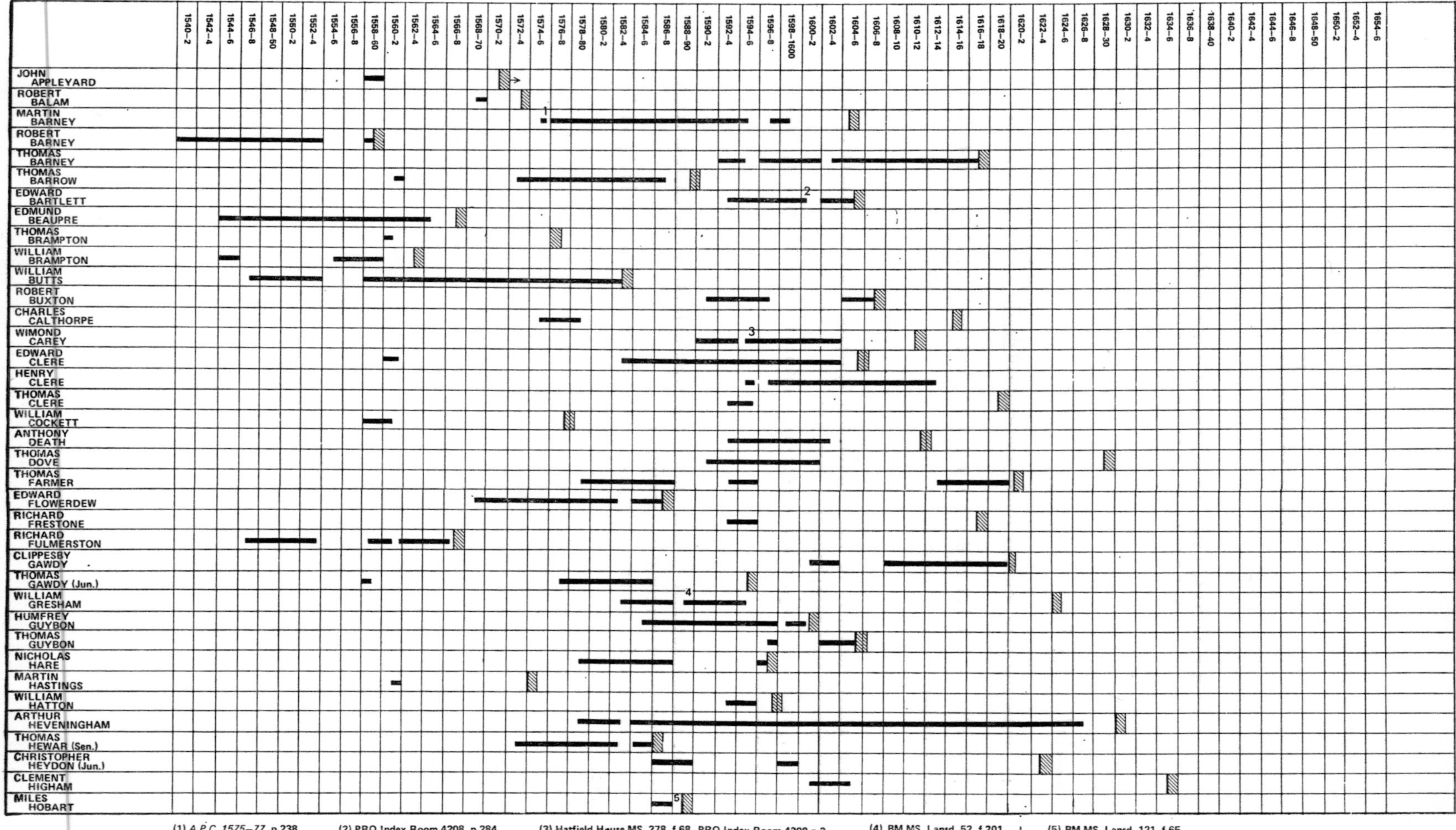

(1) *A.P.C. 1575–77*, p.238. (2) PRO Index Room 4208, p.284. (3) Hatfield House MS. 278, f.68. PRO Index Room 4208 p.3. (4) BM MS. Lansd. 52, f.201. (5) BM MS. Lansd. 121, f.65.

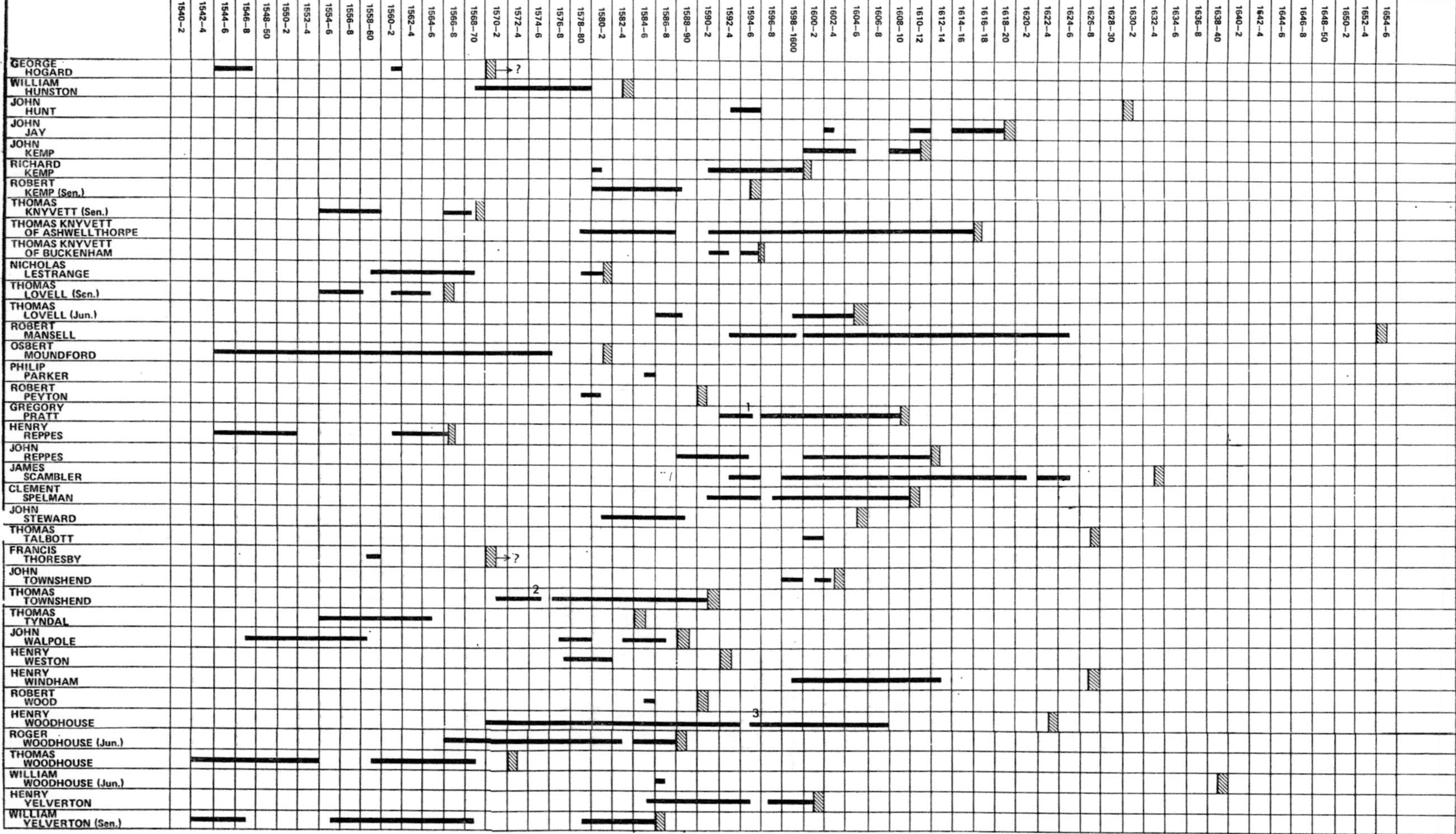

1540–2
1542–4
1544–6
1546–8
1548–50
1550–2
1552–4
1554–6
1556–8
1558–60
1560–2
1562–4
1564–6
1566–8
1568–70
1570–2
1572–4
1574–6
1576–8
1578–80
1580–2
1582–4
1584–6
1586–8
1588–90
1590–2
1592–4
1594–6
1596–8
1598–1600
1600–2
1602–4
1604–6
1606–8
1608–10
1610–12
1612–14
1614–16
1616–18
1618–20
1620–2
1622–4
1624–6
1626–8
1628–30
1630–2
1632–4
1634–6
1636–8
1638–40
1640–2
1642–4
1644–6
1646–8
1648–50
1650–2
1652–4
1654–6
GEORGE HOGARD
WILLIAM HUNSTON
JOHN HUNT
JOHN JAY
JOHN KEMP
RICHARD KEMP
ROBERT KEMP (Sen.)
THOMAS KNYVETT (Sen.)
THOMAS KNYVETT OF ASHWELLTHORPE
THOMAS KNYVETT OF BUCKENHAM
NICHOLAS LESTRANGE
THOMAS LOVELL (Sen.)
THOMAS LOVELL (Jun.)
ROBERT MANSELL
OSBERT MOUNDFORD
PHILIP PARKER
ROBERT PEYTON
GREGORY PRATT
HENRY REPPES
JOHN REPPES
JAMES SCAMBLER
CLEMENT SPELMAN
JOHN STEWARD
THOMAS TALBOTT
FRANCIS THORESBY
JOHN TOWNSHEND
THOMAS TOWNSHEND
THOMAS TYNDAL
JOHN WALPOLE
HENRY WESTON
HENRY WINDHAM
ROBERT WOOD
HENRY WOODHOUSE
ROGER WOODHOUSE (Jun.)
THOMAS WOODHOUSE
WILLIAM WOODHOUSE (Jun.)
HENRY YELVERTON
WILLIAM YELVERTON (Sen.)
?
?
1
2
3

(1) Hatfield House MS. 278, f.68. (2) *A.P.C. 1578–77*, p.238. (3) PRO Index Room 4208, p.3.

Appendix III

TABLE SHOWING CONTINUITY OF MAGISTRACY WITHIN A FAMILY

Explanatory Note

This table shows the number of families which provided a J.P. for one, two, or three generations.

The second column lists all the Elizabethan justices (with over-all dates for their appearance in the commission), except for a few justices whose families provided two or more magistrates during Elizabeth's reign. In these cases the justice who held office during the middle of the reign has been named in this column.

If the father of any justice named in column II had also been in the commission he has been named in the first column (with approximate over-all dates for his appearance in commission).

The third column lists the eldest sons of the justices who appear in column II, except that when a younger son became a justice instead of his elder brother he has been accordingly named.

Sons who became justices have been indicated in column IV by setting down the over-all dates of their appearance in the commission.

Nobility, bishops, judges, and principal officers of state have been omitted.

Over-all dates which fall within the Elizabethan period have been derived from Appendix I. Dates which fall outside this period are based upon the following sources:

(a)	*Pre-Elizabethan lists of J.P.s*
1485–1509	*CPR, 1485–94*, p. 501; *1494–1509*, pp. 659–660;
1509–1547	*L & P H VIII*, i(2), p. 1544; ii(1), p. 69; iii(1), p. 395; iv(1), pp. 168, 901; iv(3), p. 2311; v. 54; xiii(1), pp. 137, 414; xiv(1), p. 486; xviii(1), p. 133; xx(1), pp. 318, 322.
1547	*CPR, 1547–8*, p. 89.
1554	*CPR, 1553–4*, p. 24.
1555	PRO SP 11/5 no. 6, fols. 42b–43.

(b)	*Post-Elizabethan lists of J.P.s*
1603–1640	Patent roll enrolments. For refs. see *BIHR* xxxii. 241. I am indebted to Mr. Victor Morgan, who kindly allowed me to use his transcripts of these lists.

NAME OF FATHER (OR NEAR RELATIVE) IF A JUSTICE	NAME OF ELIZABETHAN JUSTICE and approx. dates of office	NAME OF SON	IF SON WAS A JUSTICE approx. dates of office
	JOHN APPLEYARD 1558–9	?	
	ISAAC ASTLEY 1596–8	Francis	1632–7
Lord Keeper Nicholas Bacon 1558–78	NATHANIEL BACON 1574–1622	None	
Lord Keeper Nicholas Bacon 1558–78	NICHOLAS BACON (Jnr.) 1578–1624	Edmund	1627–40
	ROBERT BALAM 1569–70	None?	
	JOHN BARNEY OF LANGLEY 1558–9	Richard	
Robert Barney 1540–59	MARTIN BARNEY OF GUNTON 1576–98	Henry	
	THOMAS BARNEY OF REEDHAM 1592–1616	Richard	1625–53
	THOMAS BARROW 1561–87	William	
	EDWARD BARTLETT 1593–1605	Edward	
	EDMUND BEAUPRE 1547–64	None	
Robert Bell 1564–75	EDMUND BELL 1599–1608	Robert	1621–38

NAME OF FATHER (OR NEAR RELATIVE) IF A JUSTICE	NAME OF ELIZABETHAN JUSTICE and approx. dates of office	NAME OF SON	IF SON WAS A JUSTICE approx. dates of office
	THOMAS BENNETT 1602–3	?	
	JOHN BLENNER-HASSETT OF BARSHAM 1561–9	Thomas	
	WILLIAM BLENNER-HASSETT OF PLUMSTEAD 1573–98	Edward	1606–18
William Boleyn 1485–1504	JAMES BOLEYN 1511–61		
William Brampton 1558–9	THOMAS BRAMPTON 1560–1	Thomas	
	ANTHONY BROWNE 1600–26	Thomas	1629–32
	WILLIAM BUTTS 1547–83	None	
	ROBERT BUXTON 1591–7	John (g. grandson)	1632–40
	CHARLES CALTHORPE 1575–8	None	
	WIMOND CAREY 1590–1604	None?	
John Clere 1538–47	EDWARD CLERE 1559–1604	Edward	
	HENRY CLERE OF STANFIELD 1595–1612	?	

NAME OF FATHER (OR NEAR RELATIVE) IF A JUSTICE	NAME OF ELIZABETHAN JUSTICE and approx. dates of office	NAME OF SON	IF SON WAS A JUSTICE approx. dates of office
	THOMAS CLERE OF STOKESBY 1594–5	Thomas	
	GEOFFREY COBB 1578–81	William	
Edward Cockett 1538–40	WILLIAM COCKETT 1558–61	None	
Robert Coke 1558–61	EDWARD COKE 1586–1623	Robert John	 1629–35
	RICHARD COOTE 1569–78	Nicholas	
John Corbett 1540–8	MILES CORBETT 1590–1606	Thomas	1607–15
	CHARLES CORNWALLIS 1601–29	William	
	BARTHOLOMEW COTTON 1602–12	Thomas	1617–25
	ANTHONY DEATH 1593–1603	None	
	THOMAS DOVE 1591–1601		
	HENRY DOYLEY 1575–97	Edmund	1598–1611
	DRU DRURY 1567–1612	Dru	1608–34
	EDWARD EVERARD 1593–1600	None	

NAME OF FATHER (OR NEAR RELATIVE) IF A JUSTICE	NAME OF ELIZABETHAN JUSTICE and approx. dates of office	NAME OF SON	IF SON WAS A JUSTICE approx. dates of office
William Eyer (probably not father to John) 1494–1504	JOHN EYRE 1559–61	None	
William Farmer (uncle) 1538–58	THOMAS FARMER 1579–1621	William	
	EDWARD FLOWERDEW 1569–86	None	
	RICHARD FRESTONE 1593–5	Richard	1620–25
	RICHARD FULMERSTON 1547–66	None	
Thomas Gawdy 1540–54	BASSINGBOURNE GAWDY OF HARLING 1581–9	Bassingbourne Gawdy	1590–1605
	FRANCIS GAWDY OF WALLINGTON 1564–1605	None	
	THOMAS GAWDY (sen.) OF CLAXTON 1540–88	Henry	1586–1619
	THOMAS GAWDY OF WEYBREAD 1558–86	None	
	WILLIAM GRESHAM 1583–95		
Thomas Guybon 1560–9	HUMFREY GUYBON 1585–1601	Thomas	1601–3
	RICHARD GWYNN 1601–29	Richard	

NAME OF FATHER (OR NEAR RELATIVE) IF A JUSTICE	NAME OF ELIZABETHAN JUSTICE and approx. dates of office	NAME OF SON	IF SON WAS A JUSTICE approx. dates of office
	NICHOLAS HARE 1579–96	Ralph (Brother or Nephew)	1604–22
	MARTIN HASTINGS 1560–1		
	WILLIAM HATTON 1593–5		
	ARTHUR HEVENINGHAM 1579–1626	John	1608–34
	THOMAS HEWAR 1572–86	Thomas	1589–1623
Christopher Heydon 1538–79	WILLIAM HEYDON 1570–93	Christopher	1586–1600
	CLEMENT HIGHAM 1601–5	?	
Walter Hobart 1499–1531	HENRY HOBART OF HALES HALL 1542–61	James	
	HENRY HOBART OF BLICKLING 1593–1626	John	1625–40
	MILES HOBART OF PLUMSTEAD 1584–7	Thomas	1608–22
	THOMAS HOGAN 1569–86	Henry	
Henry Hogard 1486–1511	GEORGE HOGARD 1544–61		
Robert Holdich 1531–58	JOHN HOLDICH 1581–8	Henry	1598–1618

NAME OF FATHER (OR NEAR RELATIVE) IF A JUSTICE	NAME OF ELIZABETHAN JUSTICE and approx. dates of office	NAME OF SON	IF SON WAS A JUSTICE approx. dates of office
	ROBERT HOUGHTON 1593–1624	Francis	
	WILLIAM HUNGATE 1600–5	?	
Henry Hunston 1514 (grandfather)	WILLIAM HUNSTON 1569–79	Thomas	
	JOHN HUNT 1593–5	?	
	JOHN JAY 1602–19	Suckling	
	RICHARD JENKINSON 1597–1622	Thomas	1613–25
	ROBERT KEMP 1580–6	Richard John	1579–1600 1602–10
Edmund Knyvett 1544–7	THOMAS KNYVETT OF BUCKENHAM 1554–68	Thomas	1590–94
	THOMAS KNYVETT OF ASHWELLTHORPE 1578–1616	Thomas (grandson)	1628–38
	NICHOLAS L'ESTRANGE 1558–80	Hamon L'Estrange (g. grandson)	1605–41
	WILLIAM LEWIS 1590–3		
Thomas Lovell 1554–64	THOMAS LOVELL 1585–1604		
	ROBERT MANSELL 1593–1626	None	

NAME OF FATHER (OR NEAR RELATIVE) IF A JUSTICE	NAME OF ELIZABETHAN JUSTICE and approx. dates of office	NAME OF SON	IF SON WAS A JUSTICE approx. dates of office
	LE STRANGE MORDAUNT 1602–27	Probably	
Osbert Moundford 1544–75	FRANCIS MOUNDFORD 1587–91		
	EDMUND MOUNDFORD 1591–1616	Edmund	1627–40
	RICHARD NICHOLAS 1568–72	?	
	THOMAS OXBOROUGH 1596–1622	William	
	JOHN PAGRAVE 1579–1610	Augustine	1613–38
	PHILIP PARKER 1585		
William Paston 1531–54	CLEMENT PASTON 1577–97	None	
William Paston (grandfather) 1531–54	WILLIAM PASTON 1558–1610	Christopher	
	JOHN PEYTON 1579–1626	John	
	ROBERT PEYTON 1579–80	John	
	GREGORY PRATT 1592–1608	Francis	
	ROBERT REDMAYNE 1591–1626	?	
Henry Reppes 1559–66	JOHN REPPES 1588–1612	Henry	1620–6

NAME OF FATHER (OR NEAR RELATIVE) IF A JUSTICE	NAME OF ELIZABETHAN JUSTICE and approx. dates of office	NAME OF SON	IF SON WAS A JUSTICE approx. dates of office
	JOHN REYNOLDS 1579–80	?	
	WILLIAM RUGG 1578–1615	Thomas	
	JAMES SCAMBLER 1593–1626	Adam Scambler (Brother)	1618–40
John Shelton 1510–54	RALPH SHELTON 1566–80	Thomas	
	THOMAS SIDNEY 1581–4	Henry	1607–12
Thomas Southwell 1567–8	ROBERT SOUTHWELL 1585–98	Thomas	1618–35
John Spelman 1512–42	JOHN SPELMAN OF NARBOROUGH 1579–80	Clement	1590–1606
	HENRY SPELMAN OF CONGHAM 1598–1641	Clement	
	THOMAS STENINGS 1558–80	?	
	JOHN STEWARD 1581–8	Humfrey	
	THOMAS TALBOTT 1600–1	Thomas	1628–40
	FRANCIS THORESBY 1558–9	?	
	THOMAS THROWER 1560–1	?	

NAME OF FATHER (OR NEAR RELATIVE) IF A JUSTICE	NAME OF ELIZABETHAN JUSTICE and approx. dates of office	NAME OF SON	IF SON WAS A JUSTICE approx. dates of office
	ROBERT TILNEY 1598–1601		
	JOHN TOWNSHEND OF RAYNHAM 1598–1602	Roger	1627–35
Robert Townshend 1531–44	THOMAS TOWNSHEND OF BRACONASH 1570–91	Roger	
John Tyndall 1531–38	THOMAS TYNDALL 1554–63	William	
	JOHN WALPOLE 1577–86	Edward	
	EDWARD WARNER 1563–4	Edward	
	HENRY WESTON 1577–82	Richard	1628–35
Edmund Wyndham 1531–69	FRANCIS WYNDHAM 1569–91	None	
	HENRY WINDHAM 1599–1612	Thomas	1628–40
	ROBERT WOOD 1585		
Roger Woodhouse (grandfather) 1531–60	ROGER WOODHOUSE OF KIMBERLEY 1566–88	Philip	1587–1623
Thomas Woodhouse 1542–69	WILLIAM WOODHOUSE 1554–64	Henry William	1570–1608 1586
William Yelverton 1540–86	HENRY YELVERTON 1586–1601	William	1601–34

No. of families providing Justices	114
No. of families providing a Justice for one generation	54
No. of families providing a Justice for two generations	44
No. of families providing a Justice for three generations	16

Index

Abbreviations

AG	Attorney General
B	Baron of the Exchequer
CB	Chief Baron of the Exchequer
CJCP	Chief Justice of the Common Pleas
CJQB	Chief Justice of the Queen's Bench
JCP	Justice of Common Pleas
JKB	Justice of the King's Bench
JQB	Justice of the Queen's Bench

Note. Wherever possible I have given the dates of birth and death and the places of residence of all JPs in Elizabethan Norfolk.